THE LEGAL GUIDE TO DEVELOPING, PROTECTING, AND MARKETING SOFTWARE

THE LEGAL GUIDE TO DEVELOPING, PROTECTING, AND MARKETING SOFTWARE

Dealing with Problems
Raised by Customers,
Competitors, and Employees

THOMAS J. SMEDINGHOFF

McBride, Baker & Coles
Chicago, Illinois

JOHN WILEY & SONS

New York • Chichester • Brisbane • Toronto • Singapore

Library of Congress Cataloging in Publication Data:

Smedinghoff, Thomas J., 1951–
    The legal guide to developing, protecting, and marketing
software.

    1. Copyright—Computer programs—United States.
2. Computer programs—Patents.   3. Computer contracts—
United States.   I. Title.

KF3024.C6S58   1985   346.7304'82   85-17829
ISBN 0-471-81027-4   347.306482

Printed in the United States of America

10 9 8 7 6 5 4 3 2 1

To my wife, Mary Beth

PREFACE

This book is designed to provide a single, comprehensive explanation of the basic legal concepts and issues relevant to the development, marketing, protection, and use of computer software. I hope this will provide the reader with practical and useful information that is directly relevant to his or her particular involvement with software. The book is designed to be read cover to cover for an overall understanding of the legal issues facing the software industry, and then to be used as a reference manual for specific information in a given context. It is my intent that it will serve as a guide to making business decisions relating to the protection, development, and marketing of software, by helping readers recognize the legal issues they face in a given situation and to more fully understand their options and the consequences of their actions. It is not a substitute for competent legal counsel, but hopefully will be a valuable tool in working with an attorney.

The book is designed for software entrepreneurs, data processing professionals, software businesses, and their attorneys. The text is written for the nonlawyer, but extensive citations to authorities are provided for attorneys or other readers who would like to obtain further information.

As the role of the computer expands into virtually every aspect of our society, I believe that it is important for those involved in this process to understand its legal ramifications. The book covers what I consider to be the primary legal issues facing the software industry today: software protection, problems arising in the employer-employee relationship, the contracts that govern software transactions, and the potential liabilities to which a software vendor is exposed. Because computer law is a new and rapidly changing field, a comprehensive legal analysis of these issues is not readily available in an easily understood manner from a single source. My hope is that this book will fulfill the software industry's need for accessible, understandable, and current legal information.

I am interested in any comments you may have. Please direct them to me c/o McBride, Baker & Coles, Three First National Plaza, 38th Floor, Chicago, Illinois 60602.

THOMAS J. SMEDINGHOFF

Chicago, Illinois
January 1986

ACKNOWLEDGMENTS

I would like to gratefully acknowledge the assistance of my partners and colleagues who have so generously given of their time to help in the preparation of this book. In particular I would like to thank my partner Geoffrey G. Gilbert, who generously gave of his time reviewing the manuscript and who provided invaluable assistance in editing and commenting on it. I would also like to thank Malcolm H. Brooks, for his assistance in the preparation of the trade secrets material; Paul D. Frenz, for his assistance in the preparation of the criminal law material; Thomas J. Kinasz, for his assistance in the preparation of the tax material; Elizabeth S. Perdue, for her assistance in the preparation of the trademark material; and G. Gale Roberson, Jr., for his editing and helpful comments. My thanks to Marian Kriz, Karen Kupka, and Peggy Weimer for their considerable efforts in typing and updating the manuscript on our word processor. I would also like to acknowledge the assistance of Bruce H. Benson, Kristin A. Binder, Walter C. Clements, William J. Cooney, Beth Gillingham, Morgan J. Ordman, John P. Ryan, Jr., and Suzanne M. Timble. Finally, a special thanks to my sisters-in-law, Linda Smedinghoff and Jean Reimer, for their comments and criticisms.

CONTENTS

THE LEGAL GUIDE
TO DEVELOPING,
PROTECTING, AND
MARKETING SOFTWARE

CHAPTER ONE

INTRODUCTION

Computers play an increasingly important role in our society. There is almost no activity that is not involved with the computer in some way. They touch virtually every aspect of our lives, from the monitoring of our financial transactions and the controlling of industrial processes to video games. As the cost of hardware continues to fall, and the amount of available software continues to increase, this trend will only accelerate.

As our dependence on the computer grows, there is a strong need for an orderly, efficient, and well-understood set of rules which will encourage the further development of this technology and also insure the smooth operation of the transactions that make computer technology available for our use. The incentive to spend the time and money necessary to develop new software depends, to a large extent, on the ability to recoup that investment and earn a profit from subsequent sales. If the market erodes because of software piracy, the incentive to develop new products erodes with it.

1

In many ways, the nature of software is both a cause of the problem and the reason for its success. The ease of copying lowers the cost of marketing, but also makes piracy attractive. The low capital requirements for software development encourage employees to leave their jobs and start competing businesses, thereby expanding the productivity of the industry. However, this is often accomplished with the help of their former employers' software. And the inevitable errors that plague any new software product increase the risk of liability. Those capable of further developing the technology need some assurance that if they spend the time and money necessary to develop a new product they will be free to exploit that product in the market and recover their costs, along with a reasonable profit, without unfair interference by others. Similarly, those involved in both the selling and purchasing of computer products need a well-defined set of rules by which to govern their transactions.

What has come to be called "computer law" is the legal system's attempt to formulate a set of rules designed to govern the computer world. In many cases, it is nothing more than the application of existing law to a new technology—something which does not always work very well. In an ever increasing number of areas, however, the law is slowly beginning to adapt itself to the specific problems raised by the computer revolution. Because computer technology is relatively new and different, and something with which the legal system has never before had to deal, the process is slow and often imperfect.

Software, in particular, presents the legal system with the most unusual set of problems. It is not tangible, yet it must reside on physical media in order to exist. It is not a machine, yet it is used to control the operation of a machine. In a sense, it is what the law refers to as "intellectual property," yet it is more than a mere idea—it actually directs a machine to perform a series of functions. It is a very labor intensive and often expensive product to create, yet it can be copied for mere pennies, in a matter of seconds, and without the knowledge of its owner. These factors and others present significant legal issues. Although the technicalities of our legal system and the reasons for its difficulties in dealing with software directly are beyond the scope of this book, suffice it to say that the law has had a hard time accommodating this new technology.

The legal issues raised by software are frequently encountered problems, and they touch everyone who has any involvement with a software transaction. This includes not only the developer of the software, but the distributor, the customer, and the ultimate end-user. Failure to understand and appreciate the significance of these legal issues and the manner in which they are currently treated by the law can have potentially serious consequences in terms of lost protection, increased liabilities, and, in general, additional cost.

1.1. SCOPE OF THIS BOOK

This book describes the current state of the law as it applies to computer software. It is intended to provide practical information for the businessperson or entrepreneur who is developing, marketing, or acquiring software. Sufficient detail is provided to allow the reader to make intelligent business decisions and to recognize issues that may require the advice of an attorney.

The legal issues of primary concern to a software business are those relating to software protection, software contracts, and potential liabilities for software malfunctions. Consequently, these are the subjects that will be discussed in greatest detail in the chapters to follow.

Software protection is probably the most important. Copyright, trade secret, patent, and trademark law are all, to varying degrees, used for the protection of computer software. However, the protection afforded by each is limited, and thus they are often used in combination with each other. Consequently, an understanding of the scope of each of the different types of legal protection available, and the requirements for obtaining their coverage, is essential.

The contracts that govern software transactions are equally important. This includes contracts for the sale or licensing of software, contracts for its distribution, and contracts for its development. They must be structured to accurately memorialize the bargain that both sides have made, while at the same time insuring that the legal protection for the software is not compromised.

When marketing software, a vendor must also give careful consideration to the potential liabilities to which it is exposed. Certain steps can and should be taken to limit that liability, although in many cases simple awareness of the risks is the best protection possible.

The federal tax treatment of software-related expenses, and the imposition of taxes on software transactions by the various states, are also important issues, although they are often overlooked. The federal tax laws allow advantageous treatment of software costs in many situations. States, on the other hand, are continually looking for additional sources of revenue and in many cases have turned to software transactions as a new source of sales tax revenues.

The criminal law has also been struggling to keep up with the new problems associated with computer technology. Software pirates and so-called hackers have created a whole new set of legal problems with which the law is in many ways unable to cope. Accordingly, most states have now passed computer crime statutes to deal with this and other software-related crime problems.

1.2. GUIDE TO USING THIS BOOK

The purpose of this book is to provide practical, understandable, and useful information on the current state of the law as it relates to software. It is designed to assist those individuals and businesses who are developing or marketing software to recognize and deal with the legal issues they inevitably face, and to insure that their interests are adequately protected.

This book is designed to be used in two ways: first, to be read cover to cover in order to gain a general understanding of the law that applies to software; and second, to be used as a reference book to provide answers to specific questions. This will assist the software entrepreneur in selecting a particular course of action, and provide a background in the legal issues that will be invaluable when dealing with his or her attorney.

Each substantive area of the law has been set forth in one or two self-contained chapters, but there is often a significant interrelationship among what may appear to be separate and distinct legal issues. Trade secret law, for example, is frequently used to protect software, but this means it plays an important role in employee agreements and software contracts. Thus the chapters covering these topics should be considered in conjunction with the trade secret chapter. Appropriate cross references are provided where necessary.

When reading any chapter it is important to realize that, while it sets forth a number of seemingly simple and straightforward rules, there are always exceptions and special circumstances which could change the result. It is somewhat like saying that it is against the law to kill someone. This is certainly true, but there are exceptions for self defense, insanity, mistake, execution of a convicted criminal, and so forth. This book tries to indicate the main exceptions to any rule, but there are always other unique factual situations which will change the result. This is where the advice of an attorney familiar with computer law can be invaluable.

The reader should also be aware that a number of the issues discussed in this book are governed by state rather than federal laws. In particular, trade secret law, the law governing employer–employee relationships, general contract law, the law relating to liability for software malfunctions, sales and use tax laws, and the computer crime statutes, are all governed by state rather than federal law. This means, of course, that the rules will differ somewhat from state to state. This presents somewhat of a problem, since it is impossible in a book of this nature to thoroughly analyze the differences in the laws of all 50 states. Moreover, because computer law is so new, many states have simply not resolved a number of the issues raised in this book.

Accordingly, the reader should be aware that discussions of issues governed by state law draw on whatever limited materials (i.e., statutes and court decisions) are available from all of the states, and thus may not completely cover all of the unique rules in any given state. Where the text cites a California case for a particular proposition, for example, that may be the only case in the nation having been decided on that particular subject. Therefore, it is entirely possible that a court in another state will reach a different conclusion when faced with the same issue. It should be noted, however, that it is common for courts in one state to look to the decisions made in another state for guidance when an issue comes up for the first time. Thus, for example, it is entirely possible that a court in Illinois will rely upon a California court's opinion in reaching a decision on a particular issue which has not previously been decided in Illinois. However, there is no assurance that this will occur.

This book will present the general legal principles as they have evolved to date. However, a reader who is contemplating taking particular action in reliance on those principles should consult with legal counsel in his or her state to determine whether the law varies in the state involved, whether the law has changed, or whether the unique facts of the transaction will alter the outcome.

It is assumed that the reader is familiar with the data processing concepts and terms used throughout the book, so these are not explained. It is not assumed, however, that the reader is familiar with all of the legal terms that have been used. Accordingly, a glossary has been included to provide a definition of those terms.

Many of the statements made throughout the book are annotated by footnotes. They are included to indicate the authority for the referenced statement, or to provide additional information. They will usually refer to the statute, government regulation, court opinion, or other authority on which the statement is based, in order to allow the reader to locate further information. The referenced material is available in most law school and county court libraries, and at a number of larger public libraries. This will be of assistance to attorneys and anyone else researching a particular issue.

The footnotes are not necessary to an understanding of the text and can be totally ignored. However, because the law relating to software is so new, it is important to provide citations to the material that is available. If they are needed, an explanation of the terms used in most of the citations can be found in the glossary.

A word of explanation regarding the terms used throughout the book is also in order. The words "owner," "developer," "vendor," and "distributor" have been used interchangeably, depending on the circumstances, to refer to the person or entity who owns, markets, or develops software. The words "user," "customer," and "client" have been used to refer to those who acquire software in a given transaction.

CHAPTER TWO

OBTAINING COPYRIGHT PROTECTION FOR SOFTWARE

A computer program is automatically protected by federal copyright law from the moment it is written. The programmer or author is not required to fill out any forms, register with the U.S. Copyright Office, spend any money, wait any specified amount of time, or, for that matter, take any other action whatsoever. The protection applies automatically.

But this is only the beginning. Because copyright protection is automatic, it is important for anyone dealing with software to understand its implications. The owner of the copyright[1] should be aware of the nature of this protection, its limitations, how it can be utilized to its fullest extent, and how to keep from losing the protection. Similarly, the software user must understand the restrictions that the copyright imposes on use of the software.

This chapter will explain the nature of copyright and how it can and cannot be used to protect computer software. It will then set

---

[1] The question of who owns the copyright is an issue in and of itself. See Section 3.1.

out the procedures that must be followed in order to maintain that copyright protection.

2.1. WHAT IS A COPYRIGHT—AN OVERVIEW

A copyright is a form of protection provided by the laws of the United States (and most other countries) to those who create what the law refers to as "original works of authorship."[2] It is, in essence, a grant of certain exclusive rights to authors in order to allow them to commercially exploit their works.

The types of "works of authorship" protected by copyright are numerous and include literary works (such as novels and poems), dramatic works (such as plays), musical works (such as songs), artistic works (such as drawings, paintings, sculptures, television broadcasts, and movies), and certain other types of intellectual property. Most important for present purposes is that copyright protection extends to computer software.

Copyright protection is the most easily obtained and probably the most commonly used legal form of protection for software. But it does not necessarily provide all of the protection that the software owner requires. To use copyright protection effectively, the software owner must understand what it does and what it does not protect, and how it provides that protection. Thus it is important to begin with an explanation of the nature of this thing called copyright.[3]

2.1.1. Scope of Copyright Protection for Software

Copyright protection for software helps programmers protect the *literary expression* of the ideas embodied in their programs. And as the term "copyright" implies, one of the ways it achieves this goal is by prohibiting anyone else from copying the programmer's work; that is, only the programmer has the right to make a copy of

---

[2] 17 U.S.C. §102(a).

[3] Before proceeding, please note that the Copyright Act currently in effect (the Copyright Act of 1976) became effective on January 1, 1978. Prior to that time, the governing law was the Copyright Act of 1909. The discussion that follows will be limited to the Copyright Act of 1976, and thus, will only apply to software created on or after January 1, 1978.

his or her own software.[4] But this prohibition is not as all encompassing as it might appear.

A copyright protects only the *literary expression* of an author's ideas. It does *not* protect any of the author's underlying ideas, procedures, processes, systems, methods of operation, concepts, principles, or discoveries.[5] This constitutes an important limitation on the protection it provides for computer programs.

The distinction between the literary aspects of a program and the underlying ideas, procedures, or concepts can be illustrated through this simple example. Suppose that someone develops a new, unique, and foolproof technique for rating race horses which is guaranteed to pick the winner every time. If he writes a book to explain his technique in step-by-step fashion, he can obtain copyright protection for the "literary expression" of the technique (i.e., the choice and organization of the words used to explain it), but not for the technique itself. A second person is free to read the book, learn the technique, and then write his own book describing the same technique *in his own words*. He does not infringe the copyright in the first book as long as he does not use the first author's "literary expression." Similarly, if someone writes a computer program that implements this horse rating algorithm, copyright law allows him to prohibit others from copying the literal text of his code, as well as its structure, sequence, pattern, and organization. It does not, however, allow him to prohibit others from reading his program to gain an understanding of his algorithm and then writing their own program to perform the identical function.

This was one of the issues that arose in a copyright infringement case filed by Apple Computer against Formula International, a company marketing an Apple look-alike computer called the "Pineapple." In that case, there was evidence that the Apple software had been copied, and the court issued a preliminary injunction prohibiting such copying. In its opinion, the court explained the scope of Apple's copyright protection by stating that Formula had the right "to market programs which perform the

[4] Unless the programmer is an employee, in which case the employer is the exclusive owner of this right. See Section 3.1.3.

[5] 17 U.S.C. §102(b). Note that trade secret or patent protection may be used, in some cases, to protect the algorithm, procedure, process, *etc.* See Chapters 4 and 5.

exact same function or purpose as do Apple's own programs," but
that it could not market programs "which perform the same function in the *exact same manner*" as Apple's. That is, Formula is
"free to produce programs which result in the machine performing the same calculations, set-ups, memory loading, etc. as [Ap-
ple's] software does, [but it is not] free to do so by copying the
exact number and sequence of bytes or items by which [Apple's]
program causes the machine to operate."[6] In other words copyright protection for a computer program covers the manner in
which a particular algorithm is expressed or coded, but does not
cover the algorithm itself. One is always free to write a program
that will perform the same function as someone else's copyrighted
program, but only by his own independent creative effort rather
than by piracy.[7]

Distinguishing between the "ideas" embodied in a program
(which are not protected by copyright), and the "expression of
those ideas" through the way the program is written (which is
protected by copyright) is often a difficult task. Currently very few
guidelines exist to help in making this distinction in the context of
software and the issue is still being debated in the courts.

There is little doubt that the copyrightable "expression" of a
programmer's ideas includes his choice of variable names, the
way he phrases comments within the code, and his overall programming style. But these elements can easily be changed by
someone seeking to copy the code. In one case, for example, a text
editor was used to systematically change each occurrence of a
specific name in the plaintiff's source code in an effort to disguise
copying.[8] This did not, however, relieve the defendant of liability
for copyright infringement, because the copyrightable "expression" of a programmer's ideas goes much deeper than this. It
extends at least to the organization and structural details of the
program itself.

As one court has pointed out, in the preparation of a program

[6] *Apple Computer, Inc. v. Formula International, Inc.*, 562 F. Supp. 775, 782 (C.D. Cal. 1983), *aff'd*, 725 F.2d 521 (9th Cir. 1984).
[7] Final Report of the National Commission on New Technological Uses of Copyrighted Works (1978) at 20, 21. (Hereinafter cited as the CONTU Report.)
[8] *SAS Institute, Inc. v. S & H Computer Systems, Inc.*, 605 F. Supp. 816, 823 (M.D. Tenn. 1985).

the author is faced with a virtually endless series of decisions as to how to carry out the assigned task. Beginning with a broad and general statement of the overall purpose of the program, the author must decide how to break the assigned task into smaller tasks, many of which might in turn be broken down into successively smaller and more detailed tasks. At every level, the process is characterized by choice, often made arbitrarily, and only occasionally dictated by necessity.[9] Where there are so many different ways to write a program, copying the organizational scheme of someone else's work (i.e. copying their set of arbitrary decisions), constitutes infringement of copyrightable expression. This is so regardless of whether or not the variable names are changed,[10] the software is written in a different language,[11] or the code is written independently if done so pursuant to the detailed outline of arbitrary decisions followed by the original author.[12]

Conversely, it is clear that neither the *idea* of using a computer to perform a specific function (e.g. accounts payable processing) nor the ideas behind the algorithms or processes used to perform such a function are in and of themselves subject to copyright protection. For example, in one particular case, a court held that the copyright laws do not protect the idea of a video game in which a player symbol being guided through a maze appears to gobble up dots in its path while being chased through the maze by several opponents. Consequently, the video game "Jawbreaker" did not infringe the copyright in the game "Pac-Man" because the way in which it "expressed" that idea was not the same as the expression used in Pac-Man.[13] In most cases, however, drawing the line between the copyrightable expression found in the organizational scheme of a program and an algorithm not protected by copyright will not always be an easy task, and one that will frequently be left up to the courts.

---

[9] *Id.* at 825.

[10] *Id.* at 823.

[11] *Whelan Associates, Inc. v. Jaslow Dental Laboratory, Inc.*, 609 F. Supp. 1307, 1320 (E.D. Pa. 1985).

[12] *SAS Institute, Inc. v. S & H Computer Systems, Inc.*, 605 F. Supp. 816, 826 (M.D. Tenn. 1985).

[13] *Atari, Inc. v. Williams*, Copr. L. Rep. (CCH) ¶25,412 (E.D. Cal. 1981).

2.1.2. Exclusive Rights Granted to Software Authors

To achieve the goal of protecting a programmer's literary expression of his or her ideas, and to allow it to be commerically exploited, the Copyright Act grants the author of a program what is, in effect, a limited monopoly on the use of the software. To accomplish this, the Copyright Act gives the author of the software (the copyright owner) a number of *exclusive rights*, the three most important of which are as follows:[14]

1. *Right to Copy the Software.* Only the copyright owner can make a copy of the software or authorize someone else to make a copy. Under Copyright law, a "copy" is defined as any material object in which the software is fixed and from which it can be perceived, reproduced, or otherwise communicated, either directly or with the aid of a machine.[15] Software stored on disk, tape, or Read Only Memory (ROM) chips, printed on paper, or even punched on cards is considered a copy of the original version of the software. Thus reproducing software encoded on ROM chips is just as much a copyright infringement[16] as making a copy of software stored magnetically on a diskette or making a photocopy of a source code listing. Moreover, it makes no difference that the original program is in one fixed form (e.g., a source code listing) and the copy is in another form (e.g., on a diskette). There is, however, a special exception that allows someone who is not the copyright owner to make backup copies in some cases. See Section 3.2.2.

2. *Right to Prepare Derivative Versions of the Software.* Only the copyright owner can prepare a derivative version of the software or authorize someone else to do so. A derivative version is software that is based on preexisting software. It could be a revision of the original version to add

---

[14] 17 U.S.C. §106.

[15] 17 U.S.C. §101.

[16] *Tandy Corp. v. Personal Micro Computers, Inc.*, 524 F. Supp. 171, 173 (N.D. Cal. 1981); *Williams Electronics Inc. v. Artic Int', Inc.*, 685 F.2d 870, 874–75, 876–77 (3d Cir. 1982).

new features or to alter the way the existing functions are performed, a translation from one language to another (e.g., PL1 to Cobol), or any other way in which the original software can be recast, transformed, or adapted.[17] In one case, for example, a court held that a statistical analysis software package written for a DEC computer, which incorporated some of the copyrightable elements of a similar package written for an IBM system, was a derivative work which infringed the copyright of the original package even though significant new material had been added to it.[18] In another case, a court concluded that a "speed-up" kit, which was used to increase the speed of a video game called "Galaxian," resulted in the creation of a derivative work which infringed the copyright.[19]

3. *Right to Distribute the Software.* Only the copyright owner has the right to distribute the software by sale, lease, license, or lending. It is generally illegal for anyone else to do so regardless of whether they own a copy of the software, unless they have permission from the copyright owner.[20] There is one exception to this rule, called the "first sale doctrine" which is discussed in Section 3.2.6.

If someone infringes on these exclusive rights by copying, modifying, or marketing the software without permission from the copyright owner, the Copyright Act provides the copyright owner with the right to obtain an injunction to stop the infringement, and the right to recover damages, lost profits, costs, and attorneys' fees from the infringer. In an extraordinary case the infringer may also be subjected to criminal penalties.[21] These exclusive rights are subject to certain limitations, however, which are discussed in Section 3.2.[22]

---

[17] 17 U.S.C. §101.

[18] *SAS Institute, Inc. v S & H Computer Systems, Inc.*, 605 F. Supp. 816, 830 (M.D. Tenn. 1985).

[19] *Midway Mfg. Co. v. Artic Int', Inc.*, 547 F. Supp. 999, 1014 (N.D. Ill. 1982), *aff'd*, 704 F.2d 1009, 1013 (7th Cir. 1983).

[20] 17 U.S.C. §501.

[21] 17 U.S.C. §§502–06. See discussion at Section 3.5.6.

[22] 17 U.S.C. §§107-18 establish limitations on these rights. *See also* 17 U.S.C. §106.

2.1.3. Term of Protection

Copyright protection lasts for the life of the author plus 50 years. If there is more than one author, the copyright lasts for 50 years after the death of the last surviving author. In the case of works done "for hire,"[23] the copyright lasts for 75 years after the year of first publication, or 100 years after the year of creation, whichever comes first.[24] The length of this protection is clearly more than enough to provide adequate protection for software, which has a much shorter life cycle.

2.1.4. Owning the Copyright versus Owning a Copy

When examining the nature of copyright protection for software, it is important to distinguish between ownership of the copyright and ownership of a copy of the copyrighted software. The mere ownership of the media on which copyrighted software resides (e.g., a diskette) is not the same as ownership of the copyright itself. When one purchases a book, for example, he or she owns that particular copy of the book but not the copyright in the book itself. The right to make copies of the book, to prepare derivative works based on the book, or to do any of the other exclusive rights reserved to the copyright owner is not transferred when a copy of the book is sold. The purchaser of a copy is merely the owner of the media upon which the copyrighted work is stored. The same is, of course, true with software. Ownership of a diskette containing copyrighted software does not of itself convey rights in the copyright.[25]

2.2. WHAT SOFTWARE CAN BE COPYRIGHTED?

Virtually all software qualifies for copyright protection under the category of "literary works."[26] The Copyright Act defines literary works as works that can be "expressed in words, numbers or other

---

[23] The concept of a "work for hire" is discussed in Section 3.1.3.
[24] 17 U.S.C. §302. The concept of "publication" is discussed in Section 2.4.
[25] 17 U.S.C. §202.
[26] 17 U.S.C. §102(a)(1).

verbal or numerical symbols or indicia, regardless of the nature of the material objects, such as tapes, disks, or cards in which they are embodied."[27] This clearly includes computer programs,[28] which are further defined in the Copyright Act as a "set of statements or instructions to be used directly or indirectly in a computer in order to bring about a certain result."[29]

2.2.1. General Requirements to Qualify

To qualify for copyright protection, a computer program must meet two requirements: (1) it must be an original work of authorship, and (2) it must be fixed in a "tangible medium of expression," from which it can "be perceived, reproduced, or otherwise communicated, either directly or with the aid of a machine or a device."[30] Fulfilling these requirements is not difficult.

Software will qualify as an original work of authorship, and thus meet the first requirement, as long as there is some degree of originality in the way the statements or instructions are expressed.[31] But the level of "originality" required is minimal. The "author" must simply contribute something more than a "merely trivial" variation, something recognizably "his own." Originality in this context "means little more than a prohibition of actual copying."[32] The product does not have to be a literary masterpiece. In one case, for example, a court held that a preprinted form answer sheet for standardized mutliple choice tests which was designed to be read by an optical scanner met the originality requirement of the Copyright Act.[33]

The fact that software performs a common function (e.g. a sort, payroll processing, etc.) does not deprive it of the originality re-

---

[27] 17 U.S.C. §101.

[28] In *Tandy Corp. v. Personal Micro Computers, Inc.*, 574 F. Supp. 171, 173 (N.D. Cal. 1981), the court specifically held that "a computer program is a 'work of authorship' subject to copyright."

[29] 17 U.S.C. §101.

[30] 17 U.S.C. §102(a).

[31] Compendium of Copyright Office Practices §322, hereinafter cited as "Compendium II" (see Glossary).

[32] *Alfred Bell & Co. v. Catalda Fine Arts, Inc.*, 191 F.2d 99, 102–03 (2d Cir. 1951); CONTU Report at 25.

[33] *Harcourt Brace World, Inc. v. Graphic Controls Corp.*, 329 F. Supp. 517, 523 (S.D.N.Y. 1971).

quired for copyright protection. An example of the application of this rule arose in a case involving the operating system for the Basic Four computer.[34] The defendant in that case, who was accused of infringing the Basic Four copyright, argued that the process of controlling disk and memory access was commonly used throughout the industry, and thus that the software designed to perform those functions did not qualify for copyright protection because it was not "original." The court disagreed, however, ruling that the software was "original" (for copyright purposes) even if other companies used software to perform the same types of functions, as long as it was independently written and not copied from someone else. In other words, the copyright concept of originality refers not to what the software does, but rather to the way in which it was created—i.e. whether it was copied or originally developed. As long as the software owes its origin to the author, that is, that it was independently created and not copied from other works, it will be considered original.[35] But this does not mean that everything within the software must be original. A copyright is not invalidated merely because some parts of the whole were not independently conceived, but were taken from material in the public domain.[36]

The second requirement, that software be fixed in a tangible medium of expression,[37] is also easily fulfilled. Under the Copyright Act, this occurs whenever software is embodied in a copy that "is sufficiently permanent or stable to permit it to be perceived, reproduced, or otherwise communicated for a period of more than transitory duration."[38] Thus if a program is recorded on paper, tape, disk, cards, silicon chips,[39] or any other media, in a

---

[34] *Hubco Data Products Corp. v. Management Assistance Inc.*, 219 U.S.P.Q. 450, 453–454 (D. Idaho 1983).

[35] *Synercom Technology Inc. v. University Computing Co.*, 462 F. Supp. 1003, 1010 (N.D. Tex. 1978).

[36] *Id.* at 1010.

[37] 17 U.S.C. §102(a).

[38] 17 U.S.C. §101.

[39] In *Tandy Corp. v. Personal Micro Computers, Inc.*, 524 F. Supp. 171, 173 (N.D. Cal. 1981), the court held that "a silicon chip is a 'tangible medium of expression,' within the meaning of the statute, such as to make a program fixed in that form subject to the copyright laws." The court reached the same result in *Williams Elec., Inc. v. Artic Inter'l, Inc.*, 685 F.2d 870, 877 (3d Cir. 1982); and in *Apple Computer, Inc. v. Franklin Computer Corp.*, 714 F.2d 1240, 1249 (3rd Cir. 1983).

manner that permits it to be perceived directly or with the aid of a machine (such as a computer-generated printout listing the program), it is considered to be fixed in a tangible medium of expression sufficient to meet the requirements of the Copyright Act.

2.2.2. Source Code versus Object Code

Although there has been debate in the past, it is now firmly established that copyright protection extends to both the source and object code versions of a program. There has never been much question about the copyrightability of source code, and now a number of cases have specifically held that object code is copyrightable as well.[40]

Probably the most famous of these cases is the one brought by Apple Computer against Franklin Computer for copyright infringement.[41] Franklin had introduced a new Apple-compatible computer called the Ace 100, and Apple brought suit alleging that it contained copies of 14 of Apple's operating system programs. Franklin did not deny that it had copied Apple's software, but instead claimed that the Apple software was not copyrightable. One of the arguments advanced in support of this position was that object code is not copyrightable—a position that was rejected by the court.[42] In fact, as one other court has stated, because object code is the encryption of the copyrighted source code, the two are to be treated as one work; therefore, copyright of the source code protects the object code as well.[43] The Copyright Office has also

---

[40] *See Tandy Corp. v. Personal Micro Computers, Inc.,* 524 F. Supp. 171, 173 (N.D. Cal. 1981); *GCA Corp. v. Chance,* 217 U.S.P.Q. 718, 720 (N.D. Cal. 1982); *Williams Elec., Inc. v. Artic Int'l, Inc.,* 685 F.2d 870, 876–77 (3d Cir. 1982); *Apple Computer, Inc. v. Franklin Computer Corp.,* 714 F.2d 1240, 1246–49 (3d Cir. 1983); *Hubco Data Prod. Corp. v. Management Assistance Inc.,* 219 U.S.P.Q. 450, 454 (D. Idaho 1983).

[41] *Apple Computer, Inc. v. Franklin Computer Corp.,* 714 F.2d 1240, 1246–49 (3d Cir. 1983).

[42] A number of theories have been advanced in support of the argument that object code is not copyrightable, including the following: (1) object code is not a "literary work" and thus is not covered by the Copyright Act; (2) object code is not a work of authorship because it is created by a machine rather than by humans, and thus does not satisfy the requirements for copyrightability; and (3) object code is not designed to be read by a human, and thus is not copyrightable subject matter. These have all been rejected.

[43] *GCA Corp. v. Chance,* 217 U.S.P.Q. 718, 720 (N.D. Cal. 1982).

taken the position that source code and object code are two representations of the same computer program.[44]

2.2.3. Application Software versus Operating System Software

There have also been some attempts in the past to distinguish application software from operating system software and to argue that the latter is not copyrightable because it functions as a machine, that is, it serves a utilitarian purpose, rather than being a literary work of art. This was the main argument made by Franklin Computer in defense of its copying of the Apple operating system software.[45] This argument involves a somewhat complicated analysis of the copyright law, which is beyond the scope of this book, but it was clearly rejected by the court. As the court pointed out, Franklin's argument that operating system software is not copyrightable seems inconsistent with its concession that application software is copyrightable. Both types of programs instruct the computer to do something. It should make no difference whether these instructions tell the computer to help prepare an income tax return (the task of an application program), or to translate a high-level language program from source code into its binary language object code form (the task of an operating system program). Other courts have come to the same conclusion.[46]

2.2.4. Documentation, Manuals, and Sales Literature

There is no question that documentation of all types, user manuals, sales brochures, flowcharts, and other descriptive literature qualify for copyright protection. They are considered as literary works, just as any other printed or written material. In one case, for example, a court found that Telex Corporation had copied portions of a number of copyrighted IBM hardware manuals and

---

[44] Compendium II at §321.03.

[45] *Apple Computer Inc. v. Franklin Computer Corp.*, 714 F.2d 1240, 1249–54 (3d Cir. 1983). ·

[46] *Apple Computer, Inc. v. Formula Int'l, Inc.*, 562 F. Supp. 775, 780 (C.D. Cal. 1983), *aff'd*, 725 F.2d 521, 523–24 (9th Cir. 1984).

included the copied text in its own manuals. This was held to constitute copyright infringement and Telex was required to destroy all of the infringing manuals in its possession and to pay damages to IBM.[47] In another case, a similar result was reached as to instruction manuals for computer software.[48]

2.2.5.   Software that Does Not Qualify for Copyright

Despite the preceding discussion, there are probably some computer programs or routines that do not qualify for copyright protection because they are not "the fruits of intellectual labor." Blank forms for recording data and simple and obvious instructions such as "Apply hook to wall" are not copyrightable for this reason.[49] Thus a computer program consisting of a few very obvious steps might not be protected by copyright.[50] Similarly, a computer program written or generated by another computer program might not qualify.

According to regulations issued by the Copyright Office, the following are examples of works that are *not* subject to copyright protection: words and short phrases such as names, titles, and slogans; familiar symbols or designs; blank forms such as time cards, graph paper, account books, diaries, bank checks, scorecards, address books, report forms, order forms, and the like which are designed for recording information and do not in themselves convey information; and works consisting entirely of information that is common property containing no original authorship, such as standard calendars, height and weight charts, tape measures and rulers, schedules of sporting events, and lists or tables taken from public documents or other common sources.[51]

2.3.   HOW TO OBTAIN A COPYRIGHT FOR SOFTWARE

Copyright protection for computer software is obtained automatically as soon as the program is created.[52] There is no need to

---

[47] *Telex Corp. v. International Business Machines Corp.*, 367 F. Supp. 258, 363 (N.D. Okla. 1973).

[48] *Synercom Technology, Inc. v. University Computer Co.*, 462 F. Supp. 1003, 1014 (N.D. Tex. 1978).

register the software with the Copyright Office,[53] and initially it is not even necessary to attach a copyright notice to the program.[54] However, the copyright protection can be lost if the software is "published"[55] without the notice. See Section 2.5.3.

A computer program is considered to have been created, and thus automatically protected by copyright, when it is "fixed in a copy . . . for the first time."[56] A copy is any material object in which the computer program is fixed, by any method, and with sufficient stability, and from which the program can be perceived or reproduced, either directly or with the aid of a machine.[57]

Thus a computer program is "created" whenever it is written or printed on a sheet of paper, keypunched on cards or paper tape, or otherwise input to a magnetic disk or tape, or onto a ROM chip. In any of these formats, one can either read the text of the program directly or use a machine to display or print out a readable listing. If a program is created over a period of time, undergoing a great many iterations, the portion of it that has been fixed in a copy at any particular time constitutes the copyrighted work as of that time, and where the program has been prepared in different versions, each version constitutes a separate copyrighted work.[58]

Although copyright protection is automatically obtained, it can be lost if additional steps are not taken to protect the copyright. Protecting the copyright requires consideration of three issues. First, has the software been "published," as that term is used in the Copyright Act, or will it be published in the future? Second, has a proper copyright notice been included? If software is "published" without a proper copyright notice, the protection may be lost. Third, will the copyright be registered with the Copyright

---

[49] *See* CONTU Report at 20.

[50] CONTU Report at 20.

[51] 37 C.F.R. §202.1.

[52] 17 U.S.C. §302(a) provides that "Copyright in a work . . . subsists from its creation
. . . ."

[53] 17 U.S.C. §408(a) provides that "Subject to the provisions of section 405(a), such registration is not a condition of copyright protection."

[54] 17 U.S.C. §401(a) requires only that the notice be placed on "published" copies.

[55] When a program is considered to have been "published" is discussed in Section 2.4.

[56] 17 U.S.C. §101.

[57] *Id.*

[58] *Id.*

Office? As is discussed in Section 2.6, registration of the copyright is optional, and, depending upon whether the software is to be published, use of the copyright notice may also be optional. However, failure to include a proper copyright notice, or failure to register the software, can result in loss of the copyright protection in certain cases. Each of these three concepts is discussed in the sections that follow.

2.4. PUBLICATION AND ITS CONSEQUENCES

The requirements of the Copyright Act and the scope of the protection it provides depend in large part upon whether a computer program is published or unpublished. "Publication" is a term of art under the Copyright Act. It does not necessarily have anything to do with the marketing of the software through a software publisher. "Publication" occurs when copies of the software are distributed "to the public by sale or other transfer of ownership, or by rental, lease, or lending," or when the software is offered "to a group of persons for purposes of further distribution."[59] Selling copies of the software, giving away promotional copies, providing copies to beta test sites, and renting copies on a trial basis are all examples of publication. However, such a distribution does not constitute a publication if it is done to a select group for a limited purpose in a way which prohibits "disclosure" and transfer of the contents of the program.[60] Thus, for example, a computer program distributed under a restrictive licensing agreement which prohibits transfer or disclosure to third parties is considered to be unpublished, whereas software sold or licensed with no such restrictions is considered to be published. Similarly, if the software is displayed publicly, but does not change hands, it is not a publication no matter how many people are exposed to it.[61] Thus, a demonstration of software to prospective customers does not constitute publication.

When publication does occur, however, important conse-

---

[59] *Id.*

[60] *Hubco Data Prod. Corp. v. Management Assistance, Inc.*, 219 U.S.P.Q. 450, 454–55 (D. Idaho 1983); *GCA Corp. v. Chance*, 217 U.S.P.Q. 718, 720 (N.D. Cal. 1982).

[61] 17 U.S.C. §101.

quences follow. First, all published copies of the software must bear a notice of copyright which meets the requirements of the statute, or the copyright protection may be lost.[62] Second, although registration with the Copyright Office is not a condition of copyright protection,[63] certain rights (such as the right to recover attorneys' fees in litigation) are lost if the copyright is not registered within a certain period of time after publication.[64] Third, publication of a program may trigger a requirement that it be deposited in the Copyright Office for the use and disposition of the Library of Congress.[65] These factors are discussed in Sections 2.5 and 2.6.

2.5. COPYRIGHT NOTICE ON SOFTWARE

A copyright notice is not required in order to obtain copyright protection in most countries, including the United States. In the United States, however, whenever a computer program is published, the law requires that all publicly distributed copies include a copyright notice.[66] The notice serves three basic functions: it informs everyone who comes into contact with the work that it is protected by copyright; it identifies the owner of the copyright; and it states the year in which the work was first published.

2.5.1. Format of the Notice

The copyright notice must contain three basic elements:[67]

1. The symbol © (the letter "c" in a circle), or the word "Copyright," or the abbreviation "Copr."

---

[62] 17 U.S.C. §401(a). The notice requirements for software are discussed at Section 2.5.

[63] 17 U.S.C. §408(a).

[64] 17 U.S.C. §§405(a), 411(a), 412. The registration requirements are discussed at Section 2.6.

[65] 17 U.S.C. §407. The Library of Congress deposit requirements are discussed at Section 2.6.6.

[66] 17 U.S.C. §401(a).

[67] 17 U.S.C. §401(b).

2.   The year of first publication of the software

3.   The name of the owner of the copyright

Thus, for software first published in 1986, any of the following would constitute a proper copyright notice:

Copyright 1986 [*name of owner of copyright*]
Copr. 1986 [*name of owner of copyright*]
© 1986 [*name of owner of copyright*]
Copyright © 1986 [*name of owner of copyright*]

When preparing a copyright notice, the following rules should be kept in mind:

Copyright Symbol.   Use of the copyright symbol "©" is recommended wherever possible, since this symbol is also recognized by most foreign countries under the terms of a treaty known as the Universal Copyright Convention.[68] Consequently, if the software is marketed in a foreign country, use of the symbol "©" will make the software eligible for whatever copyright protection (if any) that the country provides for software developed by its own citizens. But beware of using "(c)" as a substitute for the symbol "©". The symbol "(c)" does not literally comply with the statutory requirements in this country or in any foreign country, and the Copyright Office has taken the position that it is not an acceptable substitute for the symbol "©".[69] However, in one case involving a video game, a court ruled that a copyright notice consisting of the letter "c" surrounded by a hexagonal figure was acceptable because, unlike the symbol "(c)", it completely surrounded the letter c, and resembled a circle.[70] Notwithstanding this decision, however, if it is desirable to use some variation of the symbol "©" because of either hardware or software limitations, it is advisable

---

[68] The Universal Copyright Convention is an international treaty that extends the copyright protection granted by the laws of each signatory country to citizens of other signatory countries. To obtain such protection, the work should contain the international copyright symbol "©," the year of first publication, and the name of the copyright owner.

[69] 46 Fed. Reg. 58,310 (1981).

[70] *Videotronics, Inc. v. Bend Electronics*, 586 F. Supp. 478, 481 (D. Nev. 1984).

to use either the word "Copyright" or the abbreviation "Copr." along with it to be sure that the notice is not considered invalid.

Year of Publication.   Remember that the statute requires that the notice contain the year of first publication, which is not necessarily the same as the year in which the software was written. The important date is the year in which the software was first published (see Section 2.4). If the software is a derivative version of previously published software (see Sections 2.1.2. and 2.6.5.), the year of first publication of the modified version is sufficient for the notice. When the year of first publication is not known for sure, use the earliest possible year. If the year used in the notice turns out to be more than one year *after* the year in which first publication actually occurred, the work is considered to have been published without notice.

Owner of the Copyright.   Be sure to use the correct name for the owner of the copyright. The person who wrote the software is not necessarily the owner of the copyright. Generally, the owner of the copyright will be either the person or persons who wrote the software, their employer, or a person or entity to whom the copyright has been transferred. The issue of who owns the copyright is discussed in detail in Section 3.1.

2.5.2.   Location of the Notice

The copyright notice must be applied to the software in such a manner and location so as to give reasonable notice of the claim of copyright.[71] The acceptability of the notice depends upon its being permanently legible to an ordinary user of the software under normal conditions of use and otherwise not concealed from view upon reasonable examination.[72] To fulfill this requirement the notice for software should appear on all source listings; it should be imbedded within the corresponding object code in a manner that will cause it to appear to the user of the software no matter how it is used; and it should appear on any physical media in

---

[71] 17 U.S.C. §401(c).
[72] 37 C.F.R. §201.20(c)(1).

which the software is stored, sold, licensed, or transported, such as tapes, disks, or semiconductor chips.[73]

Source Code. With respect to source listings, the copyright notice should be prominently displayed as a note or comment within the program, preferably on the first page, the last page, or the page containing the name of the program and the name of the author or publisher.[74] In a Cobol program, for example, the notice might be included as a remark in the identification division. Such a program comment will give reasonable notice of the copyright to anyone examining the source listing. It will not, however, produce the necessary notice in the object code.

Object Code. With respect to the object code, the notice requirements are somewhat more complex. There the notice should appear to the user no matter how he or she uses the program. Consequently, it is necessary to include the notice as a data element within the program, so that it will appear in an object code version. Then, if the program aborts, or if someone attempts to decompile the software, the notice will appear in any memory dump or other listing that might be produced.

Terminal Display. When software is designed to produce a display on a user's terminal (such as an interactive screen for input of accounting data, a video game, etc.), the copyright notice should be displayed at the user's terminal, either continuously or at sign-on.[75] And it is important that the notice be displayed each time the terminal is used to access the software. Display of the notice on a random and infrequent basis does not constitute a reasonable notice. In one case, for example, a court held that a video game copyright notice which appeared randomly once in every 5 to 10 games played did not constitute reasonable notice.[76]

Printouts. When the software produces any sort of printout, it may also be a good idea to include a header or trailer page con-

[73] CONTU Report at 14.
[74] 37 C.F.R. §201.20(d).
[75] 37 C.F.R. §201.20(g).
[76] *Videotronics, Inc. v. Bend Electronics*, 586 F. Supp. 478, 481–82 (D. Nev. 1984).

taining the copyright notice. If the output is itself independently copyrightable (such as copyrighted text retrieved from a data base), a notice should be included to protect the copyright in the printed material. It should appear either with or near the title, or at the front or end of the printout.[77] On the other hand, if the output is a report containing data generated by the user (which is not copyrightable by the vendor of the software), a copyright notice is not necessary. Nonetheless, it is sometimes included, along with the name of the software, since it constitutes one more opportunity for the vendor to notify the user of its software copyright claim.

Disks, Tapes, and Other Media. With respect to the medium on which any published copy of the software is located, the rules are similar. Any tape reel, diskette, or disk pack used to transfer a copy of software to a buyer or licensee should contain the copyright notice. The notice should be reproduced on a label designed to withstand normal use, and securely attached to the copy itself, or to the box, reel, cartridge, diskette, or other container used as the permanent receptacle for the software.[78]

Documentation. The notice on documentation, user manuals, flowcharts, and other literature should be treated the same as a notice on a book. It should appear on the title page, the page immediately following the title page, the first or last page of the main body of the work, or either side of the front or back cover.

As a general rule, the more places the notices appear, the better the protection will be. For, as noted in Section 2.5.3, lack of an adequate notice may be fatal to any copyright protection.

2.5.3. Omission of the Notice

As a general rule, if the copyright notice is omitted from the software at the time it is published, the copyright protection is for-

---

[77] 37 C.F.R. §201.20(d).
[78] 37 C.F.R. §201.20(g).

feited and the work is released to the public domain.[79] However, the Copyright Act provides for three exceptions to this rule.

If the copyright notice has been omitted from no more than a relatively small number of copies of the software distributed to the public, the copyright will not be invalidated.[80] It is unclear what constitutes a "relatively small number of copies," but one court has held that a distribution of 250 to 300 video games without an adequate copyright notice constituted more than a relatively small number of copies and thus did not fall within this exception.[81] Further guidance in this area will have to await future court decisions.

Failure to incorporate an adequate copyright notice in the software will not invalidate the copyright if: (a) it is registered with the Copyright Office within five years after publication without notice, and (b) a "reasonable effort" is made to add the notice to all copies of the software that are distributed to the public in the United States after the omission has been discovered.[82] What constitutes a "reasonable effort" is not defined, although one recent case involving a video game provides some help.[83] According to the court, the statutory requirement of a "reasonable effort" implicitly recognizes that there are limits to what the copyright owner can do to add the notice. For example, it would be unreasonable to expect the copyright owner to engage in a futile attempt to add the notice to all copies of the software that had already been distributed to the public. However, the court also felt that a "reasonable effort" required a greater expenditure of time and money than would be made in the normal course of business, something which was not done in the case being considered. The facts in that case involved the marketing of a video game which was not programmed to display a copyright notice on the screen. At the time that it learned that the notice should be added, the manufacturer was planning to convert the design of its product from two circuit boards to one. Accordingly, it decided

---

[79] *Beacon Looms, Inc. v. S. Liptonberg & Co.*, 552 F. Supp. 1305, 1309–10 (S.D.N.Y. 1982).

[80] 17 U.S.C. §405(a)(1).

[81] *Videotronics, Inc. v. Bend Elecs.*, 586 F. Supp. 478, 483 (D. Nev. 1984).

[82] 17 U.S.C. §405(a)(2).

[83] *Videotronics, Inc. v. Bend Elecs.*, 586 F. Supp. 478, 483 (D. Nev. 1984).

that it would be cheaper to wait until the conversion took place before reprogramming the game to display the notice. In the interim it continued to produce games without the notice. Consequently, the court concluded that the manufacturer's failure to make any effort to add the notice during the interim period was not within the spirit of the "reasonable effort" requirement.

The third circumstance under which omission of the notice may be excused is when the notice has been omitted by a distributor in violation of an express written requirement that, as a condition of the copyright owner's authorization of public distribution of copies, they bear the prescribed notice.[84]

Any person who innocently copies a program from which the copyright notice has been ommitted is not liable for damages for any infringement committed before he or she receives actual notice that the program had been registered. However, the innocent infringer must prove that he or she was misled by the omission of the notice in order to escape liability.[85]

2.5.4. Notice on Unpublished Software

A copyright notice is not required on an unpublished version of a computer program.[86] Nevertheless, for maximum protection, the notice should be included on all copies of unpublished software. It will put any potential infringer on notice of the copyright claim, and will guard against loss of the copyright as a result of inadvertent or unapproved disclosure or publication. This might occur, for example, if a computer program was inadvertently sold or licensed to a customer who did not sign a restrictive license agreement. Thus use of a notice is a good way to be sure that copyright protection of an inadvertently published program will not be diminished or lost.

There is a problem, however, in putting a notice on unpublished software. The rules for preparing a copyright notice require that the notice include the year of first publication (see Section 2.5.1.). If the software is unpublished, there is no year of first

---

[84] 17 U.S.C. §405(a)(3).
[85] 17 U.S.C. §405(b).
[86] 17 U.S.C. §401(a).

publication to be used. The best solution is to use the year in which the program was written. If the program is eventually published in a later year, but the notice is not corrected, the continued use of the incorrect year will have only a minor impact on the term of the copyright protection. That is, if the software was a work for hire (see Section 3.1.3.) the 75 year term of protection will run from the date in the notice rather than from the date of any subsequent publication.[87]

A more worrisome problem is the possibility that a copyright notice on unpublished software may interfere with trade secret protection for that software under state law. Because the year in the copyright notice is supposed to be the year of publication, it has been argued that when one puts a copyright notice on a computer program, this action constitutes an admission that the software has been published. Were such an argument to be sustained it could preclude the owner from claiming any trade secret protection for the software, since such protection cannot exist in a published work. (See Section 4.4.2.) Fortunately, this argument has been rejected in three recent cases.[88] Nevertheless, a cautious owner would be well advised to add the following text to the copyright notice for unpublished works:

Copyright © 1986 ABC Software Corp. as an unpublished work.
This software constitutes a trade secret of ABC Software Corp.

This negates any inference that the notice itself is an admission of publication or that the owner intends to waive trade secret protection.

2.6. COPYRIGHT REGISTRATION AND DEPOSIT OF SOFTWARE

In general, copyright registration is a legal formality intended to make a public record of the existence of a particular copyright.

---

[87] 17 U.S.C. §406(b). The problem is more serious if the date in the notice is later than the actual date of publication. Where the year date used in the notice is more than one year after the year in which the publication first occurred, the work is considered to have been published without any notice. 17 U.S.C. §406(b).

[88] *Management Science America, Inc. v. Cyborg Sys., Inc.*, 6 Computer L. Serv. Rep.

Both published and unpublished software can be registered although it is not necessary to register either. But even though registration of computer software is not a condition of copyright protection,[89] except in one specific situation,[90] the copyright law is designed to encourage registration.

2.6.1. Advantages and Disadvantages of Registration

There are several advantages to registering software (which apply to both published and unpublished software). They can be summarized as follows:

1. Registration establishes a public record of the copyright claim.

2. Registration is necessary before an infringement suit may be filed.[91]

3. If the software is registered within five years of publication, registration will establish prima facie evidence in court of the validity of the copyright and of the facts stated in the certificate of registration.[92] This is important because it makes the plaintiff's burden of proof in a lawsuit easier and because it increases the likelihood of obtaining a preliminary injunction against an infringer.

4. If the software is registered prior to any infringement (or within three months of publication if infringement occurs after publication), statutory damages and attorneys' fees will be available to the copyright owner in court actions. Otherwise, only actual damages may be recovered.[93]

921, 924 (N.D. Ill. 1978); *Technicon Medical Information Sys. Corp. v. Green Bay Packaging, Inc.*, 687 F.2d 1032, 1039 (7th Cir. 1982); *M. Bryce & Assocs. v. Gladstone*, 319 N.W.2d 907 (Wis. App. 1982).

[89] 17 U.S.C. §408(a).

[90] Under sections 405 and 406 of the Copyright Act, copyright registration may be required to preserve a copyright that would otherwise be invalidated because of the omission of the copyright notice from the published program or because of a defect in the notice. See Section 2.5.3.

[91] 17 U.S.C. §411.

[92] 17 U.S.C. §410(c).

[93] 17 U.S.C. §412. Statutory damages are discussed in Section 3.5.4.

The main drawback of registration is that the owner of the copyright is required to deposit a copy of a portion of the source code as part of the registration process. That copy becomes available for public inspection[94] and could lead to disclosure of any trade secrets contained in that portion of the software deposited with the Copyright Office. The Copyright Office requires a deposit of only the first 25 and last 25 pages of the source listing, which may be useless information to a competitor. Nonetheless, for those many programs which contain 50 pages or less, registration would result in disclosure of the entire program and, very possibly, result in a waiver of any trade secret claim to the program. Copying of the program is, of course, prohibited, but a competitor is free to inspect the program at the Copyright Office and then to write another program using any new ideas disclosed by the deposited portion of the copyrighted program. If registration presents such a risk, the owner should consider registration pursuant to the special relief procedures outlined in Section 2.6.3, or foregoing registration altogether. This decision is best made in consultation with a qualified attorney.

2.6.2. Registration and Deposit Procedure

A computer program can be registered at any time before the copyright expires, either before or after it has been published.[95] When a number of computer programs are marketed as a single software package, they should be registered as a single unit with the Copyright Office.[96] Each individual computer program in a software package need not be registered separately.

The process of registering a software copyright is very simple. Three things are required: (1) a properly completed application form, (2) the filing fee, and (3) a deposit of the software being registered.[97] All three items must be sent to the Copyright Office in the same package.

---

[94] 17 U.S.C. §705(b).

[95] 17 U.S.C. §408(a). Remember, however, that late registration results in a waiver of the right to obtain statutory damages or attorney's fees in the event of infringement. See Section 2.6.1.

[96] This is spelled out in the copyright regulations found at 37 C.F.R. §202.3(b)(3)(i).

[97] 37 C.F.R. §202.3(c)(2).

Application Form. The Copyright Office uses a variety of different application forms, depending upon the copyrighted item being registered. For computer software, manuals, other documentation, and advertising brochures, the Copyright Office requires that applications for registration be submitted on Form TX. Copies of this form can be obtained free of charge by writing to the Information and Publications Section LM-455, United States Copyright Office, Library of Congress, Washington, D.C. 20559, or by calling the forms hotline at (202) 287-9100. A copy of Form TX, as well as instructions for filling out the form, can be found in Section A.1.

Filing Fee. The filing fee is $10. The fee should be paid by check or money order payable to the Register of Copyrights.[98]

Deposit. A deposit of the work being registered must accompany each application for registration. If the work being registered is a manual, any other form of documentation, or a brochure, the deposit rules are simple. Send one copy of the complete work if it is unpublished, and two copies if it is published. With respect to software, however, the rules are more complex. In determining what software to send to the Copyright Office, four issues must be addressed: (1) what media containing the software (*e.g.,* paper, diskette, etc.) is acceptable; (2) what form of software (source or object code) is required; (3) how much and what parts of the code should be sent; and (4) how many copies does the Copyright Office require?

1. *Media.* The Copyright Office regulations require that all software deposits be in a visually perceptible form rather than in machine-readable form.[99] In particular, the regulations require a listing of the software printed on paper or reproduced on microfilm. Disks, diskettes, tape, ROMs, and the like are not acceptable.

2. *Format—Source or Object Code.* The Copyright Office considers source code and object code as two representa-

---

[98] This fee is, of course, subject to change.
[99] 37 C.F.R. §202.20(c)(2)(vii); Compendium II §324.

tions of the same computer program.[100] Therefore, when software is registered, the Copyright Office takes the position that the copyright claim is in the computer program, rather than in any particular representation (*i.e.*, source or object code) of that program. Consequently, one registration covers both source and object code.[101]

Separate registrations of the two forms are not appropriate. When software is registered, however, the law requires that the "best edition" of the work be deposited with the Copyright Office. The Copyright Office has interpreted this to require that source code rather than object code be deposited.[102] Thus, as a general rule, source code should be deposited for registration. However, because copyright owners are concerned that a deposit of source code may result in a disclosure of trade secrets, object code may be deposited in certain cases (see Section 2.6.3).

3. *Amount of Code.*   In most cases, it is not necessary to deposit a printout of the entire source code listing. How much code should be deposited, and which portion of the code should be selected, depends upon three factors: (a) whether the software is published or unpublished; (b) if it is published, whether it is marketed only in machine-readable form (e.g., tape, disk, etc.) or whether it is also marketed in a visually perceptible form, (e.g., a printed listing); and (c) whether the version being registered is the first version to be registered, or is a revision of a version previously registered.

If the software is (a) either unpublished or published only in machine-readable form, *and* (b) being registered for the *first time*, the regulations require the copyright owner to deposit one copy of the "identifying portions" of the program.[103] The term "identifying portions" is defined as the first 25 and last 25 pages of the program together with the page containing the copyright notice,[104] and the page

---

[100] Compendium II §324.03.

[101] Compendium II §321.03; *GCA Corp. v. Chance* 217 U.S.P.Q. 718, 720 (N.D. Cal. 1982).

[102] Compendium II §324.03.

[103] 37 C.F.R. §202.20(c)(2)(vii); Compendium II §324.

[104] 37 C.F.R. §202.20(c)(2)(vii)(A); Compendium II §324.02.

containing the title of the software.[105] When the software being registered is less than 50 pages in length, the entire program must be deposited. If the Copyright Office receives a deposit of less than 50 pages, it will consider the deposit as constituting the entire program for which registration is sought. However, if there is information to the contrary (such as missing page numbers or obvious gaps in line numbers), the office will contact the registrant and inquire as to the completeness of the material.[106]

If the software is (a) either unpublished or published only in machine-readable form, *and* (b) being registered as a *revised version* of software previously registered, the regulations are the same as above, except that they require that the 50 pages to be deposited include the revisions. If the revisions occur throughout the entire computer program, the deposit of the first and last 25 pages will suffice. However, if the revisions are not contained in the first and last 25 pages, the deposit should consist of any 50 pages representative of the revised material.[107] (See Section 2.6.5 for a discussion of when revised versions of software may be registered.)

Finally, in the relatively rare case where the software is published in a visually perceptible form (i.e., the source code is published in a printed or microfilm form), either by itself or along with a machine-readable copy, the entire text of the software must be deposited.[108] This is true for both original and revised versions.

4. *Number of Copies.* When software is being registered as an unpublished work, only one copy of the "identifying portions" software must be deposited.[109] Similarly, if the software has been published only in the form of machine-readable copies (such as magnetic tapes or disks, punch cards, or the like) from which the work cannot ordinarily be perceived without the aid of a machine, only one copy of the "identifying portions" of the software need be depos-

---

[105] Compendium II §324.01.
[106] Compendium II §324.06(4).
[107] 37 C.F.R. §202.20(c)(2)(vii).
[108] 37 C.F.R. §202.20(c)(1)(i).
[109] 37 C.F.R. §202.20(c)(2)(vii).

ited with the Copyright Office.[110] Note, however, that when software is published in human-readable form, such as in printed source code listings, two copies of the software must be deposited with the Copyright Office.[111]

The registration will be effective as of the date that the application form, filing fee, and deposit are received by the Copyright Office. Upon receipt, the Copyright Office examines the registration form and deposited software to ensure that it is copyrightable subject matter, that there is a sufficient amount of authorship present in the deposited software, and that all of the formalities have been complied with. If there are any problems, the Copyright Office will contact the applicant. Otherwise, a certificate of registration will be issued in two to four months.

2.6.3. Alternate Deposit Rules

As described in Section 2.6.2, copyright registration normally requires a deposit of source code that is 50 pages in length. These deposit requirements have generated concern among software owners that registration will result in disclosure of the trade secrets embodied in the software. (See Section 2.6.1.) In situations where there is a risk that depositing 50 pages of source code will disclose valuable trade secrets, there are two alternatives: (1) deposit object code instead of source code; or (2) apply to the Copyright Office for "special relief" from the 50 page requirement.

Despite its preference for source code, the Copyright Office will register object code, if properly submitted, under its so-called "Rule of Doubt."[112] The Rule of Doubt simply means that the Copyright Office believes that there is a reasonable doubt as to whether the object code represents copyrightable subject matter or whether the other legal and formal requirements of the statute have been met.[113] Because the copyright examiners are not trained to read object code, they simply have no way of knowing whether it represents a computer program or merely a list of num-

[110] *Id.*
[111] 37 C.F.R. §202.20(c)(1)(iii).
[112] Compendium II §324.04.
[113] Compendium II §108.07.

bers. Consequently, to register object code, a cover letter should accompany the deposit stating:

1.   The reason that object code is being deposited rather than source code (e.g., fear of disclosure of trade secrets)
2.   That the object code deposited is in fact a work of authorship and that it represents the object code version of the program in which the copyright is claimed
3.   That the registrant is aware that the object code will be registered under the rule of doubt

In addition, if the copyright notice is encoded within the object code so that its presence and content are not readily discernable, the notice should be underlined or highlighted and its contents decoded.[114] Finally, it should be noted that no court has yet ruled on the effect that a Rule of Doubt registration has upon enforcement of the copyright. Consequently, it is best to deposit source code if that can be done without disclosing any trade secrets.

An alternative to object code deposit under the Rule of Doubt is to use the Copyright Office procedure for "special relief."[115] Special relief allows the Register of Copyrights to grant the requester the option of depositing less than or other than that which is required under the general deposit provisions. Thus when a computer program to be registered contains trade secrets or other confidential material that will be disclosed by depositing the first and last 25 pages of the source code, the Copyright Office is willing to consider a special request from the applicant to deposit less than or other than the usual 50 pages of source code.[116]

Special relief is granted only on request. Upon receipt of the applicant's written request for special relief, the Copyright Office will usually grant permission for one of the following three deposits instead of the normal deposit:[117]

1.   The first and last 25 pages of source code with some portions blocked out, provided that the blocked-out portions are proportionately less than the materials still remaining;

---

[114] Compendium II §324.02.
[115] Compendium II, §324.05.
[116] 37 C.F.R. §202.20(d)(1).
[117] Compendium II, §324.05(a).

2. At least the first and last 10 pages of source code alone (with no blocked-out portions); or

3. The first and last 25 pages of object code plus any 10 or more consecutive pages of source code (with no blocked-out portions).

Requests for special relief should be made in writing to the Chief, Examining Division of the Copyright Office, should be signed by or on behalf of the person signing the application for registration, and should set forth the specific reasons why the request should be granted and the form of relief desired.

Any decision as to whether special relief will be granted will be made by the Register of Copyrights. When an application for special relief is granted, the application for registration will bear an annotation stating that fact.

2.6.4. Expedited Registration

The copyright registration process normally takes two to four months. Occasionally, however, it is necessary to obtain a Certificate of Registration on much shorter notice. This is particularly important when a lawsuit is to be filed, since a Certificate of Registration must be attached to the complaint.

To accommodate such cases, the Copyright Office has adopted a special handling procedure for expedited registration, under which it will make every effort to process the claim within five working days after the request has been approved.[118] A special handling request will be granted, however, only in cases involving pending or prospective litigation, customs matters, or contract or publishing deadlines.[119]

Special forms are available for expedited registration although it is not necessary that such forms be used. To obtain expedited registration, a payment of $200 (in addition to the $10 filing fee) is required in the form of a certified check, accompanied by the special handling form or a suitable letter requesting special handling. If special handling is requested by letter, the following questions must be answered: (1) Why is there an urgent need for special handling? (2) If it is because of litigation, is the litigation

---

[118] Copyright Office Announcement ML-319, reported in 49 Fed. Reg. 39,741 (1984).
[119] Id.

actual or prospective? (3) Is the applicant or his or her client the plaintiff or defendant? (4) What are the names of the parties and the name of the court in which the action is pending or to be filed? It is also necessary for the applicant to certify that the answers to these questions are correct to the best of his or her knowledge.[120]

Mailed requests and any later correspondence for special handling should be sent to the Library of Congress, Department DS, Washington, D.C. 20540, Attention: Acquisitions and Processing Division Office. The outside of the envelope and the letter should clearly indicate that it is a request for special handling.[121]

2.6.5. Registering Modifications to Software

Once software has been registered, the question arises as to whether modifications to that software should also be registered. After software has been released to the market, it constantly undergoes revisions designed to correct errors that are discovered by users. Should each revised version of the software be registered?

Unfortunately, there are no hard-and-fast rules for resolving this dilemma. Generally, the answer is dependent on the scope of the modifications, since only the additions, changes, or other new material appearing in the program for the first time may be registered.[122] If the modifications to the software are significant, registration is advisable. However, where only a few minor revisions or additions have been made, or where those that were made are of a rote nature predetermined by the functional considerations of the hardware, registration for the new material will not be allowed by the Copyright Office.[123]

When modifications to previously registered software include substantial new code that enables it to perform functions not included in the original version, the Copyright Office will register the new program as a derivative work. Similarly, when a program has been translated from one language to another, the Copyright Office will register the resulting translation as a copyrightable derivative work.[124] However, when program code is changed merely to adapt the software to run on a different brand of com-

---

[120] *Id.*
[121] *Id.*
[122] Compendium II §323.01.
[123] *Id.*
[124] *Id.*

puter, registration will be refused if the changes were functionally predetermined by the nature of the new hardware.[125] Likewise, registration is generally not recommended for mere corrections of program errors.

2.6.6. Deposit for the Library of Congress

In addition to the requirement that a copy of the software be deposited for purposes of registration, there is a separate requirement that, within three months after copyrighted software has been published with notice, the owner of the copyright must deposit two copies of the software in the Copyright Office for the use of the Library of Congress.[126] However, there is no such requirement for unpublished software.

The deposit of software in connection with registration fulfills this requirement. Thus, it is only when software is published but not registered that the rule applies. If the copyright owner of the published software does not deposit the required copies, the Register of Copyrights may demand them although this is rarely done.[127] Failure to comply could subject the owner to fines,[128] although it would not invalidate the copyright. The Register of Copyrights, however, has adopted regulations which exempt from these additional deposit requirements all "computer programs and automated data bases, published in the United States *only in the form of machine-readable copies* (such as magnetic tapes or disks, punched cards, or the like) from which the work cannot ordinarily be visually perceived except with the aid of a machine or device."[129] Thus if software is published only by giving the customer a disk or a tape, no deposit is required. If, however, the customer is also given a human-readable copy of the software (e.g., a printed listing), deposit of additional copies for the Library of Congress could conceivably be required within three months of publication.

---

[125] *Id.*
[126] 17 U.S.C. §407.
[127] 17 U.S.C. §407(d).
[128] *Id.*
[129] 37 C.F.R. §202.19(c)(5). (Emphasis added.)

CHAPTER THREE

ENFORCING COPYRIGHT PROTECTION FOR SOFTWARE

Obtaining copyright protection for software is easy, but that is only half the battle. A copyright simply gives the software owner a weapon to use in a legal battle with an infringer, should he or she decide to follow that course. But in many cases, the benefit to be gained from enforcing a copyright against an infringer may not be worth the cost involved. For example, it may not be worth the cost in money and goodwill to file a copyright infringement lawsuit against an individual user of a $100 copy of personal computer software just because he or she makes a copy for a neighbor. However, the right to file that lawsuit may suddenly become very important if that same infringer goes into business and starts selling thousands of copies per month. By taking the steps to preserve the copyright protection which were outlined in Chapter 2, software owners are left with a viable option. When evidence of an infringement comes to their attention, they are then free to either pursue it or not, depending on their assessment of the situation at the time.

Before examining the legal options available to a copyright owner confronted with an act of copyright infringement, there are two preliminary matters which deserve attention. Because only the owner of the copyright can file a lawsuit against an infringer, the first question to be answered is: Who owns the copyright? It may not be the person who wrote the software, or it may be more than one person. The second important question relates to whether or not the person suspected of infringing the copyright has actually done so. Just because someone has made a copy without the software owner's permission does not necessarily mean that they have infringed the copyright. There are a number of limitations on the exclusive rights granted to copyright owners[1] which must be analyzed in order to ensure that what appears to be an infringement is, in fact, an infringement. This chapter will examine those preliminary concerns and then outline the options available to the software owner when filing a lawsuit for copyright infringement.

3.1. WHO OWNS THE SOFTWARE COPYRIGHT?

The software copyright is ordinarily owned by the author of the computer program.[2] But who is the author? The "author," as that term is used in the Copyright Act, is not necessarily the person who wrote the program. Nor is it necessarily the person who commissioned the program to be written and who paid for the time and materials necessary to write it. It depends on the facts of each case. But remember, only the copyright owner has the right to copy the software, modify the software, or sell or license the software. (See Section 2.1.2.) Therefore, the identity of the owner (i.e. the "author") is an issue that deserves serious consideration.

3.1.1 Software Written by an Individual on His or Her Own Behalf

When someone writes a computer program individually, with no assistance from anyone else, and outside the scope of any employment obligations, there is no question that he or she is the author

---

[1] These exclusive rights are discussed in Section 2.1.2.
[2] 17 U.S.C. §201(a).

of the software, and consequently the owner of the copyright.[3] This is the easiest case to deal with.

3.1.2. Software Written by More than One Individual

In many cases, it is common for a group of individuals to work together in the preparation of a software package. If they all intend that their separate contributions be merged into inseparable or interdependent parts of the final product, the resulting package will be considered a "joint work,"[4] and all of the co-authors will be co-owners of the copyright in the resulting product.[5] This means that each co-author has the right to use the software for his or her own purposes, as well as to license others to use the software on a non-exclusive basis without obtaining the consent of the other joint owners.[6] However, each joint owner may be accountable to the others for a ratable share of any profits he or she may realize on licensing the software.

It is important to distinguish a joint work from a collective work. The Copyright Act defines a collective work as a work "in which a number of contributions, constituting separate and independent works in themselves, are assembled into a collective whole."[7] Anthologies and encyclopedias are examples of collective works. If a software package was created by assembling a number of independent program modules previously written by a variety of programmers, the result would be a collective work. The copyright in each individual module would remain the property of the programmer who wrote it, while at the same time there would be a separate and distinct copyright in the collective computer system as a whole (*i.e.*, the compilation of these modules). The separate copyright in the collective work as a whole is owned by the person who, with the permission of the individual copyright owners, prepared the compilation.[8] However, the owner of the copyright in the entire computer system (*i.e.*, the collective

---

[3] 17 U.S.C. §201(a).

[4] 17 U.S.C. §101.

[5] 17 U.S.C. §201(a).

[6] *See* H. Rep. No. 94–1476, 94th Cong., 2nd Sess. at 121 (1976); *Nimmer on Copyright* §§6.08–6.12 (1985).

[7] 17 U.S.C. §101.

[8] 17 U.S.C. §201(c). *See also* 17 U.S.C. §103(b).

work), acquires only the right to reproduce and distribute the individual program modules as part of the entire computer system.[9]

In the case of a joint work, the authors intend at the time of the creation of the work that their separate contributions will be merged into a single work. In the case of a collective work, the parties are merely collecting and assembling preexisting materials. There is one copyright in a joint work which is co-owned by all of the joint authors. There are multiple copyrights involved with collective works. Each individual author retains his copyright in his original contribution to the collective work, and in addition, there is a copyright in the entire compilation itself. The author of a component module in a collective work (for example, the author of one short story in an anthology) is free to use his or her contribution in any way that he or she desires. Such authors are not, however, free to use the compilation without the permission of its copyright owner.

The implications for software are obvious. When many independent programmers[10] work to create a single software package, two possible results can occur, depending on the circumstances. If they are working together to create a single unified product, the resulting software package will be considered a joint work, in which case all of the programmers will jointly own the single copyright in the software. Alternatively, if the software package is created by combining independent stand-alone contributions, the resulting product can be considered as a collective work, in which case each programmer will retain ownership of the separate copyright in his or her contribution, but will not own the copyright in the entire software package. The copyright in the compilation is owned by the person who assembled it, with the permission of the individual contributors.

3.1.3. Software Written by Employees for Their Employer

When software is written by an employee for his or her employer, the rules are somewhat different. Software written by an em-

---

[9] 17 U.S.C. §201(c).

[10] This assumes that they are not working as employees. The rules for employees are different. See Section 3.1.3.

ployee within the scope of his or her employment is considered to be a "work made for hire."[11] In such a case, the Copyright Act states that the employer (rather than the employee who actually wrote the software) is considered to be the "author" of the software.[12] As a consequence, the employer owns all of the rights comprised in the copyright.[13] The only way in which an employer will not own the copyright in these circumstances is if the parties expressly agree to the contrary in a written document signed by them.[14] Without an express written agreement, the copyright in software written by an employee will automatically be owned by his or her employer.

Unfortunately, it is not always easy to determine whether an individual is an "employee" for purposes of the "work made for hire" doctrine, or merely an independent contractor. The determining factor is whether the employer possessed the right to direct and supervise the manner in which the work was being performed, as is customary in the true employer–employee relationship, or whether the employer simply specified the task to be completed but retained no right to control the manner in which it was accomplished.[15] The latter is typical of the consultant or independent contractor relationship.

Additional factors to be considered include the question of at whose insistence, expense, time, and facilities the work was created, and the nature and amount of compensation received by the individual for his or her work. However, when compared with the element of supervision and control, these additional factors are of minor importance.[16]

In one case, for example, a programming consultant, under contract to develop software, worked at his own place of business, worked on his own computers, was paid per program, and had no social security or income tax deducted from his pay. His client had no right to control the manner in which he performed his work. Given those facts the court concluded that the software he created

---

[11] 17 U.S.C. §101.
[12] 17 U.S.C. §201(b).
[13] *Id.*
[14] *Id.*
[15] *Scherr v. Universal Match Corp.*, 417 F.2d 497, 500 (2d Cir. 1969).
[16] *Id.*

was *not* a "work made for hire," and the consultant was allowed to continue using the software he had developed, notwithstanding his client's claim that it owned the copyright.[17]

If an individual is determined to be an "employee," only software written by that individual within the scope of his or her employment will be governed by the "work made for hire" doctrine. Work that is done outside normal business hours and outside the normal scope of his or her employment will not usually be covered.[18] Generalizations in this area can be misleading, however, and in case a dispute arises over ownership, both parties should seek the advice of competent legal counsel.

3.1.4. Software Written by Independent Consultants

When software is written for clients by independent consultants, the issue of copyright ownership of the resulting product becomes complex. Generally, because independent consultants are not employees, their work is *not* considered as a "work for hire," and consequently they will own the copyright in any software that they develop for their clients. There are, however, two exceptions to this general rule:

1. When the independent consultant specifically transfers the copyright to his or her client via a written agreement.

2. When the work performed by the independent consultant is deemed by the Copyright Act to be a "work made for hire" because it is one of a select group of "specially ordered or commissioned" works.

The subject of transferring copyright ownership is dealt with in Section 3.1.5. The balance of this section will deal with whether work performed by an independent consultant may be deemed a "work made for hire," in which case the client, rather than the consultant, will automatically own the copyright in the resulting software.

Under the Copyright Act, two criteria must be satisfied before

---

[17] *BPI Sys., Inc. v. Leith,* 532 F. Supp. 208, 210 (W.D. Tex. 1981).
[18] *See Nimmer on Copyrights* §5.03(B)(1)(b) (1985).

the work of an independent consultant will be considered a work made for hire:[19]

1. The work must be specially ordered or commissioned for use as (a) a contribution to a collective work, (b) part of a motion picture or other audiovisual work, (c) a translation, (d) a supplementary work, (e) a compilation, (f) an instructional text, (g) a test, (h) answer material for a test, or (i) an atlas; and

2. The parties must expressly agree in a written instrument signed by both of them that the work will be considered a work made for hire.

Unless both of these qualifications are fulfilled, the copyright in software written by an independent consultant will be owned by the independent consultant rather than the client.

As should be apparent from these two requirements, merely signing a contract with an independent contractor specifying that the software is to be deemed a work made for hire (the second of the two requirements) will not deprive the consultant of his or her copyright. The work must also fulfill the first requirement by falling within one of the nine above-listed categories specially enumerated in the copyright statute. Although a number of these categories do not relate to computer software, it is possible that a computer related work will fall within the scope of some of them. For example, if a consultant is retained to do a small independent portion of a much larger system, his or her work may be considered as a "contribution to a collective work."[20] Similarly, if a consultant is hired to convert software from one language to another, his work would probably be considered a "translation" under the statute. But, unless the work of an independent consultant falls clearly within one of these special categories, it is unlikely that it will be deemed to have met the first of the two requirements for retention of copyright ownership by the client.

Even if the work performed by a consultant meets the first part of the two-part test, it is important to remember that the Copyright Act also requires a written agreement between the parties specifi-

---

[19] 17 U.S.C. §101.
[20] Collective works are discussed in Section 3.1.2.

cally stating that the software to be written by the consultant is a "work made for hire." If work performed by an independent consultant cannot be fitted within the "work made for hire" doctrine, but the client would nonetheless like to obtain the copyright ownership in the resulting product, the only alternative is for the consultant to execute a written transfer of his or her copyright to the client.

3.1.5 Transfer of Copyright Ownership

Ownership of a software copyright may be transferred in whole or in part by written agreement.[21] Any one or more of the exclusive rights granted to the copyright owner, such as the right to make copies, the right to make derivative works, and the right to distribute the software (discussed in Section 2.1.2) may be transferred. No particular form is required, but the transfer will not be valid unless it is in writing and is signed by the owner of the copyright or his or her duly authorized agent.[22] It should also specifically identify the copyright work to which it pertains and the specific rights transferred.

The transfer agreement should also be recorded in the Copyright Office.[23] If the copyright owner attempts to transfer the same copyright to two separate persons, the person who received the transfer that was executed first is entitled to the copyright if the transfer is recorded in the Copyright Office within one month. If the transfer is not recorded within this period, then the person who received the second transfer will be entitled to the copyright, so long as the transfer is recorded first and was received in good faith and without knowledge of the earlier transfer. Recording of the transfer document is also a prerequisite to an infringement suit brought by the transferee.[24] To record the transfer, the original copy of the transfer contract should be sent to the Copyright Office, along with a fee of $10 plus 50¢ for each page of the agreement in excess of six.[25]

---

[21] 17 U.S.C. §201(d).
[22] 17 U.S.C. §204.
[23] 17 U.S.C. §205(a).
[24] 17 U.S.C. §205.
[25] 17 U.S.C. §708(a)(4). A copy of the document can be sent instead of the original if it is accompanied by a sworn or official certification that it is a true copy of the original signed document. 17 U.S.C. §205(a).

3.2. LIMITATIONS ON COPYRIGHT PROTECTION FOR SOFTWARE

As noted in Section 2.1.2, the Copyright Act gives the owner of a copyright in a computer program the *exclusive right* to:[26]

1. Make copies of the program
2. Prepare derivative programs based upon it
3. Distribute copies of the program publicly by sale, rental, lease, or lending

When someone other than the copyright owner—or a person acting with the owner's permission—performs one of those acts, it is an infringement of the copyright unless it comes within an exception provided by the law.[27] The copyright law contains a number of such exceptions, three of which relate specifically to software.

3.2.1. Right to Load a Copy Into a Computer

When a customer obtains a copy of a software package, it usually comes on a disk or a tape. It is impossible to use that software, however, unless it is loaded into the computer's memory—an act which constitutes the making of another copy, and which thus appears to be a copyright infringement.[28] To deal with this somewhat technical problem, the Copyright Act specifically provides that the *owner of a copy* of software has the right to make such a copy (*i.e.*, to load the software into the machine's memory) when it is done as an essential step in the utilization of the program in conjunction with the machine.[29] This right has been limited by one recent court decision, however, to permit only the act of inputting the software into the copy owner's own computer.[30] That is, the owner of a copy cannot load it into the memory of a multiple number of computers owned by others.

---

[26] 17 U.S.C. §106.

[27] 17 U.S.C. §501(a).

[28] CONTU Report at 13,22; *Micro-Sparc, Inc. v. Amtype Corp.*, 592 F.Supp. 33, 35 (D. Mass. 1984).

[29] 17 U.S.C. §117(1). (Reproduced in Section A.2.)

[30] *Apple Computer, Inc. v. Formula Int'l, Inc.*, No. CV 82-5015-IH (C.D. Cal. October 1 1984).

3.2.2. Right to Make Backup Copies

One of the most important exceptions contained in the copyright law that specifically relates to software is the right granted to the *owner of a copy* of software to make additional copies for archival purposes.[31] This exception is important, since software backup is critical to almost every data processing application.

There are, however, three significant limits on the right to make backup copies. First, and most important, this right is granted only to someone who actually *purchases* a copy of software. If the software is licensed rather than purchased (as it is in most cases), the copyright law does *not* give the licensee the right to make an archival copy.[32] Therefore, unless the license agreement provides such authorization, or it is excused under the doctrine of fair use,[33] the making of a backup copy by a licensee constitutes copyright infringement.

The second limit on the right to make archival copies is that they must remain with the original copy in the event the owner decides to transfer the software to someone else. That is, the owner cannot sell the original copy and keep the archival copies, since this would defeat the intent of the law.[34] Conversely, the owner of a computer program who makes archival copies is also prohibited from selling, leasing, or otherwise transferring any of the copies unless he or she also transfers all of his or her rights to the original program.[35]

A third limit on the right to make archival copies appears to be determined by the medium in which the software is stored. According to two recent court decisions, the right to make backup copies is limited to computer programs stored on media in which they are subject to destruction or damage by mechanical or electrical failure—for example, programs stored on disks, diskettes, or tapes. Software stored on media which is not subject to destruction by mechanical or electrical failure (e.g., software printed on paper) may not be copied. On the basis of this theory, one court

---

[31] 17 U.S.C. §117(2). (Reproduced in Section A.2.)
[32] *GCA Corp. v. Chance*, 217 U.S.P.Q. 718, 720 (N.D. Cal. 1982).
[33] See Section 3.2.4.
[34] 17 U.S.C. §117. (Reproduced in Section A.2.)
[35] *Id.*

held that using a device called a "PROM Blaster" to copy Atari game cartridges would constitute a copyright infringement of the game software since the ROMs that it is designed to copy were not susceptible to destruction or damage by mechanical or electrical failure.[36] Similarly, another court held that a company which offered a typing service to purchasers of a computer magazine infringed the publisher's copyright on programs listed in the magazine when it put those programs on a disk and duplicated and sold those disks to purchasers of the magazine. The right to make backup copies was held not to apply because the programs printed in the magazine were not subject to destruction or damage by mechanical or electrical failure.[37]

Finally, it should be noted that the right to make backup copies, by its very nature, places a limit on how the copies are used. That is, they may be used as backup when the original copy is damaged or destroyed. They may not, however, be used to run multiple copies on multiple machines, or for any other purpose.

3.2.3. Right to Modify Software

Normally, the act of modifying software constitutes the preparation of a derivative work. If this is done without the permission of the copyright owner, it can constitute an infringement of the copyright. (See Section 2.1.2.). However, in certain limited cases the *owner of a copy* of software may modify the software without obtaining permission from the owner of the copyright.[38]

Generally, the *owner* of a copy of software may modify it if the modification is necessary to enable the software to be used on a particular machine. This is intended to cover the situation in which the purchaser of a computer program plans to use it on a machine other than the one for which it was designed, and must make minor changes to accommodate the requirements of the alternative hardware.[39] The conversion of a program from one higher-level language to another to allow its use on a particular computer also falls within this exception. It is unclear how far this

---

[36] *Atari, Inc. v. JS&A Group*, Copyright L. Rep. (CCH) ¶25,613 (N.D. Ill. 1983).
[37] *Micro-Sparc, Inc. v. Amtype Corp.*, 592 F. Supp. 33, 35 (D. Mass. 1984).
[38] 17 U.S.C. §117. (Reproduced in Section A.2.)
[39] CONTU Report at 13.

right to modify extends, although it has been suggested that it includes the right to add features to the program that were not present at the time the program was purchased.[40]

Nevertheless, the right to modify software is limited. First, as with the right to make backup copies, the right is available only to those who purchase software. A licensee has no such right unless it is granted under the terms of the license. Second, if the owner of a copy of the program has modified the original program, he or she cannot sell the modifications without the copyright owner's approval.[41]

3.2.4. Fair Use

In addition to the three exceptions specifically provided for computer software, the Copyright Act also contains a general exception known as the doctrine of "fair use." This exception applies to all copyrighted works, and permits the copying and use of a copyrighted work "for purposes such as criticism, comment, news reporting, teaching, scholarship, or research."[42]

The law sets forth four factors to be considered in determining whether an act which would otherwise constitute an infringement may be permitted by the doctrine of fair use:

1. The purpose and character of the use, including whether such a use is of a commercial nature or is for nonprofit educational purposes

2. The nature of the copyrighted work

3. The amount and substantiality of the portion used in relation to the copyrighted work as a whole

4. The effect of the use upon the potential market for or value of the copyrighted work.[43]

Each case must be decided on its own facts. But once it is determined that the use made of the software is a "fair use," then,

---

[40] *Id.*
[41] 17 U.S.C. §117. (Reproduced in Section A.2.)
[42] 17 U.S.C. §107.
[43] *Id.*

notwithstanding the exclusive rights of the copyright owner, the use will not be deemed an infringement of the copyright.

It is unclear exactly how "fair use" will be applied to computer software. It can be argued that it is fair use for a licensee to make a backup copy of software, but since the Copyright Act specifically gives only owners of copies the right to make backup copies, it seems apparent that Congress did not intend licensees to have this right as well. In fact, it has been suggested that the application of fair use to computer software has been preempted by the specific statutory exceptions for software discussed in Sections 3.2.1–3.2.3. Future court decisions can be expected to address and resolve this question over time.

3.2.5. Idea–Expression Identity

Another situation in which one is also allowed to copy all or a portion of software without the permission of the copyright owner arises when there is only one way in which to express the idea contained in the coding. This is known as idea–expression identity and represents a complex legal doctrine under the copyright law.[44] Essentially, what this means is that if there is only one way to write code to perform a particular function, then anyone is free to copy a previous version of that code written by someone else. Otherwise, the first person to write the code would have a monopoly not only on his or her expression of the idea (*i.e.*, his or her particular way of coding), but also on the idea itself, since, by definition, there is no other way in which the idea can be expressed. Consequently, when a specific series of computer instructions, even though previously copyrighted, is the only and essential means of accomplishing a given task, its later use by another will not amount to an infringement.[45]

The idea–expression argument has been raised as a defense to a charge of copyright infringement in a number of computer cases, but so far, without much success. The issue was raised by Franklin Computer, for example, as one of its defenses in a suit for copyright infringement filed by Apple Computer. Franklin

---

[44] 17 U.S.C. §102(b).
[45] CONTU Report at 20. *See* 17 U.S.C. §102(b).

claimed that it was justified in copying the Apple operating system software because that was the only method by which it could obtain software that would perform exactly the same functions as the Apple operating system. The appellate court appeared to reject this argument, although it did not expressly rule on its applicability in that case, because the trial court had not made the necessary findings of fact.[46] In another case, however, the argument was raised by the manufacturer of another Apple-compatible system that had been sued by Apple for copyright infringement. In that case, Apple was able to show that there were many ways to write programs that would be 98 percent compatible with an Apple computer without infringing Apple's copyrights. Thus the defendant was not allowed to copy Apple's software.[47]

This exception to copyright protection has been most successfully applied in connection with data formats. In one case, the court held that the ideas embodied in data input formats were inseparable from the expression of the formats and that copying of the formats was thus not an infringement.[48]

3.2.6 First Sale Doctrine

As discussed in Section 2.1.2, the software copyright owner has the exclusive right to distribute copies of the software to the public by sale, rental, lease, or lending.[49] There is a limit on this right, however. After the copyright owner has sold a copy of its software (i.e. made the "first sale" of that copy), it has no right to control further disposition of that copy by the purchaser.[50] That is, it is not a copyright infringement for the purchaser to sell or rent his or her copy to someone else (as long as he or she does not retain a copy as well). This is known as the "first sale" doctrine. If the owner of the software copyright wants to prohibit subsequent transfer of that copy of the software, it must license rather than sell copies of

---

[46] *Apple Computer, Inc. v. Franklin Computer Corp.*, 714 F.2d, 1240, 1253 (3d Cir. 1983).

[47] *Apple Computer, Inc. v. Formula Int'l, Inc.*, 562 F. Supp. 775, 782 (C.D. Cal. 1983), *aff'd* 725 F.2d 521, 525 (9th Cir. 1984).

[48] *Synercom Technology, Inc. v. University Computing Co.*, 462 F. Supp. 1003, 1011-14 (N.D. Tex. 1978).

[49] 17 U.S.C. §106(3).

[50] 17 U.S.C. §109.

the software and insert appropriate restrictive language in the license agreement. (See Section 9.3.6.)

3.3. WHAT CONSTITUTES INFRINGEMENT?

Anyone who exercises any of the exclusive rights which are reserved to the owner of a copyright without the permission of the owner (unless excused by one of the exceptions discussed in Sections 3.2.1–3.2.6) will be guilty of copyright infringement. The more common methods by which a software copyright may be infringed are described in Sections 3.3.1–3.3.4.

3.3.1. Copying

The most obvious of all forms of copyright infringement is the act of copying. Every time software is copied by someone other than the copyright owner, and is done without the owner's permission, the copyright has been infringed, unless the copy is made pursuant to one of the exceptions described in Sections 3.2.1–3.2.6. Exact copying is not required for infringement. If someone takes a copyrighted program, for example, and simply changes variable names and rearranges some of the code in order to disguise the copying, it will still be a copyright infringement. A plagiarist will not be allowed to escape punishment by making immaterial variations. The problem, however, is in determining what level of similarity short of verbatim copying will constitute copyright infringement. This is a question that must be decided by the courts on a case-by-case basis. See discussion in Section 2.1.1.

3.3.2. Modifications

Modifying software, like copying, constitutes copyright infringement, unless authorized by the copyright owner or one of the statutory exceptions described in Sections 3.2.1–3.2.6. Remember, one of the exclusive rights reserved to the owner of the software copyright is the right to prepare derivative works, that is, the right to make modifications to the software. This includes translations. Thus, translating software from COBOL to PL1 is just as much a copyright infringement as translating a book from English to French or making a movie based on a book.[51]

3.3.3. Disassembly and Decompilation

Disassembly and decompilation of object code would also appear to constitute infringement of the copyright because, in essence, they involve both copying and modification of the object code. To date, this conclusion has been supported by the opinion of one court, where the work was done for financial gain.[52]

3.3.4. Distribution

The marketing of unauthorized copies of software is also an infringement of the copyright owner's exclusive right of distribution. Except for the rights the owner of a copy has under the first sale doctrine (See Section 3.2.6), no one is allowed to sell, license, or in any other way market software without permission of the copyright owner.

3.4. PROVING INFRINGEMENT

In order to prove infringement by copying, two things must be established: (1) that the plaintiff is the owner of a valid copyright, and (2) "copying" by the defendant. The Certificate of Copyright Registration is used to prove ownership of a valid copyright,[53] so that element is quite easily established. Direct evidence of copying, on the other hand, is rarely available. It is unusual for there to be a witness who can testify that he or she actually saw the defendant make a copy. Moreover, persons copying software frequently attempt to disguise the fact of copying so that their software will not appear to be a line-by-line duplicate of the software they copied. This is frequently done by changing variable names, rear-

---

[51] *Synercom Technology, Inc. v. University Computing Co.*, 462 F. Supp. 1003, 1013 n. 5 (N.D. Tex. 1978).

[52] *Hubco Data Prods. Corp. v. Management Assistance, Inc.*, 219 U.S.P.Q. 450, 455–456 (D. Idaho 1983).

[53] 17 U.S.C. §410(c).

ranging the order in which the program is executed, using a different programming language, and so forth. Therefore, copying is usually established through circumstancial evidence.

In copyright infringement cases, circumstantial proof of copying is accomplished through a two-step procedure. First, the plaintiff shows that the defendant had access to the software that was allegedly copied. Second, the plaintiff proves that the defendant's software is "substantially similar" to its own. If these two elements are proven, courts will permit a finding of copyright infringement.

The first part of the test, proving that the defendant had access to the plaintiff's software, is usually relatively easy. In many cases, the defendant is a former employee of the plaintiff or is a licensee or purchaser of the plaintiff's software. If such is the case, there is no doubt that the defendant had access to the software. In one case involving a video game, for example, the plaintiff was able to establish that the defendant actually purchased the copies of its product.[54] In another case, the court held that the defendant had access to plaintiff's video game because it was widely circulated throughout the country.[55]

The second aspect of an infringement case, showing that there is "substantial similarity" between the plaintiff's software and the defendant's software, is much more difficult to prove. Substantial similiarity is not proven merely because there are some similarities between the two copies. However, the fact that there are differences between the two programs will not preclude a finding of infringement. Exact reproduction of the software is not necessary for there to be copyright infringement. If a defendant really has copied the plaintiff's software, but has attempted to disguise his or her copy by making trivial variations in the software, by rearranging the code, or even by using a different programming language, he or she will still be guilty of infringement.

The standard of substantial similiarity is basically a test as to whether an average observer would recognize the alleged copy as

[54] *Stern Elecs., Inc. v. Kaufman*, 523 F. Supp. 635, 639 (E.D.N.Y. 1981), *aff'd*, 669 F.2d 852 (2d Cir. 1982).

[55] *Nintendo of America, Inc. v. Bay Coin Distributors, Inc.*, Copyright L. Rep. (CCH) ¶25,409 (E.D.N.Y. 1982).

having been appropriated from the copyrighted work.[56] This is also referred to as the "ordinary observer test."[57] How this test will be applied depends on the circumstances of each case. In software cases, it is very common to have an expert compare both program listings, in either source or object code, to determine the similarities. In one case, for example, the owner of the software for a video game called DEFENDER brought a copyright infringement suit against a competitor marketing a virtually identical game. The court found that there was overwhelming evidence that the software had been copied, based on the fact that the video games produced by each program were essentially identical, both programs contained an identical error, both programs contained the plaintiff's copyright notice buried in the object code, and in excess of 85 percent of the code in each program was identical.[58] Similarly, in a case involving copyright infringement of the software for the video game PAC–MAN, the evidence showed that 97 percent of the bytes in the object code for the PAC–MAN software appeared, without change, in the object code version of the allegedly infringing software. Based on this evidence, the court concluded that the high degree of identity of the two programs, and the virtual impossibility that two programmers working independently would write so nearly identical programs, compelled the conclusion that the defendant's software had been created by copying the PAC–MAN software.[59]

Remember, however, that identical copying of code is not required to prove infringement. Substantial similiarity between the organizational schemes of two programs can also support an inference of copying, even though the code itself may not be identical. When a very high proportion of the many arbitrary programming decisions that go into designing a program are resolved the same way in a second program, there is a strong inference of copying. In one case, for example, the court found copyright infringement where the defendant's software followed the organizational structure of the original software down to a detailed level, and em-

---

[56] *Id.*

[57] *Atari, Inc. v. North American Phillips Consumer Elecs. Corp.*, 672 F.2d 607, 614 (7th Cir. 1982).

[58] *Williams Elecs., Inc. v. Artic Int'l, Inc.*, 685 F.2d 870, 876 n. 8 (3d Cir. 1982).

[59] *Midway Mfg. Co. v. Strohon*, 564 F. Supp. 741, 752–53 (N.D. Ill. 1983).

ployed a very close paraphrase of the structure and organization of the original. And in that case there were only 44 examples of copying of code from over 186,000 total lines.[60]

3.5. REMEDIES FOR INFRINGEMENT

What remedies are available to the software owner who can prove that its copyright has been infringed? A court may allow the owner, in appropriate circumstances, to stop (or enjoin) the infringement, to impound and destroy all infringing copies, to obtain compensation for damages, and, in certain cases, to obtain reimbursement for its attorneys' fees. In addition, criminal penalties may be involved. Thus, at least in theory, the copyright owner may bring an impressive array of sanctions to bear upon a copyright infringer.

3.5.1. Injunction

The first goal of the copyright owner is to stop the infringement. This is accomplished by obtaining a court-ordered injunction prohibiting the defendant from continuing to copy, and (where appropriate) from continuing to market the infringing copies of the plaintiff's software.[61] If the owner of the copyright—that is, the plaintiff—can demonstrate that it is likely to prevail on its claim of infringement, the court has the power to issue a temporary injunction at the beginning of the lawsuit which will remain in effect while the case is being decided.[62] At the conclusion of the lawsuit, if it is determined that the defendant has infringed the plaintiff's software, the court has the authority to make the injunction permanent[63] and to provide the other relief discussed in the following sections.

---

[60] *SAS Institute, Inc. v. S & H Computer Systems, Inc.,* 605 F. Supp. 816, 822, 825–26, 829–30 (M.D. Tenn 1985). *See also Whelan Associates Inc. v. Jaslow Dental Laboratory, Inc.,* 609 F. Supp. 1307, 1320–1322 (E.D. Pa. 1985), and discussion at Section 2.1.1.

[61] For a more detailed discussion of injunctions see Section 4.11.1.

[62] 17 U.S.C. §502.

[63] *Id.*

3.5.2. Impoundment of Infringing Copies

The Copyright Act authorizes the court to order the impoundment of all allegedly infringing copies of the defendant's software at any time during the pendency of a copyright infringement lawsuit.[64] This is done to insure that all infringing copies of the software can be destroyed at the conclusion of the lawsuit if the plaintiff prevails. An order issued in one case, for example, required the defendant to deliver all copies of the software in its possession to the court for the duration of the litigation.[65]

3.5.3. Destruction of Infringing Copies

At the conclusion of the lawsuit, if the court determines that the defendant has infringed the plaintiff's copyright in its software, it may, as part of the final judgment or decree, order the destruction or other reasonable disposition of all copies of the software found to have been made or used in violation of the copyright owner's exclusive rights, as well as all disks, tapes, masters, or other articles by means of which such copies may be reproduced.[66]

3.5.4. Damages

A plaintiff whose software has been misappropriated is also entitled to an award of money damages as compensation for the financial injury caused by the misappropriation. Generally, two alternative damage measures are available to the plaintiff: damages measured by the sum of the plaintiff's actual losses and the defendant's profits, or statutory damages.

The plaintiff has the right to recover any damages that it suffered as a result of the infringement, plus any profits made by the infringer.[67] Actual damages may include lost profits as well as the reduced market value of the software caused by the unauthorized distribution of infringing copies. In addition, the plaintiff may

---

[64] 17 U.S.C. §503.
[65] *Videotronics, Inc. v. Bend Elecs.*, 586 F. Supp. 478, 487–88 (D. Nev. 1984).
[66] 17 U.S.C. §503(b).
[67] 17 U.S.C. §§504(a), (b).

recover the profits made by the defendant on the marketing of the infringing software to the extent they are not taken into account in calculating the plaintiff's actual damages.[68]

If it is difficult for the plaintiff to prove the exact dollar amount of its losses resulting from the defendant's infringement, the plaintiff may elect, at any time during the lawsuit, to recover "statutory damages." Then there is no need to prove the actual loss. Under the Copyright Act, the court may award statutory damages to the plaintiff of $250 to $10,000.[69] And, if the court finds that the defendant acted willfully, it may increase the award of statutory damages to as much as $50,000.[70] Remember, however, that the option to take statutory damages is not available to a plaintiff unless the software has been registered within the time period required by the statute. (See Section 2.6.1.)

3.5.5. Costs and Attorneys' Fees

The Copyright Act specifically allows the court to award the costs of the litigation, including reasonable attorneys' fees, to the prevailing party.[71] It is important to note, however, that attorneys' fees are available to the prevailing party only if the software has been registered within the time period required by the statute. (See Section 2.6.1.)

3.5.6. Criminal Penalties

In certain cases, individuals who infringe a copyright may be liable for criminal as well as civil penalties. Specifically, the copyright law makes it a criminal offense to infringe a copyright "willfully and for purposes of commercial advantage or private financial gain." The penalty can be up to one year in prison and a fine of up to $25,000.[72] Thus anyone who is infringing a software copyright for purposes of marketing the infringing copies may be guilty of criminal copyright infringement.

---

[68] 17 U.S.C. §504(b).
[69] 17 U.S.C. §504(c)(1).
[70] 17 U.S.C. §504(c)(2).
[71] 17 U.S.C. §505.
[72] 17 U.S.C. §506; 18 U.S.C. §2319.

In addition to infringement, the Copyright Act also makes it a criminal offense to place a false copyright notice on any article (such as software), or to publicly distribute an article bearing such a notice with fraudulent intent.[73] Similarly, it is a crime to remove a copyright notice with a fraudulent intent.[74] Finally, it is also a criminal offense to knowingly make a false representation of a material fact in the application for a copyright registration.[75] The penalty for all of these activities is a fine of up to $2,500.

---

[73] 17 U.S.C. §506(c).
[74] 17 U.S.C. §506(d).
[75] 17 U.S.C. §506(e).

CHAPTER FOUR

TRADE SECRET PROTECTION FOR SOFTWARE

Copyright protection for software prohibits unauthorized copying. But copying is not the only form of software piracy.

In many cases, the most valuable aspect of the software is the methodology that it uses to perform its various functions. The algorithms it contains, the processes it utilizes, its overall design and structure, or other of its characteristics, may allow the software to do something never done before, or to perform a routine task faster or in a more efficient manner. Protecting the secrecy of these elements can be as important as preventing the distribution of unauthorized copies. But the copyright law only prohibits copying of expression; it does not prohibit the theft of the secret of how the software works. Preventing the theft of this type of information falls within the realm of the law of trade secrets.

Trade secret protection is governed by state law, not federal law. Consequently, the definition of a trade secret and the scope of its protection may vary from state to state. This chapter will explain the general principles of trade secret law, but the reader should be aware that the law in a particular state may be different in some respects.

4.1. WHAT IS A TRADE SECRET—AN OVERVIEW

Any formula, pattern, device, process, plan, tool, mechanism, compound, or compilation of information can qualify as a trade secret provided that (1) it is kept a secret and (2) it gives the person who possesses it an advantage over his or her competitors who do not.[1] One of the best known examples of a trade secret is the formula for Coca-Cola. Customer lists, product designs, manufacturing processes, and business plans are also frequently kept as trade secrets. Basically any idea, formula, process, and so forth can qualify as a trade secret if it is not obvious, is valuable to its owner, is kept secret, and would require a substantial investment of time or money by another to produce the same result independently.

Most importantly, the courts have recognized that computer software can qualify for trade secret protection. In the reported cases to date, a wide variety of software has been found to contain trade secrets, including an inventory control system;[2] a time sharing system monitor and a programming language;[3] an on-line business system;[4] direct mail software;[5] software for the diagnosis, checking, and debugging of various devices within a com-

---

[1] Restatement (First) of Torts §757, comment b (1939).

[2] *University Computing Co. v. Lykes-Youngstown Corp.*, 504 F.2d 518, 535 (5th Cir. 1974) (applying Georgia law).

[3] *Com-Share, Inc. v. Computer Complex, Inc.*, 338 F. Supp. 1229, 1238 (E.D. Mich. 1971) (applying Texas law), *aff'd per curiam*, 458 F.2d 1341 (6th Cir. 1971).

[4] *Cybertek Computer Prods., Inc. v. Whitfield*, 203 U.S.P.Q. 1020, 1024 (Cal. Super. Ct. 1977).

[5] *Computer Print Sys., Inc. v. Lewis*, 422 A.2d 148, 152–53 n. 3 (Pa. Super. Ct. 1980).

puter system;[6] and software for solving structural analysis problems.[7]

Theoretically, trade secret protection can last forever, but the protection can also be lost in an instant. This is because a trade secret is protected only as long as it is kept a secret and so long as no one else duplicates it by legitimate, independent research or reverse engineering.[8] But, as in the case of the Coca-Cola formula, if proper steps are taken to preserve secrecy, trade secret protection can last indefinitely.

4.2. WHAT SOFTWARE QUALIFIES AS A TRADE SECRET

The trade secret laws will not protect all software. To qualify as a trade secret, the software must have two basic characteristics: It must be secret, and it must provide its owner with an advantage over competitors who do not have it.

4.2.1. Secrecy Requirement

The secrecy requirement may be somewhat obvious, but is also of critical importance. In the absence of secrecy, there is no trade secret protection. The concept of "secrecy" is really a term of art; it is determined by whether experts in the industry also possess the same information. Information which is general knowledge within the data processing industry, such as the COBOL programming language or the concept of an indexed sequential file structure, cannot be a trade secret even though it may not be known to most people. Software does not qualify for trade secret protection merely because the customers to whom it is marketed are unable to figure out how it works. It must also be secret from other competitors within the industry.

---

[6] *Telex Corp. v. International Business Machines Corp.*, 367 F. Supp. 258, 325–26 (N.D. Okla. 1973), *trade secret aspects aff'd*, 510 F.2d 894, 930 (10th Cir. 1975).

[7] *Structural Dynamics Research Corp. v. Engineering Mechanics Research Corp.*, 401 F. Supp. 1102, 1117–1118 (E.D. Mich. 1975).

[8] *University Computing Co. v. Lykes-Youngstown Corp.*, 504 F.2d 518, 534 (5th Cir. 1974) *reh'g denied*, 505 F.2d 1304 (5th Cir. 1974).

To determine whether software incorporates a trade secret, it is necessary to examine the extent to which the allegedly secret aspect of the software is known to anyone other than the software owner, the extent to which it is known to the software owner's employees, the extent of the measures taken by the software owner to guard the secrecy of the information, and the ease or difficulty with which the information could properly be acquired or duplicated by others.[9] Absolute secrecy, however, is not required. When one develops software that he or she considers to be a secret, it may be disclosed to persons legally obligated to keep it secret, such as employees, and to persons who expressly agree to keep it secret, such as customers, without affecting the trade secret protection. As long as the disclosure is made in confidence, and is so understood by both parties, the veil of secrecy will not be deemed to have been broken.

A disclosure of the secret is made "in confidence" when the person to whom the secret is disclosed signs a written agreement acknowledging that the material is secret and that he or she will not disclose it to others.[10] (See Sections A.13–A.15 for samples of confidentiality agreements.) However, a written confidentiality agreement is not always necessary since the law will deem certain disclosures to have been made in confidence even without a written agreement. This is the case, for example, when the owner of a trade secret discloses it to his or her employees.

Courts frequently evaluate the secrecy of software in terms of its novelty. For trade secret purposes, this novelty can relate either to the function performed by the software or to the method by which it performs a routine function. If a new software package is developed which performs a function never before accomplished with a computer, it will certainly be considered novel. But even software of a routine nature can qualify. For example, a newly developed payroll system can qualify for trade secret protection even though the function it performs is certainly not novel. Moreover, this is true even if the new software makes use of some generally known techniques, algorithms, and information. Al-

---

[9] Restatement (First) of Torts §757 comment b (1939).

[10] Such a confidentiality agreement should be included in a license allowing a customer to use the software. (See Section 9.9.) See Section A.7 for an example of such a license.

though the concept of a payroll system and many of the processes used to implement it are not themselves trade secrets (they are not secret), a specific program using those generally known ideas can be, because of the unique logic and coherence by which it is designed and programmed.[11] In other words, while generally known concepts cannot be protected, a specific implementation involving a unique combination of general concepts may well amount to a trade secret.

This was recognized by a court in an early trade secret software case.[12] There a company accused of selling software which it had promised to keep secret argued that the software was not unique, and therefore could not be a trade secret. The software involved was a time-sharing system, which the court held to embody a trade secret. In doing so, it acknowledged the fact that all time-sharing software contains certain elements which perform similar functions and which utilize certain similar fundamental concepts of a general nature. What is different (or novel) about each of these systems is their specific engineering, their particular underlying technology and design, what has been referred to as their "logic and coherence," and their speed, accuracy, cost, and commercial feasibility. These qualities will differ greatly from system to system, and will inevitably reflect the peculiar and unique accomplishments and technical skills of the developers. Trade secret novelty (or secrecy) requires only that the particular architecture of a program is valuable and that it is not a matter of common knowledge or readily duplicated.[13]

In addition to the requirement that the software be secret within the industry, the law also imposes a burden on the owner of the software to take steps to maintain its secrecy. In essence, the law says that the software must not only be secret, but that the owner must also act as if it is a valuable secret and guard it accordingly. Otherwise the protection provided by the trade secret laws may be lost, even though the information is not otherwise known in the industry. In one case, for example, a court held that soft-

---

[11] *Cybertek Computer Prods., Inc. v. Whitfield*, 203 U.S.P.Q. 1020, 1024 (Cal. Super. Ct. 1977).

[12] *Com-Share, Inc. v. Computer Complex, Inc.*, 338 F. Supp. 1229, 1234 (E.D. Mich. 1971), *aff'd*, 458 F.2d 1341 (6th Cir. 1972).

[13] *Dickerman Assocs. v. Tiverton Bottled Gas Co.*, 594 F. Supp. 30, 35 (D. Mass. 1984).

ware used in the design and manufacture of class rings was not a trade secret because, among other things, the plaintiff never proved that it intended to keep the relevant information secret.[14] This conclusion was based in part on the fact that when the software was installed, no policy was established to keep it secret, and that the plaintiff had allowed one of its employees to write an article explaining the system to other experts in the field.

Depending on the circumstances, fulfilling this obligation to maintain secrecy may require the establishment of an affirmative course of action reasonably designed to insure that the software will remain secret.[15] Steps that can be taken to insure protection of software are described in Section 4.5.

4.2.2. Competitive Advantage Requirement

In addition to being a secret, the software must provide its owner with an advantage over its competitors who do not have it. Otherwise, there really is not anything worth protecting. For example, if a word processing vendor were to develop software capable of printing documents backwards, it might represent an accomplishment of sorts, and the way in which it is done may very well be secret, but it is doubtful that it would provide its owner with any advantage over its competitors in the office systems market. Another example is the case of a woman who created a set of "I Ching" cards, using better colors and paper than the original.[16] The court said that these "improvements" were not trade secrets, since they were minimal and gave her no competitive advantage.

Courts frequently analyze the competitive advantage of a trade secret by looking at the time and effort that has gone into its development. It is the time and money that goes into a finished software product that frequently gives its owner a big "head start" over any competitor who is only beginning the process of developing similar software. The essence of trade secret law is to protect the value of this head start by requiring competitors to spend their own time and money to create a competing product. In this

---

[14] *Jostens, Inc. v. National Computer Sys., Inc.*, 318 N.W.2d 691, 700 (Minn. 1982).

[15] *Amoco Prod. Co. v. Lindley*, 609 P.2d 733, 743 (Okla. 1980).

[16] *Walker v. University Books, Inc.*, 602 F.2d 859, 865 (9th Cir. 1979).

way, the law protects the trade secret owner's investment in the product.

4.3. SCOPE OF TRADE SECRET PROTECTION

Trade secret protection is in some ways broader than that afforded by copyright, but at the same time it is also more restrictive. In general, it will protect more aspects of software than copyright, but will do so in fewer situations. To utilize the trade secret law effectively, it is important to understand its scope.

4.3.1. Idea and Expression

Trade secret law protects both ideas and the expressions of those ideas. Thus it is much broader than copyright, which protects only the expression of an idea. The scope of trade secret protection is best explained by comparing it to the protection provided by copyright. Remember the example (in Section 2.1.2.) of the individual who developed a foolproof technique for rating horses in order to pick a winner at the races? If instead of writing a book to describe his technique, he keeps it a secret and writes a computer program to implement it, he will surely have an advantage over his competitors at the race track betting windows. In short, the technique qualifies as a trade secret. Copyright law protects the way he wrote the code to implement his secret algorithm, but it does not prevent others from reading his code, learning the algorithm, and writing their own code to implement it. This is where trade secret protection is important. In this example, the trade secret is the algorithm (i.e., the idea), not the way it was coded (i.e., the way the idea was expressed). Trade secret law will protect that idea; anyone who reads the code and then uses it without authorization or discloses it to others may be liable for trade secret misappropriation.

4.3.2. Confidential Relationship

Although the scope of trade secret protection is broader than the scope of copyright protection, its application is somewhat more limited. Whereas copyright prohibits any unauthorized copying of the software, trade secret protection prohibits the unauthorized use of a trade secret only when it is done in violation of a confidential relationship, that is, a relationship in which one is legally bound not to use or disclose the secret information without the owner's permission.

A confidential relationship between an owner of software and someone else can arise in two ways: It can be implied by law, or it can be expressly agreed to in a contract. The best example of an implied obligation of confidentiality occurs in the employer–employee relationship. Employees are automatically bound not to disclose or use for their own benefit the trade secrets disclosed to them by their employer. No written contract is necessary to create this obligation.

Conversely, when a trade secret is disclosed to a customer, there is no obligation of confidentiality implied by law. Thus to establish a relationship of confidentiality which will preclude the customer from exploiting a vendor's trade secret, it is normally necessary to enter into a written contract to this end. It is for this reason that virtually all software license agreements impose a confidentiality obligation on the user. (The confidentiality provision itself is discussed in Section 9.9, and examples may be found in the sample contracts set forth in Sections A.7, A.9, A.11, A.13, A.14, and A.15.)

Imposing an obligation of confidentiality is very important. In one case, for example, Data General had made confidential design drawings for its Nova 1200 computer available to approximately 6,000 customers for use in maintaining the equipment. When a competitor obtained a copy of these documents and attempted to use them to design a new computer, Data General filed suit for trade secret misappropriation. The competitor argued that Data General had made an unrestricted disclosure of these documents (thereby forfeiting its trade secrets), but the court disagreed, because the documents had been given only to customers who had signed confidentiality agreements.[17] Consequently, Data General was able to prevail on its claim.

---

[17] *Data General Corp. v. Digital Computer Controls, Inc.*, 357 A.2d 105, 110–11 (Del. Ch. 1975).

When there is no confidential relationship between the owner of a trade secret and someone who learns of it, the latter is free to use it in any way he or she desires. Thus, independent development of the same secret and reverse engineering of products purchased on the open market are perfectly proper. If someone independently develops the secret, they are, of course, under no obligation to anyone else who may also have the same secret. Similarly, if the owner discloses the secret to an outsider without any confidentiality restrictions, there is nothing wrong with using it. This frequently occurs when products are placed on the market and the trade secrets are disclosed by the product itself or are discernible through reverse engineering.

An example of the rather unfortunate consequences that can occur when software or any trade secret is disclosed to someone not bound by an obligation of confidentiality is illustrated by the facts of a recent case brought by two game inventors against Milton Bradley Company.[18] The two plaintiffs, Coleman and Burten, had developed a new electronic game which they called "Triumph." It contained a microprocessor which, with the plaintiff's software, was capable of providing private visual cues to individual players, storing information that could be kept secret from other players, and providing public sound cues for all players. The structure of this game was the trade secret.

Coleman and Burten submitted this game to Milton Bradley for its consideration, and although they received an initially positive response, the game was ultimately rejected about a month later. At the time they submitted their prototype, however, they were asked to sign a document titled "Disclosure Record" which contained the following language:

> I submit my idea or item voluntarily and I understand that this submission by me and its acceptance by Company does not, in whole or in part, establish or create by implication or otherwise any relationship between Company and me not expressed herein. I further understand and agree that Company, in its own judgment, may accept or reject the idea or item submitted and shall not be obligated to me in any way with respect to my idea until Company

---

[18] *Burten v. Milton Bradley Co.*, 592 F. Supp. 1021 (D.R.I. 1984); *rev'd* 763 F.2d 461 (1st Cir. 1985). (applying Massachusetts law).

shall at its own election enter into a properly executed written agreement with me and then, only according to all of the terms of said agreement. If no agreement is concluded, I shall rely solely upon such rights as I may have under U.S. Patent laws.

Approximately 11 months later Milton Bradley introduced a new electronic game called "Dark Tower," which had the same structure as plaintiffs' "Triumph" game and performed the same functions. It enjoyed enormous commercial success.

Coleman and Burten sued Milton Bradley claiming trade secret misappropriation. After a trial, the jury found that Coleman and Burten's game did in fact contain a trade secret, that they did disclose the secret to Milton Bradley, and that Milton Bradley did take and use that trade secret in developing its own game, to the plaintiffs' detriment. But there was one important issue left to be decided—that is, did there exist a confidential relationship between the inventors and Milton Bradley? If such a relationship did exist, Milton Bradley would be liable for trade secret misappropriation. If not, then Milton Bradley was free to use the invention disclosed to it.

Milton Bradley argued that the language of the Disclosure Record signed by the inventors clearly disclaimed the existence of any relationship between it and the inventors, including a confidential relationship. Therefore, it claimed, there was no trade secret misappropriation. The trial court agreed with this conclusion, and entered judgment in favor of Milton Bradley. The inventors appealed this decision, however, and court of appeals reversed the trial court. It agreed that the Disclosure Record could be read to waive the existence of a confidential relationship, but held that other factors surrounding the transaction, including a handwritten addendum to the agreement, allowed the jury to find that a confidential relationship did exist. But both the trial court and the appeals court clearly agreed that if a confidential relationship had not been established, Milton Bradley would have been free to use the inventors' trade secret.

Thus, as illustrated by the *Milton Bradley* case, establishing a confidential relationship with everyone who will receive the software is critical to protecting its trade secrets. However, it should be noted that an unauthorized user of a trade secret can also be held liable for misappropriation, in the absence of a confidential relationship with the owner, if he knew that the trade secret had been disclosed to him by someone else in violation of their obligation of confidentiality, or was subsequently informed of that fact.[19]

This problem will most likely arise in the case of a customer who either knowingly or innocently obtains software from someone who has wrongfully misappropriated a copy from its rightful owner. This scenario did occur in one reported case involving a customer of a data processing service bureau.[20] There, the service bureau customer had requested a backup copy of the software being run on its behalf because it doubted the ability of the service bureau to remain in business. An employee of the service bureau provided such a copy, but, unbeknown to the customer, this was done in violation of company policy. Before the customer could use the software, however, it was put on notice by the service bureau that the programs were its exclusive property. This notice, the court held, subjected the customer to trade secret liability for its subsequent use of the software for which it had paid no money.

4.4. HOW TRADE SECRET PROTECTION CAN BE LOST

Although trade secret protection is broader than that offered by copyright, it is also very fragile. It is automatically lost whenever it is disclosed or becomes generally known within the industry. There are two ways this can happen—independent discovery and unrestricted disclosure.

4.4.1. Independent Discovery

A trade secret is protected only as long as competitors fail to duplicate it by legitimate independent research.[21] Once someone independently discovers a trade secret, that person is free to use or disclose it. It will remain a trade secret, even though known to

---

[19] Restatement (First) of Torts §§757, 758 (1939).

[20] *Computer Print Sys., Inc. v. Lewis*, 281 Pa. Super. 240, 422 A.2d 148, 155 (1980).

[21] *University Computing Co. v. Lykes-Youngstown Corp.*, 504 F.2d 518, 534 (5th Cir. 1974).

two persons instead of one, if both keep it secret. If either discloses it to the industry, however, the secret is lost to both.

Independent discovery can occur in two ways. First, another person can serendipitously happen on the same idea or solution, or can do the work and spend the money necessary to independently develop it. Second, another person can purchase the product, take it apart, study it, and figure out how it works. This latter process is known as reverse engineering and is perfectly legal once a product is sold on the market. The mere fact that a product is on the market and available for reverse engineering, however, will not permit others to steal its trade secret by improper means. The law requires all trade secrets to be obtained honestly if at all.[22] If it will require an extensive period of time and/or a large expenditure of money in order to reverse-engineer the product, even after it is out in the market, then the trade secret can be protected to the extent of this time and cost advantage.

Although reverse engineering is legal in most cases, it may not be allowed in some cases in connection with software. If a customer obtains a copy of a package pursuant to a license agreement, that agreement may prohibit reverse engineering, and in any event, will prohibit the customer's disclosure of the vendor's secrets to third parties (see Section 9.9). Moreover, even when software is purchased rather than licensed, reverse engineering may constitute copyright infringement if it is done through process of disassembling or decompiling the object code (see Section 3.3.3).

4.4.2. Unrestricted Disclosure

Disclosure of a trade secret in the context of a confidential relationship will not result in the loss of trade secret protection. For example, an employer is free to disclose trade secrets to its employees, because by law, employees are legally bound to keep all of their employer's trade secrets confidential. Similarly, the owner of software can disclose it to anyone who will sign a contract specifically agreeing to keep the trade secrets confidential. In fact,

---

[22] *Digital Dev. Corp. v. International Memory Sys. Inc.*, 185 U.S.P.Q. 136, 141 (S.D. Cal. 1973); *Thermotics, Inc. v. Bat-Jac Tool Co.*, 541 S.W.2d 255, 260–61 (Tex. Civ. App. 1976); *Colony Corp. of America v. Crown Glass Corp.*, 430 N.E.2d 225, 227 (Ill. App. 1981).

this is the way that software must be marketed if the trade secret is to be protected: that is, all customers must agree to keep the software confidential and not to disclose it to anyone else. (See Section 9.9).

On the other hand, unrestricted disclosure of a trade secret will forfeit its protected status. An unrestricted disclosure of a trade secret is a disclosure to anyone who is not legally obligated to keep it confidential. This frequently occurs through simple carelessness on the part of the trade secret owner. In one case, for example, trade secret protection was lost when a company allowed one of its employees to publish an article explaining its system to other experts in the field. The trial court found that the information in the article was sufficient to enable an experienced engineer to duplicate the software without too much difficulty.[23] The *Milton Bradley* case discussed in Section 4.3.2 is another example of the problems that can arise when a secret is disclosed to someone who is not legally obligated to keep it confidential. Disclosures like these should never be allowed to occur.

Another way that unrestricted disclosure can occur is through marketing. Any product which has been sold on the market is generally open to duplication by skilled engineers.[24] If software is sold outright instead of being licensed, and if the trade secret can be determined by an inspection of the software itself (such as if source code were provided), the trade secret will be lost when that occurs. If the software is licensed, however, and the licensee is contractually bound to keep it confidential, this will constitute a protected disclosure and trade secret protection will not be waived. In other words, the party to a confidentiality agreement will not be permitted to obtain rights in the trade secret, even by reverse engineering.

4.4.3. Registration of Copyright

Many commentators feel that copyright registration can also result in the loss of trade secret protection. As discussed in Section 2.6.2, when software is registered with the Copyright Office, the "identifying portions" of the software must be deposited with the Copy-

---

[23] *Jostens, Inc. v. National Computer Sys., Inc.*, 318 N.W.2d 691, 700 (Minn. 1982).
[24] *Analogic Corp. v. Data Translation, Inc.*, 358 N.E.2d 804, 807 (Mass. 1976).

right Office where it will become available for public inspection. To the extent that these identifying portions would disclose any trade secrets, it would be an unrestricted disclosure resulting in the loss of protection.

4.5. HOW TO PROTECT SOFTWARE AS A TRADE SECRET

The major risk of relying on the trade secret laws to protect proprietary technology is that once the secret is out, the protection is gone. The secret may be revealed through carelessness, the independent discovery of a third party, or theft. While there is no way to prevent independent discovery, it is possible to guard against theft and careless or inadvertent disclosure. In fact, the failure to take steps to prevent inadvertent disclosure, may, itself, result in waiver of the protection. The ease with which allegedly proprietary information can be obtained from its owner may furnish a valid defense to a charge of trade secret misappropriation. Thus whether an owner of proprietary software has taken adequate steps to protect its secrecy is frequently one of the key issues in trade secret litigation. Simply put, to maintain trade secret protection for software, it must be treated as a trade secret. A software developer who freely distributes "trade secret" information within his or her own firm may find that the courts will deny protection. Courts will generally not enforce trade secret protection for software unless there is evidence that the owner has taken clear action to protect its secrecy. If the owner does not treat it like a valuable secret and try to protect it, why should the courts?

Standard measures which can be taken by a software owner to protect trade secrets involve both the use of contractual safeguards for customer relationships and the establishment of internal controls within the owner's organization. The level of effort and expense required to protect a trade secret varies widely, depending on the circumstances. Consequently, a decision as to whether to implement any particular procedure should be based on (1) an analysis of the value of the software and (2) the likelihood that it will be subject to misappropriation. There is no requirement that any specific procedures be implemented; the test is simply whether the owner treated the software as one would treat a valuable secret. The following sections discuss the most widely used and commonly recognized techniques for protecting a trade secret.

4.5.1. Notice of Trade Secret Claim

One of the first and most important steps to be taken in maintaining trade secret protection for software is to notify anyone who comes into contact with it (such as employees and customers) that the owner considers it to be a valuable trade secret. One who is truly unaware that particular software contains a trade secret will be more difficult to prosecute for misappropriation.

Providing notice that software is considered to contain a valuable trade secret is easy to do. For example, confidentiality notices can be inserted as comments in source code listings, and displayed at the terminal when the software is executed. Such a notice might read as follows:

> Warning—This software is a trade secret of ABC Software Corp., and is to be kept confidential at all times. Anyone who wrongfully uses or discloses this software may be subject to civil and/or criminal penalties.

Trade secret notices can also be ink-stamped on the top of any sensitive program listings or applied by gummed label to binders containing source code, as well as to disks, tapes, manuals, or diskettes containing machine-readable copies of the software. Appropriate notices should also be inserted in any sensitive documentation.

It is also advisable to inform employees, customers, and anyone else to whom sensitive material is to be disclosed, both verbally and by written contract, of the fact that the owner considers it to be a valuable trade secret. Such notice in employee confidentiality agreements is discussed in Section 7.2; similar notice in customer contracts is discussed in Section 9.9.

The primary goal is to be sure that everyone who comes into contact with the software is aware of the fact that its owner considers it to be a valuable trade secret. This will encourage individuals to whom it has been disclosed in confidence to treat it as a trade secret, and will make it easier for a court to punish anyone who discloses what he or she knows to be a trade secret.

4.5.2. Restricting Access to the Software

Perhaps the primary method available for protecting a trade secret in software is to restrict the number of individuals who have access to it to the absolute minimum. Access to the trade secret may be obtained on-line, via tape, disk, or diskette kept in a storage area, via source code listings, or via documentation. No one who is not directly working with the software, and authorized to do so, should have access to any of these sources.

On-line access can be restricted through the use of passwords which should be changed periodically, restricted libraries, or other similar procedures. Access to the physical tapes, disks, and diskettes containing the software should be carefully controlled by keeping such media in a secure and locked area. Only authorized personnel should be allowed access to this media, and sign-out procedures should be instituted where appropriate. All use of the software residing in this media should be carefully monitored.

Access to source code listings and documentation should be similarly restricted. If possible, sensitive program listings should be kept under lock and key. Allowing programmers to take source code listings home, or, for that matter, to access the computer via home terminals, can lead to the loss of a trade secret and should be carefully controlled, if allowed at all. Furthermore, all source listings and other documentation relating to programs should be stamped with legends such as "Secret," "Confidential," "For Use By Authorized Personnel Only," "Return to Office Safe," or "Not for Publication." And if programs are disclosed to third persons such as customers or technicians, a written record of such disclosure should be kept and the third party should execute a written commitment not to reveal the information to anyone else.

Accurate and detailed record keeping is one of the cornerstones of adequate software protection. The owner should make a written record of all procedures and policies implemented to restrict access to trade secret software, and be sure that they are enforced. Like all methods of protecting trade secrets, carefully restricting access makes disclosure less likely, and puts a software thief at a distinct disadvantage in the eyes of a court.

The extent to which these procedures are implemented depends, of course, on the nature of the business, the value of the software, and the likelihood of misappropriation. Large corporations with extremely valuable products may go to the extent of installing closed-circuit cameras, keeping the software in safes, and having guards patrol the premises. A one-person operation, on the other hand, might just simply refrain from allowing anyone else to use the software, and keep the copies in a locked drawer.

4.5.3. Protecting Trade Secrets Disclosed to Employees

The law implies the existence of a confidential relationship between every employer and employee. In other words, the law implies an agreement which prohibits employees from disclosing any trade secrets revealed to them in the course of their employment, and from using those trade secrets for their own or someone else's benefit.[25] But an employee is also entitled to fair notice of the confidential nature of the relationship and what material is to be kept confidential.[26] Consequently, the implied obligation of confidentiality may apply only to trade secrets of which (1) the employee has been expressly made aware, such as through specific designation by the employer; or (2) the employee can be said to have "constructive knowledge," such as from the context in which the information was disclosed, from the measures taken by the employer to protect the secret, or from the knowledge which an employee can reasonably be expected to possess as to what provides one business with an advantage over its competitors.[27]

Consequently, it is often wise to have employees sign confidentiality agreements in which they expressly acknowledge that the software and documentation with which they will be working is considered to be a trade secret belonging to the employer, and that they will not improperly use or disclose it. An employee confidentiality agreement serves to demonstrate that the em-

[25] *Jostens, Inc. v. National Computer Sys., Inc.*, 318 N.W.2d 691, 701 (Minn. 1982).
[26] *Id.* at 702.
[27] *Id.*

ployer considers its developments to be secret and valuable. It is also the most persuasive possible evidence that employees were informed from the outset that they would not be permitted to use the company's software except in its business.

If an employee leaves his or her employer to work for a competitor, a confidentiality agreement gives the first employer a sound legal basis for preventing the employee from taking or using software or its unique constituent elements in his or her new job. The existence of a confidentiality agreement, if made known to the new employer, may also help to reduce its enthusiasm for exploiting the employee's confidential knowledge.

Employee confidentiality agreements are discussed in detail in Section 7.2. Sample employee agreements which contain confidentiality provisions are set out in Sections A.13. and A.14.

Employee noncompetition agreements are also used, in some states, in conjunction with confidentiality agreements. A noncompetition agreement is a contract that prohibits an employee from going to work for a competitor (or starting his or her own competing business) for a certain period of time in a particular geographical area after leaving his or her current employer. Its purpose is to preclude the employee from using or disclosing the former employer's trade secrets. A noncompetition agreement is particularly recommended where:

1. It is difficult to distinguish between an employee's general knowledge and skills in the industry and the trade secrets he or she knows; and

2. By working for a competitor, it will be virtually impossible for an employee to refrain from disclosing the trade secrets of his or her former employer.

The theory behind a noncompetition agreement is that, notwithstanding an employee's best intentions, if he or she goes to work for a competitor on a similar project, it will be virtually impossible for the employee not to use or disclose trade secrets obtained from his or her former employer. Consequently, one solution to this problem is simply to prohibit the employee from going to work for a competitor.

Although noncompetition agreements are recognized in most states, they are not favored. This means that courts will not enforce agreements that are overly restrictive. Moreover, some states prohibit all noncompetition agreements by law. Thus state law must be consulted before this device is used.

Noncompetition agreements are discussed in detail in Section 7.3. A sample employee agreement which contains a noncompetition provision is set out in Section A.13.

Finally, when an employee announces his or her intention to leave, it is also appropriate to conduct an exit interview. The purpose of such an interview is to remind the employee of his or her obligations with respect to trade secrets and to insure that the employee has returned all software, documentation, and any other materials that belong to the employer.

4.5.4. Protecting Trade Secrets Disclosed to Customers

There are, of course, many good reasons for disclosing trade secrets to persons other than employees. The most obvious example is the licensing of software to a customer, which in many cases will require disclosure of the trade secret. Similarly, trade secrets may be disclosed to others for evaluation, or potential purchase, or as "advertising." In all of these cases, it is extremely important that those to whom the software is to be disclosed execute a confidentiality agreement in which they agree (1) to limit their use of the software as specified in the contract, and (2) not to disclose the software to any other party without the express permission of the owner. The necessary element of secrecy is not lost if the holder of the trade secret reveals it to another "in confidence" and under an obligation not to disclose it.[28]

The effectiveness of such an agreement was illustrated in a case involving two computer service corporations, Com-Share, Inc. and Computer Complex, Inc. They had entered into a time-and technology-sharing agreement in which they agreed to provide confidential technology to each other, but which also specifically

---

[28] *Management Science America, Inc. v. Cyborg Sys., Inc.*, 6 Computer L. Serv. Rep. 921, 925 (N.D. Ill. 1978) (applying Illinois law and quoting *Kewanee Oil Co. v. Bicron Corp.*, 416 U.S. 470, 475 (1974) (applying Ohio law)).

prohibited the disclosure of secret information to third parties. When Computer Complex subsequently sold its assets plus some of Com-Share's software to a third party, Com-Share filed suit. The court enforced the nondisclosure agreement and issued a preliminary injunction prohibiting disclosure or transfer of the Com-Share software by Computer Complex.[29]

When software is licensed to a specific customer, an appropriate confidentiality provision should be inserted in the contract. In addition, to assist in enforcing this confidentiality requirement, the software contract should clearly define (1) the vendor's rights to any trade secrets, and (2) the responsibilities of the customer to protect against misappropriation of those trade secrets. This may require imposing restrictions on the customer's use of the software and a prohibition against copying the software, manuals, or other materials licensed for their use. Confidentiality clauses for software contracts are discussed in detail in Section 9.9, and the imposition of various restrictions on use of the software is discussed in Section 9.3.

4.5.5.　Defensive Software Development

"Defensive software development" is an all-encompassing phrase which covers two general areas. The first refers to the coding techniques which can be used to inhibit disclosure of the software, such as copy protect routines, destruction routines, date bombs, and the like. These techniques are best left to the ingenuity of the author of the software. One word of caution, however. If date bombs or similar destruction routines are included within the software, it is advisable that the customer be informed of their existence (especially if this device is used to enforce payment). Otherwise, the customer may have a claim against the developer for damages incurred when the software suddenly ceases to run.

The second aspect of defensive software development refers to methods of coding which, although they will not prevent misappropriation of a trade secret, will make proof of misappropriation much easier. This involves, in essence, the concept of

---

[29] *Com-Share, Inc. v. Computer Complex, Inc.*, 338 F. Supp. 1229, 1240 (E.D. Mich. 1971).

"fingerprinting" the software so that a court can examine software allegedly misappropriated from its rightful owner and determine whether it was taken from the original version of the software. The number of ways to fingerprint software is limited only by the creativity of the programmer. Examples include the use of arbitrary sequences of code, the inclusion of harmless errors, the use of unreferenced variables or encrypted messages, and other similar techniques. Serial numbers can also be included within software, preferably in an encrypted manner, which will not only identify an infringing copy but may also reveal the source of the original disclosure.

A good example of fingerprinting occurred in a case involving the copying of software for a video game called "DEFENDER."[30] The owner of the software had buried a copyright notice in the object code, which, sure enough, also showed up in the object code of the allegedly copied software. There was not much doubt about the fact of copying.

4.5.6. Business Records

In addition to defensive software development, it is also important to keep appropriate business records to assist in proving the existence of a trade secret and its misappropriation. Records should be kept which will identify the trade secret, establish the history of its development, document the procedures taken to preserve its secrecy, and document the cost of developing it in order to provide a current indication of its value. A careful record should also be kept of all confidential disclosures made of the software, in order to rebut any claims that the software was not treated as a secret.

4.5.7. Method of Marketing

Ideally, when software is marketed, only object code should be distributed. By keeping the source code secret, the vendor is taking a major step in preserving its trade secret status.

This is especially important when software is sold rather than

---

[30] *Williams Elecs., Inc. v. Artic Int'l., Inc.*, 685 F.2d 870, 876 n. 6 (3d Cir. 1982).

licensed, because in a sale transaction the customer will not be bound by the obligation of confidentiality that is normally included in a license agreement. The customer is therefore free to try to reverse engineer the software in order to discover its trade secrets.[31] And whenever the secret nature of software is discovered through analysis of the product marketed, the secret is lost to the person who performed the analysis.[32] Thus when software is sold, it should be packaged in a form that makes reverse engineering as difficult as possible. This means that, at a minimum, software should be sold in object code form only. Any other procedures which can be employed to discourage reverse engineering should also be considered.

Ideally, however, software should be licensed rather than sold, and the license should include an appropriate confidentiality agreement, as discussed in Section 9.9.

4.6. TRADE SECRETS AND AN EMPLOYEE'S KNOWLEDGE

When employees leave one employer to work for another they are free to take with them the general skills and knowledge acquired during their tenure with their former employer to the extent they are derived from generally known sources.[33] A computer programmer, like any other person trained for a particular occupation, must be free to practice his or her skills in order to earn a living. As one court put it:

> [T]he right of an individual to follow and pursue the particular occupation for which he is best trained is a most fundamental right. Our society is extremely mobile and our free economy is based upon competition. One who has worked in a particular field cannot be compelled to erase from his mind all of the general skills, knowledge and expertise acquired through his experience. These skills are valuable to such employee in the market place for his services.[34]

---

[31] That is, of course, as long as the reverse engineering does not involve any copyright infringement. See Section 3.3.3.

[32] *Analogic Corp. v. Data Translation, Inc.*, 358 N.E.2d 804, 807 (Mass. 1976).

[33] *J & K Computer Sys., Inc. v. Parrish*, 642 P.2d 732, 735 (Utah 1982).

[34] *ILG Indus., Inc. v. Scott*, 49 Ill.2d 88, 273 N.E.2d 393, 396 (1971).

Employees are not, however, free to take their employer's trade secrets. The problem lies in drawing the line between the employee's general skills and knowledge and the employer's trade secrets. Although this is often difficult to do, some general rules have been developed.

4.6.1. Knowledge Available Elsewhere

During the course of employment, a programmer will usually learn new skills. He or she may, for example, learn a new programming language, or a new operating system, or the operation of a new machine, or perhaps the use of a particular software product such as a program generator or a data base management system. If the employee could have learned such information in the course of similar employment elsewhere, the information cannot be protected as a trade secret, and the employee is free to use it on a new job.[35] But, if an employee learns something known only to his or her employer, the employer has a right to protect it and to prohibit its subsequent use.

4.6.2. Knowledge About a Particular Industry

Frequently, software designed to perform rather common functions (such as general ledger, inventory control, billing, etc.) is specifically tailored for a particular type of business (e.g., automobile dealerships, medical clinics, etc.). In such a case, a developer who understands the way that a particular industry works has an important edge over those who do not. Nonetheless, knowledge of a particular type of business gained by an employee in the course of designing or developing software constitutes general information which the employee is free to use in any later efforts to develop a competing system.

This principle is illustrated by the facts of a trade secret misappropriation case filed by Automated Systems, Inc. (ASI) against Service Bureau Corp. (SBC).[36] ASI had developed an inventory

---

[35] *Wilson Certified Foods, Inc. v. Fairbury Food Prods., Inc.*, 370 F. Supp. 1081, 1087 (D. Neb. 1974).

[36] *Automated Sys., Inc. v. Service Bureau Corp.*, 401 F.2d 619, 625 (10th Cir. 1968).

control system for automobile dealerships and entered into a contract with SBC whereby SBC would attempt to market the system. Pursuant to the contract SBC sent a programmer to ASI to help with documentation. He had no experience in the automobile parts business, but received intensive indoctrination in the general business of automobile parts distribution while at ASI. Consequently, when the contract was terminated and this same employee subsequently designed a competing automobile inventory control system for SBC, ASI sued. However, the court held that SBC was entitled to use the "general information" gained through its association with ASI, including information about the automobile parts business.

In another case, a programmer learned a lot about the banking industry while working for his employer to develop a shareholder's record system for a bank. When he left to form his own business, a court held that he was free to use this knowledge, since it was information about the banking industry, not a secret of his employer.[37]

To prohibit a former employee's use of information, it must be shown that it constitutes the particular secrets of the complaining employer, not general secrets of the trade in which he or she is engaged.

4.6.3. Employee-Developed Software

There is some dispute over the issue of whether an employee who actually designs and develops proprietary software has a right to use and disclose any trade secrets that may be involved. In one case involving complex structural analysis software, a Michigan federal district court said that an employee may have such rights. The court distinguished between trade secrets disclosed to an employee by the employer and trade secrets developed by the employee himself, and reached the following conclusion:

> If the subject matter of the trade secret is in being and an employee learns about it in the course of his employment in a relationship of confidence, the duty not to use or disclose trade secret knowledge

---

[37] *Trilog Assocs., Inc. v. Famularo*, 455 Pa. 243, 314 A.2d 287, 292 (Pa. 1974).

adversely to his employer arises. On the other hand, if the subject matter of the trade secret is brought into being because of the initiative of the employee in its creation, innovation or development even though the relationship is one of confidence, no duty arises since the employee may then have an interest in the subject matter at least equal to that of his employer or in any event, such knowledge is a part of the employee's skill and experience. In such a case, absent an express contractual obligation by the employee not to use or disclose such confidential information acquired during his employment adverse to his employer's interest, he is free to use or disclose it in subsequent employment activity.[38]

Note, however, that under this court's decision employees have such rights in software they develop only if they have *not* signed a written confidentiality agreement. The court made one further distinction within the category of employee-developed secrets that is worth noting:

Where the employer assigns the employee to a specific development task and commits considerable resources and supervision to the project, a confidential relationship arises that prevents the employee from using or disclosing the fruits of his research. When, on the other hand, the developments are the product of the application of the employee's own skill, "without any appreciable assistance by way of information or great expense or supervision by [the employer], outside of the normal expenses of his job," he has "an unqualified privilege" to use and disclose the trade secrets so developed.[39]

Remember that this is the opinion of a court sitting in Michigan. A similar result has also been reached by a court in Oklahoma.[40]

Most other courts disagree, however. In Connecticut a court held that "[t]he fact that it was the defendants who developed the [trade secret] process gives them no greater right to use it in competition with the plaintiff than that of any other employee."[41] In elaborating on this ruling, the court stated that:

---

[38] *Structural Dynamics Research Corp. v. Engineering Mechanics Research Corp.*, 401 F. Supp. 1102, 1111 (E.D. Mich. 1975).

[39] *Id.* at 1112.

[40] *Amoco Prod. Co. v. Lindley*, 609 P.2d 733, 744–45 (Okla. 1980).

[41] *Sperry Rand Corp. v. Rothlein*, 241 F. Supp. 549, 564–65 (D. Conn. 1964).

Where, as in the present case, the trade secret was one developed by the defendants themselves as employees of the plaintiff, they are entitled to take with them the skills learned and the knowledge acquired in the many months of trial and error devoted to the development of the marketable Sperry silicon alloy junction transistor. For example, how certain chemicals affect certain metals, what procedures insure a clean environment and what do not, etc., are things learned from their experiences at Sperry and become a part of their intellectual equipment. But their knowledge of the end products of their work there, the combination of apparatus and equipment, materials and procedures which made up the Sperry process for the manufacture of its superior quality transistor, in short, the things about the process which were the secret of Sperry's success, were information which the defendants could not use or impart to others without breaching their fiduciary duty to Sperry.[42]

Except in exceptional circumstances, the latter view is more generally accepted. However, to insure exclusive ownership in the employer, it is advisable to use a confidentiality agreement.

4.7. WHO OWNS THE TRADE SECRET IN SOFTWARE?

It frequently occurs that a software development company obtains a contract to design and program a system for a client, and then uses its own employees or independent consultants to develop that software. After the transaction has been completed, the question often arises of who owns the software—the development company, its employees, the independent consultants, or the client? The same question may also arise when a business uses its own employees (or hires independent consultants) to develop software for its own use. The best way to resolve this question is to state, in a written contract signed by each of the appropriate parties, exactly who shall own the software. (See Section 7.1.) All too frequently this is not done, however.

In the absence of a written agreement, the law is not completely clear as to who will own the trade secrets. The result will often depend upon the particular factual situation involved, and a court's attempt to balance an employee's need to use the knowl-

---

[42] *Id.* at 564.

edge he or she has obtained against the potential harm to the employer's business. In certain cases employees will retain limited rights to use the trade secrets they develop (see Section 4.6.3). On the other hand, many courts hold that the facts give rise to an implied contract for employer ownership. Accordingly, the best rule to follow is to decide the issue in advance and put it in writing before a dispute develops.

4.8. BASES OF LIABILITY FOR MISAPPROPRIATION

Trade secret law does not prohibit the use or disclosure of another's trade secrets per se. Thus the mere fact that someone else uses or discloses trade secret software does not necessarily mean that the software owner can successfully bring a lawsuit for misappropriation. The law only prohibits the unauthorized use and disclosure of trade secrets obtained under an obligation of confidentiality, or by improper means.

If one's possession, use, and/or disclosure of another's trade secret does not fall into one of these categories, then he or she has done nothing wrong. For example, if an individual obtains a copy of trade secret software without signing a confidentiality agreement (such as by purchase), he or she is free to try to reverse engineer that software in order to learn the secret and use it or disclose it to others (provided there is no copyright infringement—see Section 3.3.3). And, of course, anyone who discovers a trade secret through independent work is free to do whatever they would like with it.

It is the improper conduct in obtaining, using, or disclosing a trade secret that gives rise to liability for misappropriation. In many cases, the improper conduct will relate to the way in which the trade secret was obtained. Theft of software is an obvious example. More often than not, however, the trade secret will have been obtained legitimately. For example, it may be disclosed to an employee on the job or to a customer who has signed a confidentiality agreement. In this case, liability for trade secret misappropriation occurs only if the employee or the customer uses or discloses the trade secret in a way that breaches the obligation of confidentiality. This would occur if either of them used the trade secret to assist in starting a competing business, or gave it away to a third party.

If someone wrongfully obtains a trade secret, or uses or discloses a trade secret in violation of a confidential obligation, he or she will be liable to the owner of the trade secret for damages regardless of the way in which the trade secret was used. Thus, for example, if someone improperly obtains software and then modifies or improves it to produce a new product which is totally unrelated to the original product, he or she will still be liable for misappropriation of the original trade secret. Improper "use" of a trade secret does not require precise duplication or copying. Modifications or improvements to the original trade secret will still subject one to liability if the secret of the original owner is substantially involved.[43]

Additionally, if a trade secret was obtained wrongfully, neither the fact that it could have been discovered by legitimate means, nor that it might have been independently developed, is a defense. This issue arose in a lawsuit in which IBM charged Telex Corporation with misappropriation of its trade secrets, and the judge stated the law rather clearly:

> Telex obtained these trade secrets from IBM by a massive and persuasive program designed to induce the breach of known obligations of IBM employees or former employees. That such information or part of it could have been subsequently procured by Telex, given enough time and expense, by independent investigation, research or experience, did not justify Telex's conduct. That subsequent to the invasion of IBM's trade secrets a portion of the information in the course of marketing of IBM products became available to the public, including Telex, did not excuse Telex's conduct in the first instance nor insulate it from liability to both monetary and equitable relief.[44]

It is the improper conduct that is the key to liability in a misappropriation case.

---

[43] Restatement (First) of Torts §757 comment b (1939); *M. Bryce & Assocs., Inc. v. Gladstone*, 319 N.W.2d 907, 912 (Wis. App. 1982); *Digital Dev. Corp. v. International Memory Sys.*, 185 U.S.P.Q. 136,141 (S.D. Cal. 1973).

[44] *Telex Corp. v. International Business Machines Corp.*, 510 F.2d 894, 929–30 (10th Cir. 1975).

A question that frequently arises in connection with software protection is whether appropriating a trade secret by memorizing it, as opposed to taking a physical disk, tape, source listing, or copy of the documentation, falls within the protection of the trade secret laws. The answer is clearly "yes." Employees may be able to memorize algorithms, plans, techniques, formulae, and so on, but this does not mean that they can claim the information as their own knowledge. It is as much a breach of confidence for employees to reproduce their employer's trade secrets from memory as to copy them directly.

In one case, the court found that the defendants had over the years actually memorized the plaintiffs' plans and drawings, that they actually had a mental picture of these trade secrets. This, the court held, was no different than having a copy or picture on paper. Since these "mental pictures" were obtained by the defendants while in the plaintiffs' employ, the court concluded that "to carry them away in this manner was [as much] a violation of a confidence reposed in them by their employer, as if they had made copies or photographs and carried them away."[45]

In another case, involving misappropriation of on-line business software, the defendant, a former employee, defended the charge by claiming that he had not taken any documentation or other physical material away from his employer.[46] He contended that his software was independently developed, not copied. However, the court said that it made no difference whether he had taken the documentation or not, since misappropriation by memory is also forbidden. Moreover, the court pointed out that it was not necessary that his software be an exact copy in order to impose liability.

4.9. DETECTING MISAPPROPRIATION

Trade secret protection for software is of little value if the trade secret owner is unable to detect and prosecute those who are misappropriating the trade secret. Unfortunately, detecting mis-

---

[45] *Schulenburg v. Signaltrol, Inc.*, 33 Ill. 2d 379, 212 N.E.2d 865, 868 (1965).

[46] *Cybertek Computer Products, Inc. v. Whitfield*, 203 U.S.P.Q. 1020, 1024–25 (Cal. Super. Ct. 1977); *see also Jostens, Inc. v. National Computer Sys., Inc.*, 318 N.W.2d 691, 702 (Minn. 1982).

appropriation is often a difficult task in which luck plays a large role.

Nonetheless, there are some steps that can be taken. One of the most important is to watch the situations with the greatest potential for misappropriation. The factual settings in which most trade secret cases arise can be categorized as follows:

1. An employee changes jobs or leaves to form a competing company, and takes his or her employer's trade secrets with him or her;
2. An independent contractor misuses proprietary information disclosed to it for purposes of evaluating or developing a product for the owner of the trade secret;
3. A licensee of software develops a competing product using trade secrets disclosed to it in confidence pursuant to the license agreement;
4. A competitor gains access to the trade secrets through merger or acquisition of a licensee.

If a trade secret is misappropriated, the result of that misappropriation will frequently be a product which is similar to and competitive with the misappropriated product. Thus another important technique for detecting misappropriation is to analyze all new competing products. Announcements and advertisements in trade journals, as well as information obtained from customers and potential customers, are all excellent sources of leads.

Obviously, the mere appearance of a new competing product does not, by itself, suggest that there has been a misappropriation of trade secrets. Suspicions should be raised, however, if (1) the source of the new product appears to be someone who has had access to the trade secret; or (2) information indicates that the competing product was developed in a very short time or that the expense of its development was very low. Under these circumstances, further investigation is warranted.

The owner of the trade secret should contact a qualified attorney before initiating an in-depth investigation. It is important that no unfounded accusations be made which might lead to charges of libel, tortious interference with business relations, or antitrust violations.

The investigation should attempt to obtain as much information as possible about the company marketing the suspect product, and about the product itself. If possible, a copy of the competing software should be legitimately obtained for further examination.

4.10. PROVING MISAPPROPRIATION

In order to prove that a trade secret has been misappropriated, it is necessary to prove (1) the existence of a trade secret, (2) that the trade secret was acquired by the defendant by improper means, or properly but subject to an obligation of confidentiality, and (3) that the defendant used or disclosed the trade secret in a manner not authorized by its owner (i.e., that the defendant violated the obligation of confidentiality). In many cases, the issue in dispute is whether the person who used the trade secret was free to do so, or whether he or she was bound by an obligation of confidentiality prohibiting such conduct. In most cases, however, the issue is whether the defendant actually used or disclosed the plaintiff's trade secret.

4.10.1. Direct Evidence

Direct evidence of misappropriation is, of course, the best method of proof. Although situations in which such evidence is available are rare, they have occurred.

In one such case, University Computing Co. was able to establish that the defendant obtained a copy of its software by bribing a customer's employee to deliver magnetic tapes of the software.[47] And in another case IBM was able to prove that one of its employees, hired by Telex, took a copy of the source code with him to Telex, which Telex subsequently used in the development of its own product.[48]

Finding copies of stolen trade secret software in the defendant's possession also provides excellent evidence. In one crimi-

---

[47] *University Computing Co. v. Lykes-Youngstown Corp.*, 504 F.2d 518, 529 (5th Cir. 1974).

[48] *Telex Corp. v. International Business Machines Corp.*, 510 F.2d 894, 911 (10th Cir. 1975).

nal case, for example, the defendant copied his former employer's source code by accessing the computer through his home terminal. The phone call was traced, and the FBI obtained a search warrant. Upon searching his house, they found 40 rolls of computer paper containing the stolen source code.[49]

4.10.2. Circumstantial Evidence

If direct evidence of misappropriation is not available, it may still be proved by circumstantial evidence. There are a number of ways to do this. One of the most common methods by which misappropriation is proved is by comparing the time and expense of development incurred by both parties. Such a circumstantial case would consist of the following evidence:

1. The plaintiff spent large sums of money and/or a great deal of time and effort to develop a specific software package;

2. The defendant, in some way, had access to the plaintiff's software; and

3. The defendant produced a functionally similar package in a fraction of the time and/or at a fraction of the cost.

In one such case, the court concluded that Telex had misappropriated IBM's trade secrets in a disk storage system upon a showing that a former IBM employee familiar with the trade secret developed an equivalent device for Telex in 18 months, although it had taken IBM five years.[50] In another case, the plaintiff spent more than $100,000 over an 18-month period to develop software that the defendant was able to develop in a few months for only $2,500.[51] The court had no trouble finding misappropriation.

Misappropriation may also be established by showing that the defendant's software duplicates some of the errors or arbitrary sequences of code contained in the plaintiff's software. In one case the court found misappropriation based on the testimony of

---

[49] *United States v. Seidlitz*, 589 F.2d 152, 155 (4th Cir. 1978).

[50] *Telex Corp. v. International Business Machines, Corp.*, 510 F.2d 894, 911 (10th Cir. 1975).

[51] *Analogic Corp. v. Data Translation, Inc.*, 371 Mass. 643, 358 N.E.2d 804, 806 (1976).

plaintiff's experts who had "made a careful analysis of the two programs and found not only similarity in the overall structure and organization (some of which might be explainable on functional grounds), but they found identical segments of code which were solely arbitrary and, most significantly, deviations or quasi-mistakes which, in their judgment, could only be explained by copying."[52] In another case, the court found that the defendants had copied trade secret blueprints, noting that they "have even copied some of the plaintiff's mistakes."[53]

Misappropriation may also be proved by a detailed comparison of the two programs, if such comparison establishes similarity of an unlikely number of program elements that would otherwise be arbitrarily decided. Such elements might include input and output formats, program call routines, the sequence of processing, error detection procedures, subprogram structures, optimization techniques, field and file sizes, and particular formulas. Thus, in one case, expert testimony that "it would be very unlikely that two computer programmers would be capable of drafting an accounts receivable program with as many similiarities as are contained in the plaintiff's and defendant's programs," and testimony that the two programs had such "great similarity and likeness to the point where the programs are a copy, one of the other," was used to establish misappropriation.[54]

It should also be noted that the amount of the plaintiff's code that is appropriated by the defendant is not really important. The fact that only a small percentage of the plaintiff's routines may have been used by the defendant does not, in and of itself, provide a defense. A small portion of a program may make it unique.[55]

Frequently, all of the above factors are used, in combination, to establish trade secret misappropriation. A good example is a case filed by the owner of a jobber management system, called "JMS," against an employee of one of its customers.[56] The employee,

[52] *Structural Dynamics Research Corp. v. Engineering Mechanics Research Corp.*, 401 F. Supp. 1102, 1117 (E.D. Mich. 1975).
[53] *Schulenberg v. Signatrol, Inc.*, 33 Ill. App. 2d 379, 212 N.E.2d 865, 869 (1965).
[54] *J & K Computer Systems, Inc. v. Parrish*, 642 P.2d 732, 735 (Utah 1982).
[55] *Josten, Inc. v. National Computer Sys., Inc.*, 318 N.W.2d 691, 703 (Minn. 1982).
[56] *Dikerman Associates, Inc. v. Tiverton Bottled Gas Co.*, 594 F. Supp. 30 (D. Mass 1984).

along with another individual, had developed a comparable package called "FuelPak." The evidence at trial established that the two developers of Fuel Pak had access to the JMS manual, and used it; that JMS had taken 22 months to develop, whereas FuelPak took only 3–4 weeks; that JMS cost $400,000 to develop, whereas most of the money spent for FuelPak (the amount of which was never proved) went for marketing rather than development; that some of the design notes for FuelPak were remarkably similar to the JMS design; and that (as established by expert testimony) there were a great number of similarities between the two programs which were not accidental, and a certain number of cosmetic differences which were incorporated in FuelPak to disguise copying. On the basis of this evidence, the court concluded that the JMS trade secrets had been misappropriated.

4.11. REMEDIES FOR MISAPPROPRIATION

Once misappropriation of trade secret software has been proven, the owner of the trade secret wants to accomplish three things—to stop the misappropriation, to recover the losses sustained to date, and to deter future acts of misappropriation. Each of these remedies is available to the owner in an appropriate case.

4.11.1. Injunction

Putting a stop to the damages flowing from a misappropriation is usually accomplished by obtaining an injunction. An injunction is a court order prohibiting one party from doing a wrongful act that he or she is threatening to do, or to stop him or her from continuing to perform a wrongful act. For example, a court-ordered injunction could be used to prevent someone from marketing software utilizing misappropriated trade secrets.

There are essentially three types of injunctions which can be issued by a court. All three have exactly the same effect in terms of prohibiting certain conduct by the defendant, but they are issued at different stages of a lawsuit and have different durations.

The first type of injunction is called a temporary restraining order (TRO). A trade secret owner may seek a TRO at the very beginning of a lawsuit in order to prevent the occurrence of some imminent action by the defendant which is likely to cause immediate and irreparable harm to the plaintiff. A TRO, however, typically lasts for a very short time, usually no more than 10 days. The purpose of such an injunction is simply to preserve the status quo and prevent additional injury to the plaintiff until the court can conduct a preliminary hearing into plaintiff's allegations.

After the preliminary hearing has been held, the court may be persuaded to issue a preliminary injunction. The purpose of such an injunction is to prevent the defendant from disclosing, marketing, or continuing to market the allegedly misappropriated software until the issues are finally resolved at a trial.[57] In order to obtain such an injunction, the following must be proved to the court's satisfaction:

1. That the plaintiff will suffer "irreparable injury"[58] if the defendant is allowed to continue its activities or threatened activities while the case is waiting to go to trial; and

2. There is a strong likelihood that the plaintiff will win its case at trial.

Although in theory the court's disposition of a plaintiff's request for a preliminary injunction does not end the lawsuit, it frequently has that effect. This often occurs if the preliminary injunction has been granted because the judge will be viewed as having sent a strong signal to the defendant that the defendant is likely to lose the case for good when it come to trial, and because the defendant will be prevented from continuing its challenged conduct during the interim. By the same token, if the court refuses to enter the preliminary injunction and the plaintiff is the losing party, the plaintiff often decides that the cost of continued litiga-

---

[57] It was this type of an injunction which Apple Computer sought against Franklin Computer during the course of its litigation in the Pennsylvania district court. (See Sections 2.2.2 and 2.2.3.)

[58] In legal parlance, an injury is "irreparable" if it cannot be remedied through the payment of money damages. This is frequently the case with the misappropriation of trade secrets since it is often difficult (if not impossible) to calculate the true extent of the plaintiff's loss.

tion is not justified by the prospect of winning at trial years hence, by which time the trade secret may well have become obsolete. The preliminary injunction procedure thus can provide a very expeditious (and relatively inexpensive) resolution of a trade secret dispute.

If the case goes to trial, and if the defendant is successful in establishing that he or she did not misappropriate any of the trade secrets of the plaintiff, any preliminary injunction that was entered will be "dissolved" and the defendant will be free to continue doing business as before. However, whether or not a preliminary injunction was entered, if the plaintiff wins at the trial, the court will enter a "permanent" injunction prohibiting the defendant from doing whatever it is that was found to be wrongful. In trade secret cases, however, the use of the term "permanent" injunction is somewhat misleading. For the duration of such an injunction is generally limited to the amount of time that it would take the defendant to discover the trade secret independently, or to develop it by reverse engineering, rather than through misappropriation.[59] There are, however, some cases in which truly permanent injunctions have been entered in a trade secret misappropriation action.[60]

4.11.2. Damages and Profits

The courts have employed a variety of theories in calculating the measure of damages in a trade secret misappropriation case,[61] but they fall into two general categories: The first looks at how much the plaintiff lost as a result of defendant's wrongdoing (compensatory damages), and the second looks at how much the defendant gained (an "accounting").

The first approach represents an award of money "damages" to

[59] See Analogic Corp. v Data Translation, Inc., 371 Mass. 643, 358 N.E.2d 804, 807–08 (Mass. 1976); K-2 Ski Co. v. Head Ski Co., Inc., 506 F.2d 471, 474 (9th Cir. 1974); Anaconda Co. v. Metric Tool & Die Co., 485 F. Supp. 410, 431 (E.D. Pa. 1980); C-E-I-R v. Computer Dynamics Corp., 183 A.2d 374, 381 (Md. App. 1962).

[60] These include Data General Corp. v. Digital Computer Controls, Inc., 357 A.2d 105, 114 (Del. Ch. 1975), and BMC Software, Inc. v. Data-Base Technology Corp., No. 830-C-9026, slip op. (N.D. Ill. May 16, 1984) (consent judgment).

[61] See Telex Corp. v. International Business Machines Corp., 510 F.2d. 894, 930–31 (10th Cir. 1975).

compensate plaintiff for its injury; the plaintiff must demonstrate how much money (i.e., profits) it lost because of the defendant's unlawful conduct. Thus, under this theory if the plaintiff cannot show any loss, it will recover nothing, even if the defendant has made money from the misappropriation.

However, courts can measure compensatory damages in a number of different ways. One way is by calculating what would amount to a reasonable royalty for the use of the plaintiff's trade secret by the defendant.[62] Another way to measure compensatory damages is to determine what an investor would pay for the projected return that would be realized by virtue of owning the trade secret, and to have the defendant reimburse the plaintiff for this amount.[63] A third approach is to compensate the plaintiff for the sales that it lost as a result of the misappropriation.[64] One final approach, applicable where the defendant has in some way destroyed the value of the trade secret, such as through unrestricted disclosure, is to determine the value of the information to the plaintiff as a secret, compared to its "value" after disclosure, and to award the plaintiff the difference.[65]

Under the second approach, often referred to as an "accounting," a court will determine the profits (not gross sales) made by the defendant by virtue of its misappropriation, and will then require the defendant to pay those profits to the plaintiff.[66] Alternatively, the development costs that were saved by the defendant as a result of the misappropriation are awarded to the plaintiff.[67]

In some cases, the plaintiff will be allowed to recover both its losses and the defendant's gains if it can establish that this will not result in a double recovery.[68]

[62] Cases using this approach have included *Structural Dynamics Research Corp. v. Engineering Mechanics Research Corp.*, 401 F. Supp. 1102, 1120 (E.D. Mich. 1975); *University Computing Co. v. Lykes-Youngstown Corp.*, 504 F.2d 518, 539 (5th Cir. 1974).

[63] See *Precision Plating & Metal Finishing, Inc. v. Martin-Marietta Corp.*, 435 F.2d 1262, 1263–64 (5th Cir. 1970).

[64] See *Telex Corp. v. International Business Machines Corp.*, 510 F.2d 894, 931 (10th Cir. 1975).

[65] See *University Computing Co. v. Lykes-Youngstown Corp.*, 504 F.2d 518, 535 (5th Cir. 1974).

[66] This sales approach was used in the case of *Telex Corp. v. International Business Machines Corp.*, 510 F.2d 894, 931–32 (10th Cir. 1975).

[67] See *Koehring Co. v. National Automatic Tool Co.*, 257 F. Supp. 282, 291 (S.D. Ind. 1966), aff'd 385 F.2d 414 (7th Cir. 1967).

[68] This was allowed in *Telex Corp. v. International Business Machines Corp.*, 510 F.2d

In addition to actual damages suffered by the plaintiff, or actual gains made by the defendant, the plaintiff may also be entitled to punitive damages. When Telex was found to have misappropriated IBM's trade secrets, IBM was awarded $17.5 million in compensatory damages and $1 million in punitive damages.[69] Punitive damages are awarded, not to compensate the plaintiff for its injury (though they are paid to the plaintiff), but solely to punish the defendant for particularly outrageous wrongdoing.

4.11.3.　Criminal Penalties

A number of states have enacted criminal statutes which expressly deal with trade secret theft. California, for example, has a comprehensive statute imposing criminal liability for the wrongful appropriation of trade secrets.[70] Four different types of conduct are specifically prohibited under the statute: the taking of an article representing a trade secret, the "fraudulent appropriation" of a trade secret entrusted to an individual, the copying of a trade secret to which the individual has unlawfully obtained access, and the copying of a trade secret to which the individual has obtained access through a "relationship of trust and confidence." Thus anyone who delivers a trade secret owned by his or her employer to any other person not authorized to receive it can be punished by up to one year in jail and a fine of up to $5,000. This statute has already been applied to the theft of computer software.[71] (See Section 12.1.) In another case, an IBM employee was convicted of theft of trade secrets from his employer.[72]

The subject of software protection and the criminal law is discussed in more detail in Chapter 12.

894, 930–33 (10th Cir. 1975); and *Try-Tron Int'l., v. Velto*, 525 F.2d 432, 437 (9th Cir. 1975). However, this approach was not allowed in the case of *Sperry Rand Corp. v. A-T-O, Inc.*, 447 F.2d 1387, 1393 (4th Cir. 1971).

[69] *Telex Corp. v. International Business Machines Corp.*, 510 F.2d 894, 933 (10th Cir. 1975); *see also Try-Tron Int'l. v. Velto*, 525 F.2d 432, 437–38 (9th Cir. 1975); *Sperry Rand Corp. v. A-T-O, Inc.*, 447 F.2d 1387, 1394-1395 (4th Cir. 1971).

[70] Cal. Penal Code §499C.

[71] *Ward v. Superior Court*, 3 Computer L. Serv. Rep. 206 (Alameda, Cal. Super. Ct., 1972).

[72] *People v. Serrata* 133 Cal. Rptr. 144; 62 Cal. App. 3d 9 (1976).

CHAPTER FIVE

PATENT PROTECTION FOR SOFTWARE

Written with the assistance of Russell J. Barron, Foley & Lardner, Milwaukee, Wisconsin.

Patent protection for software offers the most comprehensive form of protection available. However it is more expensive in the first instance than copyright or trade secret protection, is time consuming to obtain, and requires the assistance of a patent attorney. Nonetheless, because patent protection is the only form of protection that permits suit against innocent infringers, that is, no proof of copying or misappropriation is necessary, it is worth considering in nearly every situation, especially for mass-marketed software. Unlike copyright and trade secret protection, however, patent protection is not available for most software. Only when the software meets certain requirements can it qualify.

5.1. WHAT IS A PATENT?

A patent is a grant by the government to an inventor that gives the inventor the right to exclude others from making, using, or selling his or her invention throughout the United States.[1] In essence, a patent is like a legal monopoly. During the life of a patent, no one is allowed to make, use, sell, or license the invention without the inventor's permission. It makes no difference whether they copy the inventor's invention or develop it independently.

When compared with the protection afforded by copyright and the law of trade secrets, patent protection is plainly the strongest of the three. Copyright prohibits only the actual copying of the author's expression of an idea. It does not protect the idea itself, nor does it protect an independent creation of the same expres-

---

[1] 35 U.S.C. §154.

sion, as long as there is no copying. Trade secret law goes a little farther, protecting both the idea and the expression of that idea, but such protection is only available as long as everything is kept secret. Once the secret is out, everyone is free to use it. Moreover, reverse engineering of a trade secret is a legitimate form of competition, and trade secret law does not provide any protection against independent development of the same product or idea. A patent, on the other hand, precludes all forms of copying, all uses of the ideas embodied in the patent, and all independent development of the same invention.

There is, however, a cost associated with obtaining the all-encompassing protection provided by a patent. In exchange for a patent, an inventor is required to make a complete and public disclosure of the invention with sufficient detail to enable one skilled in the art relating to the invention to practice the invention. Thus where a patent is granted for software, the inventor–programmer is required to disclose enough detail about the system so that another programmer could write a program which functioned in accordance with the claims of the patent.

Fortunately, depending upon the level of detail at which the inventiveness of the software lies, disclosure of actual code is not necessary. A copy of U.S. Patent 4,460,975 issued for a software-implemented invention is set forth in Section A.3. Note that no code is described in this patent. Indeed, it would be fair to say that this patent is directed at protecting the software at a high flowchart level. Moreover, for mass-marketed and mass-distributed software, disclosure will occur in any event when the products are put on the market. Thus, the disclosure requirement of the Patent Law should not stand in the way of using patent protection for such software.

The reason for this disclosure requirement is rooted in the purposes of the patent laws. Basically, patent laws were set up to advance the arts and sciences. The theory is that inventors will be encouraged to disclose information concerning their inventions and their discoveries, and the sum of useful knowledge available to our society will be increased if, in exchange, inventors are given a limited monopoly on the use of their inventions. In exchange for a disclosure of his or her invention, the inventor is given the right to prevent anyone else from creating the same invention for a period of 17 years. At the end of those 17 years, however, the patent expires. Anyone is then free to reproduce the inventor's publicly disclosed invention with no liability to the original inventor. Since the commercial lifetime of nearly all software is much less than 17 years, this is not a genuine impediment.

5.2. WHAT SOFTWARE MAY BE PATENTED?

Most inventions, and most software, will not qualify for patent protection. Under the patent law, an invention must meet a number of more or less strict criteria before it will qualify for patent protection.

Software that meets the standards set forth in the patent law may be patented so long as the patent claims do not "preempt the algorithm"—that is, as long as they do not appear to prohibit someone from performing the program steps with a paper and pencil. In practice this requirement is often dealt with by skilled drafting of the patent application.

5.3. REQUIREMENTS TO OBTAIN A PATENT

In order to obtain a patent for software, or for any other invention or discovery, the invention must meet the following five requirements:

1. The inventor must be the first person to invent or discover the invention
2. The invention must be what is known as "patentable subject matter"
3. The invention must be novel
4. The invention must have utility
5. The invention must be nonobvious.

Each of the these requirements presents a hurdle on the road to obtaining a patent. Typically, the "nonobviousness" hurdle is the one of greatest consequence. These tests will be examined in detail in the following sections.

5.3.1. First Inventor

A patent may be issued only to the actual inventor (not his or her employer or assignee), and only if the inventor was the first person to create the invention.[2] Thus if two persons independently create the same invention, the patent will not be issued to the first one who applies for it, but rather, to the first one who actually created it.

To qualify as the first inventor, the invention must be both conceived and reduced to practice with diligence. An invention is conceived when the inventor has in his or her mind a definite and permanent idea of the complete invention, including all of the steps necessary to create it. The invention is reduced to practice when it is actually created and working. However, the date a patent application is filed is considered as constructive reduction to practice.[3] If someone subsequently asserts that he or she made the invention first, it will become necessary to determine who was, in fact, first. Such determinations are normally made in a Patent and Trademark Office proceeding called an "interference" which requires the assistance of a lawyer skilled in interference practice.

5.3.2. Patentable Subject Matter

Only certain types of inventions may be patented. The general categories of patentable inventions are described in the Patent Act as "any new and useful process, machine, manufacture, or composition of matter, or any new and useful improvement thereof."[4] Which inventions fall within these broad and general categories, and which do not, has been the subject of much controversy, particularly in the case of computer software. The problem arises from the fact that ideas, abstract principles, laws of nature, scientific truths, and algorithms are not patentable, whereas, as may be seen from the definition, concrete manifestations which utilize certain principles, ideas, laws of nature, and

[2] 35 U.S.C. §§102(f), (g).
[3] Manual of Patent Examining Procedure §715.07 (1983).
[4] 35 U.S.C. §101.

scientific truths are patentable. The problem lies in distinguishing between the two.

Most of the controversy over the patentability of computer software used to center around whether the particular software involved was merely an expression of an algorithm, which may not be patented, or whether it represents something more, which may be patentable. This controversy was essentially put to rest by the Supreme Court decision in *Diamond v. Diehr*[5] and subsequent administrative rulings by the Patent and Trademark Office. The basic rule now is that, as long as the claims do not preclude manual performance of the claimed software process steps, software is patentable subject matter.[6]

5.3.3. Novelty

To be patentable, software must be "novel" as that term is defined in the Patent Act. This means that if the process steps performed by the software were (a) known or used by others in this country, or (b) patented or described in a printed publication in this or a foreign country, the claimed invention is considered to have been "anticipated" by the prior art, and thus is not considered to be novel.[7] In essence, novelty requires that the software in question must be different from programs previously in existence.

Because "total" newness is rare in any technical field, the patent law recognizes the appropriateness of patenting "improvements" on existing processes. Hence, rejections of patent claims for lack of novelty are relatively rare and problems with this issue are often overcome during the examination process.

5.3.4. Utility

The requirement of utility refers to the usefulness of the invention. Essentially, the utility requirement is met if the software works and is useful for any beneficial purpose. The utility requirement does not mean, however, that the software must be a commercial success, or even that it be commercially practicable. Lack

---

[5] 450 U.S. 175 (1981).
[6] Manual of Patent Examining Procedure §2110 (1983).
[7] 35 U.S.C. §102(a).

of utility is a very infrequent reason for the rejection of patent claims.

5.3.5. Nonobviousness

In addition to the requirements of novelty and utility, the software must also be what the patent law terms "nonobvious." If the invention is obvious, that is, if the differences between the subject matter sought to be patented and the prior art are such that the subject matter as a whole would have been obvious at the time the invention was made to a person having ordinary skill in the art to which the subject matter pertains, the invention may not be patented.[8]

This requirement is essentially a requirement that the invention be a contribution to the art sufficient to merit patent protection. There are four elements that go into making the nonobviousness determination:

1. The scope and content of the pertinent prior art
2. The differences between the prior art and the claimed invention
3. The level of ordinary skill in the pertinent art
4. The extent other factors indicative of nonobviousness are present. These include:
   a. Commercial success of the patented invention
   b. Overwhelming acceptance, recognition, or adoption of the patented invention by the industry
   c. Copying or imitation of the patented invention
   d. Long-felt need in the industry for a solution to the problem solved by the patented invention and the failure of others to solve the problem.[9]

As a result of recent court decisions, the "other factors" category is now considered by the courts to be as important as the first three factors in the non-obviousness equation.[10]

---

[8] 35 U.S.C. §103.

[9] *Graham v. John Deere Company of Kansas City & Co.*, 383 U.S. 1 (1966).

[10] *Simmons Fastener Corp. v. Illinois Tool Works, Inc.*, 222 U.S.P.Q. 745 (Fed. Cir. 1984).

5.4. PROCESS OF OBTAINING A PATENT

Patent rights in the United States are obtained only by grant from the federal government. Following the creation of an invention (e.g., software), the process of obtaining a patent begins with the patent application. It is a time-consuming process and may be expensive. The time between first submission of the application and issuance of the patent may often span several years, and the cost can exceed $10,000. However, the payments are typically spread out over a period of time and should be compared with the cost of other types of protection, such as the cost of providing the security necessary to protect trade secrets, and the enhancement of market value potentially resulting from being able to exclude all infringers from the marketplace. Also, the nature of the patent application process is a step-wise one. Hence, there are a number of points in the process at which the application may be dropped if it is decided that it is no longer economical.

Although the use of a patent attorney is not required by law, it is a practical necessity in order to assure that a patent application is properly drafted and prosecuted before the Patent and Trademark Office. The following sections describe the patent application process in general, but do not attempt to provide the detailed information necessary to apply for a patent. That is best done in consultation with a competent patent attorney.

5.4.1. Who May Apply for a Patent?

As a general rule, the only person who may apply for a patent for software or any other type of invention is the inventor.[11] When two or more persons are involved in the creation of software to be patented, all of them must join in the patent application and sign the required oath or declaration.[12]

Where patentable software or other patentable inventions are created by employees in the scope of their employment, the employer often requires them to sign a patent assignment agreement, whereby they agree that any and all inventions that they make are

---

[11] 35 U.S.C. §111; 37 C.F.R. §1.41.
[12] 35 U.S.C. §116; 37 C.F.R. §1.45.

assigned to the employer. Such an agreement is normally effective to assign all rights in the patent to the employer (see Sections 5.5 and 7.1), but such an assignment will normally not allow the employer to apply for the patent itself. The employee who created the software must execute the patent application, except in very limited situations.[13]

5.4.2. Time Limits for Patent Applications

The right to obtain a patent in a given invention can be lost forever if the patent application is not filed within a certain time. The Patent Act requires the inventor to file his or her application within one year of the date in which the invention is first (a) in public use, (b) on sale in this country, (c) described in a printed publication in this or a foreign country, or (d) patented in a foreign country.[14] Private use of the invention will not trigger the one-year limitation period. However, any nonsecret use of the invention (other than for experimental purposes), either by the inventor or by another person with the inventor's permission, is considered a "public use." The experimental use exception is a treacherous area in which there has been much recent change in the law. Consequently, no field testing or other experiment outside of the inventor's workplace or home should be done without first consulting a qualified patent attorney.

To preserve foreign patent rights in most of the commercially significant countries, *no* delay following commercial or public use or publication is permitted. The safest practice is to file a U.S. Patent Application (which preserves for one year the right to file in most foreign countries) before any field testing or attempt to sell is made.

5.4.3. Form and Content of the Patent Application

A patent application can be a lengthy and complex document. An example of some of the material required in a patent application, as incorporated in a patent ultimately issued, is reproduced in

---

[13] 35 U.S.C. §118.
[14] 35 U.S.C. §102(b).

Section A.3. Moreover, much care must be taken in drafting the patent application, since the way in which it is framed will determine the scope of the patent rights to be granted, and in some cases, may even determine whether a patent will be granted at all.

A complete patent application must include the following elements:[15]

1. A specification describing the invention and the manner and process of making and using it, including one or more "claims"

2. An oath or declaration by the applicant that he or she believes himself or herself to be the original and first inventor[16]

3. Drawings, when necessary for an understanding of the subject matter to be patented[17]

4. The prescribed filing fee, which is at least $170 for "small entities" and $340 for everyone else.[18] Additional fees are charged for applications which contain many claims, and/or certain categories of claims.

The heart of the patent application is found in the specification section. Basically, this section of the patent application must do two things. It must disclose the operation of the invention with enough detail so that someone familiar with the particular art (e.g., computer programming) could reproduce the invention.[19] Second, it must set forth the claims which are to be the subject of the patent, that is, the specific claims for which the applicant wishes to be granted a limited monopoly.[20] The claims define what it is that has been invented, and delimit the extent of the monopoly granted by the patent. Consequently, it is very important that the claims be properly drafted. If they are too broad, the

---

[15] 35 U.S.C. §§111, 112, 113, 115; 37 C.F.R. §1.51.

[16] 35 U.S.C. §115 and 37 C.F.R. §1.63.

[17] 35 U.S.C. §113 and 37 C.F.R. §§1.81–1.88.

[18] 37 C.F.R. §1.16. A "small entity" is defined as "an independent inventor, a small business concern or a non-profit organization." A "small business" concern is one with fewer than 500 employees.

[19] 35 U.S.C. §112; 37 C.F.R. §1.71.

[20] 37 C.F.R. §1.75.

patent will not be issued; if too narrow, the protection provided by the patent will be reduced accordingly.

An example of the content of the specification section for a software related patent, which includes 52 claims, is set out in Section A.3.

5.4.4. Examination by the Patent Office

Once a patent application is filed with the Patent and Trademark Office, it is assigned for examination to an examiner for the appropriate class of invention to which the application relates.[21] Applications are taken up for examination by the examiner to whom they have been assigned in the order in which they have been filed.[22] The patent examiner reviews the application to determine whether it complies with applicable statutes and rules and also to determine the patentability of the claimed invention. This examination requires a thorough study and investigation of the available prior art relating to the subject matter of the claimed invention.[23]

At the conclusion of this examination, if the patent examiner determines that the invention is not patentable, the applicant will be notified of the examiner's rejection of the application.[24] The applicant then has the right to require reconsideration of the patent application by the Patent and Trademark Office.[25] The reconsideration process also permits the applicant to modify (amend) his or her claims in an effort to meet the examiner's objections. In practice, most patent applications have most or all of their claims initially rejected.

The application process is such that the applicant can, in effect, negotiate the language of allowable claims with the examiner. If the applicant and the examiner are unable to reach agreement on allowable claims, the Patent and Trademark Office issues a Final Rejection.[26] The applicant may appeal the Final Rejection within

---

[21] 37 C.F.R. §1.101(a).
[22] Id.
[23] 37 C.F.R. §1.104(a).
[24] 37 C.F.R. §1.104(b).
[25] 37 C.F.R. §1.111.
[26] 37 C.F.R. §1.113(a).

the Patent and Trademark Office or to federal court if he or she so desires.[27]

If a patent application is approved, the applicant will be so notified, and upon payment of the patent issue fees,[28] the patent will be granted. The grant of a patent is evidenced by a printed document called Letters Patent. An example is reproduced in Section A.3.

While a patent application is pending, secrecy is maintained by the Patent Office. Thus no trade secrets which may be embodied in the software are compromised until the patent has actually been issued, at which time the contents of the application become public knowledge.

It takes approximately two years for the Patent and Trademark Office to process a patent application. The cost to the applicant for the preparation of the patent application, an initial patent search, prosecution of the patent application before the Patent and Trademark Office, and the necessary fees, can easily run in excess of $10,000. Thus even with respect to software that qualifies for patent protection, it may not be worth obtaining the patent unless the useful life of the software, and its value, justify the time and expense required. However, for software that does have a sufficient useful life and a substantial potential market, the advantages of patent protection are such that patent protection ought to be seriously considered with the assistance of a qualified patent lawyer.

5.4.5. Patent Notice

A patent notice consists merely of the word "patent" or the abbreviation "pat." followed by the number of the patent.[29] In the case of a patent application which is pending but not granted, the notice may be simply the phrase "patent pending." A penalty may be imposed for an improper notice,[30] so one should not be used unless appropriate.

There is no requirement that a patented invention be marked

[27] *Id.*
[28] 37 C.F.R. §1.18.
[29] 35 U.S.C. §287.
[30] 35 U.S.C. §292.

with a patent notice. However, if the notice has not been used, and someone infringes the patent, the patent owner will be allowed to recover money damages only for the period subsequent to the date on which the infringer received actual notice that the invention was patented.[31]

5.5. WHO OWNS THE PATENT?

Under the patent law, the inventor or discoverer of patentable subject matter owns the patent.[32] Even if the invention was made within the scope of the inventor's employment, the employer will not own the patent unless it is assigned to the empoyer by the inventor. Thus, as a general rule, the patent rights in any patentable software will be owned by the employee or the independent consultant who developed the software. However, where someone is hired or retained for the specific purpose of inventing patentable subject matter, the invention will belong to the employer.[33]

Normally, an assignment from the inventor to the employer will not be implied and must be in writing.[34] However, there are certain situations where the law may imply the existence of such an assignment. This could occur in the case of inventions made by officers or directors of a corporation,[35] and in the case of employment specifically for the purpose of inventing patentable subject matter.[36] However, even under these circumstances, it is still possible that patent rights will remain with the inventor in the absence of an express written assignment.

Thus, if an employer wishes to own all patents on any software invented by any of its employees or independent contractors, it should enter into an appropriate written assignment agreement with the individuals involved. Such agreements are valid if re-

---

[31] 35 U.S.C. §287.
[32] 35 U.S.C. §101.
[33] *United States v. Dubilier Condenser Corp.*, 289 U.S. 178, 187, 53 S.Ct. 554 (1933).
[34] *Id.*
[35] *Dowse v. Federal Rubber Co.*, 254 F. 308 (D. Ill. 1918).
[36] *Lyon Mfg. Corp. v. Chicago Flexible Shaft Co.*, 106 F.2d 930 (7th Cir. 1939); *Dinwiddie v. St. Louis & O'Fallon Coal Co.*, 64 F.2d 303, 306 (4th Cir. 1933).

quired as a condition of employment, but may require additional consideration if entered into after the employment has commenced. Moreover, the laws in some states impose restrictions on the scope of such assignment agreements. These restrictions, and assignment agreements in general, are discussed in Section 7.1.

Even if an employee or independent contractor does not assign his or her patent to the employer, the employer will in most cases still have the right to use the patentable invention under what is known as the "shop rights" doctrine. This doctrine provides that the employer has a perpetual, royalty-free license to use in its business any patented invention created by an employee in the course of his employment.[37] This right, however, is not exclusive, and the employee or independent contractor is still free to market the patented invention. On the other hand, the employer may use the patented invention only in the course of its business and may not sell or license it to anyone else.

5.6. INFRINGEMENT OF PATENTS

Once a patent has been granted for software, if anyone other than the holder of the patent or his or her licensee develops and/or markets software that performs the patented functions, they will be guilty of patent infringement.[38] Also guilty of infringement are those who contribute to or induce infringement.[39] It makes no difference whether the infringing software was developed independently and without knowledge of the patent, or whether the infringing software was stolen or copied from the patented software. In either case, the owner of the patent has the right to sue the infringer in order to obtain a court-ordered injunction prohibiting production, use, and marketing of the infringing software, and to recover any applicable damages.[40] In appropriate cases of

---

[37] *Annot.*, 61 A.L.R. 2d 356 (1958); *United States v. Dubilier Condenser Corp.*, 289 U.S. 178, 188–189, 53 S.Ct. 554 (1933).
[38] 35 U.S.C. §271(a).
[39] 35 U.S.C. §§271(b), (c).
[40] 35 U.S.C. §§283–284.

willful infringement the damages may be trebled.[41] In "exceptional" cases, attorneys' fees may also be awarded.[42]

Of importance to the software developer is the patent infringement concept of "equivalency" which provides protection against those who attempt to disguise patent infringement. As the Supreme Court has pointed out:[43]

> One who seeks to pirate an invention, like one who seeks to pirate a copyrighted book or play, may be expected to introduce minor variations to conceal and shelter the piracy. Outright and forthright duplication is a dull and very rare type of infringement. To prohibit no other would place the inventor at the mercy of verbalism and would be subordinating substance to form.

The doctrine of equivalents evolved in response to this problem, and provides a penumbra around patent claims that will result in an infringement finding even if the accused software is not precisely described by the patent claims. The rules surrounding the doctrine of equivalents are complex and have been in a state of flux. However, the rule is generally stated as follows: infringement by equivalency exists if the infringing device or process and the patented device or process perform substantially the same function in substantially the same way to achieve substantially the same result.[44] The more of a breakthrough or pioneering an invention is, the greater the scope of the penumbra of equivalency around the patent claims for that invention.

5.7. CONCLUSION

Patents offer the software developer a potentially powerful tool for defending his or her product and enhancing its value, but the protection is not available for all software, and where available can be expensive to obtain. The cost of obtaining one or more

[41] 35 U.S.C. §284.
[42] 35 U.S.C. §285.
[43] *Graver Tank & Mfg. Co. v. Linde Air Products Co.*, 339 U.S. 605, 607–08, 70 S. Ct. 854, 856 (1950).
[44] *Id.*

patents for a software module should be weighed against the value of exclusivity in the market place, the relief from the complexities and cost of maintaining trade secrets and confidentiality for software, and the enhancement of the software developer's value as a business entity which comes from owning exclusive rights.

Evaluation of the merits of patents for specific software is best done in close consultation with a qualified patent lawyer.

CHAPTER SIX

TRADEMARK PROTECTION FOR SOFTWARE

In addition to copyright, trade secret, and patent protection for software, trademark protection may be available in certain cases. Unlike the other forms of protection, however, a trademark will not protect the software itself from piracy, and cannot be used to punish anyone who wrongfully copies the software or steals the ideas it contains. Trademark rights will only protect the word, name, symbol, slogan, or other device used by the vendor to identify its software and distinguish it from software marketed by others. Trademark law protects a vendor from one form of unfair competition in which others attempt to market competing software using a mark that is the same or deceptively similar to the vendor's.

Trademarks are primarily marketing tools which, over time, can become valuable assets. They serve to identify the products to which they are applied, and to distinguish them from similar products marketed by competitors. In doing so, trademarks identify the origin of the product and denote to the customer a certain level of quality that can be expected based on the goodwill symbolized by the trademark. A trademark also helps to protect the public from confusion and deception. "IBM" is a good example of a successful trademark. There is little doubt that customers will frequently purchase products carrying the "IBM" trademark solely because they associate that mark with quality products; and there can be no doubt that the right to use that mark is a valuable asset of International Business Machines Corporation.

6.1.   WHAT IS A TRADEMARK?

A trademark can be any word, name, symbol, or slogan used by a vendor to identify its products and to distinguish them from similar products marketed by someone else.[1] "Visicalc," "Apple," "Microsoft," "IBM," "dBASEII," "CP/M," "DEC," and "Multiplan" are all examples of trademarks. However, as discussed in Sections 6.2 and 6.5, not all words, names, or symbols will qualify as trademarks.

In addition to trademarks, trademark law also protects service marks.[2] The only difference between a service mark and a trademark is that a service mark is used to identify services, whereas trademarks are used to identify products. "The Source," "Radio Shack," "McDonald's," "Safeway," "American Express," and "Greyhound" are all examples of service marks.

Note that trademarks and service marks identify products and services. They do not identify businesses. It is important to distinguish trademarks and service marks from trade names. A trade name is usually a company name used to identify a business. Examples of computer-related trade names include International Business Machines Corporation, Burroughs Corporation, Apple Computer, Inc., Visicorp, Microsoft Corporation, and Digital Equipment Corporation. Trade names are not protected by the federal trademark law. However, in some cases a trade name may also be used as a trademark when it is applied to products or services. Thus Apple Computer, Inc. markets computers with the trademark "Apple." In addition, some state laws afford protection to trade names.

The process of acquiring a trademark usually involves the following four steps:

1. Selecting a mark
2. Determining that the mark has not already been taken by someone else
3. Using the mark in commerce
4. Registering the mark

Each of these steps will be discussed in detail in Sections 6.2–6.6.

---

[1] 15 U.S.C. §1127.
[2] *Id.* Generally, the references in this chapter to "trademarks" include service marks, unless the context otherwise indicates.

6.2. SELECTING A TRADEMARK—WHAT QUALIFIES?

The process of selecting a trademark involves more than simply
deciding on a name for a product. Some marks can be protected as
trademarks, whereas others cannot. And of those that can be protected, some are stronger than others. If properly selected, a trademark can be a valuable asset to a business. If not, it may be worthless, or worse, may embroil its owner in litigation. To begin the
selection process, we look at what qualifies for trademark protection.

6.2.1. Form of Trademark

Any number of items can constitute a trademark. The most commonly used forms of trademarks are:

1. *Words and Phrases.* Examples include "Visicalc," "Xerox," "Multiplan," "Wordstar," "dBASEII," "Apple," and
   "Microsoft—The High Performance Software."
2. *Pictures and Symbols.* Examples include the rainbow-col-
   ored apple used by Apple Computer, the "eye" used by
   CBS Broadcasting, the "Playboy" bunny, and the RCA figure of a dog listening to "his master's voice."
3. *Numerals and letters.* Examples include "IBM," "RCA,"
   "GE," "DEC," "CP/M," "XT," and "1–2–3."

In some cases, other items can also qualify as trademarks. One
company, for example, was able to register a narrow colored band
mounted on its computer tape reels as a trademark.[3]

6.2.2. Distinctiveness

In order to qualify as a trademark, a mark that falls into one of
these categories discussed must also have the quality of being
"distinctive"; that is, it must distinguish or be capable of distinguishing the products on which it is applied from other similar

[3] *See Application of Data Packaging Corp.,* 453 F.2d 1300 (C.C.P.A. 1972).

products.[4] The more distinctive a mark is, the stronger it will be, and the more likely it is to be accepted for registration and protected against use by others.

Whether a particular mark is distinctive depends on a variety of circumstances. Distinctiveness may be inherent in the mark itself because the mark is a newly-created word (such as "Xerox" or "Exxon"), or it may be acquired through public identification of the mark with a particular manufacturer's product or service (such as "Eveready" for batteries, or "National Geographic" for a magazine). Moreover, a mark may be distinctive when applied to one product (such as the trademark "Apple" when used on computers), but not on another product (such as the word "apple" used in connection with the fruit).

Trademark law attempts to categorize the distinctiveness of a mark in order to determine the scope of protection that will be provided. The intrinsic "strength" of a mark may be rated (from weakest to strongest), as follows:

Generic: A term which is the common descriptive name for a product is considered generic and is not entitled to trademark protection. A generic term, by definition, identifies a type of product to the public by answering the question "what is it?" Consequently, it cannot also function as a trademark, since it cannot identify the source of a specific product or distinguish it from the same products made by others; that is, it cannot also answer the question "whose is it?" Thus terms such as "software,"[5] "computer," "word processing," "data base," or "video"[6] will not qualify for trademark protection when they are used on products that they generically describe. For example, in one case a court held that the terms "Software" and "Software News" were both generic and could not be registered as trademarks. Thus the plaintiff, which published a trade journal called "Software News,"

---

[4] *Westward Coach Mfg. Co. v. Ford Motor Co.* 388 F.2d 627, 634 (7th Cir. 1968); *In re Swift & Co.* 223 F.2d 950, 954–55 (C.C.P.A. 1955); *American Basketball Assn. v. AMF Voit, Inc.,* 358 F. Supp. 981, 984–85 (S.D.N.Y. 1973).

[5] *Technical Publishing Co. v. Lebhar-Friedman, Inc.,* 729 F.2d 1136, 1140 (7th Cir. 1984).

[6] *Reese Publishing Co. v. Hampton Int'l. Communications,* 620 F.2d 7 (2d Cir. 1980) ("Video Buyer's Guide" held to be generic).

could not prevent another publisher from publishing a trade journal under the name "Computer + Software News."[7]

A word which is the common name for one class of products may, however, qualify for protection as a trademark when it is used in connection with a product it does *not* describe. For example, the term "apple" cannot be a trademark for the fruit, but does qualify as a trademark for computers.

Descriptive: A descriptive mark is one that describes the product or service itself or one or more of its functions, qualities, components, properties, or other attributes.[8] Examples of descriptive marks are "Computerland" when applied to computer stores, "Tender Vittles" when applied to pet food, and "Quik-Print" when applied to printing services. Misspelling or varying the spelling of a descriptive term will not generally prevent it from being found descriptive. For example, "Quik," a misspelling of the word "Quick," is still considered a descriptive term for speedy printing services.[9]

Descriptive marks do not automatically qualify for trademark protection. Every manufacturer is normally entitled to use appropriate descriptive words to describe its products. However, once the public has come to associate a descriptive mark with a particular vendor's product or service, it is considered to have acquired a "secondary meaning" and then it may be protected as a trademark. For example, "Hair color so natural only her hairdresser knows for sure" is a descriptive phrase that has developed sufficient "secondary meaning" for trademark protection. By contrast, a court has found that the mark "Computerland" is descriptive and even "perilously close to the generic line." In that case, the court assumed for the sake of argument that the mark was descriptive as opposed to generic, but held that the mark could not be legally protected at that time, since it had not yet acquired the level of consumer awareness required to establish a "secondary meaning."[10]

---

[7] *Technical Publishing Co. v. Lebhar-Friedman, Inc.*, 729 F.2d 1136 (7th Cir. 1984).

[8] *See Educational Dev. Corp. v. Economy Co.*, 562 F.2d 26, 28 (10th Cir. 1977); *Application of Quik-Print Copy Shops, Inc.*, 616 F.2d 523, 525 (C.C.P.A. 1980).

[9] *Application of Quik-Print Copy Shops, Inc.*, 616 F.2d 523 (C.C.P.A. 1980).

[10] *Computerland Corp. v. Microland Computer Corp.*, 586 F. Supp. 22 (N.D. Cal. 1984).

Secondary meaning is usually acquired through exclusive use and advertising by one person over a long period of time so that, in the public's mind, the descriptive mark serves to identify and distinguish that person's goods from those of another. For example, all software vendors are free to use the term "user friendly" in their advertisements to describe their software. No potential customer would now associate that term with any particular vendor's software. However, if one particular vendor had used the term "user friendly" so much that customers come to associate the term with that vendor's particular software, the term might have acquired secondary meaning.[11]

Suggestive: A suggestive mark is a mark that suggests something about the product but does not actually describe it. A mark is suggestive when imagination, thought, or perception is required to reach a conclusion about the nature of the goods or services. Examples of suggestive marks are "Ultrasuede," "Playboy," "Safeway," and "Roach Motel." In the computer area, it might be argued that "Byte" is suggestive when used for a computer magazine, that "Data Aire" is suggestive when applied to computer air-conditioning, and that "1–2–3" and "Visicalc" are suggestive when applied to software.

Suggestive marks qualify for trademark protection without the need to show secondary meaning, but they are considered to be weak marks. Moreover, it is often difficult to distinguish suggestive marks from descriptive marks, and as a consequence, a great deal of controversy may result.[12]

Arbitrary: A word that has meaning in itself, but no connection to the product on which it is used, is an arbitrary mark. An arbitrary mark can be a very strong trademark. Examples include "Apple" as applied to computers, "Camels" as applied to cigarettes, and "Shell" as applied to gasoline.

Fanciful or Coined: Marks that are invented and have no inherent meaning whatsoever are categorized as fanciful or coined

---

[11] For purposes of federal registration, secondary meaning will generally not need to be proved if a mark has been exclusively and continuously used in interstate commerce for five years prior to the registration filing. 15 U.S.C. §1052(f).

[12] *Union Carbide Corp. v. Ever-Ready Inc.*, 531 F.2d 366 (7th Cir. 1976).

marks. They enjoy the strongest trademark protection. Examples of coined marks include "Exxon," "Xerox," and "Kodak." Their strength as trademarks is due to the fact that they have no meaning other than that which has been created by the manufacturers of the products they describe.

   The stronger or more distinctive the mark, the greater the trademark protection. Strength may be derived from the intrinsic quality of the mark, or from the degree of its public recognition. Weak marks, such as descriptive or suggestive terms, or marks which are used on a variety of different products by different vendors, will usually be narrowly protected, and in general only very similar marks on almost identical products will be enjoined from use or registration. Strong marks, such as fanciful terms or marks which have acquired great public fame, enjoy a greater sphere of protection. Thus even if another mark or its product is only somewhat similar to a coined mark or its product, it may be found to be infringing or denied registration.
   It is therefore highly desirable from a trademark perspective to adopt a mark with the strongest possible protection. Although vendors often decide to use descriptive or suggestive terms for marketing purposes, it is advisable to consider the advantages of a fanciful or coined mark if the objective is to develop a distinctive product identity.

6.2.3. Deceptively Similar to Other Marks

Even though a proposed trademark is proper in form and is not generic or merely descriptive (or if descriptive, has secondary meaning), it may not be protected as a trademark if it is deceptively similiar to other preexisting trademarks. Thus, for example, one court has ruled that the mark "Pineapple," as applied to computers, could be confusingly similar to the trademark "Apple."[13] Similarly, another court has held that the mark "Thinker Toys" as applied to apparatus for electronic computer and data processing systems so resembled the mark "Tinkertoys" as applied to wooden stick toys as to create a likelihood of confusion.[14] This

---

[13] *Apple Computer, Inc. v. Formula Int'l Inc.*, 725 F.2d 521, 526 (9th. Cir. 1984).

issue of similarity is also an important issue in the context of federal trademark registration, and is discussed more fully in Section 6.5.2.

6.3. TRADEMARK SEARCH

Prior to adopting and using a new trademark, it is recommended that the records of the Patent and Trademark Office be searched in order to determine whether the proposed trademark is identical or similar to any trademark previously registered.[15] It is important that this be done before any money is spent on printing, advertising, and using the mark. This will help to avoid a possible infringement action in the future, and to insure that the mark adopted can be protected property. There are a number of trademark search firms that will conduct a trademark search, and trademark searches are routinely done by attorneys.

A trademark search will not guarantee that a particular mark is available for use. It will only determine whether the mark has previously been registered. A mark may turn out to be unavailable because another person is already using it, even though such use will not necessarily be revealed in a trademark search. Nonetheless, a trademark search will provide a reasonable degree of certainty as to the availability of the mark. Searches of state trademark registrations and telephone or business directories may also be useful.

6.4. HOW TO ACQUIRE TRADEMARK RIGHTS—
USING THE MARK

Once the mark has been selected and determined to be available for use, there are certain steps that must be taken to acquire trademark rights. It is important, however, to distinguish between ac-

---

[14] *CBS, Inc. v. Morrow*, 708 F.2d 1579, 1582 (Fed. Cir. 1983).

[15] Such a search is not required, however. *The Money Store v. Harriscorp Fin. Inc.*, 689 F.2d 666, 671 (7th Cir. 1982).

quiring trademark rights and registering a trademark. They are very different activities.

Trademark rights are *not* granted by the government or acquired through registration. They are acquired automatically by the person who is the first to appropriate and "use" a particular word, name, symbol, or combination thereof in connection with a product or service for the purpose of indicating the source of that product or service. Under U.S. law, one cannot acquire trademark protection or even file an application for registration until one actually begins using the mark.[16]

"Use" of a trademark on a product requires first that it be physically attached to the product. Merely including the mark on advertising material is not sufficient. With software, the mark should be attached by placing it on the disk or tape containing the software, or on the box or other wrapping in which the disk or tape is marketed. It can also be imbedded within the software so that it will be displayed on a terminal at sign-on, and on any printouts produced. The mark does not have to be permanently attached to the software. It is sufficient if it is there at the time the software is sold or licensed (as, for example, on the wrapper which will be discarded after the transaction is complete). A mark is "used" in connection with services by incorporating it in advertising and promotional materials.

The second requirement for "use" is that the product or service itself be marketed and sold. Merely selecting a mark with plans to use it in the future, or putting the trademark on software or an advertisement for software that is never sold or licensed is not sufficient for trademark protection under U.S. law.

The person who is first to appropriate and use a trademark is the one who owns it, at least with respect to the class of goods or services to which it is applied and the area in which the goods or services are marketed. Thus a person who merely thinks up or creates the trademark has no rights in it under trademark law unless he or she is also the first person actually to use it to identify products or services for sale.

The trademark rights which are automatically acquired by us-

---

[16] *Radio Shack Corp. v. Radio Shack, Inc.*, 180 F.2d 200, 206 (7th Cir. 1950); *United Drug Co. v. Theodore Rectanus Co.*, 248 U.S. 90, 97–98 (1918).

ing the mark are limited to the specific geographical area in which the mark was used. For example, if the mark is applied to software which is marketed only in the Los Angeles area, the trademark rights extend only to that area. If someone else were to start using the same mark in another area of the country, he or she would acquire trademark rights in the same mark with respect to that separate area. To prevent this from occurring, and to obtain trademark rights for the entire country without actually having to use it nationwide, it is necessary to register the trademark with the federal government.

6.5. FEDERAL REGISTRATION OF TRADEMARKS

Federal registration of trademarks is governed by the federal Trademark Act (also referred to as the "Lanham Act"), and is administered by the U.S. Patent and Trademark Office. The purpose of the Trademark Act is to prevent the deceptive and misleading use of marks, to protect vendors against unfair competition, and to prevent fraud and deception by the use of reproductions, copies, counterfeits, or colorable imitations of registered trademarks.[17]

6.5.1. Advantages of Registration

As indicated in Section 6.4, trademark rights are acquired by adopting and using a trademark in connection with the sale of a particular product or service. It is not necessary to register the trademark with either the state or the federal government in order to acquire those rights. In fact, as stated previously in Section 6.4, registration is not even allowed until those trademark rights have already been acquired.

Nonetheless, there are certain advantages to be obtained from registering a trademark—advantages that, in many cases, make registration highly recommended. Moreover, registration can have great practical value when it comes to protecting trademark rights.

---

[17] 15 U.S.C. §1127.

Trademarks are registered with the U.S. Patent and Trademark Office on either the Principal Register or the Supplemental Register. The difference between these two registers is discussed in Section 6.5.3. The most valuable advantages that flow from federal registration of a trademark are available only for registration on the Principal Register. They are as follows:

1. The Certificate of Registration issued by the Patent and Trademark Office is prima facie evidence of the validity of the registration, the registrant's ownership of the trademark, and the registrant's exclusive right to use the mark in commerce in connection with the goods or services specified in the certificate.[18] This means that the mere fact of registration is sufficient to prove these elements, unless and until the contrary is established.

2. Registration constitutes constructive notice to everyone else of the registrant's claim of ownership of the trademark.[19] This means that those who subsequently use the same trademark cannot defend themselves by claiming that they did not know that the trademark rights were already owned by someone else. Everyone is presumed to have notice of the existence of trademark rights for trademarks which have been registered. (This is one reason why it is advisable to conduct a federal trademark search prior to adopting a mark.)

3. If the owner of the trademark continues to use the trademark in commerce for five consecutive years after it has been registered, and complies with certain other formalities required by the Trademark Act, the right of the trademark owner to use the registered mark in commerce for the goods or services for which it has been registered becomes "incontestable." This means that, with certain exceptions specified in the Trademark Act, no one can challenge the validity of the trademark or the owner's exclusive rights thereto, for example, by asserting that they used the same or

---

[18] 15 U.S.C. §1057(b).
[19] 15 U.S.C. §1072.

a similar mark prior to the time that it was first registered by the trademark owner.[20]

4. Imported goods bearing an infringing trademark can be prevented from entering the country.[21]

5. Any attempt by another person to register a conflicting mark will be blocked where there is a likelihood of confusion.[22]

6. The owner may bring suit for trademark infringement in the federal courts.[23]

7. In certain cases, treble damages and attorneys' fees are available to registrants who have been injured by an infringer.[24]

8. Finally, federal registration on the Principal Register will serve to expand the registrant's exclusive rights to include the entire United States, even if actual use has taken place only in a portion of the country.[25]

6.5.2. Qualifying For Federal Registration

With certain exceptions, any mark which is used in interstate commerce may be registered on the Principal Register, and will enjoy the benefits described in Section 6.5.1, provided that it is distinctive of the applicant's goods (or services). The requirement that the trademark be used in interstate commerce means that it must be affixed to goods actually sold or licensed in interstate commerce, that is, across state lines. Merely advertising software in interstate commerce does not constitute "use" sufficient to qualify for trademark registration. Advertising will, however, constitute sufficient use to qualify for registration of a service mark, as long as the services are sold in interstate commerce.

There are certain types of marks that will not qualify for registration. For example, a mark which is descriptive or is a person's

[20] 15 U.S.C. §§1065, 1115. However, if an innocent party has used the mark prior to the registrant's registration, the innocent party's geographic area of use will be carved out and reserved for its exclusive use. *Burger King v. Hoots*, 403 F.2d 904 (7th Cir. 1968).
[21] 15 U.S.C. §1124, 19 U.S.C. §1526.
[22] 15 U.S.C. §1052(d).
[23] 15 U.S.C. §1114.
[24] 15 U.S.C. §1117.
[25] *John R. Thompson Co. v. Holloway*, 366 F.2d 108, 115 (5th Cir. 1966).

surname may not be registered on the Principal Register, unless it has acquired secondary meaning.[26] Other exceptions to registration include marks that are immoral, deceptive, or scandalous, marks consisting of a government flag or other insignia, and marks which consist of a person's name, portrait, or signature used without his or her consent.[27]

Finally, an otherwise eligible mark cannot be registered if there is a likelihood that it will be confused with an existing trademark; that is, if it so resembles a mark already registered or used in the United States "as to be likely, when applied to the goods of the applicant, to cause confusion, or to cause mistake, or to deceive . . . ."[28] The question of when a proposed trademark is likely to cause confusion or mistake with respect to another trademark is often difficult to answer since it depends upon the facts of each case. However, when comparing two marks to determine whether the second mark can be registered, the following factors should be considered:

1. The similarity or dissimilarity of the goods or services on which the two marks are used (including a comparison of price ranges)

2. The similarity or dissimilarity of the two marks with respect to appearance, sound, connotation, and commercial impression

3. The similarity or dissimilarity of the market being served (e.g., wholesale or retail, sophisticated or unsophisticated consumers)

4. The number and nature of similar marks in use on similar goods

5. The nature and extent of any actual confusion that may already have arisen between the two marks

6. The length of time during which and the conditions under

---

[26] 15 U.S.C. §§1052(e), (f). However, as discussed in Section 6.5.3, a descriptive or surname mark which has not acquired secondary meaning may be registered on the Supplemental Register.

[27] 15 U.S.C. §1052.

[28] 15 U.S.C. §1052(d).

which there has been concurrent use of the two marks without evidence of actual confusion

7. The variety of goods on which a mark is used

8. The extent of potential confusion.[29]

The first factor listed, a comparison of products or services in connection with which the marks are used, is a major one in determining likelihood of confusion. In one case, a court denied registration of the mark "Digicom" in connection with computer consulting services where a similar mark, "Digicon," had been previously used by another company in the same business.[30] In another case, Computer Communications, Inc. tried to register a mark consisting of a small block "c" within a larger block "C" to be used on computer peripheral equipment. Registration was refused, however, because Graphic Controls Corp. had previously registered a mark consisting of a small round "c" within a larger block "G". The Graphic Controls mark was used to identify computer accessories, and these products were sufficiently similar to the products of Computer Communications to create a reasonable likelihood of confusion, mistake, or deception if the two marks were allowed to coexist.[31] In another case, however, the court found that the use of the trademark "PTS" in connection with computerized tax preparation services did not create a likelihood of confusion with another's use of the same mark in connection with computers. The court noted that the products or services of the two companies did not compete with each other, and concluded that there was no likelihood of confusion. There, one of the determinative factors was that the plaintiff's services cost between $6.75 and $50, whereas the defendant's cheapest computer cost $6,000.[32]

---

[29] *Application of E.I. DuPont DeNemours & Co.*, 476 F.2d 1357, 1361 (C.C.P.A. 1973).

[30] *Digicom, Inc. v. Digicon, Inc.*, 328 F. Supp. 631, 635–36 (S.D. Tex. 1971).

[31] *Application of Computer Communications, Inc.*, 484 F.2d 1392, 1393–94 (C.C.P.A. 1973).

[32] *Programmed Tax Sys., Inc. v. Raytheon Co.*, 439 F. Supp. 1128, 1133 (S.D.N.Y. 1977). This was a case involving trademark infringement rather than the right to registration; however, the same general principles of likelihood of confusion are applied in infringement cases and registration proceedings.

6.5.3. Principal versus Supplemental Register

Certain marks which are not registrable on the Principal Register, but which are still capable of distinguishing the applicant's goods or services, may be registered on the Supplemental Register if they have been used in interstate commerce for one year prior to the time of registration.[33] Marks registered on this register are primarily marks which fall into the descriptive or surname categories and which have not yet attained secondary meaning. Registration on the Supplemental Register does not provide many benefits, but will preclude registration of similar marks.[34] Thus if a descriptive mark does not qualify for registration on the Principal Register, it may be advisable to register it on the Supplemental Register, and then, after five years of constant use, to apply for registration on the Principal Register. After five years of use in interstate commerce, the trademark examiner may assume that there is secondary meaning and may permit registration on the Principal Register.

6.5.4. Application for Registration

An application for registration of an eligible trademark on the Principal Register may be filed at any time after the trademark has been used in interstate commerce. An application for registration on the Supplemental Register, however, cannot be filed until the mark has been used in interstate commerce for at least one year.

To register a trademark with the federal government, the following items are required:

1. A written application
2. A drawing of the trademark (in many cases a typewritten version will suffice)
3. Five specimens of the mark as actually used (i.e., five actual labels, or, for services, five actual brochures or advertisements)
4. A filing fee of $175[35]

---

[33] 15 U.S.C. §1091.
[34] *In re Clorox Co.*, 578 F.2d 305 (C.C.P.A. 1978).
[35] 15 U.S.C. §1051; and 37 C.F.R. §§2.21, 2.31–2.58. The filing fee is, of course, subject to change at any time.

Applications can be made on forms supplied by the Patent and Trademark Office or on plain paper. A copy of the application form is set forth at Section A.4. The application itself is relatively simple and does not necessarily require the services of an attorney. However, because of a number of other complexities inherent in the trademark registration process, the use of a trademark attorney is recommended.

6.5.5. Registration Process

The trademark registration process usually takes one to two years to complete. The process begins when the completed application and the other required documents are received in the Patent and Trademark Office. This information will be reviewed by a trademark examiner familiar with the appropriate class of products or services to which the mark applies in order to determine whether the trademark is appropriate for registration. Several months after the application has been filed, the examiner will make a decision as to whether the registration is to be allowed or rejected. If the mark is to be rejected, an appropriate notice is sent to the applicant, who then has six months to respond and/or to provide any additional information requested.

If the mark is determined to be registrable, it will then be published in an official publication of the Patent and Trademark Office known as the "Official Gazette." The purpose of this publication is to provide notice to the public that the Patent and Trademark Office intends to register the listed trademarks. Any persons who believe that they will be injured by the issuance of the registration have 30 days to file a notice of opposition. If no objections are received within 30 days of publication in the *Official Gazette*, the registration will be issued.

6.5.6. Trademark Notice

After a trademark has been registered by the Patent and Trademark Office, the law allows the owner of the trademark to give notice that the mark has been registered, in any one of three ways:

1. By displaying the mark as used with the words "Registered in U.S. Patent and Trademark Office"

2. By displaying the mark as used with the words "Reg. U.S. Pat. & TM. Off."

3. By displaying with the mark the letter "R" enclosed within a circle, as ®[36]

The use of such a notice is not required by the law, but if the notice is not included, a trademark owner will not be able to recover the infringer's profits or its own damages from an infringer who did not have actual notice of the registration.[37] Therefore, it is advisable to use the notice with all federally registered trademarks.

It is important to note that these trademark notices may *not* be used prior to the issuance of a trademark registration by the Patent and Trademark Office. However, the owner of an unregistered trademark should give notice of its claim of trademark ownership by use of the term "TM" for trademarks and "SM" for service marks. Neither of these designations confers any legal status but by serving as some notice of a claim of trademark ownership, it may deter a potential infringer.

6.5.7. Term of Registration

Each certificate of registration issued by the Patent and Trademark Office remains in force for 20 years.[38] The registration will be canceled after six years, however, unless the owner of the trademark files an affidavit between the fifth and sixth year after registration which states that the mark is still in use in interstate commerce.[39]

Assuming the affidavit has been filed, the trademark registration may be renewed for additional 20-year terms, provided that the trademark is still in use in interstate commerce at the time the application for renewal is filed.[40] Thus the registration of a trade-

---

[36] 15 U.S.C. §1111. This notice may be used whether the registration is on the Principal or Supplemental Register.

[37] 15 U.S.C. §1111.

[38] 15 U.S.C. §1058(a).

[39] 15 U.S.C. §1058.

[40] 15 U.S.C. §1059. The renewal application may be filed within six months prior to the expiration date, or, for an additional fee, within three months after the expiration date.

mark can be renewed indefinitely, so long as the trademark continues to be used in interstate commerce.

6.6. STATE REGISTRATION OF TRADEMARKS

In addition to the federal Trademark Act, each of the 50 states also has its own trademark laws. If a trademark is registered with the federal government, however, there is generally no need for state registration.

In most of the states, the laws are patterned after a model state trademark bill. This law is, in many ways, similar to the federal trademark law, and provides for trademark registration at the state level. The benefits of state registration apply only to the state in which registration is made, and are not nearly as extensive as the benefits of federal registration. For example, state registrations do not generally carry a presumption of trademark validity and do not operate as nationwide constructive notice of the rights of the registrant. Federal registration will generally include all benefits granted by state registration, and more.

State registration can usually be accomplished more quickly than federal registration, however, and is thus often utilized while a federal application is pending. In addition, if the software is marketed only in one state, and thus does not qualify for federal registration, state registration may be advisable.

The model state trademark bill provides that registration is for a 10-year term, which may be renewed indefinitely. The application fee generally ranges from $5 to $25.

Several states also have what are known as anti-dilution laws which may be invoked to protect a trademark owner. Anti-dilution laws generally provide for the entry of an injunction against another's use of a mark in a manner that is likely to cause injury to the trademark owner's business reputation or to cause dilution of the distinctive quality of the mark. Thus, even if the products on which the two marks are used are so dissimilar that the public will not likely be confused as to their source, and therefore trademark infringement cannot be proved, an anti-dilution statute may be invoked to protect the mark on the grounds that such use is likely to dilute the owner's mark. For example, in one case a court found that Polaroid was entitled to an injunction against the defendant's use of the term "Polaraid" in its refrigeration and heating system installation business under state unfair competition and anti-dilution laws. The question of trademark infringement was not addressed.[41]

6.7. LOSS OF TRADEMARK—ABANDONMENT

Trademark rights can be lost through abandonment. Abandonment can occur either: (1) when use of the trademark is discontinued with an intent not to resume use or (2) when any course of conduct of the registrant causes the mark to lose its significance as an indication of origin.[42] Once the trademark is abandoned, anyone else is free to use it.

Abandonment through nonuse does not occur solely as a result of not marketing products containing the trademark. The nonuse must be coupled with an intent to abandon the trademark. However, intent not to resume use of the trademark may be inferred from the circumstances. Under the Trademark Act, nonuse of a trademark for two consecutive years is considered prima facie evidence of abandonment.[43]

A trademark can also lose its significance as an indication of origin when the mark becomes generic, that is, when the public begins to use the trademark to identify the particular type of product itself, rather than to identify the brand of the product produced by the trademark owner. This has happened to "aspirin," "thermos," "escalator," "formica," and "cellophane," as well as many other marks, all of which were at one time trademarks identifying specific product brands. However, there are a number of steps that can be taken by the trademark owner to police the use of its mark to insure that its trademark does not become generic. These are described in detail in Section 6.8.

The reader may be familiar with a recent case holding that the name "Monopoly" as applied to a board game had become an

---

[41] *Polaroid Corp. v. Polaraid, Inc.*, 319 F. 2d 830 (7th Cir. 1963).
[42] 15 U.S.C. §1127.
[43] *Id.*

unprotectible generic term.[44] The court applied an unusual purchaser-motivation test and held that "Monopoly" was generic because it "primarily denotes a product, not the product's producer." This decision, which was widely criticized, threatened the trademark rights of producers of unique products, whose customers are motivated to buy because they want the particular product rather than because they are interested in who made it. The Supreme Court declined to review the case, but steps were taken by Congress to amend the Trademark Act and overturn the decision so that the purchaser-motivation test would not be applied in future cases. As a result, the Trademark Clarification Act of 1984 was signed into law on November 9, 1984, to provide that a trademark would not be considered generic merely because it is used to identify a unique product, and that the purchaser-motivation test should not be applied. This amendment should protect trademark owners in future cases like the one involving "Monopoly."

6.8. PROTECTING THE TRADEMARK

In order to maintain the valuable property rights acquired in a trademark, it is important that steps be taken to insure that the mark does not become generic, and that others are not permitted to infringe on the mark. If a mark becomes generic, it is no longer the exclusive property of the original owner, and in essence becomes public property. If others are permitted to infringe on the mark without objection, the value of the mark may be diminished.

First and foremost, the owner should use the trademark in a proper and consistent manner. The mark should be printed in initial or all capital letters; in correspondence, the use of quotation marks is suggested. If the mark is registered, it should always be used in the form registered and the symbol "®" should immediately follow the mark. Prior to registration, it is a common practice to use the symbol "TM" after the mark; while this does not confer any special legal status to the mark, it will demonstrate that the mark is being claimed as a trademark.

[44] *Anti-Monopoly, Inc. v. General Mills Fun Group, Inc.*, 684 F.2d 1316, 1326 (9th Cir. 1982).

The mark should always be used as an adjective followed by a common name for the product. It should never be used as a noun or verb. For example, the Xerox Corp. is careful to phrase its advertisements to refer to a "Xerox brand plain paper copier," or a "Xerox computer," rather than to "making a xerox" or "xeroxing a copy."

Second, the owner of the trademark should take steps to prevent generic or improper use of the trademark by others. This generally involves monitoring the trademark's use by dealers, distributors, and licensees, and objecting to any misuses that occur. Such misuses could include improper format, lack of trademark notice, or generic use, as well as any infringing use.

In developing an approach to misuse by persons outside its own distribution network, the trademark owner should assess the value of the trademark, the need to prevent loss of distinctiveness, and its financial ability to maintain a lawsuit to protect the trademark. Protecting against misuses by outsiders may involve monitoring trade and other print media, publishing advertisements informing the general public of the proper way to use the trademark, and following up on misuses by letters, personal contacts, and, if necessary, lawsuits. The owner should recognize that a trademark infringement suit can be quite costly, but, depending on the type of misuse and the value of the mark, a suit may be the advisable course, not only to prevent the current misuse, but to demonstrate a willingness to protect the mark and thus deter future misuses.

6.9. INFRINGEMENT AND REMEDIES

The owner of a federally registered trademark has the right to prevent others from using a reproduction, counterfeit, copy, or colorable imitation of that mark in a manner that is likely to cause confusion, to cause mistake, or to deceive. The owner may also be entitled to damages for unauthorized use. Similar rights exist for unregistered trademarks and state-registered trademarks. The following discussion is intended to provide some general background on infringement issues. In any case where infringement is claimed or is believed to exist, however, it is advised that a lawyer be consulted.

6.9.1. Factors Relevant to Infringement

Unlike copyright protection, which is concerned with protecting the owner's authorship rights, trademark law has the dual goal of protecting the owner from unfair competition and protecting the public from confusion. While copyright law would prevent any and all copying of the protected item, trademark law only protects against confusing or deceptive copying. Thus the same or similar mark may be used by someone else, as long as there is no likelihood of confusion as to the source of the goods or services. For example, in one case discussed earlier, the court found there was no likelihood of confusion, and therefore no infringement, between the trademark "PTS" used in connection with computers and the same mark used in connection with computerized tax preparation services.[45]

In determining whether there is a likelihood of confusion in an infringement case, the courts will generally consider the same factors as the Patent and Trademark Office considers when reviewing an application for registration. These factors are described in Section 6.5.2. Thus the courts will compare the marks themselves, the products or services with which they are identified, and the markets in which the marks are used. The courts will also examine all other relevant facts and circumstances, including any incidents of actual confusion. For this reason, it is advisable to maintain accurate records regarding the kinds of goods and services on which the trademark is and has been used, copies of infringing marks, and customer correspondence or other contacts regarding infringing goods. For example, records of customer inquiries to the trademark owner about an infringer's goods may help to establish that consumers were actually confused as to the source of the goods.

In an infringement action, the strength of the disputed mark, discussed in Section 6.2.2, may become important. This is because a weak mark will generally be given a narrower scope of protection than a strong one. The owner of a weak mark thus may not be able to prevent its use on another product which is significantly different from its own, whereas if the mark were fanciful or

---

[45] *Programmed Tax Sys., Inc. v. Raytheon Co.*, 439 F. Supp. 1128, 1133 (S.D.N.Y. 1977).

coined, or had acquired great public fame, the owner might be able to prevent its use on a variety of different products. For example, the owner of the strong arbitrary mark "K2" used on skis was able to enjoin use of the same mark on a totally different product, cigarettes,[46] whereas the owner of the weak mark "Mustang" for campers was unable to prevent its use on a similar product, automobiles.[47]

Even though trademark validity and ownership are prima facie established by trademark registration, these issues are often brought up and contested in an infringement suit. In such a suit questions of descriptiveness or genericness, secondary meaning, priority of use, and abandonment may be addressed. Even after trademark registration is obtained, it is therefore important to maintain records of use, sales, advertising, and customer correspondence relating to the mark.

6.9.2. Remedies for Infringement

If the trademark owner can prove infringement, a court will generally enjoin the infringement and award the owner the infringer's profits, its losses, and the costs of suit.

As with copyright infringement, the first goal of the trademark owner is to stop the infringement. Assuming the owner has not been successful in persuading the infringer to cease using the mark without litigation, this is accomplished by obtaining a court-ordered injunction against continued use of the infringing mark. The Trademark Act gives courts the authority to enter a preliminary injunction at the initiation of the lawsuit, which will remain in effect for the duration of the lawsuit.[48] If the suit is successful, the court may make the injunction permanent. In some cases, courts have tailored injunctions to fit the particular case without prohibiting use of the infringing mark. For example, an injunction might specify that a label be altered to make clear that particular

---

[46] *Philip Morris Inc. v. K2 Corp.*, 555 F.2d 815, 816 (C.C.P.A., 1977).
[47] *Westward Coach Mfg. Co. v. Ford Motor Co.*, 388 F.2d 627, 634–35 (7th Cir. 1968). In this case, the weakness of the mark was demonstrated by the use of that term by different persons on a wide variety of items over time.
[48] 15 U.S.C. §1116.

software was produced by the defendant rather than by the plaintiff.

As an additional remedy for infringement, the owner may be awarded the defendant's profits from the sale of goods using the infringing mark. The owner may also get treble the amount of damages it has suffered, that is, sales or profits lost because of the infringement. This type of recovery is available only if the owner has given the proper notice or the infringer had actual notice of registration.[49]

The court may order the destruction of all infringing labels, signs, prints, packages, wrappers, receptacles, and advertisements bearing the infringing mark, as well as all plates, molds, or other means of making copies of the infringing mark.[50]

Finally, the Trademark Act prohibits the importation of any goods which bear a copy or simulation of a federally registered trademark.[51] Such goods are to be stopped by customs officials at the border and prevented from entering the country.

[49] 15 U.S.C. §§1111, 1117.
[50] 15 U.S.C. §1118.
[51] 15 U.S.C. §1124.

CHAPTER SEVEN

EMPLOYERS AND EMPLOYEES

When a company hires talented and creative individuals to develop valuable software, it must consider the possibility that those employees will someday leave, and may very well use what they have learned to go to work for competitors, or to start their own competing businesses. This is an especially common occurrence in the software industry. In situations where this is a very real possibility, the employer must face two very critical issues. First, how can the employer insure that it is the exclusive owner of all rights to software developed by its employees? Second, what steps can the employer take to insure that its proprietary rights in software, however developed, are not compromised?

The best way to resolve both of these issues is through the execution of an appropriate written contract between employer and employee. Such a contract can be designed to protect the employer by: (1) requiring the employee to assign to the employer all rights in any software he or she develops; (2) binding the employee to an obligation of confidentiality; and (3) where permitted by law, restricting the employee's right to compete with the employer following termination of the relationship. A contract of this nature also helps to make employees aware of the need for confidentiality with respect to their work. It must be carefully drafted, however, because a court will refuse to enforce such an agreement if it is deemed to work too great a hardship on the employee.

Sample employee agreements addressing these issues are included in Sections A.13 and A.14. Each of the primary issues addressed in such agreements is analyzed in the sections that follow.

7.1. ASSIGNMENT OF RIGHTS

When there is no written agreement between an employer and its employees, it is sometimes unclear who owns the rights to software developed by employees. The employer clearly owns the copyright under the work for hire doctrine (see Section 3.1.3), but the employee who develops software may own any patent rights that exist (see Section 5.5), and may, under certain circumstances in some states, also retain the rights to use any trade secrets (see Section 4.6.3).

The best way to insure that the employer will own all rights in software developed by its employees is for the employer to require the employees to assign to the employer their rights in any software that they develop. If this is clearly set forth in a written document, there can be no controversy at a later date.

The following is an example of a contract clause in which the employee acknowledges that the employer will automatically own the copyright, and agrees to assign all other software rights to the employer:

> Employee acknowledges that all software, documentation, and other works created by him within the scope of his employment are "works made for hire" and that Employer will own any resulting copyrights. Furthermore, Employee hereby assigns to Employer any and all patent and trade secret rights in and to all software, documentation, and other works created by Employee within the scope of his employment.

When requiring employees to assign all of their rights in any software they develop, the contract must specify which software is covered. Note that this contract clause covers software developed by an employee "within the scope of his employment." Obviously, software written "outside" the scope of employment is not covered, but distinguishing between the two is often a problem.

It is clear that software written during working hours under the direction of the employer and for which the employee is being compensated is within the scope of employment. But what about software that is developed by an employee after hours, that is, on the employee's own time? If such software is totally unrelated to the employer's business, a strong argument can be made that the employer should have no right to it.

Two questions should be asked when addressing this issue: (1) is the software that is written by employees on their own time related to the software they are being paid to write on their employer's time, and (2) are the employees using any of their employer's time, money, facilities, or trade secrets to develop it? For example, suppose that Softco hires Bob Lewis to work 9 to 5 writing an accounts payable system for mainframe computers that it intends to market to manufacturing businesses. Suppose further that Lewis spends his evenings and weekends writing video game software that he intends to sell in the personal computer market. Does Softco have a right to claim ownership of the video game software or to require Lewis to assign his rights to Softco? Would it make any difference if Lewis wrote his game software while at work, and used the Softco computer to test it? Does this give Softco a better claim to ownership? Alternatively, what if Lewis writes an accounts payable package that he himself intends to market? Does the fact that this is the same type of product as the one he was hired to develop affect Softco's ownership rights?

As you can see from this example, what is within or without the "scope of employment" can be a tricky issue. Some employers attempt to deal with this problem by requiring their employees to assign all rights in any software they develop, regardless of whether the software is written on the employee's own time, and regardless of whether it bears any relationship to the employer's business. But this is a rather harsh restriction to impose on an employee and may not be enforceable.

Some states now have laws that prohibit an employer from requiring an assignment of ownership rights in any invention (including software) developed on an employee's own time and with his or her own resources, especially if the invention does not relate to the business of the employer. In Illinois, for example, a statute provides as follows:

> A provision in an employment agreement which provides that an employee shall assign or offer to assign any of the employee's rights in an invention to the employer does not apply to an invention for which no equipment, supplies, facilities, or trade secret information of the employer was used and which was developed entirely on the employee's own time, unless (a) the invention relates (i) to the business of the employer, or (ii) to the employer's actual or demonstrably anticipated research or development, or (b) the invention results from any work performed by the employee for the employer. Any provision which purports to apply to such an invention is to that extent against the public policy of this State and is to that extent void and unenforceable. The employee shall bear the burden of proof in establishing that his invention qualifies under this subsection.[1]

Similar statutes have been passed in several other states as well.[2] Some of these statutes also require that employees be informed of

---

[1] Ill. Rev. Stat. ch. 140, §302(1).
[2] *See also* Cal. Labor Code §2780, Minn. Stat. §181.78, and Wash. Rev. Code Ann. §49.44.140.

the applicable law. In Illinois, for example, if an employment contract requires employees to assign their rights in any invention to the employer, the employer must also give the employees written notification, at the time the agreement is made, that it does not apply to inventions for which no equipment, supplies, facility, or trade secrets of the employer were used and which were developed entirely on the employee's own time.[3]

Where the software relates to the business of the employer, however, the employer has a legitimate interest in obtaining ownership of it, even if it was developed on the employee's own time. For example, if Mr. Lewis was using his evenings to develop his own accounts payable system, there would be no way to prove that he was not using his employer's trade secrets to do it. Moreover, his employer is entitled to have Lewis' talents directed exclusively to the project he is being paid to work on, which he is not likely to get if Lewis has got something similar going "on the side."

These arguments lose much of their force when applied to software developed by Lewis on his own time which is completely unrelated to his employer's business. The arguments have no force at all when applied to software an employee may have developed *before* his or her employment began. Being mindful of these limtations will help employers to draft fair and enforceable employment agreements.

7.2. CONFIDENTIALITY AGREEMENT

All employees are under an obligation imposed by law not to disclose to others, or to use for their own benefit, the trade secrets which may be disclosed to them during the course of their employment. (See Section 4.5.3.) In some states, however, employees may be entitled to the benefit of trade secrets they themselves have developed, and the prohibition may not apply at all to confidential information which does not rise to the level of a trade secret. Consequently, to insure that every employee is bound by an obligation of confidentiality with respect to *all* trade secrets and confidential information, and to insure that all employees are

---

[3] Ill. Rev. Stat. ch. 140, §302(3).

aware of this obligation, it is best to enter into a written confidentiality (or nondisclosure) agreement.

Such an agreement was a key factor in protecting software in an important case that arose in Michigan. In that case, a company called Structural Dynamics Research Corp. (SDRC) developed software capable of solving some unique structural analysis problems. The two employees responsible for its development left SDRC before development was complete and formed their own company, which thereafter began marketing an almost identical package. The former employees were sued by SDRC for trade secret misappropriation and ultimately found to be liable. In its decision, the court said that, because they were the developers of the software at SDRC, they would normally have been free to use the trade secrets in the software they developed, but for the fact that they had signed an appropriately worded confidentiality agreement with their employer. Thus, the key to SDRC's protection in that case was the confidentiality agreement. Because they had breached its terms, the former employees were required to pay damages equal to 15 percent of their gross sales for a three year period.[4] Although the court's insistence on a confidentiality agreement to protect employee-developed trade secrets represents a minority view, the result in that case emphasizes the need for such agreements.

A confidentiality agreement should be designed to accomplish two things. First, because an employee is entitled to fair notice of what is considered confidential, the agreement should identify, as specifically as possible under the circumstances, the confidential and trade secret information to be covered by the agreement. Second, the agreement should clearly state that the employee cannot disclose the trade secrets and confidential information to anyone, or use them for his or her own benefit, without the permission of the employer.

7.2.1. Identifying the Information to Be Protected

The first step, identifying the "confidential information," is very important, but not always easy to do. An employee is entitled to

---

[4] *Structural Dynamics Research Corp. v. Engineering Mechanics Research Corp.*, 401 F. Supp. 1102 (E.D. Mich. 1975).

fair notice of what material is to be kept confidential. It may not be possible to define the confidential information with particularity, but a good faith effort should be made to at least define the categories of information involved, in order to insure that employees are made aware of which information is truly confidential at or before the time they actually learn it. If this is done, employees will not be able to defend a trade secret misappropriation claim on grounds that they did not know what they were doing.

The employer should also resist the temptation to claim that all information provided to an employee is confidential, since it may result in an unenforceable contract.[5] The general knowledge and skills of a trade or profession, even if learned from one's employer, cannot qualify as trade secrets, and no matter how carefully drafted, a confidentiality agreement cannot be used to prevent an employee from using that kind of knowledge for his or her own benefit.[6] One who has worked in a particular field cannot be compelled to erase from his or her mind all of the general skills, knowledge, acquaintances, and overall expertise acquired during his or her tenure with a former employer.

This can be illustrated by the following example. Assume that Dentalsoft, a company that develops and markets software for dentists, needs a PL1 programmer to help with a new patient management system. Unable to find a qualified PL1 programmer who has any knowledge of the dental business, it hires George Schuster, a recent college graduate who knows COBOL but not PL1. After requiring him to sign a confidentiality agreement, Dentalsoft trains Schuster to program in PL1, and teaches him the ins and outs of the dental business. Nevertheless, when Schuster later decides to quit Dentalsoft and start his own business, the confidentiality agreement he signed with Dentalsoft will not prevent him from writing software in PL1. This is because PL1 is a commonly known language in the industry, and Schuster could have learned how to use it from many different sources. (See Section 4.6.1.)

What if Schuster wants to compete with his former employer and write his own software for dentists? Is he prohibited from

---

[5] See, e.g., Disher v. Fulgoni, 464 N.E.2d 639, 644 (Ill. App. Ct. 1st Dist. 1984).
[6] Trilog Assocs., Inc. v. Famularo, 455 Pa. 243, 314 A.2d 287, 292 (1974).

using his knowledge of the dental industry (which he learned at Dentalsoft) in designing his software? Again, the answer is no. Information about the dental industry that he learned at Dentalsoft was information he could have learned elsewhere. There is nothing secret about it, and thus he cannot be prohibited from using or disclosing it. (See Section 4.6.2.)

But what about Schuster's knowledge about the design and structure of the Dentalsoft package itself and the techniques and algorithms it utilizes; information he learned because he designed and developed it? If this is information which Dentalsoft took care to keep a secret, and if it is not, in fact, generally known in the industry, it is the type of information which Dentalsoft is entitled to have protected as a trade secret. Thus, Schuster would be prohibited by an appropriately worded confidentiality agreement from using this information, or from disclosing it to anyone else.

In light of this example, consider the following somewhat detailed definition of confidential information which might be included in an employee agreement:

Confidential Information

The term "Confidential Information" refers to any information, not generally known in the relevant trade or industry, which was obtained from Employer, or which was learned, discovered, developed, conceived, originated or prepared by Employee in the scope of his or her employment and which falls within the following general categories:

(a) information relating to Employer's existing or contemplated products, services, technology, designs, processes, and formulae, including computer systems, computer software, algorithms and related research or developments;

(b) information relating to Employer's business plans, sales or marketing methods, methods of doing business, customer lists, customer practices and/or requirements, and supplier information;

(c) any other information which is identified as confidential by Employer.

This definition covers information not generally known in the relevant trade or industry which falls into three general categories. It does not specifically identify any trade secrets, but at least gives the employee some guidelines, albiet very vague ones. Note also that this definition covers information discovered or developed by the employee as well as information disclosed to him or her by the employer. It makes no difference how the employee learned the information. He or she is still obligated to keep it confidential.

There are, of course, an unlimited number of ways to define what it is that employees must keep confidential. This should be tailored to meet the needs of the particular situation.

7.2.2. Employee Obligations

The second part of a confidentiality agreement is a clear and concise statement setting forth the employee's obligations. Four main points should be covered:

1. The contract should cover confidential information discovered or developed by the employee as well as information merely disclosed to him or her by the employer.
2. The contract should prohibit the employee from using confidential information for purposes outside the scope of his or her employment.
3. The contract should prohibit the employee from disclosing the confidential information to anyone outside of the company, or anyone within the company not authorized to receive it.
4. The confidentiality obligation should remain in effect after the employee leaves.

An example of a confidentiality provision designed to accomplish these goals may be written as follows:

> During Employee's term of employment with Employer, and at all times thereafter, unless Employee shall first secure Employer's written consent, Employee agrees that he or she will not disclose to others, or use for his or her own benefit, any Confidential Information, whether or not developed by Employee, except as required for the performance of his or her duties to Employer. This para-

graph shall apply only so long as the information in question does not become generally known in the trade or industry other than by breach of this agreement.

The term "Confidential Information" which is used in this clause is, of course, a reference to a definition of that term contained elsewhere in the contract. Note the use of the phrase "at all times thereafter" at the beginning of the paragraph. Words to this effect are important to make it clear that the obligation of confidentiality continues indefinitely even after termination of employment, or as the last clause makes clear, until the information is no longer a secret.

A confidentiality agreement that is appropriate in one situation may not be appropriate in another. Because the public policy in most states favors competition and seeks to avoid restrictions on an individual's right to earn a living, courts give careful scrutiny to confidentiality agreements and tend to construe them most strongly *against* the employer. Thus it is important that such an agreement not be overly broad in scope or duration, that the information to be protected is really confidential, and that the restriction is reasonably and realistically necessary for the protection of the legitimate interests of the employer.

This analysis was applied in one recent case, where a court felt that an employee was required to sign a confidentiality agreement that imposed an inordinate duty of confidentiality, and thus could be invalidated on that basis.[7] The employee had signed an agreement with Information Resources, Inc. (IRI), which prohibited him from disclosing IRI's trade secrets and confidential information to any third party. The restricted subject matter included, but was not limited to, client lists, marketing and business plans, computer programs and systems, test designs, specifications, models, and financial data. The contract also stated that the obligation of confidentiality survived termination of his employment. Under the facts of that case, the court felt that this agreement could be invalidated because the lack of a restriction on the time or geographical scope of the confidentiality obligation may have exceeded what would have been necessary for the protection of

[7] *Disher v. Fulgoni*, 464 N.E.2d 639 (Ill. App. Ct. 1st Dist. 1984).

IRI's legitimate interests. The court also cited the fact that the duty of nondisclosure extended to any third party, and that the subject matter of the obligation of confidentiality was explicitly left open-ended.

This case was decided under Illinois law, and the result might have been different in another state. However, it does illustrate the need for competent legal counsel when it comes to the drafting of confidentiality agreements.

7.3. NONCOMPETITION AGREEMENT

As a general rule, employees are free to compete with their former employer, or to go to work for a competitor, as long as they do not use any of their former employer's trade secrets.[8] A noncompetition agreement can alter this general rule.

A noncompetition agreement prohibits an employee from starting a business which competes with his or her employer, and from going to work for a competitor of the employer. Noncompetition agreements are designed to be used as an additional measure to insure that an employee does not misappropriate his or her employer's trade secrets and confidential information.

These agreements are used because, in many cases, it is virtually impossible for an employee to work on a competitive project with a new employer without using or disclosing the trade secrets of his or her former employer. Take George Schuster, the Dentalsoft employee in the earlier example. Absent a noncompetition agreement, he would be free to go into competition with Dentalsoft after he resigns, although he cannot use any of Dentalsoft's trade secrets in doing so. This raises a very practical problem. How will Schuster develop his own dental software without using any of the trade secrets embodied in the Dentalsoft software that he also developed? In reality, he probably cannot.

This very problem arose in a case where an employee left Electronic Data Systems Corp. (EDS) to go work for a competitor.[9] While at EDS the employee had helped to develop software for

---

[8] *Trilog Assocs., Inc. v. Famularo*, 455 Pa. 243, 314 A.2d 287, 291 (1974); Restatement (Second) of Agency §396 (1957).

[9] *Electronic Data Sys. Corp. v. Powell*, 524 S.W.2d 393, 398 (Tex. Civ. App. 1975).

processing private health care claims, and he was assigned to perform a similar function for his new employer. Because he had signed a noncompetition agreement, EDS filed suit to prevent him from working for a competitor. In its opinion, the court acknowledged that a mere confidentiality agreement in such a case would, as a practical matter, be unenforceable. As the court pointed out, even in the best of good faith, a technical or "creative" employee working for a competitor can hardly prevent his knowledge of his former employer's confidential methods from showing up in his work. The mere rendition of service in the same area would almost necessarily impart knowledge obtained from his former employer in some degree in his subsequent employment. In an effort to avoid this problem, employers will often require employees to enter into a noncompetition agreement prohibiting subsequent employment as or with a competitor.

One problem with noncompetition agreements is that they are not enforceable in all states. States such as Alabama, California, Florida, Louisiana, Montana, North Dakota, Oklahoma, and South Dakota have enacted laws prohibiting noncompetition agreements except in very limited circumstances, such as the sale of a business.[10] But even in states where noncompetition agreements are valid, they must be drafted very carefully or they will not be enforced. If such an agreement would unreasonably impair the employee's ability to earn a living in his or her chosen field, or if its scope goes beyond what is reasonably necessary to protect the legitimate interests of the employer, it will not be enforced.

The following is an example of a noncompetition clause which might be used as part of an employment agreement in states in which it is allowed:

Noncompetition Agreement

During the period of his employment with Company, and for a period of ___ years[11] after its termination, Employee agrees that, within the area of _____ ,[12] he will not:

---

[10] *See* Ala. Code tit. 9 §§22–23; Cal. Business & Professions Code §§16,600–16,602; Fl. Stat. §542.12; La. Rev. Stat. §23:921; Mont. Rev. Code §28–2–703; N.D. Cent. Code §9–08–06; Okla. Stat. tit. 15 §§217–18; S.D. Comp. Laws, Ann. tit. 53 §§9–8 to 9–11.

[11] See Section 7.3.2.

[12] See Section 7.3.3.

(a) render any services as a consultant or as an employee to any business which is a competitor of any part of the business of Company for which employee worked during the 12 months immediately preceding his termination.

(b) be engaged in the ownership or management of any business or activity which is a competitor of any part of the business of Company for which employee worked during the 12 months immediately preceding his termination (except as an investor in securities publicly held and listed on a national securities exchange).

To determine whether this or any other noncompetition clause will be enforced (in the states in which such agreements are allowed), the critical test to apply is one of "reasonableness." In analyzing the reasonableness of a noncompetition agreement, a court will question whether the scope of the restraints imposed on the employee is reasonable when measured against the employee's need to earn a living in his or her chosen field, and the employer's need to protect its proprietary rights. In performing this analysis, courts will take the following factors into consideration:

1. What the employee received in exchange for entering into the noncompetition agreement
2. How long the restraint on competition lasts
3. The geographic scope of the noncompetition agreement
4. Whether or not the noncompetition agreement is necessary to protect the employer's legitimate rights in its proprietary information, such as trade secrets.

These factors are not all weighed equally in a given case, and a court's analysis will depend heavily on the particular facts involved. What follows is a general discussion of how courts analyze these factors when deciding whether to enforce a noncompetition agreement.

7.3.1. Consideration

A noncompetition agreement will not be enforced unless there is some consideration flowing from the employer to the employee in exchange for the employee's commitment. When the agreement is executed at the time the employee is hired, this is not a problem.[13] The employer is agreeing to give the employee a job and to pay him or her a wage in exchange for the employee's labor and commitment to be bound by the noncompetition agreement.

Frequently, however, an employer will request its employees to sign noncompetition agreements after they have been on the job for some period of time. In many states, unless the employee is given a new or extra benefit in exchange for signing the agreement, the agreement may later be deemed unenforceable for lack of consideration.[14] In one case, for example, Burroughs had one of its employees sign a noncompetition agreement four years after he started work, but did not give him anything extra for doing so. Subsequently, when the employee left to start a competing business and Burroughs tried to stop him, a federal court in Pennsylvania ruled that because Burroughs had given him nothing in return for signing this agreement, there was no consideration and it was not binding.[15]

In other states the courts consider the employee's continued employment to be sufficient consideration to support the agreement not to compete, on the theory that the employer could have ended the employment at any time. Thus the employer's agreement to continue employing the employee constitutes consideration for the employee's agreement to be bound by the noncompetition agreement.[16] The lesson to be learned is that, if the noncompetition agreement is not signed at the time the employee is hired, legal counsel should be consulted to determine whether, and under what circumstances, an agreement signed at a later date can be made enforceable. If continuing to employ the employee is not sufficient, the employer should consider providing some additional benefit to the employee in exchange for signing the agreement. This could be a small bonus or salary increase, or

[13] *Burroughs Corp. v. Cimaksky,* 346 F. Supp. 1398, 1399 (E.D. Pa. 1972).

[14] *Jostens, Inc. v. National Computer Sys., Inc.,* 318 N.W.2d 691, 703–04 (Minn. 1982); *Modern Controls, Inc. v. Andreadakis,* 578 F.2d 1264, 1267 (8th Cir. 1978); Annot., 51 A.L.R. 3rd 825, 833–35 (1973).

[15] *Burroughs Corp. v. Cimakasky,* 346 F. Supp. 1398, 1399 (E.D. Pa. 1972).

[16] *Matlock v. Data Processing Sec., Inc.,* 607 S.W.2d 945, 948 (Tex. Civ. App. 1980); *Puritan-Bennet Corp. v. Richter,* 657 P.2d 589, 592 (Kan. Ct. App. 1983); Annot., 51 A.L.R. 3d 825, 835–39 (1973).

perhaps a change of jobs which would be viewed as desirable by the employee.

7.3.2. Time Restrictions

A noncompetition agreement must be written so that it is binding for a period of time that is no longer than is necessary to protect the reasonable and legitimate interests of the employer. Otherwise, there is a risk that a court will not enforce it.[17] The time period should normally not extend beyond one or, at most, two years, although it is impossible to set forth any specific rules. How much time is "reasonable" will depend to a large extent on the facts of each case. Such facts may include the "life" of the secret material, market conditions, the nature of the employee's relationship to the company, the employer's lead time in the particular market involved, and other similar factors. In one case, a court stated that a contract which prohibited a systems engineer from working for a competitor for three years after his employment ended was reasonable.[18] In another case, a one-year restriction was found to be acceptable.[19]

7.3.3. Geographical Restrictions

Courts will also refuse to enforce noncompetition agreements if the geographical area in which the employee is prohibited from competing is excessively broad in relation to the employer's interests to be protected. However, as with the question of the duration of the restriction, there are no set rules for determining what is and what is not acceptable.

Courts consider factors such as: the area in which present and prospective customers are located; the likelihood that a former employee will contact any of these customers or potential customers; the nature of the market; and other factors relating to the

[17] In some states the courts will reduce the restricted time period rather than refusing to enforce the entire agreement.

[18] *Electronic Data Sys. Corp. v. Kinder*, 360 F. Supp. 1044, 1050 (N.D. Tex. 1973) (dicta) *aff'd*, 497 F.2d 222 (5th Cir. 1974).

[19] *Business Intelligence Servs., Inc. v. Hudson*, 580 F. Supp. 1068, 1072 (S.D.N.Y. 1984).

effect that any former employee's competition would have on his or her former employer.

If the employer is a consulting business that operates solely in one city, for example, any restriction on competition by former employees which extends beyond the boundaries of that city will probably be viewed as unreasonable. As long as an employee goes outside of the city before competing with his or her former employer, there is no competition in the market in which the former employer operates, and thus no injury to the former employer. On the other hand, if the employer is a software firm marketing its products on a nationwide basis, a noncompetition provision which restricts the former employee from competing anywhere in the United States may be viewed as a reasonable restriction. The key is that the scope of the geographical restriction must be reasonably necessary to provide the protection to which the employer is entitled.[20]

In one case a court upheld a noncompetition clause containing no geographical limitation whatsoever. The case involved a programmer who left Business Intelligence Services, Inc. (BIS) to work for a competitor, Management Technologies, Inc. (MTI)[21] Both companies developed and marketed software for use by international financial institutions engaged in international multicurrency transactions, and were vigorous competitors. BIS required its employees to sign a one-year noncompetition agreement which had no geographical limit. When a BIS programmer left to go to work for MTI, BIS filed a lawsuit seeking an injunction to prohibit her from working for MTI for one year. The court expressed some concern about the unlimited geographical scope of the noncompetition agreement, but decided that it was not unreasonable due to the fact that BIS's business was worldwide in scope and that the time restriction (one year) was sufficiently limited.

In another case, however, a court refused to enforce a noncompetition agreement because there was no limit on the territory covered.[22] In that case, a programmer had agreed "not to develop

---

[20] *Matlock v. Data Processing Sec., Inc.*, 607 S.W.2d 946, 950 (Tex. Civ. App. 1980).

[21] *Business Intelligence Servs., Inc. v. Hudson*, 580 F. Supp. 1068, 1073 (S.D.N.Y. 1984).

[22] *Trilog Assocs., Inc. v. Famularo*, 455 Pa. 243, 314 A.2d 287, 294 (1974).

or assist in developing a shareholder's record system for himself or anyone else." The court held this agreement void because there was no limit on territory. As the court pointed out, enforcement of the agreement would have prevented the employee from practicing his profession almost anywhere for anyone in developing a shareholder's record system—something that was much broader than necessary to protect his employer. Other courts have also found that noncompetition agreements with no geographical limitation were too broad, and have refused to enforce them.[23]

7.3.4. Employer's Need for the Protection

A noncompetition agreement will not be enforced unless it is necessary for the protection of the employer's business. Public policy favors employee mobility, and courts are generally reluctant to prohibit an employee from working. A good example is a case brought by Electronic Data Systems Corp. (EDS) against a former employee who had signed an agreement not to compete with EDS.[24] EDS had developed software to process Medicare payment claims, one of only two such packages on the market. The EDS Plan was proprietary to EDS, whereas the other software package, the Model Plan, had been developed by the Social Security Administration and was public information available to anyone for the asking. When an EDS employee went to work for another firm that also processed medicare payments, but which utilized the Model Plan, the court refused to enforce the noncompetition agreement. The court reasoned that, because of the difference in the software used by the two companies, prohibiting the EDS employee from working for the other firm was not necessary for the protection of EDS's business.

Another example of this attitude can be seen in a case involving a Burroughs employee who sold and serviced checkwriters.[25] The employee had signed a noncompetition agreement which prohibited him from competing with Burroughs "in selling, leasing,

---

[23] *On-Line Sys., Inc. v. Staib,* 479 F.2d 308, 310 (8th Cir. 1973); *see also Direction Assocs., Inc. v. Programming & Sys., Inc.,* 412 F. Supp. 714, 720 (S.D.N.Y. 1976).

[24] *Electronic Data Sys. Corp. v. Kinder,* 360 F. Supp. 1044, 1050 (N.D. Tex. 1973), *aff'd,* 497 F.2d 222 (5th Cir. 1974).

[25] *Burroughs Corp. v. Cimakasky,* 346 F. Supp. 1398, 1400 (E.D. Pa. 1972).

renting, servicing, and programming and from selling business forms and supplies which he had sold while at Burroughs" to persons who were Burroughs customers within his last year of employment. After leaving Burroughs, the employee went into business for himself servicing Burroughs checkwriters and selling supplies to customers he had previously serviced for Burroughs. He was sued by Burroughs, but the court refused to enforce the noncompetition agreement on the ground that it prohibited him from doing things that were not related to his experience at Burroughs (such as programming). Because the contract prohibited more than was necessary for the protection of Burroughs' interests, the court refused to enforce it.

Some companies have even tried to prohibit their employees from working for organizations without regard to whether they were in competition. In one case, for example, a data processing company called Trilog Associates was party to an agreement which prohibited its employees from working for any Trilog customer or anyone else with whom the employee had come into contact through his employment with Trilog.[26] This was void, the court said, because there was no restriction on the kind of employment prohibited. It covered work totally unrelated to the work the employee had performed for Trilog; for example, although they were data processing employees, they were barred from working as janitors, bank managers, or truck drivers for any Trilog customers, or anyone they happened to meet while on Trilog's business. This, the court said, was broader than necessary for the protection of the employer's interest.

Plainly, it is important not to try to accomplish too much with a noncompetition agreement. There is a real risk that, in trying to get too much, the employer will come away with nothing.

7.4. RISKS IN HIRING EMPLOYEES OF COMPETITORS

The preceding sections have emphasized the importance of assignment, confidentiality, and noncompetition agreements to employers. But employers must also be sure that they do not partici-

---

[26] *Trilog Assocs., Inc. v. Famularo*, 455 Pa. 243, 314 A.2d 287, 294 (1974).

pate in the violation of any such agreements their employees may have entered into with previous employers. Care must also be taken when hiring employees of competitors to insure that they do not bring with them any trade secrets of their former employer. If they do, and those trade secrets are subsequently used in work for the new employer, the new employer may be liable, along with the new employee, for misappropriation of the competitor's trade secrets.

In the most obvious case, if an employer hires employees away from a competitor for the purpose of obtaining the competitor's trade secrets, the employer will be liable to the competitor for trade secret misappropriation. This is exactly what Telex did with some IBM employees in the early 1970s. As a court later determined, Telex deliberately set out to misappropriate certain IBM trade secrets, hired a number of IBM engineers for this purpose, and succeeded in misappropriating a number of those secrets and incorporating them into Telex products.[27] For this conduct, the court awarded IBM approximately $21 million in damages.[28]

In another case, a company called Pentronix deliberately hired a number of Sperry Rand Corp. employees in order to obtain Sperry's trade secret process for manufacturing magnetic memory cores.[29] For this, both Pentronix and the former Sperry employees were ordered to pay Sperry for the damages it suffered.

An employer can even run into problems when it hires employees innocently, and without any intent to misappropriate trade secrets. If the employees improperly disclose any such trade secrets to their new employer, the new employer may be liable after it learns that the information was someone else's trade secret which was wrongfully disclosed. The liability would be based on use or disclosure of the trade secrets by the employer after it received such notice.

An example of this occurred in a case involving a service bureau and one of its customers. The service bureau had developed

---

[27] *Telex Corp. v. International Business Machines Corp.*, 367 F. Supp. 258, 323, 327, 358 (N.D. Okla. 1973), *trade secret aspects aff'd*, 510 F.2d 894, 929–930 (10th Cir. 1975).

[28] *Id.* at 363. This was reduced to $17.5 million on appeal. 510 F.2d at 933. The case was subsequently settled by the parties.

[29] *Sperry Rand Corp. v. Pentronix, Inc.*, 311 F. Supp. 910, 923 (E.D. Pa. 1970). *See also Sperry Rand Corp. v. Electronic Concepts, Inc.*, 325 F. Supp. 1209, 1219 (E.D. Va. 1970).

software for direct mail advertising and used it to perform services for its clients. At some point one of its clients became concerned about the service bureau's financial stability, and demanded a copy of the software as security. An employee of the service bureau delivered the source code to the client, although, unbeknown to the client, this was a violation of company policy. When the parties subsequently broke off their relationship, the former client used this software to develop its own system after being informed that the source code was a trade secret owned solely by the service bureau. Notwithstanding that it had initially acquired the source code innocently, the court ruled that use of the software after the client was informed of its trade secret status subjected the client to liability for misappropriation.[30]

It is therefore important for employers to be sure that their employees are not bringing trade secrets of their former employers with them. Otherwise the new employer may inherit an additional liability for trade secret misappropriation.

---

[30] *Computer Print Sys., Inc. v. Lewis*, 281 Pa. Super. 240, 422 A.2d 148, 155 (1980).

CHAPTER EIGHT

BASIC SOFTWARE CONTRACTS

At the heart of the software industry are the contracts that govern the terms of the various transactions relating to the development, marketing, and use of software products. Although there are many different types of software transactions between two parties, most of them can be grouped into four general categories: sales, licensing, distribution, and development. Most of the transactions which do not fall in these general categories will resemble them to some degree. Consequently, the contracts applicable to those transactions will tend to be hybrids of the contracts applicable to the primary categories. A turnkey system contract, for example, is basically a combination of a software license and a hardware sale.

This chapter will discuss the nature and purpose of each of the software transactions that typify the market today. Chapter 9 will analyze the provisions which should be considered for inclusion in the agreements that govern these transactions and will identify the considerations that are relevant to determining how such provisions should be structured.

8.1. SOFTWARE SALE

When software is transferred from one party to another, the transaction may take the form of either a sale or a license. If the transfer is a sale, the owner of the software loses all rights of ownership and control over the software after it is sold. If the transaction is a license, the owner of the software retains its ownership rights, and, as discussed in Section 8.2, retains some degree of control over the customer's use and disposition of that software. For this reason, most software transactions are structured as licenses rather than sales. Nonetheless, software can be, and certainly is, sold.

There are two ways to sell software. An owner can sell all of its rights in the software, or it can merely sell a copy. If it sells only copies, it can make as many sales as possible, but if it sells all of its rights, it can sell the software only once. This is analagous to the sale of a book. A bookstore sells only copies, and tries to sell as many copies of the book as possible. When authors sell their books to a publisher, however, they frequently sell all of their rights in it, that is, the right to make and sell copies and the right to modify or update the book. Similarly, if a software owner wants to market its software to a large number of customers, it will sell only copies. If, however, an owner wants to obtain a large one-time payment for the software, it may sell all rights to one buyer, such as a distributor or publisher, who will then market the copies.

When an owner of software sells all of its rights in the software, it relinquishes the right to possess, use, copy, and modify the software. It also transfers any copyrights, trade secrets, and patent rights that it has to the buyer. The original owner retains nothing, except, hopefully, a good price for the software. While most sales of software do not take this form, such sales do occur in the context of a distribution or publishing agreement, and as part of the sale of all of the assets of a software business.

Normally, if an owner chooses to sell its software, it will sell only a copy. In this type of a transaction, a software owner will lose only the right to control any subsequent use or disposition of the particular copy that has actually been sold. The owner will retain the right to make, sell, and modify additional copies of the software.

An individual who purchases a copy of the vendor's software may use it in any way that he or she sees fit, provided, of course, that such use does not violate the copyright laws which, in general, forbid the making of additional copies (except backup copies as discussed in Section 3.2.2). The purchaser may, however, resell the copy purchased, provided he or she does not keep an extra copy. (See Section 3.2.6.)

Like the sale of a copy of a book, a sale of a copy of software is usually an over-the-counter transaction in which the copy is exchanged for cash and thus is generally not governed by a written contact. The owner's sale of all of its rights to the software, however, will normally involve a written contract.

8.2. SOFTWARE LICENSE

A software license is the most basic, the most common, and one of the most important of all computer software transactions. The vast majority of all software available in the market today (except, perhaps, for mass-marketed software for personal computers), is licensed rather than sold. The software license agreement forms the basis of virtually all transactions in which one party is given the right to use software by another party.

Strictly speaking, a "license" is a grant of permission to do something which would not otherwise be allowed, or to use something the user does not own. A software license is a contract by which the owner of the software (or the owner's agent) grants to the licensee (the user) the permission or right to use a particular copy of the software. A software license might also be compared to a lease or rental agreement whereby the owner of the software "rents" a copy to the user for a specified fee.

It is important to distinguish the concept of a license from that of a sale. In the case of a license, the user does not become the owner of either the copy of the software received, or of any other rights in the software that are not specified in the license contract. The copy is still owned by the licensor, and the user merely obtains the right to use it, subject to all the restrictions imposed by the license agreement. In the case of a sale, title to a particular copy is transferred to the buyer, who is then able to use that copy of the software in any manner he or she desires—free from any restrictions imposed by the seller, and subject only to the restrictions imposed by the copyright laws.

From the software owner's perspective, the primary benefit of the license format is that it provides a vehicle through which the owner can market its products and at the same time protect its trade secrets by imposing restrictions on the use and dissemination of the software by the user. Without a license agreement to impose an obligation of confidentiality on the user, the software owner would waive protection for any trade secrets in the software which are disclosed to the user or discovered through its use. (See Section 4.3.2.) By licensing copies of the software, software owners are able to retain ownership of the copies, protect their proprietary rights, control third-party use of the software, and prevent unauthorized exploitation of the software[1] —controls not possible when the copies are sold.

The two most important issues to be addressed when drafting provisions in a software license agreement to protect the software owner's trade secrets are: (1) what rights are granted to, and what restrictions are imposed on, the user; and (2) what obligations are imposed on the user to keep the software confidential. With respect to the first issue, owners will want to limit the use of their software according to their marketing plan and their need to protect the software from theft. Users, on the other hand, will want to

---

[1] The courts have recognized that the customer's right to use the software is governed by the express terms of the license agreement. *S & H Computer Sys., Inc. v. SAS Institute, Inc.*, 568 F. Supp. 416, 421 (M.D. Tenn. 1983).

insure that they obtain rights to use the software that are sufficiently broad to accommodate their own needs. Thus, while the
license will grant the user the right to use the software, a major
concern is the scope of that use. For example, will the user be
granted the right to copy, modify, or transfer the software? Will
the user be permitted to grant others access to the software on a
time-sharing basis? These and other considerations relevant to
drafting this section of the contract are discussed in Section 9.3.

With respect to the issue of confidentiality, it is important to
remember that a primary function of a software license agreement
is to protect the software owner's trade secrets after they have
been disclosed to its customers. Accordingly, it is necessary that
the license impose a clearly defined obligation of confidentiality
on the licensee which, if complied with, will prevent the unauthorized use or disclosure of proprietary information. The obligation of confidentiality is discussed in detail in Section 9.9.

There are, of course, many other important issues that must be
addressed in a software license, but they depend, to a large extent,
on the nature of the particular transaction involved. Some of the
major contract terms that appear in license agreements are analyzed in Chapter 9, and a detailed checklist of questions to consider in preparing or analyzing a license is set forth in Section A.6.
An example of a software license agreement is included in Section
A.7.

8.3.   SHRINK-WRAP LICENSE

Another form of software license that deserves mention is the so-
called shrink-wrap license. This type of license is identical in all
respects to a standard software license, except that it is never
signed by the user. For this reason, its validity as a binding contract is open to question.

Most licenses are contracts signed by both the software vendor
and the user. Their signatures signify their agreement to the terms
of the license and impose on them a legal obligation to be bound
by those terms. Negotiating the terms of the license and obtaining
the user's signature on the license agreement are feasible in software transactions involving substantial sums of money and signifi-

cant commitments by both sides. But this is not true for low-priced high volume software that is marketed to a large customer base through distributors who cannot justify the extra expense of obtaining signed license agreements. To deal with this problem, many vendors have begun using so-called shrink-wrap or tear-open license agreements.

The shrink-wrap license is a relatively new concept, and one that is heavily used for mass-marketed software for personal computers. The shrink-wrap license is a preprinted form agreement that is placed or printed on the top of the package containing the software to be marketed and encased in a cellophane wrapper (i.e., shrink-wrapped). A warning label on the outside of the cellophane wrapper informs the customer that by opening the cellophane wrapper (or in some cases, by actually using the software) he or she accepts the terms of the license agreement, which are visible through the cellophane. Frequently, the notice will also state that if the user is unwilling to agree to the terms of the license agreement, he or she may return the package to the vendor, unopened, for a full refund. The theory is that the act of opening the cellophane wrapper (or the act of using the software) is legally equivalent to signing the contract—that is, both acts indicate acceptance of the contract terms.

The legality of this technique has not yet been tested in the courts, and thus the ultimate viability of this mechanism as a procedure for securing the customer's agreement to the terms of the license agreement remains to be seen. However, the States of Louisiana and Illinois have enacted legislation specifically making such contracts enforceable,[2] and similar legislation has been introduced in several other states.

If the courts ultimately decide that shrink-wrap licenses are enforceable contracts, customers will be bound by their terms just as they would be bound by the terms of any license agreement that was actually signed. On the other hand, if shrink-wrap licenses are held not to be binding contracts, the transaction will be considered as a sale of the copy of software involved, and the vendor will lose its right to control the customer's use of that copy.

---

[2] La. Rev. Stat. Ann. §§51:1951–1956 (enacted in 1984); Ill. Pub. Act No. 84-901 (Enacted in 1985).

8.4. SOFTWARE DISTRIBUTORSHIP

When a software developer does not have the desire or the resources to market its own software, a distributorship agreement is
often an acceptable alternative. In exchange for accepting a
smaller fee for each copy of its software licensed, the developer is
relieved of the need to make what is often a substantial investment in advertising and promotion.

A software distributorship agreement is thus a marketing arrangement between the software owner and a separate entity who
will undertake to market (or distribute) the software and to pay the
owner a royalty. A software distributorship agreement is also commonly referred to as a software publishing agreement. But regardless of what it is called, a software distributorship agreement is
simply another form of license agreement. The software license
discussed in Section 8.2 was a license to use a particular copy of
the software. The software distribution agreement is broader—it
is a license to market and sublicense copies of the software to
others.[3]

As with the software license, the software distributorship agreement must be carefully structured so that the owner obtains optimum distribution of its software and prompt payment of all revenues due, while insuring that its trade secrets in the software are
not compromised. With respect to its trade secrets, the owner
must not only insure that confidentiality is protected at the distributorship level, but must also be concerned about unauthorized
disclosures by the distributor's customers. This may require a
contractual provision in the distributorship agreement specifying
the commitments that must be made by any customer to whom the
software is to be sublicensed, including the precise contract language to be used. Satisfaction of these needs may require exten-

---

[3] It is also common, especially in publishing agreements, for the owner to transfer all
rights in its software to the publisher in exchange for either a lump-sum payment or
royalties on each copy of the software that is subsequently sold or licensed by the publisher. Likewise, it is common for software owners, especially in the personal computer
market, to sell copies of their software to distributors, who merely resell them at whatever
price they choose to their customers. In software designed for larger computers, however,
it is much more common for the distributor to obtain the software via a license to market it,
and for the owner to specify the terms of a sublicense agreement which the distributor's
customer must accept.

sive documentation to permit verification that the distributor is using its best efforts to market the software, is obtaining a signed license agreement from each of its customers before disclosing the software to them, and is paying the royalties due on all user sales or licenses.

Another important issue to consider in negotiating or drafting a software distributorship agreement is the matter of the fees or royalties to be paid by the distributor to the owner for each copy of the software that it sublicenses. A royalty scheme must be established, and a procedure must be agreed upon for keeping records of all sublicenses so as to insure the accurate payment of fees.

These and other issues of importance to a software distributorship agreement are analyzed in Chapter 9. In addition, a detailed checklist of questions to consider when preparing or analyzing a distribution agreement is set out in Section A.8. An example of a software distribution agreement is reproduced in Section A.9.

8.5. SOFTWARE DEVELOPMENT

Frequently firms will contract with outside vendors for the development of new software or the modification of existing software. Such a transaction is normally governed by a software development agreement. The purpose of such an agreement is to specify exactly what work will be done by the developer, the price to be paid, and each party's rights in the resulting product. The very nature of a software development transaction, however, makes the contract very difficult to draft, and even more difficult to implement and enforce. This is a reflection of the basic problem with the task at hand: it is hard to define. Thus whether the developer agrees to develop or modify software (1) pursuant to previously defined specifications, (2) pursuant to specifications to be developed during the course of the contract, or (3) merely agrees to develop software to meet a general goal with undefined specifications, it will usually be difficult to determine whether the goal has been achieved.

Although it is easier said than done, the key to structuring a successful software development agreement is to sufficiently define the product to be developed so that, by reference to the contract, both parties will be provided with an objective standard to determine whether and when the contract has been completed. As long as such an objective standard exists, future disputes between the parties will be minimized. Consequently, until all parties have agreed on the detailed software specifications, it is normally unwise to attempt to proceed to a finished product. The contract must also accommodate the changes which will inevitably occur during performance, and provide a mechanism to identify and correct problems as soon as they arise. These issues are addressed in more depth in Section 9.4.

The software development agreement must also address the difficult question of ownership. If the developer is to retain ownership rights, then the user must be given a license to use the software. If the user will own all of the rights, the contract should reflect a transfer of ownership to the user, and should specify what rights, if any, the developer will retain. The issue of ownership in this context is further discussed in Section 9.8.

Like the software license and the software distribution agreement, there are a wide variety of terms that should be included (or at least considered) when preparing a software development agreement. Many of these terms are analyzed in Chapter 9, and a detailed checklist of questions to be considered when drafting or analyzing a development agreement is set out in Section A.10. An example of a software development agreement is included as Section A.11.

CHAPTER NINE

ISSUES RAISED IN MOST SOFTWARE CONTRACTS

Chapter 8 identified the basic types of software contracts. The purpose of this chapter is to examine what goes into those contracts. Although many software transactions are the result of a unique combination of facts, circumstances, and agreements, it is the thesis of this chapter that, in every software transaction, the parties must consider a number of basic issues which are common to all software transactions. This book cannot hope to evaluate all of the unique problems and circumstances that arise in the wide variety of software deals being made today, but it will attempt to analyze the issues that can be expected to arise most frequently.

This is not to imply that a given contract must contain language dealing with all of the issues raised here, or alternatively, that no other issues are relevant. Every contract must be structured to meet the needs of the particular transaction, and should accurately reflect the agreement of the parties. However, in preparing a software contract, the issues raised in this chapter should at least be considered, although the extent to which they are relevant, and the way in which they are handled, will vary depending upon the particular situation and the type of contract involved.

To introduce these contract issues, we begin with a checklist of basic issues, an overview of the types of questions both a vendor and user should be asking when drafting or evaluating a software contract.[1]

1. *Contract Introduction.* Who are the parties to the agreement and what is the background of the transaction? (See Section 9.1.)

2. *Definitions of Terms.* Are there any special terms that need to be defined for purposes of the contract, and if so, how should the definitions be phrased? (See Section 9.2.)

3. *Rights Granted by Vendor.* If the contract is a license agreement or a distribution agreement, what rights to use and/or market the software are granted to the user or distributor, and what restrictions are placed on those rights? (See Section 9.3.)

---

[1] See also Sections A.6, A.8, and A.10 for more detailed checklists.

a. *Right to Use.* Is the user granted the right to use the software for any purpose, or is it limited in some way? (See Section 9.3.1.)

b. *Right to Distribute/Market/Sublicense.* Is the user also granted the right to market the software to others? (See Section 9.3.2.)

c. *Exclusivity.* Is the right to use (and if appropriate, the right to distribute) the software granted exclusively to the user, or is the vendor free to grant these same rights to others? (See Section 9.3.3.)

d. *Right to Copy.* What rights, if any, does the user or distributor have to copy the software? (See Section 9.3.4.)

e. *Right to Modify.* Does the user have the right to modify the software, and if so, what effect will such modifications have on the vendor's warranty and maintenance obligations? Furthermore, what rights will each party have to use and market such modifications? (See Section 9.3.5.)

f. *Right to Assign.* Does either party have the right to transfer its rights under the contract to someone else? (See Section 9.3.6.)

g. *Restrictions on Disclosure.* Is the user free to disclose the software to others, or is it bound by an obligation of confidentiality? (See Section 9.3.7.)

h. *Hardware Restrictions.* Is the use of the software restricted to a particular type and/or model of hardware, a specific CPU serial number, or some other hardware-related parameters? (See Section 9.3.8.)

i. *Operating System Restrictions.* Is use of the software restricted to machines operating under a specified operating system? (See Section 9.3.9.)

j. *Location Restrictions.* Is use of the software restricted to a specified location? (See Section 9.3.10.)

k. *Use Restrictions.* Are any other restrictions placed on the way the software is used, or on who uses it? (See Section 9.3.11.)

4. *Work To Be Performed by Developer.*   If the contract is a software development agreement, what will the developer do, what specifications will be used, and how will the parties handle changes to the project that arise after the work begins? (See Section 9.4.)

5. *Term of the Agreement.*   When does the contract begin, how long does the contract remain in effect, and under what circumstances may the contract be terminated before it expires? (See Section 9.5.)

6. *Fees, Royalties, Payments, and Bookkeeping*

    a. *Types of Charges.*   What type of fee or royalty will be charged? (See Section 9.6.1.)

    b. *Items Included in Charges.*   Do the charges cover software only, or do they also include documentation, installation, training, support, and other items? (See Section 9.6.2.)

    c. *Payment Schedule.*   When is payment due? (See Section 9.6.3.)

    d. *Bookkeeping Requirements.*   In a software distribution agreement, what record-keeping requirements are imposed on the distributor to report sublicenses or sales of the software in order to determine the royalties due to the owner? (See Section 9.6.4.)

7. *Taxes.*   Who will pay any state and local taxes applicable to the transaction? (See Section 9.7.)

8. *Ownership of Software.*   What are the ownership rights of the respective parties in the software? (See Section 9.8.)

9. *Confidentiality and Protecting Proprietary Rights.*   What obligations and restrictions are imposed on the user or distributor to keep the software confidential in order to protect and preserve the owner's copyright and trade secret rights? (See Section 9.9.)

10. *Indemnification.*   What protection does the user have in the event the software infringes any patents, copyrights, or trade secrets of any third parties? What protection does either party have against losses caused by actions of the other party? (See Section 9.10.)

11. *Delivery.* What are the vendor's obligations with respect to delivery? (See Section 9.11.)

12. *Installation.* Is the vendor obligated to install the software on the user's system, and if so, under what terms? (See Section 9.12.)

13. *Training.* Is the vendor obligated to provide training in the use of the software, and if so, under what terms? (See Section 9.13.)

14. *Acceptance Testing.* Is the software required to pass an acceptance test, and if so, how will the test be conducted? (See Section 9.14.)

15. *Warranties.* What express warranties, if any, are provided by the vendor? Will the warranties implied by law be part of the contract, or will they be disclaimed by the vendor? Are any restrictions placed on the vendor's warranty obligations? What happens if the software fails to live up to the warranties? What are the vendor's obligations? (See Section 9.15.)

16. *Limitations of Liability.* Is the vendor responsible for all damages that the user might suffer as a result of using the software, or is there a limit on the nature or the extent of the vendor's liability? (See Section 9.16.)

17. *Software Maintenance.* Will the vendor provide maintenance for the software, and if so, under what terms? (See Section 9.17.)

18. *Default.* What constitutes a breach or default of the agreement by either party, and what are each party's rights in case of a default? (See Section 9.18.)

19. *Arbitration of Disputes.* Will the parties agree in advance to submit any disputes to arbitration instead of taking them to court? (See Section 9.19.)

20. *Termination.* When can either party terminate the agreement and what happens upon termination? (See Section 9.20.)

21. *Source Code Access.* Does the user get access to the source code, and if not, is any provision made for the possi-

bility that the vendor might go out of business or otherwise become unable to perform its maintenance obligations? (See Section 9.21.)

22. *Entire Agreement.* Does the contract contain the entire agreement of the parties, or are there other understandings between the parties that have not been included? (See Section 9.22.)

23. *Choice of Law.* Do the parties want to specify the law of a particular state to govern any disputes that may arise concerning the transaction? Which state's law should be specified? (See Section 9.23.)

24. *Force Majeure (Excusable Delays).* Will performance by either party be excused in the event it is prevented by circumstances beyond its control? (See Section 9.24.)

The questions raised by this checklist will be examined in the sections that follow. Examples of the contract terms discussed in this chapter, as they might be used in different types of software contracts, can be found in the sample software contracts in Sections A.7, A.9, and A.11.

9.1. CONTRACT INTRODUCTION

The introductory paragraph of each software contract should fulfill at least one basic function—it should identify the parties to the contract. The complete name of each party should be included, and if any party is a corporation or a partnership, that fact should also be stated, as well as the name of the state under whose laws that party is organized. If abbreviations for the names of each party arc to bc used throughout the balance of the contract, those abbreviations should also be defined in the introductory paragraph.

An example of an introductory paragraph is as follows:

This agreement is made on June 1, 1986 between Jones & Smith, an Illinois partnership, located at 72 W. Madison St., Chicago, Illinois ("Vendor"), and ABC Corporation, an Illinois corporation located at 764 Industrial Drive, Elmhurst, Illinois ("Licensee").

Note that this introduction contains the complete name and address of each party, and indicates that Jones & Smith is an Illinois partnership and that ABC is an Illinois corporation. The terms to be used in the balance of the contract to refer to each party (i.e., "Vendor" and "Licensee") are set forth here as well. The date can be stated here or at the end of the contract, but regardless of where the date is placed, it is important to insure that the date is included in the contract.

In addition to this introduction, some contracts also include a section describing the background of the transaction. This is sometimes referred to as the "recitals," or the "whereas clauses."

In essence, the recitals section of a contract is designed to explain why the parties are entering into the contract. This type of background information is not essential, but may be helpful in interpreting the agreement at a later date should a dispute arise over the meaning of its terms. An example of such a background section is as follows:

This Agreement is made with reference to the following facts:

A. Vendor has designed, developed, and programmed an inventory control system;
B. Licensee desires to license this inventory control system for use on its XRT 5/215 computer;
C. Licensee has thoroughly tested and evaluated this inventory control system and determined that it is suitable for its needs; and
D. Vendor desires to license this system to Licensee.

Now therefore, the parties hereby agree as follows:

Note that this section establishes who designed, developed, and programmed the software, identifies the type of software involved, and establishes that the package has been reviewed and tested by the user prior to entering into the license agreement. If ABC (the Licensee) later sued Jones (the Vendor), claiming that the software did not work properly, the admission by ABC that it had "thoroughly tested and evaluated" the system would surely be relevant.

9.2. DEFINITIONS OF TERMS

Any important term which will be used in the contract and which does not have a standard meaning should be clearly defined. Technical terms or concepts will be frequently misunderstood by unsophisticated parties, and may even mean different things to different people within the industry. Nontechnical terms also may be subject to a variety of interpretations. Therefore, the parties should give careful consideration to the need to define the potentially ambiguous words they have decided to use in their agreement.

When defining terms it is not necessary to use a dictionary definition, or even one that bears any relationship to the way in which a dictionary would define the same term. The purpose of providing a definition is merely to state, in writing, the parties' agreement as to what each term will mean for purposes of their particular contract.

The need for clear and concise definitions was summed up by one court as follows:[2]

> After hearing the evidence in this case the first finding the court is constrained to make is that, in the computer age, lawyers and courts need no longer feel ashamed or even sensitive about the charge, often made, that they confuse the issue by resort to legal "jargon," law Latin or Norman French. By comparison, the misnomers and industrial shorthand of the computer world make the most esoteric legal writing seem as clear and lucid as the Ten Commandments or the Gettysburg Address; and to add to this Babel, the experts in the computer field, while using exactly the same words, uniformly disagree as to precisely what they mean. Such being the state of the art, the court concludes that before even discussing the contract it should make at least a preliminary attempt at computer definitions.

Terms that are not defined in the contract will be given their plain, ordinary, and popular meaning by a court unless the parties are able to present evidence showing that the words were used with a different meaning.[3] In one case, for example, source code

---

[2] *Honeywell, Inc. v. Lithonia Lighting, Inc.*, 317 F. Supp. 406, 408 (N.D. Ga. 1970).

[3] *S & H Computer Sys., Inc. v. SAS Institute, Inc.*, 568 F. Supp. 416, 421 (M.D. Tenn. 1983).

was licensed for "use" on a single CPU designated by serial number. The term "use" was not defined in the contract and a dispute arose between the parties when the licensee placed the software on a second (unauthorized) CPU in order to list the source code. The user argued that the term "use" meant "to execute" the computer program, and thus claimed that using another (unauthorized) CPU merely to list or view the source code did not violate the license. Since the term was not defined in the license agreement, the court decided to give it its common definition, that is, "the act or practice of employing something." Using this definition, the court found that the software had been "used" on the unlicensed CPU and that that constituted a breach of the license agreement. Consequently, the court held that termination of the license agreement had been justified.[4] The moral of this story is that the agreement should define all terms on which significant rights may depend.

Defining terms need not be a complicated process, but it does require giving a close look at potential ambiguities to insure that the agreement actually expresses the intentions of the parties. This is an area where a lawyer, particularly one familiar with the computer industry, can be a big help.

In any software agreement, for example, some word will have to be used to refer to the software to be licensed, developed, or marketed. Commonly used words include "software," "licensed software," "licensed materials," "computer program," or perhaps an identifying name such as the "ABC Accounts Payable Software." Regardless of the term used, however, it is important that it be used consistently throughout the contract, and that it be defined in a manner that will allow an objective observer to determine which specific computer programs are the subject of the agreement, and what form they will take. Even though everyone in the industry may believe they understand the meaning of the term "software," it may still be unclear, in the context of a specific contract, which software is involved, or whether object code or source code will be provided. Only by defining the term "software" in the contract will these questions be resolved.

The definition can be as simple as identifying the software by

---

[4] *Id.*

its title, or as complex as providing an elaborate and detailed description of all of the specifications that the software must meet. Many agreements, for example, simply indicate that the vendor will deliver its "ABC Accounts Payable System." This type of definition is appropriate in a license agreement for a vendor's standard software system which is well known in the market. However, parties who sign an agreement which merely provides for the development of an "accounts payable system" are looking for trouble. How will either party know when the software delivered by the vendor has satisfied its obligations under the contract?

To deal with this potential problem, it is advisable, in an appropriate case, to attach or incorporate by reference detailed software specifications, such as those set forth in the user's manual or other documentation provided by the vendor, or to attach an elaborate exhibit detailing the specifications agreed upon between the parties. Such specifications may include a list of the functions to be performed, and items such as screen formats, report formats, input and output formats, data file structures, error deduction capabilities, error correction and recovery procedures, through-put, response times, systems environment, operating systems, interface with other applications, programming languages used, incorporation of proposals, and incorporation of published specifications.

As an example of the different ways in which software can be defined, consider the following sample definitions:

1. The term "Licensed Software" means the object code version of Release 5.2 of the ABC Inventory Control Package, as implemented on the VX2 hardware.

2. The term "Software" refers to the source and object code versions of the computer programs to be developed by Vendor for User pursuant to the specifications attached to this Agreement as Exhibit B.

3. The term "Software" refers to the computer programs listed on Exhibit A attached to this Agreement, all updates and enhancements to those programs that may subsequently be developed by Vendor, and all of the Vendor's standard user's manuals for those programs.

Note that definition 1 refers to a specific release of a preexisting package which is identified by name, and that it makes clear that only object code is included. Definition 2, by contrast, refers to software not yet developed, and thus incorporates a series of technical specifications which are attached to the contract as an exhibit. The more carefully prepared and detailed these specifications are, the easier it will be for the parties to determine whether the vendor has delivered the appropriate product. Finally, definition 3 defines "software" to include a specified list of computer programs and the user's manuals for those programs, even though documentation may not fall within the commonly accepted definition of software. Nevertheless, this is how the term will be defined for purposes of that particular contract.

"Documentation" is another term that may require a contract definition. Whatever word is chosen should be consistently used throughout the contract to refer to the specific documentation included (such as "documentation," "user manuals," "program description," etc.). The words chosen must be properly defined. For example, is the documentation to be provided limited to "user" documentation which merely tells the end-user how to operate the software, or does it also include the "technical" documentation necessary for a programmer to maintain and modify the software? It is important that clear and precise definitions be used so that both parties understand exactly what the other is saying.

Additional examples of definitions are included in the sample contracts in Sections A.7, A.9, and A.11.

9.3. RIGHTS GRANTED BY VENDOR

This section will examine the rights commonly granted and the restrictions commonly imposed in software license and distributorship transactions.

When software is licensed rather than sold, the vendor retains title to each copy of the software delivered, and merely grants the customer the right to use (and in some cases, distribute) the software. Because the vendor retains ownership, it can limit the rights granted to the user and can make delivery of the software subject to a contractual agreement by the user to abide by specified restrictions. The vendor does this to protect its trade secrets and its market for the software. Consequently, one of the most important sections in a license or distribution agreement is the one in which the vendor grants the right to use or market the software, and imposes restrictions on that right.

A typical license grant to an end-user, complete with many of the commonly used restrictions, may be written as follows:

> Vendor grants to User, during the term of this Agreement, a nonexclusive, nontransferable license to use the Licensed Software solely on an AJAX Model 55/10 CPU, serial number 5273612, running under the OVS operating system. The Licensed Software may be used only for processing User's own data. This license does not include the right to modify or sublicense the Licensed Software.

Similarly, a grant of the right to market and distribute software may be written as follows:

> Vendor grants to Distributor, during the term of this Agreement, a nonexclusive, nontransferable license to use, modify, market, and sublicense the Licensed Software within the Territory defined on Exhibit B.

The appropriateness of these contract clauses will, of course, depend upon the circumstances of each transaction. They are included here simply to raise the issues discussed in the following sections.

9.3.1. Right to Use

The right to use the software is the primary right that the vendor grants to the user in every software license agreement. Without it, the contract is of no value to the user. In many cases, no restrictions are imposed on the way in which the software can be used. It is not uncommon, however, for the license to limit use in a number of ways. For example, many licenses allow the software to be executed only on a CPU with a designated serial number, or only under a specified operating system. In other situations, the customer's use of the software may be limited to processing its own data, or to serving a specific location. The right to use the software is also frequently granted to the distributor in a software distribution agreement, although it is often limited to use for demonstration purposes only.

9.3.2. Right to Distribute/Market/Sublicense

The right to market and sublicense software to others is the primary right that a vendor grants to a distributor in a software distribution agreement. This is what sets a distribution agreement apart from the ordinary end-user license agreement. Nevertheless, the grant of the right to distribute, sublicense, publish or market software is, in essence, simply another form of a license. The licensor retains its ownership rights in the software and merely grants the distributor certain rights to market it.

When granting the right to market software, the distributorship agreement should also specify the terms of any sublicense agreement that the distributor's customer, that is, the end-user, will be expected to sign as a condition of obtaining the software. The owner must do this if the software embodies trade secrets, in order to insure that everyone who has a copy of it is at least under a contractual obligation to keep it confidential.

9.3.3. Exclusivity

A license to a user or distributor can either be exclusive or nonexclusive. If the vendor grants an exclusive license, it forfeits its right to license the software to anyone else. For this reason, the grant of an exclusive license to an end–user is very rare. Normally an end-user license agreement states that the license granted is "nonexclusive," as this gives the vendor the right to grant similar licenses to as many other customers as possible. If nothing is said about exclusivity, the law will usually assume that only a nonexclusive license was intended.

In a software distribution agreement, an exclusive right to market the software is more common. If exclusivity is intended, it should be specifically stated in the contract. Normally, however, a software owner who wishes to maintain marketing flexibility should consider entering into only a nonexclusive distributorship so that it will retain the flexibility to supplement the distribution efforts of one licensee with those of another or of itself.

Sometimes, when a distributor is granted the exclusive right to solicit customers, that right is confined to a specific geographical territory. Whether a license is structured in this manner is a business decision which depends on the software owner's assessment of how a particular distributor can be most effective, and on the owner's desire to license other distributors. However, there may be antitrust constraints on the allocation of exclusive territories, and legal counsel competent to give advice in this area should be consulted with respect to this issue.

9.3.4. Right to Copy

A user's right to make copies of licensed software is a subject which should always be considered. The user has a legitimate need to copy the software for backup purposes. But the vendor also has a legitimate need to reduce the risk that copies of its software will be passed along to users who might otherwise have become paying customers. If the issue is not covered in the contract, the user will not have the right, at least in theory, to make any copies. This is because the software is protected by copyright, and the provision in the copyright law allowing a user to make backup copies applies only when the user owns a copy, not when it merely licenses one. (See Section 3.2.2.) However, it is nevertheless a good idea to make the restriction on copying explicit so that there can be no misunderstanding by the licensee concerning its rights.

Thus, while the user may properly insist upon a provision affording some limited right to copy the software, the vendor can properly impose restrictions on this right. This is typically done by restricting the purposes for which extra copies may be made, and by specifying the number of extra copies which the user can have in existence at any one time. For example, the contract might allow the user to make no more than three copies, and specify that those copies are to be used only on a designated CPU, and are to be used only for backup purposes, to replace a worn copy, or for purposes of error verification and maintenance. A simple contract provision allowing a limited right to make copies might be written as follows:

> User may make no more than three copies of the Licensed Software, and these copies may be used only for backup purposes on the licensed CPU. User agrees to reproduce Vendor's copyright notice on all copies.

If the user violates a contractual provision like this and makes unauthorized copies, it will constitute a breach of the license agreement and, depending on the other terms of the agreement, may justify termination by the vendor.[5] It will also constitute an infringement of the copyright.

In a distribution agreement, the distributor's right to copy the software may need to be somewhat broader. This will depend upon whether the distributor is to make copies of the software for its customers, or whether the software owner is to ship each copy after the distributor has placed an order. If the distributor is allowed to make copies for customers, the contract should restrict the right to make copies to this limited purpose.

9.3.5. Right to Modify

As with the right to copy, the Copyright Act also prohibits a user or distributor from modifying licensed software unless the vendor gives its express permission. (See Section 2.1.2).[6] Whether such permission to modify the software, it is often a good idea to include parties before their agreement is signed. When granting permission to modify, however, the vendor should consider two important issues: (1) what effect any user modifications will have on the vendor's warranties and maintenance obligations; and (2) what rights both the user and the vendor will have to use and market the modifications.

From the vendor's point of view, user modifications can lead to serious performance problems. Thus if the vendor grants the user

---

[5] *S & H Computer Sys., Inc. v. SAS Institute, Inc.*, 568 F. Supp. 416, 421 (M.D. Tenn. 1983) (applying Tennessee law).

[6] When a copy of the software is "sold," the purchaser has a limited right under the Copyright Act to make modifications. But this does not apply to a license. (See Section 3.2.3.)

permission to modify the software it is often a good idea to include a clause in the contract stating that any modifications will void the warranties and relieve the vendor of any maintenance obligations. Alternatively, the contract can be structured to continue the vendor's warranty and maintenance obligations in force, but also to provide that if any problem with the software is caused by user modifications, the vendor will charge the user for the time and expenses incurred in locating and correcting the problem.

If user-prepared software modifications are likely to be a valuable and marketable product, the second issue must be faced: what rights each party has to use those modifications. Because the user has no right to modify the vendor's software without permission, the vendor can surely attach conditions to that permission. For example, if the vendor is concerned about the user selling its modifications to the vendor's other customers, thereby depriving the vendor of a market for its own enhancements, it might be wise to prohibit the user from marketing its modifications. Thus many contracts will provide that user modifications can be used by the user solely for its own internal use, and solely on the equipment for which the software was originally licensed.

Alternatively, if the vendor believes that it would like to use or market the user's modifications, it might be appropriate to require the user to furnish the vendor with copies of all modifications and grant the vendor a license to market them, either for a fee or royalty-free. Some vendors even go as far as insisting that the user transfer title to its modifications to the vendor. In any event, to avoid disputes, the right to use modifications should be expressly stated in the contract if the parties believe there is a chance that they will be significant.

9.3.6. Right to Assign

An assignment is a transaction whereby one party to a contract transfers all of its rights and obligations to someone else. For example, if a user has licensed a software package from a vendor, and the user wishes to transfer its right to use that software to a third party, it would accomplish this by assigning its license agreement to the third party. The third party then steps into the shoes of the user with respect to the contract. Note that because all of the user's rights under the license are transferred by an assignment, the user can make this transfer only once.

Does the user have the right to transfer or assign its software license or distributorship agreement to someone else without the vendor's consent? The user may desire such a right, so that in the event it decides to sell its computer system, to go out of business, or to license an alternate software package to perform the same functions, it will have the ability to transfer its software license and recoup at least a portion of the license fee originally paid to the vendor. The vendor, however, will normally prefer that the license not be transferable in order to maintain maximum control over the use of the software and to market as many copies as possible. Particularly in cases involving highly proprietary software, the vendor needs to know the identity of everyone who has a copy so that it can monitor compliance with confidentiality requirements and discover potential infringers. Moreover, out of concern over the trustworthiness of potential transferees, the vendor may not want the software arbitrarily transferred to a user whose integrity it has not had a chance to evaluate.

As a general rule, unless the contract states otherwise, a party may assign its rights under a contract, but may not assign its duties or obligations. Thus in a software development contract the developer may assign its right to receive money from the client, but may not assign its obligation to develop the software. It may be free to have someone else perform those obligations, as in a subcontract arrangement, but the developer will remain liable to the client in the event that they are not properly performed.

It is therefore wise for a vendor to insert a clause in the contract prohibiting assignment. The clause may be tailored to meet a user's need to assign the license in the event that it decides to sell its entire computer system or its entire business, or in the event that it desires to transfer the software to another division or affiliate corporation. This is commonly done by allowing a transfer of the license only if the user gets the vendor's written permission. To protect the user, the contract frequently provides that such permission will not be unreasonably withheld. This procedure will inform the vendor of the identity of the new user and allow the vendor to object if it has legitimate grounds for doing so.

In a software distribution agreement, however, the vendor will normally want to prohibit all assignments. The vendor will have entered into a contract with the particular distributor because it felt that the distributor would do a good job marketing the software and protecting the vendor's interests. The vendor depends heavily on its distributors, and will want to be sure that the distributorship is not transferred to someone with whom the vendor does not want to do business.

9.3.7. Restrictions on Disclosure

A confidentiality clause prohibiting disclosure of trade secrets embodied in the software is an essential element of every license and distribution agreement. If it is not included, the user is under no obligation to keep the software confidential, and the vendor risks losing its trade secrets. Because of the importance of this provision, it is discussed separately in Section 9.9.

9.3.8. Hardware Restrictions

Vendors will frequently restrict use of software to a single CPU. In some cases, the vendor will go to the extent of designating the serial number of the CPU on which the software may be executed. This is done primarily to maximize income by requiring a separate license for each machine, but is also used to maintain control over the number of copies that have been disseminated. In one case in which such a restriction was imposed, a court held that, by executing the software on an unauthorized CPU, the user had breached the license, thereby giving the vendor the right to terminate the license, repossess the software, and recover damages.[7]

Licensees which use many CPUs will typically seek to obtain a license for all of the computers located at a particular site, or, in some cases, for all of the computers they own or use, regardless of where they are located. These are matters to be negotiated between the parties. However, it is important for the vendor to have

---

[7] *S & H Computer Sys., Inc. v. SAS Institute, Inc.*, 568 F. Supp. 416, 421 (M.D. Tenn. 1983).

some control over the number of copies the user is allowed to use in exchange for the license fee that it has paid.

The use of software is also frequently restricted on the basis of hardware capacity. This allows vendors to price software on the basis of the level of its anticipated use and its presumed value to the customer. For example, a license for a particular software package might restrict the customer's use to a particular make and model of hardware that will support no more than 8 terminals and 512 K of memory. If the customer wants to run the software on hardware supporting 32 terminals and 1 MB of memory, it will presumably have more value, and consequently can be priced at a higher level.

9.3.9. Operating System Restrictions

It is also common for software to be licensed for use only with a specific operating system. Although some software can easily be modified for use on different operating systems, such modification and use may be prohibited unless the user obtains an additional license and pays the appropriate fee. Again, this is a device that can allow the vendor to maximize its revenues by charging a larger fee to users with a more extensive operating system. For example, consider a computer that will support two operating systems, one that allows for multiple terminals at remote locations, and one that does not. Because the former will allow more people to access a single copy of the software, thereby depriving the vendor of potential additional license fees, it may be appropriate for the vendor to charge a higher fee. The operating system restriction is one means whereby the vendor can achieve this marketing objective.

9.3.10. Location Restrictions

Some license agreements will restrict the location at which the software can be executed, for example, to the location for which the software was originally licensed. A variation on this type of provision will limit use of the software to one location at a time. Whichever alternative is selected, location restrictions are designed to deal with the situation in which the user will allow access to the software from remote locations through a network, rather than license additional copies. This will serve to protect the vendor's trade secrets, control the proliferation of its software, and maximize its income.

9.3.11. Use Restrictions

In order to preserve the confidentiality of its software and to maximize license revenues, vendors also will frequently insert a clause in the contract stating that the software may be used only to process the user's own internal data. This prohibits the user from acting as a service bureau, or from allowing third parties to access the software to process their own data on a time-sharing basis. Vendors who have a product that is in sufficient demand to form the basis for a service bureau or time-sharing operation may prefer to reap the benefits of that demand for themselves.

If the user is free to allow others to access the software on a time-sharing basis, a potentially large group of people who are not contractually bound to an obligation of confidentiality will be given access to the software. Any third party who has access to the software on a time-sharing basis may be able to use, copy, and/or disclose the software in ways that could seriously jeopardize the owner's trade secrets. In order to protect these rights, vendors often prohibit the user from allowing access on a time-sharing basis, or require that the user's time-sharing customers sign a license and/or confidentiality agreement in a form approved by the vendor, to try to insure that the trade secrets and copyrights in the software are not compromised.

The confidentiality problem is not as acute with respect to a service bureau arrangement because in that case the customer of the user does not have access to the software. Nonetheless, a service bureau arrangement may deprive the vendor of additional license fees.

Another way of dealing with the problems that could result from allowing third parties (who are not contractually obligated to keep the software confidential) to have access to the software is to provide in the license agreement that the software may be used solely by the one to whom it is licensed. Thus even though the software is installed on a single computer within the user's office,

the user is required to agree that no one other than its own employees will have access to it, either on a time-sharing basis or
otherwise. Appropriate exceptions can always be made to accommodate the user who has hired consultants to develop additional
software for its business, or whose software must be examined by
its auditors.

9.4.   WORK TO BE PERFORMED BY DEVELOPER

When two parties contract for the development of new software,
one of the most important parts of the contract is the one that
defines the work to be performed by the software developer. Not
surprisingly, it is also one of the most difficult sections to draft.
Frequently, the party who needs the software—the client—does
not know exactly what it wants. All too often, the client is unfamil-
iar with the world of data processing, and the developer is unfa-
miliar with the client's business. Adding to this confusion is the
fact that both parties' perception of a project will frequently
change during its lifetime, often with disastrous effects on the
original timetable and cost estimates. A simple example will illustrate this problem.

Consider the case of Ebenezer, a software developer. He has
agreed in principle to write an inventory control system for Freddie's Fast Foods, a new soyburger chain. Having agreed on the
job to be done, at least in principle, and knowing the perils of an
entirely oral agreement, Ebenezer and Freddie might typically
execute one of two types of agreement. The first, and unfortunately most common, is a short letter agreement in which Ebenezer will agree to create an inventory control package in exchange
for either an hourly rate (if Ebenezer has his way) or a fixed fee (if
Freddie prevails). The second type of agreement is a detailed
contract specifying each of the features of the desired system.
However, Freddie, like many businesspeople, knows relatively
little about software design, and, as a result, is unaware of this
option. Since Ebenezer does not want to be constrained by a long
contract, he happily signs the engagement letter he receives from
Freddie. The engagement letter provides that Ebenezer will be
paid $40 per hour and that the entire project is *estimated* to take
200 hours, but does not specify an upper limit.

After 300 hours of work, Ebenezer reports that a couple of unexpectedly difficult problems have been resolved and that the package should be completed with another 50 hours of work. Freddie, although angered by the delay and the additional cost, needs the system badly enough that he reluctantly agrees to wait the additional week and to pay for the additional work. Three weeks (and 150 sleepless hours) later, Ebenezer presents Freddie with the "system" and gives a demonstration. Much to Freddie's dismay, the software neither accounts for the costly ginseng strips served with every soyburger nor gives Freddie the option of shaving the amount of soybean meal used in each burger. In effect, the system which cost significantly more than Ebenezer projected will allow Freddie to do substantially less than he expected.

This is an all-too-common outcome in transactions like this. It results from two basic problems: Ebenezer does not adequately understand the soyburger business and Freddie does not understand the programming options available to him. Because of this mutual ignorance, many software development agreements are woefully inadequate to enable the contracting parties to accomplish their legitimate objectives.

From the developer's point of view, vagueness may be perceived as an advantage, since this will leave it more freedom to perform the contract in any way that it desires. Ultimately, however, the problem of vagueness works to the disadvantage of both parties. Due to the inevitable fact that each party will have differing expectations, vagueness can only lead to disputes and dissatisfaction. For the developer, this can mean problems collecting its money; for the user, this can mean a significant adverse impact on its business, as well as additional costs. For both parties, the prospects of expensive and time-consuming litigation are heightened.

The key to structuring a successful software development agreement lies in defining the product to be developed well enough so that, by reference to the contract, both parties will be able to determine whether and how well the contract has been completed. As long as such an objective standard exists, future disputes between the parties will be minimized.

Unfortunately, as in the case of Ebenezer and Freddie's, the parties frequently fail to adequately define in advance the significant features of the software to be developed. This is particularly true with an unsophisticated user or with a user who has not taken the time to define its needs. If, instead of simply requesting "an inventory control system," Freddie had requested that a system be developed in accordance with previously agreed-upon functional specifications which described the input and output formats and the record and file layouts to be used, and the calculations and analysis to be performed upon each field within each record, Ebenezer would not have missed the ginseng strips and probably would have completed his work in significantly less time.

To handle this "education" problem, users and developers alike should consider dividing software development projects into two or more distinct phases. First, the developer should prepare a comprehensive set of program specifications which will force it to learn enough about the client's business to be able to identify the important functions which the software must perform. Second, the client must approve the specifications in detail before any actual programming work begins. This will force the client to learn enough about the available programming options to make critical choices in advance, before elaborate routines have been developed. Third, once the parties have a detailed mutual understanding of the task at hand, the financial arrangements for the actual programming work can be made and the software developed. Until both parties are agreed on the detailed software specifications, however, it is generally unwise for them to proceed with the balance of the project.

The work to be performed should be defined so clearly that a neutral third party (such as a judge) could easily decide whether the developer had completed the job and is entitled to full payment. This is not always an easy task, but careful negotiations and drafting at the beginning of a project will pay substantial dividends in time and money by minimizing the chances of a dispute at the end. When the scope of the work is thoroughly defined, each party can more easily enforce its rights and meet its obligations than would otherwise be the case. An ambiguous or otherwise poorly drafted development agreement is, in other words, an "accident just waiting to happen."

Once the parties have agreed to a contract which adequately defines the scope of the work to be done, usually by reference to appropriately detailed specifications, the parties must face another issue, namely, how they will deal with changes that arise during the course of performance.

In a software development contract, the specifications for the software and the documentation are frequently changed while the agreement is being performed. Just as with the construction of a family residence, the client's needs and desires evolve as the project takes shape, and new and better ways of doing things occur to the developer. It is important that the software development agreement contain the flexibility to accommodate such changes. By the same token, the agreement should contain a mechanism for insuring that both parties are protected from unfair surprises. Specifically, if the developer has committed to do the work for a fixed price, or to complete it by a particular date, those commitments may have to be modified in order to accommodate changes. Similarly, the developer's client is entitled to know, in advance, the cost and the delay that will be associated with any requested change. Accordingly, the contract should specify a procedure for handling requests for changes.

One approach is to require that any request for a change in specifications be made in writing, with the developer being given a specified period of time within which to evaluate the change and to advise the client of its impact on the schedule and on the cost of the project. Thereafter, if the parties agree to the change, the contract should be amended accordingly. For the protection of both parties, no change in specifications should be made unless this procedure or something like it is followed.

There are, of course, a variety of other ways in which changes to the original specifications can be handled. It is important that the parties and the contract be flexible enough to allow for such changes, but it is equally important that the procedure agreed upon be followed punctiliously.

9.5. TERM OF THE AGREEMENT

In any software agreement in which the vendor grants rights to use or distribute the software to others, it is wise to specify the length of time for which those rights are granted. The term of the contract is an issue often overlooked, but one which can be of critical importance. In an exclusive distributorship agreement, for example, the owner of the software may subsequently decide that a different distributor can generate more revenue, or that an alternative marketing scheme would be better. Absent a fixed term or the ability to terminate the contract, the owner's flexibility is severely limited.

There are many ways in which the term of the agreement can be structured. Typically, the term is for a specified period of years or until a certain date, but it can also be indefinite and subject to being terminated by either party upon a specified number of days' or months' advance notice. The contract may also provide that the right to market the software will continue as long as specified minimum royalties continue to be paid to the owner. Consider the following examples:

1. This agreement shall be for a term of one (1) year.

2. This agreement shall remain in force until terminated by either party by giving ninety (90) days advance written notice to the other party.

3. The license granted by this agreement shall continue in force until March 15, 1990.

4. Distributor shall have the right to market the software for one (1) year. Thereafter this contact shall be automatically renewed on a year-to-year basis provided distributor has licensed at least 15 systems in the preceeding year.

One final issue to consider is whether the user has the right to renew the contract after the term has expired. The owner will normally not want to allow renewal unless the user has satisfied the performance criteria, such as minimum royalties, embodied in the agreement. If a renewal provision is included, it should specify the appropriate fees or royalties to be paid, if any, as well as any other terms under which the agreement may be renewed. Typically such a provision will specify that the agreement may be renewed under the same terms and conditions as the existing agreement, either upon the payment of a specified fee, or upon the payment of the vendor's then prevailing charges.

9.6. FEES, ROYALTIES, PAYMENTS, AND BOOKKEEPING

The cost of the software is of primary concern to the parties in every software transaction. How much will a vendor charge a user for the right to use or market its software? How much will a developer charge for a software development project? These sound like simple questions, but in many cases the answer can become quite complex, and there is no limit to the number of ways in which the fee provision of a software contract can be structured. It is not the purpose of this book to suggest that one payment method be used over another; that is an issue best left for negotiations between the parties. Here it is important to examine the factors which should be considered in those negotiations, in structuring the fee provision within a software agreement. The payment terms, whatever they are, must be spelled out clearly and completely so that there are no disputes or disagreements between the parties.

Three questions should be considered: what type of fee structure will be used; what products and services are included in the agreed-upon fee; and when is payment due? In a distributorship agreement a fourth issue must also be addressed—what provisions are to be made for verifying the number of copies of the software sublicensed, in order to calculate royalties due?

9.6.1. Types of Charges

The types of fees or charges used in a software contract vary greatly, depending on the type of contract. In the case of a software license agreement, fees fall into three general categories. The first and probably most common category is the one-time fixed fee, although the fee may sometimes be payable in installments. Another common fee category requires the payment of a fixed fee on a periodic basis, such as monthly or yearly, in order to keep the license in effect. The third category involves a variable license fee tied to software usage. For example, a variable fee may be related to the number of terminals on the system, the length of time the software is operated in the machine, the number of operations performed by the software in an industrial or manufacturing environment, or any other mechanism by which the volume of usage can be measured. A variable fee arrangement allows customers with low usage requirements to pay reduced fees without requiring the owner to sacrifice the income which could be generated from high usage customers who would be willing to pay higher fees for the same software.

In software distributorship arrangements, the software owner's income is normally dependent upon the distributor's success in marketing the product. Thus the distributor usually pays a royalty to the owner for each copy of the software licensed or sold to its customer. Two types of royalty structures are generally utilized. The first is an arrangement under which the distributor pays a percentage of the income it receives from the licensing or sale of the software. Under this arrangement, the software owner's income will depend upon both the price charged by the distributor to its customers and on its success in the sale or license of the software. Under the second type of royalty the distributor pays a fixed fee for each copy of the software sold or licensed to a customer. In this case, the software owner is assured of receiving a set fee for each copy of the software that is sold or licensed, regardless of the price charged by the distributor. A third format is also used in which the owner receives a one-time up-front payment for allowing the distributor to market the software with no further royalties due.

In software development contracts, the vendor is being paid to develop and deliver software. Charges for this type of work are usually a fixed fee or an hourly rate for the cost of the labor plus any out-of-pocket expenses, an arrangement commonly referred to as "time and expenses."

9.6.2. Items Included in Charges

Regardless of the type of fee selected, the contract should specify what is covered by the fee. That is, what does the customer get for its money? Obviously, delivery of the software is included, but what about other items? Is the customer also entitled to the delivery of future updates and enhancements, custom modifications, documentation revisions, installation, training, support, maintenance, or technical assistance? To the extent that any of these items are included for the fee paid, they must be clearly set forth in the contract so that there can be no disagreements over what was and was not covered by the contract.

9.6.3. Payment Schedule

The third critical issue with respect to cost is the question of when payment is due. Generally, payment can be required on a specified date (such as March 15), at specified periodic intervals (such as monthly or quarterly), or upon the occurrence of specified events. Events that are often used to trigger payment obligations include the execution of the contract, the delivery of the software, the installation of the software, vendor certification that the software is "operational," determination that the software is "ready for use," completion of user training, or upon acceptance of the software by the user following a predefined acceptance test, or a specified number of days after any one of the above events.

Where payments are to be made in installments, it is important to specify the relevant installment dates. They may be set with reference to the calendar, as in weekly or monthly intervals, or they may be tied to the completion of certain tasks defined in the contract, or to some other factor. And if progress payments are to be made under a software development agreement, it may or may not be appropriate for the user to hold back a certain percentage of the payment (e.g., the percentage that represents the vendor's profit) until the project is completed and accepted.

9.6.4. Bookkeeping Requirements

Software distribution agreements present a unique problem for the vendor seeking royalties. If the contract obligates the distributor to pay a royalty for each copy of the software it licenses, then only the distributor will know how much is owed to the software owner. How can the owner insure that it is receiving all the royalties due to it?

A commonly used solution is to require the distributor to keep complete records of all of its licensing transactions and to give the owner the right to audit those records to insure that royalty payments are being promptly made. This is not a foolproof solution, but it does provide some measure of protection for the owner.

A sample contract provision designed to accomplish this goal can be found in Section A.9.

9.7. TAXES

A number of states impose a tax on transactions involving the development, distribution, and licensing of computer software. (See Section 11.6.) These taxes include sales taxes, use taxes, and personal property taxes. Therefore it is important that the software agreement specify who is to pay any taxes which may be applicable.

A typical provision to accomplish this goal reads as follows:

> User shall be liable for and pay all local, state, and federal taxes, including all sales, use, and property taxes, which may now or hereafter be levied upon this license or on the possession or use of the Licensed Software, excluding, however, all taxes on or measured by Vendor's income.

Although it is normal in the industry for the user to pay the taxes imposed on software transactions, the user will want to insure that it will not be required to pay any taxes which, although ultimately arising from the software agreement, are not specifically related to the agreement itself. Examples of such taxes are income taxes on net income received by the vendor and franchise taxes on the vendor's business. These are taxes which should properly be borne by the vendor. Note also that although this contract provision makes reference to federal taxes, there are presently none that would apply to this type of contract.

9.8. OWNERSHIP OF SOFTWARE

The issue of software ownership is an important subject which should be dealt with in every software agreement. Both the vendor and the user have a number of legitimate concerns which, if not addressed, can cause them problems.

In a software license or distributorship agreement the vendor conveys the right to use and possess a copy of its software, often for a perpetual term. Such a transaction often has all the appearances of a sale, and an unsophisticated user may actually believe that it is buying rather than licensing the software. Thus it is important to have the user expressly acknowledge, in the contract, that the vendor owns the software and is merely granting a license to use it. This simple mechanism will prevent the user from ever taking the position that the transaction was actually a sale.

The contract should also make it clear that any copies of the software which the user makes will also belong to the vendor. This is important because, under the copyright law, when the owner of a copyright authorizes another to make a copy of a particular work, the resulting copy will normally belong to the copier. To preclude an inadvertent transfer of ownership in a copy, it is therefore important that the contract specify both that the user's right to copy the software derives solely from the permission granted by the vendor and that all copies will become the property of the vendor. Such a provision may be written as follows:

> The Licensed Software and any and all authorized copies thereof made by User are and shall at all times remain the sole and exclusive property of Vendor.

The user also has legitimate concerns which must be addressed in the license and distributorship agreement. Specifically, the user should make certain that the vendor actually owns the software or is authorized by the owner to license it. Thus a user may insist that the agreement contain a warranty of ownership or authority to license, such as the following:

> Vendor warrants that it is the exclusive owner of, or has the right to license, the Licensed Software and Documentation which are the subject of this Agreement.

Such a warranty does not, however, provide absolute protection. For example, if the vendor is an individual with virtually no assets, the user will, in effect, have no remedy in the event that the warranty is not true. Accordingly, where justified by the circumstances, the user should require an independent verification of the vendor's right to license the software.

The issue of ownership is much more important in the context of a software development agreement, where the answer to the ownership question will determine each party's rights to the software after the development work has been fully performed. Nonetheless, in many software development agreements the issue is never raised.

The question of who owns the software is one that should be resolved through negotiation between the parties before the contract is signed. If the matter is not resolved by the terms of the contract, however, the law may hold that the developer is the owner of the software.[8] Although this would appear to give the developer an incentive to avoid the issue altogether, there are risks in doing this, the greatest of which is the prospect of expensive litigation over the issue. It is plainly best for both parties to have the ownership issue clearly resolved by the terms of the software development agreement itself.

Both parties to a software development agreement have legitimate concerns that favor their retention of ownership. The developer would, of course, like to exploit the potential market for the newly developed software. More importantly, however, it will want to maintain its flexibility to do similar work for other clients, utilizing the ideas, tools, and experience developed in the first project. To the extent the client in the first project obtains ownership rights in the software, the developer will be precluded from copying portions of the code for use in subsequent projects and from utilizing ideas from the first project that rise to the level of trade secrets.

The client, on the other hand, is justifiably concerned about paying for the development of a valuable software product and then being unable to exploit its marketing potential, something the developer would be free to do without compensating the client for its investment. More importantly, however, if the software is intended to give the developer's client a competitive advan-

---

[8] *See BPI Sys., Inc. v. Leath*, 532 F. Supp. 208, 210 (W.D. Tex. 1981). (For a discussion of who owns the copyright in software written by independent consultants, see Section 3.1.4.)

tage, it may be critical that the client be able to prevent the marketing of the same or similar software to its competitors.

These competing concerns can be resolved only through negotiations between the parties. There are a myriad of ways in which this can be done. One readily apparent method is to vary the price of the software development work depending on who will own the software. If ownership is to be retained by the developer, then the cost of development can be less than it would otherwise be to reflect the developer's opportunity to obtain additional revenues through the subsequent use and marketing of the software. On the other hand, if the client is to retain all ownership rights, the vendor may wish to charge a correspondingly higher fee.

Other possible resolutions of the problem include joint ownership, in which both parties have equal rights to use and market the software, or a scheme whereby one party retains ownership of the software but licenses it to the other party (either at no cost or for a specified royalty), on terms which give it the right to market the software as well.

9.9. CONFIDENTIALITY

To protect its proprietary rights in the software, the owner must insist that the user agree to maintain the confidentiality of any trade secrets embodied in the software. Without such an agreement of confidentiality, the user would be free to disclose the owner's trade secrets to any interested person, thereby destroying them. (See Section 4.3.2.) Accordingly, it is extremely important that an owner who desires to maintain its trade secret protection include a confidentiality clause in its software agreements.

A confidentiality provision in a software agreement will also help to insure that individuals who have not paid a license fee for the software, such as competitors or potential customers, will not have access to it. In the event a user breaches a confidentiality agreement by delivering the software and/or its secrets to unauthorized persons, the vendor will at least have a cause of action against the user for any resulting damages.

To provide maximum protection for the vendor, the software agreement should require the user to assume a general obligation of confidentiality, which should cover both the software licensed to the user as well as the corresponding documentation if it contains sensitive information. To implement this obligation, the contract should include an undertaking by the user to "take all reasonable precautions" to insure confidentiality or to take all of the steps to protect the software that the user would normally take to protect its own proprietary data. A general obligation of confidentiality may be written as follows:

> User acknowledges that the Licensed Software and its Documentation contain confidential information which constitutes a valuable property right of the Vendor, and agrees that it will use the Licensed Software and Documentation only in the manner allowed by this Agreement, that it will not disclose the Licensed Software or Documentation to any third parties, and that it will take all reasonable precautions to insure that such confidentiality is not breached. Such precautions shall be at least as careful as those established by User for its own confidential information.

To supplement the general obligation imposed on the user to maintain confidentiality, software agreements will often impose a number of specific restrictions and obligations on the user. The following list of restrictions is not meant to be all-inclusive, but it does cover certain of the more commonly used provisions.

1. *Acknowledgments by User.* To strengthen the obligation of confidentiality, the vendor will often obtain acknowledgments from the user that the vendor is the sole owner of the software and that the software is a confidential trade secret of the vendor. In the event of a subsequent dispute between the parties, such acknowledgments by the user will make it difficult to adopt a contrary position.

2. *Restrictions on Use.* Another commonly used device is to place restrictions on how the software may be used and on the number of people who have access to it. The contract may prohibit the user from allowing third parties to have access to the software on a timesharing basis, it may restrict use of the software to one designated machine, and it may even limit disclosure to employees of the user who have a specific need to use it. These types of restriction are based

on the assumption that the fewer people who have access to the software, the less chance there is of a "leak."

3. *Restrictions on the Right to Copy.* Another way to preserve confidentiality is to restrict the number of copies that can be made by the user. The user has a legitimate need for some backup copies of the software, but not for an unlimited supply.

4. *Prohibition of Disassembly or Reverse Engineering.* If the vendor supplies object code only and fears that the user may try to generate the corresponding source code, it may be appropriate to insert a clause prohibiting "disassembling" or "reverse engineering" of the software. Disassembling software constitutes copying and is thus both an infringement of the copyright law and a breach of the agreement if it limits copying to backup purposes. It can also be viewed as the preparation of a derivative work, which is also prohibited by the copyright law. (See Section 3.3.3.) In other words, such a contractual prohibition on "disassembly" merely clarifies an obligation which is already imposed upon the user by law.

5. *Prohibition against Competition.* In an effort to remove one of the incentives for unauthorized use and disclosure of the software, some software agreements will provide that the user may not compete with the vendor in providing functionally identical or similar software. The agreement may also prohibit the use of the software on a time-sharing or service bureau basis so as to preserve the vendor's market.

6. *Prohibition on Assignment.* In order to prevent software from being transferred to someone who will not honor the confidentiality requirements, most contracts contain a restriction on assignment. The vendor's consent to assignment may then be legitimately withheld until it has an opportunity to evaluate the transferee's reliability and to require the transferee to execute a similar license and confidentiality agreement.

7. *Preservation of Notices.* In order to insure that anyone coming into contact with the software and documentation is

made aware of the vendor's claims of copyright and trade secret protection, contracts often provide that the user may not remove any of the vendor's notices from the materials supplied by the vendor, and that the user must attach identical copyright and trade secret notices to any copies of these materials which the contract authorizes the user to make.

8. *Record-Keeping Requirements.* The vendor can also require the user to maintain records specifying both the number and location of all copies of the software. Such a provision is particularly important in a distributorship or publishing agreement. If it becomes necessary to investigate a breach of confidentiality, these records can prove to be helpful.

9. *Continuing Nature of Obligation.* The confidentiality clause should also provide that the obligation of confidentiality will remain in effect even after the contract has ended, until the information becomes public knowledge.

Whether one or more of these restrictions should be incorporated into the confidentiality clause of a given contract depends, of course, on the circumstances of the transaction. Examples of different types of confidentiality clauses can be found in the sample contracts in Sections A.7, A.9, A.11, A.13, A.14, and A.15.

9.10. INDEMNIFICATION

An indemnification provision in a contract is an agreement by one of the parties to reimburse the other for certain categories of losses or costs that it may incur. It is analogous to an insurance policy.

Indemnification clauses are primarily used for two purposes in software contracts. In the first case, indemnification is used as the computer industry's answer to the question of what happens to the user if the vendor supplies software that has been misappropriated from someone else. It is an attempt to provide some protection for the unsuspecting user who may have no way of knowing whether the vendor has a legal right to market the software.

A simple example should illustrate the problem. If a thief steals a car and then sells it to an innocent buyer, the innocent buyer does not acquire title to the car even though he paid good money to the thief. Thus when the rightful owner finds out who has his car, he has the right to repossess it, regardless of how much money the innocent buyer paid for it. However, an innocent car buyer can protect himself by insisting that the seller produce a copy of the automobile registration, which will identify the true owner of the car.

In the case of software, there is no registration certificate to identify the true owner.[9] The best that a user can hope to obtain is a warranty from the vendor that the vendor is the true owner, backed by an indemnification provision. "Indemnification" means that the vendor will pay any losses or damages suffered by the user in the event it is sued by someone else claiming to be the true owner of the software.

Even when dealing with a reputable vendor, indemnification is important to the user and is routinely granted by vendors. Indeed, the vendor, as well as the user, may not know that the software being licensed infringes on anyone else's rights. This could occur if, unbeknown to the vendor, its employees or consultants who wrote the package used proprietary information misappropriated from someone else, such as a former employer. The problem could also arise with software independently developed by the vendor which nonetheless infringes upon an existing patent of which the vendor was unaware. Finally, the problem can arise in situations in which the vendor's software does not infringe on anyone else's rights, but, because of the value of that software and its similiarity to other software, a lawsuit may nevertheless be filed by a third party in the erroneous belief that an infringement has taken place.

The typical format of an indemnification clause provides that the vendor will pay any expenses incurred or damages suffered by the user in the event that the user is sued under a certain enumerated list of theories, provided that the user meets certain requirements set forth in the clause. The clause will also typically pro-

[9] Even a copyright registration certificate will not guarantee that the software has not been misappropriated.

vide that the vendor may, at its option, either pay damages, procure for the user the right to continue using the software, or repossess the software and return a portion of the license fee to the user.

The following is an example of a short indemnification clause:

> In the event Licensee is sued on a claim that the Licensed Software infringes any patent, copyright, or trade secret of any third party, Vendor will defend such suit, at its own expense, and will pay any judgment entered against Licensee, provided that Licensee promptly notifies Vendor of such suit and allows Vendor complete control of its defense.

Examples of more elaborate indemnification clauses can be found in the sample contracts in Sections A.7, A.9, and A.11.

The second way in which indemnification clauses are used is to protect one party against the actions of the other in an ongoing relationship. A software distributorship agreement is a good example. If Dave's Software Co. licenses Mary's Marketing, Inc. to distribute a new software product, both parties will want an indemnification from the other. Dave is concerned that Mary will misrepresent the capabilities of his software and that he will then be sued by disgruntled customers when the software does not live up to their expectations. Mary, on the other hand, is concerned about whether Dave's software will do everything Dave claims it will. If the software fails to live up to Dave's promises, Mary may also end up being sued by an unhappy customer.

Thus each party needs protection from actions by the other over which it has no control. The solution is an indemnification clause like the following:

> Distributor agrees to indemnify Owner with respect to all claims, losses, and damages which Owner may suffer as a direct result of the marketing, installation, or support of the Software by Distributor, including claims arising out of (a) statements, whether oral or written, made by Distributor, (b) inadequate installation, support, or assistance by Distributor, or any (c) other act or failure to act on the part of Distributor. Owner will indemnify Distributor with respect to all claims, losses, and damages which Distributor may suffer as a direct result of any breach or claimed breach of any of the warranties and representations made by Owner in this Agreement.

One word of caution is in order: The protection provided by an indemnification clause is only as good as the financial strength of the indemnifier. In the previous example, if Mary is sued by an unhappy customer and Dave is bankrupt, Dave's agreement to indemnify Mary will probably be worthless.

9.11. DELIVERY

When is the vendor obligated to deliver the software called for in the contract? If the contract does not specify a delivery date, the law will require only that delivery be made within a "reasonable time" after execution of the contract, as determined by all of the circumstances surrounding the transaction. If, however, the user requires delivery of the software by a certain date, or if the vendor is not sure that it will be able to deliver within a "reasonable time," an explicit delivery provision should be included within the contract. In drafting such a provision the issues to be considered are the date of delivery, the place of delivery, the method of delivery, and who is obligated to pay the costs of delivery.

If the software is already written, tested, and ready to go, inserting a firm delivery date in the contract is usually no problem. Things become much more complex in the case of a software development agreement if the developer is unable or unwilling to commit to a definite delivery date. This frequently occurs when the project is large and if it is not well defined. In such a case it is important that the parties work out some sort of arrangement which will provide the user some assurance of getting the software within its timetable, while at the same time protecting the developer from an unrealistic schedule.

The user may also want the contract to specify a remedy in the event that delivery is late, such as a right to cancel and to obtain a refund of all amounts previously paid, or a provision for "liquidated damages" set at a certain amount for each day, week, or month that the delivery is late. The vendor will want a provision excusing it from liability for any delivery delays attributable to matters outside of its control.[10]

---

[10] For a discussion of "force majeure" clauses in general, see Section 9.24.

9.12. INSTALLATION

If the parties agree that the vendor will install the software, the scope of that obligation should be clearly defined in the agreement. Otherwise it will be presumed that the vendor has no such duty at all.

In preparing an installation clause, the following issues should be addressed:

1. Is there a charge for installation, and if so, what is the charge?

2. When will installation take place?

3. Will the user be expected to provide assistance, such as by designating appropriate personnel to participate in the installation, and will it be expected to make certain decisions with respect to customization of the software?

9.13. TRAINING

If training in the use of the software is to be provided by the vendor, the contract should specify the scope of this obligation. If the contract makes no reference to training it may be assumed that none will be provided.

When the vendor is to provide training, the contract should specify the fee to be charged, the amount of training to be provided, and when and where the training will take place. From the vendor's point of view, training should be limited to a specified number of days, or some other quantifiable factor, so as to insure that the obligation does not become excessively burdensome. The user, on the other hand, would like to insure that the vendor will provide sufficient training to meet the user's needs, regardless of how long that may take.

In specifying the amount of training to be provided, the parties must also consider how many of the user's employees will be trained and the level of training that will be provided. The training might be limited to the operation of the software, but it could also be extended to the technical details that would allow the user's programming staff to maintain or modify the software.

Finally, the contract should specify when and where the training will take place. If the training is to take place at the user's site, and the user and the vendor are not located in the same city, the contract should also address the question of who will pay for the travel and living expenses incurred by the vendor's personnel.

9.14. ACCEPTANCE TESTING

Software contracts (especially development agreements) frequently provide the user with an opportunity to evaluate the software before accepting it and making the final payment, in order to insure that it meets the contract specifications. There are three types of acceptance test provisions generally used. The first may be defined as a subjective acceptance criteria. Contract clauses in this category usually state that the software will be deemed to have been accepted once the user, in its sole judgment, determines that the software is satisfactory for its purposes. A time limit may be imposed upon such a provision, but in essence this amounts to granting the user a free trial period with unlimited return privileges. From the user's point of view, this is the ideal acceptance provision. For the vendor, however, it is unrealistic in many instances.

The second type of acceptance provision is an objective acceptance test that is based upon the vendor's standard diagnostic tests. This provision generally favors the vendor since it makes acceptance dependent upon standard criteria very much under the vendor's control. Typically, such a provision provides that acceptance occurs upon successful testing of the software by the vendor; when the vendor certifies that the software is installed and "ready for use"; upon completion of the vendor's standard diagnostic testing; or upon the vendor's certification that the installed software meets its published specifications.

The third category of acceptance provision requires the successful completion of a predefined acceptance test which is designed to demonstrate to the user that the software meets the agreed-upon specifications. Such a test must be tailored to the specific software transaction involved and should be designed to evaluate both the performance and the reliability of the software.

The test should be designed so that both parties know in advance what requirements must be met by the software, so that they can objectively determine whether the software has in fact met those requirements. If properly done, an acceptance test provision in a contract will allow the user to satisfy itself that the software performs properly and meets its requirements, while at the same time assuring the vendor that acceptance will be based upon objective criteria and that it will receive payment within a relatively short period of time.

In designing such a test, it is important to determine in advance the requirements and specifications that the software must meet. These may include the vendor's published specifications, additional specifications included in the contract, and actual user transaction data. Regardless of the tasks the software must perform, however, it is important that the specifications be clearly set forth so that both parties know whether the software has passed the test.

The contract must also specify when the test begins and how long it will run. A date for the start of the test, and a specified length of the test, are important for the vendor to insure that the testing does not take too long, and that it does not allow the user to utilize the software without compensating the vendor. The test can be started after the vendor certifies that the software is installed and ready for testing, or upon delivery, or upon some other mutually agreed-upon date. The length of the test is usually specified as a certain number of business days.

The contract should also specify when acceptance will be deemed to have occurred. This can be done in a number of ways. For example, the contract could indicate that acceptance occurs following a specified number of days after the beginning of the test unless the user notifies the vendor of the failure of the test. Alternatively, the date of acceptance could require positive notification from the user to the vendor, with the assumption being that acceptance has not occurred in the absence of such notification. Again, this is a subject to be negotiated between the parties.

It is also important to specify the data to be used for the test. If predesigned and specially developed test data is to be used, the parties must address the question of who will develop it. The vendor will want some control over the development of this test data, or at least the right to review it to insure that it reflects typical transactions for which the software is designed. If actual data is to be used, the issue is probably moot.

The contract should also define the obligations of each party during the test. For example, the user may have the obligation of supplying the test data, of reporting all problems to the vendor, and of rejecting or complaining in writing to the vendor if the system is not accepted. The vendor, on the other hand, may have the obligation to maintain the software during the test, to correct all problems identified by the user within a certain number of days, and to provide all other necessary support.

Finally, the contract should also specify what happens if the test fails. A number of options are available. For example, the contract could require that, upon failure, the vendor will make all necessary repairs and that the test will be redone at that time. Alternatively, the user may have the option of returning the software and canceling its order, or the parties may want to agree to appropriate modifications in the test.

9.15. WARRANTIES

The law of warranties is discussed in detail in Section 10.1. Consequently, this section will merely examine the issues that should be addressed when drafting or analyzing the warranty section of a software contract.

As software contracts have evolved over the past few years the subject of warranties has come to involve more than the answer to the question "What will the software do?" At present, there are four basic issues that both the vendor and the user must consider in analyzing the warranty section of a contract.

The first issue is the most fundamental—what does the vendor *expressly warrant* that the software will do? Although the vendor is under no obligation to make any warranties at all, if it decides to do so the contract should clearly state what they are.

Express warranties can cover almost any topic, the most important of which relates to how the software will perform. The vendor might warrant, for example, that the software will perform all functions specified in its documentation or in a list prepared by the parties and attached to the contract. Other express warranties might relate to factors such as the speed of the software, the operating system it runs under, the storage space it requires, or any other performance criteria that may be relevant to a particular transaction.

After the parties have agreed on the express warranties, if any, that will be made by the vendor, the second issue to be considered is the *warranties implied by law*. These are the warranties of merchantability and fitness for a particular purpose, which are explained in Section 10.1.2 and which can automatically become part of the contract unless they are expressly excluded. It is normally advisable for a vendor to disclaim these implied warranties, and most software contracts do so. The rules for disclaiming implied warranties, which require the use of certain contract language printed or typed in a "conspicuous" manner, are explained in Section 10.2.1.

The third issue relates to *limitations and restrictions* placed on the vendor's warranties. There should be some limits on the warranties so that the vendor can quantify its potential exposure and plan accordingly. As pointed out in Section 10.1, almost any statement made by a vendor can become an express warranty, regardless of whether it was the vendor's intention to make a warranty. Statements contained in documentation or sales brochures and statements made by sales representatives can all constitute express warranties. If the vendor does not intend to be bound by these statements, they should be expressly excluded in the contract, as discussed in Section 10.2.1. In addition, however, the vendor should seek to limit its obligations with respect to those warranties it is willing to make. For example, if the vendor warrants that its software will perform all functions specified in its published documentation, it would be reasonable to place a time limit on the warranty and to void the warranty if the user modifies the software. If a software license agreement restricts use of the software to a CPU designated by serial number, it may make sense to provide that all warranties are void if the software is used on another CPU. These limitations are discussed in Section 10.2.2.

Finally, the vendor must also consider what happens if the software does not perform as warranted—an event which, given the nature of software, is not at all uncommon. The law allows the vendor to limit its liability by specifying in the contract the user's rights in the event of a breach of warranty. This is typically done by inserting a clause in the contract providing that, in the event the software fails to perform as warranted, the user's exclusive remedy will be to require the vendor to repair it. This reduces the risk that the vendor will be required to pay money to the user if the software does not work properly. Rules for this provision are discussed in Section 10.2.3.

The four issues outlined may best be illustrated by the following software warranty provision that is typical of the industry:

(a) *Software Functions.* Vendor warrants that the Licensed Software will substantially perform all functions specified in its currently published documentation. However, User acknowledges that the Licensed Software is of such complexity that it may have inherent defects, and therefore agrees that, should the software not perform as warranted, its remedy shall be limited to that specified in part (b) of this section.

(b) *Exclusive Remedy.* In the event that the Licensed Software fails to perform as warranted, and as User's sole and exclusive remedy, Vendor shall, within a reasonable time, correct all documented errors.

(c) *Warranty Period.* This warranty shall remain in effect for one (1) year after the Date of Installation. Any warranty claim not made within this period will be irrevocably barred.

(d) *Conditions Voiding Warranty.* This warranty shall be null and void in the event that the Licensed Software is installed on any computer equipment other than the Designated Equipment, is modified by User, or is merged with other software. This warranty shall also be null and void in the event that the Licensed Software is transferred to someone else or is used by any person other than the User or its authorized employees.

(e) *LIMITATION OF WARRANTY.* VENDOR MAKES NO WARRANTIES, EXPRESS OR IMPLIED, OTHER THAN THE WARRANTIES EXPRESSLY STATED IN THIS AGREEMENT. ALL OTHER WARRANTIES, INCLUDING THE IMPLIED WARRANTIES OF MERCHANTABILITY AND FITNESS FOR A PARTICULAR PURPOSE, ARE EXPRESSLY DISCLAIMED.

In this warranty provision, the express warranty made by the vendor is stated in paragraph (a). Paragraph (e) makes clear that there are no other warranties, and disclaims all implied warranties pursuant to the rules outlined in Section 10.2.1. The warranty is limited to one year in paragraph (c), and paragraph (d) makes clear that the warranty is void if any of the events set forth there occur. Finally, paragraph (b) specifies the user's exclusive remedy in the event the software fails to perform as warranted.

9.16. LIMITATION OF LIABILITY

Every software contract should contain a clause limiting the vendor's liability for losses suffered by the user in the event the software malfunctions. Without such a limitation, the vendor's potential exposure may be so great that a claim could threaten its very existence. Vendors frequently market software to a wide variety of users who employ it for varying purposes. Vendors have no way of anticipating all of those uses and the potential losses all of those users could suffer.

An example will help to illustrate this point. If The Software Shop markets a package called Spreadsheet II, it is reasonable to assume that it will be used by corporate executives for financial planning purposes and by high school students doing a class project. If the software contains a major defect, the worst that will happen to the high school student is that he or she will get the wrong answer and perhaps receive a lower grade. The corporate executive, however, may make a major business decision on the basis of an erroneous calculation by the software, and the consequences for his or her company could be catastrophic. If The Software Shop is required to pay the damages that may be suffered by the corporate user, it will have to increase the price of the software significantly higher to cover the risk—thereby pricing the high school student out of the market. A better solution for the vendor, and probably the software consumer as well, is to limit the vendor's liability by contract. Since the risk of any major loss is then shifted to the user, the vendor can charge a lower price.

There are a number of ways to limit liability, which are analyzed in detail in Section 10.2. In the typical software contract, they usually include the following:

1. Imposing a dollar limit on the damages that the vendor must pay to the user

2. Excluding liability for any consequential damages (such as lost profits) suffered by the user

3. Reducing the time period during which the user may file a lawsuit for any losses it sustains.

These limitations are illustrated by the following sample contract language:

LIMITATIONS OF LIABILITY. IT IS UNDERSTOOD AND AGREED THAT VENDOR'S LIABILITY TO USER SHALL NOT EXCEED THE RETURN OF THE LICENSE FEE PAID BY USER, AND UNDER NO CIRCUMSTANCES SHALL VENDOR BE LIABLE FOR LOST PROFITS OR OTHER CONSEQUENTIAL DAMAGES SUFFERED BY USER OR ANY THIRD PARTY, EVEN IF VENDOR HAS BEEN ADVISED OF THE POSSIBILITY OF SUCH DAMAGES IN ADVANCE. NO ACTION, REGARDLESS OF FORM, ARISING UNDER THIS AGREEMENT OR OUT OF USE OF THE LICENSED PRODUCT(S), MAY BE BROUGHT BY USER MORE THAN ONE YEAR AFTER THE CAUSE OF ACTION HAS ACCRUED.

The limitations on this type of contractual protection are discussed in Section 10.2, and that section should be reviewed in conjunction with this one.

9.17. SOFTWARE MAINTENANCE

In any software contract the parties should consider the issue of maintenance. If the vendor is expected to provide maintenance, the contract should contain a maintenance section specifying the extent of the vendor's obligation. In some cases, vendors will commit to providing all programming assistance necessary to correct any errors reported by the user. In others, however, the vendor will merely agree to provide the user with any software corrections that it happens to release, but will make no commitment to correct all problems encountered by the user. In still other cases the vendor will commit only to providing telephone support to answer the user's questions. Whatever the type of support to be provided, it should be clearly spelled out in the contract.

If the vendor is required to perform programming work to correct problems identified by the user, the user may seek some commitment by the vendor with respect to the time it will take to do so. Because there is no way to tell in advance how much work will be required, and because the importance of the problem can vary greatly, the vendor will generally want to avoid making such a commitment. Compromise solutions include an agreement that the vendor begin work on the problem within a specified time, assign a certain number of people to work on the problem full time until it is resolved, or take all "reasonable" steps to resolve the problem.

The fee to be charged for the vendor's commitment to maintain the software should, of course, also be included in the contract. It is common to charge for maintenance on a monthly or yearly basis, and to require payment in advance.

Finally, the maintenance section of the contract should specify anything that is excluded from maintenance coverage as well as events that will void the vendor's maintenance obligation. Typically the vendor will exclude from maintenance any software that has been modified by the user, since the vendor has no control over any changes the user has made. Likewise, the vendor may only want to maintain the latest version of its software and thus will so limit its maintenance obligation. If the user fails to install any software updates supplied by the vendor, the vendor will have no obligation to provide maintenance.

A vendor-oriented contract clause to reflect these issues could be structured as follows:

(a) *Maintenance Services.* Vendor will provide all programming assistance reasonably necessary to correct any defects in the Licensed Software which are reported to Vendor by User.

(b) *Timing.* Vendor will endeavor to correct any errors reported by User as soon as possible, consistent with its other obligations, and the resources available to it.

(c) *Exclusions.* Vendor will have no obligation to maintain or correct any errors in any Licensed Software which has been modified by User. Vendor's obligation to provide maintenance will be limited to the unaltered and latest version of the Licensed Software.

(d) *Charges.* Vendor will provide maintenance for a period of one year upon payment of its then current maintenance fees, in advance. If Vendor is requested to correct any problems caused by

user modifications to the Licensed Software, User will be charged
for Vendor's time at its then-current hourly rate.

9.18.   DEFAULT

A default section is often included in software contracts in order to
specify what type of breach will constitute a default, and to define
the procedures by which the injured party can terminate the
agreement or pursue its other remedies. Specifying what constitutes a breach of the agreement is normally not necessary, since
any act contrary to the terms of the contract or any failure to do
what is required by the contract will be a breach of the agreement.
Some breaches are more serious than others, however, and the
parties may wish to specify those which will give rise to the right
to terminate the agreement or to invoke other specific types of
remedies. Moreover, the parties will frequently wish to identify
acts which, on their face, do not violate any terms of the contract
but which will nonetheless be deemed to constitute a breach of
the agreement. For example, the default section might state that if
either party becomes insolvent or goes out of business, that party
will be deemed to be in default. This gives the other party the
option of acting on the default without waiting for a failure to pay
or other similar violation of the agreement.

The main purpose of a contract section dealing with default,
however, is to specify the procedures which must be followed in
the event of a default. Normally, the contract will provide that in
the event of a breach of the agreement, the injured party must
give the breaching party written notice of the breach, whereupon
the party in default will have a specified number of days to cure
the breach. If the breach has not been cured at the expiration of
that time period, the injured party may terminate the agreement
and pursue its other remedies. However, if the breach is cured
during that time period, the contract continues in full force.

A contract clause in this format is acceptable in most cases but
does not adequately address the problems which can arise from a
breach of confidentiality. If, for example, a user sells the vendor's
software without permission or otherwise discloses its trade secrets, the damage has been done and there is no way that the user
can cure this breach. In fact, the passage of time can only make

matters worse. Accordingly, for such a situation the vendor should be entitled to pursue its remedies without delay.

The following is an example of a default provision that provides for notice and an opportunity to cure and deals with breach of confidentiality:

> In the event either party breaches any of the terms of this agreement, the non-breaching party shall, at any time thereafter, give written notice of the default to the breaching party. In the event that the breach is not cured within thirty (30) days after notice, the nonbreaching party shall have the option to terminate the agreement and/or pursue any of its other legal remedies. Notwithstanding the foregoing, in the event that User breaches any of its obligations with respect to confidentiality, Vendor shall have the right to terminate this agreement and pursue its remedies for breach immediately upon notice to User.

9.19. ARBITRATION OF DISPUTES

When a dispute arises that the parties to a contract cannot resolve between themselves, their normal recourse is to the courts. An alternative to this often lengthy and expensive process is arbitration.

Arbitration is a procedure whereby parties submit their disputes, by agreement, to one or more impartial arbitrators who will decide which side should prevail. Arbitration is not a mechanism for mediation or conciliation, but rather a procedure whereby an impartial arbitrator decides which of the parties should prevail over the other. The result of an arbitration proceeding is binding; it has the same force and effect as a decision made by a judge or a jury after a trial. If anything, it has even greater finality than the judgment of a court since it may be appealed only in very limited situations.

The parties may agree to submit a dispute to arbitration after it has arisen, or they can agree at the time they enter into their contract to submit their disputes to binding arbitration when and if they arise. In the latter case, an appropriate arbitration clause is inserted in the contract; if a dispute subsequently arises, the parties are then legally obligated to arbitrate rather than go to court.

In fact, if one party ignores the arbitration clause and files a law-suit, the other party can have the lawsuit dismissed and an order entered directing the parties to submit their dispute to an arbi-trator.

Virtually any dispute between the parties can be the subject of arbitration. However, an arbitration clause can also be limited to specified disputes or may exclude certain types of disputes.

The federal government and most states have laws regulating arbitration agreements. These laws are designed to encourage arbitration and to provide for the enforceability of arbitration deci-sions. Whether a particular agreement will be governed by federal or state law depends upon whether the contract involves inter-state commerce. Software agreements between parties in differ-ent states clearly involve interstate commerce and accordingly will be governed by federal law. Conversely, software transac-tions between parties in the same state, which have no elements of interstate commerce, will be governed solely by the law of the state in which the parties reside.

It is important to determine whether state or federal arbitration law will control and to ascertain whether any specific require-ments must be met. In Texas, for example, an arbitration clause in a contract with an individual person involving less than $50,000 must be reviewed by attorneys for both sides, and the signatures of both attorneys must appear on the contract in order for it to be enforceable.[11] Accordingly, if an arbitration provision is to be used, it is important to consult with an attorney to determine if there are any special requirements or restrictions which must be considered.

If a software agreement provides for arbitration of disputes, the parties should consider the following issues:

1. Which state's law is to be applied

2. Where the arbitration will be held

3. What types of disputes will be arbitrated or excluded from arbitration

4. How many arbitrators will be used

---

[11] Tex. Rev. Civ. Stat. Ann. Art. 224.

5. How the arbitrators will be selected

6. If more than one arbitrator will be used, whether the decision must be made by majority or unanimous vote

The American Arbitration Association (AAA) recommends that the following clause be used when the parties have agreed upon arbitration of future disputes:

> Any controversy or claim arising out of or relating to this contract, or the breach thereof, shall be settled by arbitration in accordance with the rules of the American Arbitration Association, and the judgment upon the award by the arbitrator(s) may be entered in any court having jurisdiction thereof.

Note that this clause resolves the issues specified previously by merely referring to the rules of the AAA, copies of which can be obtained from any AAA office. But the parties need not use the AAA, and should not agree to do so unless they have first reviewed the AAA rules. In many cases, it will be appropriate for the parties to design an arbitration clause that will suit their particular needs. For example, they may decide to limit arbitration to certain types of disputes, such as disputes regarding payment of fees or disputes regarding acceptance of the software, or to exclude certain types of disputes, such as disputes relating to a claimed breach of confidentiality or the infringement or misappropriation of proprietary rights. They may wish to agree on an arbitrator at the time their contract is signed and to establish their own rules of procedure. Since disputes, like death and taxes, are inevitable, the parties should give careful consideration, in advance, to how they should be resolved. If they do not, their only alternative is likely to be the courts.

The following is a brief summary of the pros and cons of the arbitration process.

1. *Speed.* Arbitration is usually concluded much faster than litigation. While litigation may take years to complete, arbitration will frequently be completed in just a few months. This results in part because of fewer pretrial hearings, limited discovery, and lack of problems with court schedules.

The speed of arbitration may be a disadvantage in certain situations. For example, if one party believes that it has a counterclaim against the other, it will have much less time to pursue and develop that counterclaim. This is especially true if the information and other documents needed to develop that counterclaim reside with the other side.

2. *Cost.*   Arbitration is generally considered to be less expensive than litigation because of the speed of the process and the minimal discovery involved. To the extent that the parties assume that the outcome of any litigation will turn upon the ability of one party to outlast the other in terms of resources, this may be perceived as an advantage to the financially weaker party and a disadvantage to the financially stronger party.

3. *Use of an Expert as an Arbitrator.*   Another major difference between litigation and arbitration is that the parties are free to select an arbitrator who has expertise in the data processing industry. This will facilitate the arbitrator's understanding of the issues involved and hopefully produce a better result. Litigation, on the other hand, is often conducted before a judge who has no knowledge of the computer field, little or no time in which to learn the technicalities, and a resulting inability to grasp the problem at hand.

  The expertise of the arbitrator may be a disadvantage, however. If the arbitrator has been in the data processing industry for a long time, he or she may have developed a number of biases which could have a significant impact upon the decision—something less likely to occur with a judge. If this is expected to be a problem, the arbitrator can be selected before the dispute arises or the parties can agree not to use an expert.

4. *Availability of Discovery.*   Although pretrial discovery is available in arbitration, it is usually more limited than what is available in court. This offers the advantage of expediting the process, but also has the disadvantage of precluding one party from learning the full extent of the other party's case and any information in the other party's possession which may help its own case. In many cases, arbitration

gives one party the ability to keep its documents hidden from the other party, something which usually operates to the advantage of the vendor and to the disadvantage of the user.

5. *Application of the Rules of Evidence.* In arbitration proceedings the arbitrator is not bound to follow the rules of evidence used in court. As a result the procedure is more informal and evidence which would otherwise be excluded by a court will be admitted. On the other hand, there is nothing to prevent the parties from specifying that the arbitrator *will* follow the rules of evidence.

6. *Confidentiality of Arbitration Proceedings.* Unlike litigation, which is a matter of public record, arbitration proceedings can be kept confidential. This can be helpful in protecting trade secrets that might be exposed during the dispute resolution process and it offers an advantage to a party whose business could be damaged by any adverse publicity that could be generated from litigation. On the other hand, the ability to threaten litigation, and its corresponding adverse publicity, is a weapon that the other party might not want to give up.

7. *Tendency to Compromise.* One criticism leveled against arbitrators is that they tend to render decisions that compromise the claims of the two parties, rather than deciding completely for one party and completely against the other party. To the extent that this occurs, it is not necessarily bad since it is frequently the case that having the dispute resolved is as or more important than the decision itself.

8. *Limited Right of Appeal.* Under the arbitration statutes the right to appeal the award of an arbitrator to a court is severely restricted. The award of an arbitrator will be enforced unless the losing party can show that the award was procured through corruption, that the arbitrator was obviously partial, that there was misconduct on the part of the arbitrator in refusing to hear certain evidence or through other prejudicial misbehavior, or that the arbitrator exceeded his or her powers in rendering the award. This can rarely be shown and, for all practical purposes, the arbitrator's decision will be final.

9.20. TERMINATION

A termination clause should be included in software agreements to describe the manner in which the contract may be ended by either party and to specify the consequences of termination. This provision should also be designed to assist the vendor in preserving its trade secrets after termination.

If the contract is for a specified term (such as one year, five years, etc.), termination will automatically occur at the end of that term. However, the parties may wish to provide for the right to terminate the contract earlier. Similarly, if the contract has no specified ending date, the parties should decide when and under what circumstances it may be brought to a close.

After defining the circumstances under which the agreement may be terminated, it is also necessary to specify what will happen upon termination. In software license and software distributorship agreements, there are two major considerations: (1) what happens to the software supplied to the user; and (2) what obligations imposed on the parties by the contract will survive its termination. Both issues relate directly to the vendor's desire to preserve its trade secrets.

For the vendor's protection, the termination clause should provide that the user will stop using the software upon termination and will either destroy all copies of the software in its possession or return them to the vendor. In such a case, using or marketing the software after termination will constitute an independent breach of the agreement.[12] The user should also be required to return all copies of the documentation and any other materials supplied by the vendor. It is also appropriate to require the user to certify, in writing, that it has complied with this provision. In order for the vendor to maintain its trade secret protection, it is important that the user not be left with any copies of this material after termination of the agreement.

The termination clause should also specify which obligations imposed on the parties will survive termination. Because the user may have learned a great deal about the vendor's software and the trade secrets it contains, it is important that the user be required to

---

[12] *S & H Computer Sys., Inc. v. SAS Institute, Inc.*, 568 F. Supp. 416, 421 (M.D. Tenn. 1983).

keep this information confidential indefinitely, notwithstanding the termination of the agreement. Also, if there are any license fees, royalties, unpaid taxes, or other similar amounts due and owing from the user to the vendor, the termination of the agreement should not relieve the user of its obligation to pay what it owes.

In a distributorship agreement, where the distributor has granted sublicenses to its customers, termination of the distribution agreement should not affect the validity of the sublicenses between the distributor and its customers. For maximum protection to the vendor, the agreement should require that those sublicenses be automatically assigned to the vendor.

In a software development agreement, termination is an entirely different issue. The user will not want to give the developer a right to terminate at all, at least after the user has started making payments toward the development of the software. The user will, however, often seek to retain the right to terminate if it subsequently decides to abandon the project. The termination provision in a development agreement should specify what happens to the work completed to date and whether any penalty payments are due to the nonterminating party. For example, if the developer has hired extra people in anticipation of a lengthy project, it may want some compensation in the event of early termination by the user.

9.21. SOURCE CODE ACCESS

One of the more important issues to be raised in software transactions is the question of the user's right to have access to source code. The vendor will typically seek to withhold source code as a means of protecting its trade secrets, as well as to limit the user's ability to transfer the software to anyone else.

When the user is only provided with object code, it must rely on the vendor for maintenance. Without access to the source code, the user faces a very real risk that when critical maintenance is needed it will be unavailable because:

1. The vendor is unable or unwilling to devote the necessary resources to performing the required maintenance;

2. The vendor has ceased doing business or filed for bank-ruptcy; or

3. All copies of the source code in the vendor's possession have been lost or destroyed.

There are two possible solutions to this problem, neither of which is completely satisfactory to the user. First, the license agreement can provide that in the event the vendor ceases to do business, a copy of the source code will be delivered to the user. Second, the parties can agree that the vendor will deliver a copy of the source code to a third party who will hold it in escrow and release it to the user only upon the occurrence of certain prede-fined events, such as the vendor's cessation of business. With either alternative, the goal is to provide the user with a copy of the source code so that it can provide its own maintenance if the vendor becomes unwilling or unable to do so.

The first approach will not protect the user in the event that all copies of the source code in the vendor's possession are either lost or destroyed. And if the vendor files for bankruptcy before the user receives a copy of the source code, all assets of the vendor will be controlled by the trustee in bankruptcy, who has a right under the Bankruptcy Code to refuse to deliver the software to the user. The source code escrow provides better protection for the user, but can get very complicated and expensive and still leave the user with an inadequate remedy.

When setting up a source code escrow, the parties must first determine what materials will be included. Simply depositing a copy of the source code may be insufficient for the user, who may need other information if it is to be able to maintain the software. This may include technical documentation, file layouts, record layouts, flowcharts, coding annotations, and other information that would help a programmer understand how the system works. Ideally, the user would like the source code escrow to contain all of the materials that would be necessary for a skilled programmer or analyst to maintain or enhance the program without the help of any other person or the need to refer to any other materials. In-deed, this is what the user will require if it ever becomes neces-sary to obtain the materials from the source code escrow.

Once the parties decide what will go into the escrow, they must agree on some method of verifying that the vendor has deposited the latest version of all of the required materials. This usually requires the assistance of a third party in analyzing the materials deposited and comparing those to the software provided to the user. A vendor must be wary of any such verification procedure, however, because it will require the disclosure of its source code and technical documentation to a third party capable of understanding and analyzing the materials. It is very important that this third party be bound by an obligation of confidentiality, and also that it not be a potential competitor of the vendor.

The parties should also consider what will happen if the software is updated or modified after the original escrow deposit. Ideally, the escrow agreement should provide for the additional deposit of any changes to the software or documentation. Again, it will be necessary to have someone verify that the proper materials are deposited into the escrow after any new releases are issued by the vendor.

The vendor may wish to place a restriction on the length of time that it is required to continue to update the escrow materials. Also, the contract should specify how long the vendor has to deposit the materials into the escrow after the changes have been delivered to the user. The agreement must also specify who will pay the costs charged by the escrow agent for holding the software and the costs charged by any third parties whose services may be required under its terms.

One of the most critical aspects of any source code escrow agreement is a definition of the events which will require the source code to be released to the user and the procedure by which that release will be accomplished. Events which have typically been used to trigger release of the source code include the following:

1. The filing of bankruptcy by the vendor
2. The dissolution or liquidation of the vendor's business
3. In the case of a sole proprietorship, the death of the vendor
4. The vendor's failure to maintain the software according to the agreement

The procedure to be used to inform the escrow agent that one of these events has occurred and to instruct him or her to release the software to the user is also an area that causes significant problems for both parties. Ideally, the user would like the right to obtain the source code merely upon notice to the escrow agent that one of the triggering events has occurred. However, this requirement will be resisted by the vendor because it gives the user too much discretion. The vendor should be notified whenever the user requests the source code so that it has an opportunity to object.

If the vendor objects to the user's request, however, the whole intent of the escrow agreement can be frustrated. Unless the parties can resolve their differences, it will be up to a court (or an arbitrator if the agreement so provides) to determine whether the escrowed materials should be released. The escrow agent, who is concerned about his or her liability to either party if he or she acts improperly, will almost certainly refuse to release the escrow materials if there is a dispute between the parties. If the user has an immediate need for the source code because of an imminent maintenance problem which the vendor has failed to resolve, or because of a pending vendor bankruptcy, the option of resorting to the courts, as well as the cost, may effectively leave the user without a remedy.

Moreover, notwithstanding the best efforts of both parties, if the vendor files for bankruptcy the trustee of the vendor's estate in the bankruptcy court may be able to prohibit the escrow agent from releasing the source code notwithstanding the terms of the escrow agreement. Under §365 of the Bankruptcy Code, the bankruptcy trustee has the "option" of refusing to allow the escrow agent to perform the terms of the escrow agreement if the trustee decides that such a prohibition is in the best interests of the bankrupt's estate.

A number of commentators have suggested ways in which an escrow agreement can be drafted to avoid this problem, but to date no court has yet ruled on the validity of any of those approaches. If the parties desire to provide for an escrow in their agreement, a knowledgeable attorney should be consulted to minimize the adverse consequences of a bankruptcy.

Finally, the source code escrow agreement should specify what rights the user has to the source code following its release. From the vendor's point of view, the user should be restricted to using the source code solely for the maintenance and enhancement of its copy of the object code, and use of the source code should be subject to all of the other restrictions contained in the license agreement. Specifically, the user should be required to keep the source code confidential and should be restricted from transferring or disclosing the contents of the source code to unauthorized persons.

9.22. ENTIRE AGREEMENT CLAUSE

Virtually every computer software agreement will contain a short and somewhat obscure clause, usually buried at the back of the contract, which contains language similar to the following:

> This contract constitutes the entire and exclusive agreement between the parties, and it supersedes all previous communications, representations, or agreements, either oral or written, between them. No representations or statements of any kind made by any representative of the vendor or its agent, which are not included in this agreement, shall be binding on the vendor.

This clause is known as an entire agreement clause, integration clause, or merger clause. Notwithstanding its apparent obscurity, it is one of the most important clauses in a computer software contract.

This clause literally means what it says. If something is not in the written contract, it is not part of the deal.[13] Promises which the vendor's sales representative made to the user, statements contained in the vendor's advertisements, statements found in letters from the vendor to the user, and statements the vendor made to the user during contract negotiations are not part of the deal and are not binding on the vendor unless they are included in the final written contract. Thus the user does not have the right to rely on any representations that are not included in the contract.

There are two fundamental reasons for the inclusion of such a clause. The first has to do with the nature of contract negotiations. During those negotiations, a number of proposals and counterpro-

---

[13] *Office Supply Co., Inc. v. Basic/Four Corp.*, 538 F. Supp. 776, 782 (E.D. Wis. 1982); *APLications, Inc. v. Hewlett-Packard Co.*, 501 F. Supp. 129, 133 (S.D.N.Y. 1980).

posals are made by both parties. In the give-and-take of these negotiations, certain representations that one party may have made will be retracted or bargained away in favor of other provisions requested by the other party. When all is said and done and a final agreement is reached, the parties, as a practical matter, should be able to know exactly what they have agreed to. To achieve this objective the parties enter into a final written agreement which clearly states that any promises or representations made during the prior negotiating process are not part of the deal unless they are included in the final written contract.

The second reason for the use of this type of clause is to enable the vendor to protect itself against unauthorized or overinflated representations made by its sales representatives. Such a clause is, in effect, the vendor's warning to the user that it should not rely on anything that is not included in the contract.

An integration or entire agreement clause is a sensible approach to dealing with the problems resulting from lengthy contract negotiations and misunderstandings resulting from statements of the vendor's sales representatives. The problem, however, is that many software contracts are entered into by the user solely on the basis of the vendor's oral representations; there are no lengthy negotiations and, in fact, the user is assuming that the vendor's oral representations are part of the deal. Such a mistaken assumption can prove costly to both parties.

For the user, an entire agreement clause makes it imperative that the final contract include any promises or representations upon which the user is relying. Thus if the vendor's sales literature contains promises that are important to the user, the literature should be attached to and made a part of the contract, that is, incorporated by reference. Similarly, if any statements made by the vendor's sales representatives are particularly important to the user, the user should insist that they are also incorporated in the contract so that it can hold the vendor to them.

The entire agreement clause can have a significant impact upon the user in the event of litigation. The user will be able to sue only on the basis of what exists in the written contract (unless the user can prove that it was induced to sign the contract on the basis of fraudulent misrepresentations by the vendor, a subject which is discussed at Section 10.3). Thus, when the user comes into court and alleges that the vendor made certain promises which were not kept, the user will lose if those promises are not contained in the contract.

The entire agreement clause will not, however, always protect the vendor, nor will it always operate to defeat any claims of the user. In situations involving fraud, unconscionability, mistake, clear evidence that the written agreement is not the entire agreement of the parties,[14] and other situations, the effect of the integration clause may be defeated. These are matters which are beyond the scope of this book, but it is important to be aware that such problems can exist and for the vendor not to place all of its reliance on the "entire agreement" clause. For the user, however, the best general rule is to be sure that everything of importance to the deal is actually included in the written contract.

9.23. CHOICE OF LAW

When both parties to a software agreement are located in the same state, a dispute arising under that contract will be governed by the laws of that state, absent an agreement to the contrary. However, when parties are located in different states, the issue of which state's law is applicable to a dispute arising under the contract may need to be decided by a court in accordance with a complex set of "choice of law" rules that vary from state to state. These rules consider factors such as the place at which the contract was signed, the place at which the software is delivered, the place at which performance is to take place, and a variety of other factors. Indeed, the issue of which state's law will apply, can, by itself, constitute a significant issue in the resolution of any dispute between the parties.

To avoid choice-of-law problems in multistate transactions, the parties can decide in advance which law will govern their disputes and memorialize that decision in the contract. That provision is typically written as follows:

---

[14] *Teamsters Sec. Fund of N. Cal., Inc. v. Sperry Rand Corp.*, 6 Computer L. Serv. Rep. 951, 966 (N.D. Cal. 1977).

This contract will be governed and construed in accordance with the laws of the State of _____ .

Note that this contract clause does not have any effect on where a lawsuit may be filed. That is determined by a different set of rules which are beyond the scope of this work. It may be possible for the parties to agree in advance where any suit may be filed, but the drafting of such a clause would require the services of legal counsel. Nevertheless, regardless of which court hears the lawsuit, it will generally be bound to apply the law of the state specified in the contract, unless the state whose law is selected has no relation to the transaction, or unless there is some other public policy reason for not applying it.[15]

Thus in selecting which state's law to apply, the parties should select a state which bears some relationship to the transaction. This is typically the state where either the vendor or the user is located. Ideally, each party would like to select a state whose laws are most favorable to its position, but this is difficult to know in advance. The vendor will typically choose the law of its own state in which it is located, because that is the law with which its counsel and management are most familiar. Moreover, while such a choice will obligate the user to abide by the law of only one other state (i.e., the vendor's state), choosing the law of the user's state could conceivably force the vendor to be responsible for abiding by the laws of 50 separate states. For these reasons, the vendor arguably has a stronger claim to using the law of the state in which it is located than the user has to the law of its state.

9.24. FORCE MAJEURE (EXCUSABLE DELAYS)

There are always events or occurrences which are both unforeseen and beyond the control of the parties which can prevent a party from performing its obligations under the contract. For example, a vendor may be unable to deliver the software by the specific date required in the contract if its offices are destroyed by

---

[15] *Triangle Underwriters, Inc. v. Honeywell, Inc.*, 457 F. Supp. 765, 768 (E.D.N.Y. 1978) (dicta), *rev'd in part on other grounds*, 604 F.2d 737 (2d Cir. 1979).

fire, if the U.S. Postal Service goes on strike after the only copy of the software has been mailed, or if a general flood prevents the vendor from gaining access to its offices. These are often referred to as "Acts of God," or "force majeure."

To guard against the possibility that the vendor will be considered to be in breach of its contract for failing to perform in such cases, it is common to insert what is called a "force majeure" clause in the contract. An example of such a clause is the following:

> Neither party shall be responsible for delays or failures in performance resulting from acts beyond the control of such party. Such acts shall include but not be limited to Acts of God, strikes, lockouts, riots, acts of war, epidemics, governmental regulations imposed after the date of the agreement, fire, commmunication line failures, power failures, earthquakes, or other disasters.

The purpose of this clause is to make it clear that a party will not be liable for things that are beyond its reasonable control. It might not be liable even in the absence of such a clause, but this is not an area where one should or needs to take chances.

CHAPTER TEN

LIABILITIES FOR SOFTWARE MALFUNCTIONS

Software development can be a very complex process, and the resulting product will frequently contain errors notwithstanding the best efforts of the developer. The effects of these errors may be obvious, causing a total failure of the system. Or they may be hidden, resulting in failure only if a certain rarely occurring condition arises. Or they may be subtle, continually generating erroneous results without giving any real indication that the software is not functioning properly.

Problems can arise as a result of errors or omissions in the way software is designed, or in the way that it is coded. But what happens if software is released with a problem, something goes wrong, and someone is damaged as a result? Does the developer have any liability for the damage that results, and if so, is there anything it can do to limit its exposure to such liability?

Alternatively, what if the software works properly, but simply does not do everything the customer was told it would do? Is the vendor responsible for the difference between the customer's expectations and reality?

The answers to these questions depend, in large part, on the legal theory on which a claim of liability is based, and on the steps taken by the vendor (if any) before the loss occurs to limit its potential liability. The main theories of vendor liability, which will be discussed in this chapter, are breach of warranty and fraud. In addition, there are two other theories of liability, which may become important in the future—negligence and products liability. Which, if any, of these are applicable in a given case will depend upon the circumstances involved.

If there is a contract between the vendor and the injured party, and the injury was caused by the failure of the software to perform as warranted in the contract, the vendor may be liable for breach of warranty. On the other hand, if the software met the contract's specifications but the customer was induced to enter into the contract by the vendor's false representations as to the software's capabilities, the vendor may be liable for fraud. For example, if a vendor falsely represents that its software will meet a customer's requirement for multiple terminal access, the damages suffered by the customer when the software fails to do so might be recoverable on a fraud theory, even though the contract may not have warranted the multiple terminal access capability.

If, when designing software, the developer fails to exercise proper caution to insure that a known risk of damage does not occur, it may be liable for negligence or for breach of the implied warranty of merchantability. Finally, if defective software causes personal injury to someone, the vendor may be liable on a products liability theory even if it was not negligent in developing the software.

10.1. SOFTWARE WARRANTIES

A warranty can be created by any statement that a certain fact with respect to the software is true, or will be true at the appropriate time. For example, a software vendor's statement that the "XYZ Spread Sheet will run on the RX211 operating system" is a warranty, as is a vendor's statement that its software will operate in 64K memory. Whenever software fails to perform as warranted, the vendor may be liable for breach of warranty.

There are two types of warranties: express warranties and warranties implied by law. Express warranties do not come into existence unless a vendor makes a statement or representation of fact to the user. Implied warranties, on the other hand, come into existence automatically and become part of the contract with a customer unless they are expressly disclaimed.

10.1.1. Express Warranties

An express warranty can be created by any explicit statement or affirmative action on the part of the vendor. Words such as "warranty" or "guarantee" are not necessary in order to create an express warranty.[1] In fact, the vendor does not even need to have an intention to make a warranty, since any statement of fact relating to the software, as opposed to a statement of opinion, may be considered a warranty. An express warranty can be created in one of three ways.

The first way to create an express warranty is by an "affirmation of fact or promise" which relates to the software and becomes part of the basis of the transaction.[2] Warranties arising in this manner can result from representations made orally by sales personnel, written representations in letters and other documents sent to the user by the vendor, claims made in advertisements, in sales literature, on packaging, and in instruction manuals, or in virtually any other form to which the user is exposed prior to entering into the contract, and which actually induces the user to enter into the contract. In one case, for example, a manufacturer purchased an NCR computer in reliance on a sales representative's oral statements that the system would include software to perform accounts receivable, payroll, order entry, inventory deletion, state income tax, and cash receipts functions. Over eight months after delivery, when payroll was the only function that had worked, the customer sued NCR for breach of warranty, and the court held that the sales representative's statements constituted a warranty.[3]

The second method by which an express warranty can arise is through a seller's description of the software,[4] such as through technical specifications, flowcharts, tables, and users' manuals.

The third type of express warranty can result from a demonstration of the product to the user.[5] Under the law, a vendor is deemed to warrant that the products it sells will perform as well as the product demonstrated.

[1] U.C.C. §2–313(2).
[2] U.C.C. §2–313(1)(a).
[3] *Chatlos Systems, Inc. v. National Cash Register Corp.*, 479 F. Supp 738, 743 (D.N.J. 1979) (applying New Jersey law), *aff'd*, 635 F.2d 1081 (3d Cir. 1980).
[4] U.C.C. §2–313(1)(b).
[5] U.C.C. §2–313(1)(c).

In short, any representation made by word or deed better be true, because it is likely to constitute a warranty. There is, however, no legal requirement that a vendor make any express warranties at all.

10.1.2. Implied Warranties

Implied warranties are warranties that become part of the transaction even though they are not expressly included in the written contract, and even though they were never discussed by the parties. They are warranties implied by the law and automatically become part of the contract unless they are specifically excluded.[6]

There are two basic warranties that can be implied by law in a software transaction. They are the warranty of merchantability and the warranty of fitness for a particular purpose. Both are explained in the following paragraphs.

1. *Merchantability.* The implied warranty of merchantability is a warranty that what is being offered for sale is fit for the ordinary purpose for which it is used, and of a quality that is commercially acceptable for products of that type.[7] In the case of software, this means that it will adequately do the job for which it is designed. For example, an automated payroll system would have to be able to calculate withholding for federal, state, and social security taxes or it could not be called a payroll system. Therefore, as applied to a payroll program, the implied warranty of merchantability would mean that, at a minimum, it will perform all of those standard functions. A payroll system which did not calculate state tax withholding for each employee would almost certainly not be worthy of the name, and its sale or license would constitute a breach of the implied warranty of merchantability.

However, the warranty of merchantibility will not be implied in a software transaction unless two conditions are met: (1) the transaction must be governed by the Uniform Commercial Code (U.C.C.), and (2) the vendor must qualify as a "merchant" with

---

[6] *Office Supply Co. Inc. v. Basic/Four Corp.*, 538 F. Supp. 776, 782 (E.D. Wis. 1982) (applying California law).
[7] U.C.C. §2–314.

respect to the product it is marketing.[8] The U.C.C. is written to govern transactions involving the sale of goods, but courts have begun applying it to software license transactions as well.[9] Accordingly, a vendor should assume that its provisions will apply in all cases. A software vendor will be considered a "merchant" if it regularly deals in the type of software involved, or holds itself out as having knowledge or skill peculiar to the software involved in the transaction.[10] Thus a software vendor whose business is the licensing of payroll programs would presumably be considered a "merchant" with respect to payroll programs. On the other hand, a widget manufacturer who decides to license its own payroll program to another widget manufacturer to make a few extra dollars would not be deemed to be a "merchant" of payroll programs, and would not be bound by the implied warranty of merchantibility.

2. *Fitness for a Particular Purpose.*   The implied warranty of fitness for a particular purpose is a warranty that a product will fulfill the specific needs of the purchaser.[11] Thus, even though a particular software package runs properly for most users, if it proves inadequate to meet the needs of a given customer, that customer may have a claim for breach of the implied warranty of fitness for a particular purpose. The circumstances which will give rise to this particular warranty are as follows:

a.   The vendor must have had reason to know of the particular purpose for which the software was being acquired;

b.   The vendor must also have had reason to know that the user was relying on the vendor's skill or judgment to select or furnish suitable software; and

c.   The user must actually have relied on the vendor's judgment in selecting software to meet its special needs.[12]

---

   [8] U.C.C. §2–314. The Uniform Commercial Code has been enacted (with some changes) in all states except in Louisiana.

   [9] *Triangle Underwriters, Inc. v. Honeywell, Inc.*, 604 F.2d 737, 741 (2d Cir. 1979); *Chatlos Systems, Inc. v. National Cash Register Corp.*, 479 F. Supp. 738, 742 (D.N.J. 1979), *aff'd*, 635 F.2d 1081, 1083 (3d Cir. 1980); *RRX Industries, Inc. v. Lab-Con, Inc.*, 772 F.2d 543, 546 (9th Cir. 1985).

   [10] U.C.C. §2–104.

   [11] U.C.C. §2–315.

   [12] *See* U.C.C. §2–315.

When these three requirements are fulfilled, the warranty of fitness for a particular purpose will be implied in the contract. Like the implied warranty of merchantability, however, the implied warranty of fitness for a particular purpose arises only in transactions governed by the Uniform Commercial Code.

This warranty can very easily arise in the data processing industry. Users are often unsophisticated, and frequently rely upon the judgment and advice given by vendors as to the suitability of various software products for particular applications. It is for this reason that the implied warranty of fitness for a particular purpose is almost universally disclaimed in computer software agreements.

A good example of what can happen if the implied warranty of fitness is not disclaimed is a case involving NCR Corporation and Chatlos Systems, Inc., a company engaged in the design and manufacture of cable pressurization equipment.[13] Chatlos was interested in purchasing a computer system and entered into discussions with NCR. NCR was apprised of Chatlos' detailed business history and operations, and recommended that Chatlos purchase a particular NCR system which it claimed would provide the accounts receivable, inventory, payroll, and order entry functions required by Chatlos. Because NCR recommended this system for Chatlos' particular "express purpose," and because NCR was aware that Chatlos was relying on its skill and judgment, the court found that there was an implied warranty that the system was fit for Chatlos' express purpose. Consequently, when the system failed to meet Chatlos' specific needs, the implied warranty was breached and NCR was required to pay damages.

10.1.3. Consumer Product Warranties

The concept of express and implied warranties applies to all software transactions. Additional rules apply to both of these types of warranties, however, when software is considered a "consumer product" and sold as part of a "consumer transaction." The federal government and a number of the states have enacted consumer

---

[13] *See Chatlos Systems, Inc. v. National Cash Register Corp.*, 479 F. Supp. 738, 743 (D.N.J. 1979) (applying New Jersey law); *aff'd*, 635 F.2d 1081 (3d Cir. 1980).

warranty statutes designed to expand the scope of warranty protection provided to consumers.[14] Generally, what these statutes do is regulate the content of express warranties and limit or prohibit any disclaimer of the implied warranties. The following discussion will focus on the most important of these statutes, the Magnuson-Moss Warranty Act.

The Magnuson-Moss Warranty Act is a federal statute that prescribes comprehensive standards for warranties on consumer products. The Act only applies in certain situations and it is not at all clear if it covers computer software. Consequently, it will only be discussed briefly. Nonetheless, because the requirements of the Act are rather strict, and the penalties for failure to comply could have serious consequences for the software vendor, compliance with its requirements is advised in any transaction which could conceivably fall within its terms.

The Act only applies to written warranties given to an end-user consumer in connection with the "sale" of "consumer products." It does not apply to software license transactions or distributorship agreements. If it applies to software at all, it only applies when software is sold, and only in situations where the software is a "consumer product."

The Act defines "consumer product" as "any tangible personal property which is distributed in commerce and which is normally used for personal, family, or household purposes . . . ."[15] Although it is clear that software will not be covered unless it is of a type used for personal, family, or household purposes, software need not be used exclusively for these purposes in order to qualify. As long as it is "not uncommon" for particular software to be used for personal, family, or household purposes, it may be deemed a "consumer product" under the Act.[16] For example, products such as automobiles and typewriters which are used for both personal and commercial purposes come within the definition of "consumer product." Moreover, where it is unclear whether a particular product falls within the definition of consumer product, any ambi-

---

[14] See 15 U.S.C. §2301; Cal. Civ. Code §§1790–1794.2; Kan. Stat. Ann. §§50–623 to–644; Minn. Stat. Ann. §325G.17–.20; W. Va. Code §§46A–6–101 to–108.

[15] 15 U.S.C. §2301(1).

[16] 16 C.F.R. §700.1(a).

guity will be resolved in favor of coverage.[17] Consequently, it is reasonable to assume that software purchased for home computer use would be covered by the Act. However, even software that falls into this category will not be covered by the Act if a court subsequently decides that software is not tangible personal property—an issue which has not yet been decided under the Act.

If it is determined that software qualifies as a consumer product, then the Act will govern certain written warranties made in connection with its sale to a consumer. The Act does not cover oral warranties, nor does the Act require that the vendor make any warranties at all. It merely governs the terms of written warranties in the event they are made.

Three general types of written warranties are covered by the Act. These are warranties that the product is free of defects, warranties that it will meet a specified level of performance over a specified period of time, and warranties undertaking to refund, repair, replace, or to take other remedial action in the event that the product fails to meet the specifications set forth in the undertaking.[18]

If a software warranty is covered by the Act, it must comply with the warranty disclosure rules contained in the regulations issued by the Federal Trade Commission.[19] Those rules are rather detailed and require that any written warranty for a consumer product must fully and conspicuously disclose a specified number of items in simple and readily understood language. In addition, the written warranty must also be clearly and conspicuously designated as either "full (statement of duration) warranty" or "limited warranty," as those terms are defined in the statute.[20]

The Act also prohibits vendors from disclaiming or modifying any implied warranties arising under state law,[21] and any attempt to disclaim or modify implied warranties in a written warranty will be deemed ineffective.[22]

---

[17] *Id.*
[18] 15 U.S.C. §2301(6).
[19] 16 C.F.R. §701.3(a).
[20] 15 U.S.C. §§2303, 2304, 2308.
[21] 15 U.S.C. §2308(a).
[22] 15 U.S.C. §2308(c); *FTC v. Virginia Homes Manufacturing Corp.*, 509 F. Supp. 51, 57 (D.Md. 1981).

In the event that a vendor fails to comply with the terms of the Magnuson-Moss Warranty Act, it will be liable to the user for all damages suffered, including costs and attorneys' fees. Thus, a software vendor contemplating any of the warranties covered by the Act would be well-advised to consult legal counsel before making them.

10.2. LIMITING LIABILITY FOR BREACH OF WARRANTY

Notwithstanding a vendor's best efforts, its software may contain defects which will, at some time, cause problems for one of its users. While most of these problems will be relatively minor and cause nothing more than inconvenience, some can have extremely serious consequences. In one case, for example, a customer of a Honeywell turnkey system brought suit alleging that the failure of the system to operate properly caused the destruction of its business.[23]

The question of which party should bear the risk that such damages will occur is a heavily debated issue. The user will argue that it was the vendor's software that caused the problem, whereas the vendor will argue it had no way of knowing or controlling the consequences that might result from the user's particular use of the software, and, therefore, that the user should bear the risk of the loss.

In any event, the risk of such significant liabilities arising from the failure of a software product to perform as warranted has led virtually all vendors to draft their contracts so as to limit their exposure to the extent possible. There are six contractual provisions that can be used to limit a vendor's liability. Each, if properly drafted, is enforceable and can be used in conjunction with the others.

10.2.1. Limiting the Number and Types of Warranties Made

As discussed in Section 10.1.1, virtually any statement or representation made by a vendor can be construed as an express war-

---

[23] *Triangle Underwriters, Inc. v. Honeywell, Inc.*, 604 F.2d 737, 739 (2d Cir. 1979).

ranty which will become part of the contract. Moreover, the law often adds a number of implied warranties to the contract. The more warranties that become part of the deal, the greater the obligations undertaken by the vendor, and the greater the vendor's potential liability.

The first step in limiting that liability is to restrict express warranties to those which the vendor specifically agrees to undertake. To do this, the written agreement between the vendor and its customer should specifically set forth all express warranties (if any) to which the vendor has expressly agreed to be bound, followed by a provision excluding from the agreement all other statements and representations which could be construed as express warranties. This can be accomplished by inserting language similar to the following immediately after the express warranties stated in the contract:

THE WARRANTIES SET FORTH IN THIS CONTRACT ARE THE ONLY WARRANTIES MADE BY VENDOR. VENDOR DISCLAIMS ALL OTHER WARRANTIES.

This language is normally used in conjunction with the disclaimer of implied warranties discussed below, and should be sufficiently conspicuous to meet the requirements of the U.C.C.[24]

A clause like this was effectively used by Hewlett-Packard to defend a claim for breach of express warranties made by a customer.[25] Hewlett-Packard and the customer had entered into an Original Equipment Manufacturer (OEM) agreement for the HP3000 Series II computer and the APL/3000 programming language. When it turned out that response time in APL/3000 proved unacceptably long for the customer, it sued Hewlett-Packard, claiming that Hewlett-Packard had represented that its APL/3000 language would provide "fast response, even with multiple users." Even though this statement did appear in a Hewlett-Packard brochure, the court dismissed the claim since the warranty was

---

[24] The U.C.C. requires that disclaimers of implied warranties be conspicuous, and, in the case of the warranty of merchantability, specifically use the word "merchantability." U.C.C. §2–316. It is best to follow this rule for all warranty disclaimers.

[25] *APLications, Inc. v. Hewlett-Packard Co.*, 501 F. Supp. 129, 133–34 (S.D.N.Y. 1980).

not included in the contract, and since the contract contained a clause limiting its warranties to those set forth in the contract.[26]

The same result was reached in a case involving a computer system sold by Burroughs.[27] The system, consisting of both hardware and applications software, was sold after Burroughs had submitted a proposal to the customer which claimed that the system would provide "more work in less time and more meaningful management information than ever before possible." The contract provided a limited three-month warranty and also contained a clause restricting express warranties to those actually set forth in the contract. Thus, notwithstanding the customer's evidence of frequent hardware failure and the failure of four of the eight application packages, the court concluded that Burroughs had effectively disclaimed all warranties other than the limited three month warranty contained in the written contract.

The second step in limiting warranty liability is to disclaim all implied warranties. Although implied warranties arise automatically, the vendor has the right to disclaim them[28] unless the software is sold as part of a consumer transaction governed by the Magnuson-Moss Act, or by the law of one of the few states which limit the right of a vendor to disclaim implied warranties in consumer transactions. Included in this group are the states of Alabama, California, Kansas, Maine, Maryland, Massachussets, Minnesota, Mississippi, Vermont, Washington, and West Virginia.[29] Remember, however, that these statutes apply only to sales to end-users (i.e., not licenses), and only when the software is deemed to be a consumer product. (See Section 10.1.3.) Consequently, if these statutes are applicable at all, they probably only apply to the sale of software for home computers.

In all other cases, a vendor is well advised to disclaim *all* implied warranties. This should be done because implied warranties create a substantial risk which the vendor cannot adequately

[26] The customer also sued Hewlett-Packard for fraud, however, and this claim was not dismissed. (See Section 10.3 for a discussion of fraud.)

[27] *Badger Bearing Co. v. Burroughs Corp.*, 444 F. Supp. 919, 922–23 (E.D. Wis. 1977).

[28] *Office Supply Co., Inc. v. Basic/Four Corp.*, 538 F. Supp. 776, 783 (E.D. Wis. 1982) (applying California law); *APLications, Inc. v. Hewlett-Packard Co.*, 501 F. Supp. 129, 133 (S.D.N.Y. 1980) (applying California law); *Badger Bearing Co. v. Burroughs Corp.*, 444 F. Supp. 919, 922–23 (E.D. Wis. 1977) (applying Wisconsin law).

[29] 15 U.S.C. §2301(7).

foresee or measure at the time the software is licensed or sold. Under the implied warranty of fitness for a particular purpose, for example, a vendor could find itself in the position of warranting that its software will perform adequately for the user in a very peculiar situation of which the vendor, in reality, has very little knowledge. If the user is actually relying on the skill and judgment of the vendor in selecting its software for a particular purpose, the competing interests of the two parties can best be served by disclaiming all implied warranties, but including specific express warranties that meet the user's requirements. This way the vendor can specifically define the risks which it is willing to assume, and the user knows exactly what is warranted.

To be effective, a disclaimer of any implied warranty must be part of a contract between the parties entered into prior to delivery of the software. A disclaimer will have no effect if made after the contract is signed and the software delivered, such as by inserting it in the documentation.

The disclaimer must also be "conspicuous."[30] That is, it must be so obvious that the user is likely to read it before entering into the transaction. To meet this requirement, disclaimers are typically printed in all capital letters and boldfaced type, often in type larger than the type used for the rest of the agreement, and captioned with a heading such as "DISCLAIMER OF WARRANTIES" which is designed to attract the customer's attention. In one case, a court found that the disclaimer of implied warranties in a contract prepared by Basic Four Corporation was invalid because it was not sufficiently conspicuous. It was buried in the middle of the contract, there was no heading to call it to the customer's attention, and, although it was printed in italics, it contrasted only slightly with the remainder of the contract.[31]

In addition, certain "magic words" are required to disclaim the implied warranty of merchantability. To be effective, the contractual language must specifically mention the word "merchantability."[32] No similar requirement exists when disclaiming the implied warranty of fitness for a particular purpose, but to be safe it

---

[30] U.C.C. §2–316(2).
[31] *Office Supply Co., Inc. v. Basic/Four Corp.*, 538 F. Supp. 776, 783–84 (E.D. Wis. 1982) (applying California law).
[32] U.C.C. §2–316(2).

should be specifically mentioned as well. An example of language which will disclaim both the implied warranty of merchantability and the implied warranty of fitness for a particular purpose, as well as all express warranties not included in the contract, is the following:

> VENDOR MAKES NO WARRANTIES EXCEPT FOR THE WARRANTIES SPECIFIED IN THIS CONTRACT. VENDOR DISCLAIMS ALL OTHER EXPRESS WARRANTIES AND ALL IMPLIED WARRANTIES, INCLUDING, BUT NOT LIMITED TO, THE IMPLIED WARRANTIES OF MERCHANTABILITY, AND OF FITNESS FOR A PARTICULAR PURPOSE.

Note that this language (1) is conspicuous by its capital letters and boldfaced type, and (2) that it specifically mentions both implied warranties to be excluded. In both the Hewlett-Packard and Burroughs cases mentioned above, language similar to this was held by the courts to be effective in excluding liability for any implied warranties.[33]

In addition to the foregoing, there are other ways to disclaim implied warranties. If, for example, the contract contains language such as "AS IS," or "WITH ALL FAULTS," or other similar language which calls the user's attention to the fact that no warranties are being made, then the implied warranties will be disclaimed.[34] Whether this approach is practical from a marketing standpoint depends upon the circumstances of the transaction involved, but if a customer is willing to accept software with no warranties whatsoever, a "no-warranty" contract can certainly be enforceable. To insure that it is enforceable, however, it should contain an appropriate disclaimer such as:

> THIS SOFTWARE IS LICENSED "AS IS." VENDOR MAKES NO WARRANTIES WHATSOEVER, EITHER EXPRESS OR IMPLIED.

It should also be noted that if a user has had an opportunity to examine the software in detail prior to its sale or license, no im-

---

[33] *APLications, Inc. v. Hewlett-Packard Co.*, 501 F. Supp. 129, 133 (S.D.N.Y. 1980) (applying California law); *Badger Bearing Co. v. Burroughs Corp.*, 444 F. Supp. 919, 923 (E.D. Wis. 1977) (applying Wisconsin law).
[34] U.C.C. §2–316(3).

plied warranty will exist as to any defects which would have been discovered pursuant to such an inspection.

10.2.2. Limiting the Scope of Warranties

Once the vendor has reduced its warranty obligations to a specified set of written warranties, it can further limit its potential liability by imposing reasonable limitations on their scope.

The most frequently used warranty limitation is a limitation on the time period during which the warranty will be effective. This can range anywhere from a few days to several years, but the important point is to set an end to the warranty obligation. Obviously, the user would like the longest warranty period possible, whereas the vendor would prefer a shorter warranty period.

Another common practice is to provide that the warranty is void if the user modifies the software. This is a limitation which a vendor must insist upon since it has no control over any changes that the user might make to its software. However, where both parties contemplate changes being made by the user, it may be appropriate for the parties to work out an agreement whereby software unaffected by user changes (if it can be isolated) remains covered by the warranty.

To enforce license provisions restricting the use of software to a single designated CPU, or imposing other hardware based restrictions, some vendors also provide that the warranty is void if the software is used on different equipment. The same approach might also be taken when software is licensed for use with a specified operating system. This also serves the practical purpose of insuring that the software is not used with an incompatible operating system, which would render the warranty impossible to fulfill.

10.2.3 Exclusive Remedy in Case of Breach

Notwithstanding the vendor's efforts to limit the number and scope of its warranties, it is still possible that the software will not live up to the warranties actually made. Because such an occurrence is likely, at least with newly released software, the vendor must consider how it can limit its potential liability for any losses the user may suffer.

One commonly used method of dealing with this problem is for the vendor to limit the types of remedies available to the user in case of breach. Otherwise, in the event of a breach of warranty the user may have a claim for money damages, for a refund of the license fees paid, or even for injunctive relief. To avoid the prospect of having to pay damages or to refund the license fees, while at the same time insuring that the user gets what it paid for, the parties can agree to a "limited remedy."[35] The "limited remedy" which is usually provided in software agreements is one in which the vendor promises to correct any defects in the event that the software fails to perform as warranted. Such a provision might be worded as follows:

> In the event that the Licensed Software fails to perform as warranted, Vendor shall, within a reasonable time, and as User's sole and exclusive remedy, correct all documented errors.

This language will protect the vendor in the event of a suit for damages, provided the vendor has corrected the defect in a timely manner. However, this paragraph will operate as a limitation on the remedies available to the user only if it specifies that it will be deemed to be the user's "sole and exclusive remedy." Otherwise, it will be considered only an optional remedy for the user, who will be free to pursue any other remedies he may have under the law, including an action for damages or, in the proper situation, an action to rescind the contract.[36]

The primary purpose of such a limited remedy is to give the vendor an opportunity to make the software conform to its warranties, while limiting its exposure to the risk of paying any damages that might otherwise be due. The user may also benefit from the vendor's incentive to provide software that conforms to the contract within a reasonable time.

A problem can arise with the "repair only" limitation when the vendor is unable or unwilling to correct the software or unreasonably delays in doing so. In that case, the exclusive remedy is said

---

[35] U.C.C. §2–719(1)(a).
[36] U.C.C. §2–719(1)(b).

to "fail of its essential purpose," and will become null and void.[37] Otherwise, the user would be left with no remedy whatsoever.

When an exclusive remedy fails of its essential purpose, the user is allowed to pursue all of the remedies it would have otherwise had under the contract. An example of this problem occurred in a case involving six custom software packages delivered by NCR to one of its customers. NCR told its customer that the software would be up and running by March, 1975, but, more than a year later, only one of the six functions was operating properly. NCR repeatedly attempted to correct the deficiencies in the system, but, a year and a half after it was supposed to be operational, NCR was still unable to make it work. The contract between the parties stated that, in the event the software failed to work properly, NCR's obligation was limited to correcting any errors. However, under the circumstances the court ruled that the repair remedy had failed of its essential purpose, and the customer was allowed to recover damages.[38]

10.2.4. Maximum Dollar Limitation on Damages

If the contract does not provide for an exclusive remedy, or if the exclusive remedy fails of its essential purpose, the vendor will be liable for damages suffered by the user. But except in the case of personal injury, the amount of the vendor's liability for those damages may be limited to a dollar amount specified in the contract,[39] provided that the dollar limitation is not so low that the user is left without a realistic remedy in the event the vendor breaches the contract.[40]

Damage limitations are frequently tied to the license fee paid for the software if the fee was paid in a lump sum, or to the fees paid by the user for a specified number of preceding months if the fees were paid on a monthly basis. If the amount chosen is reason-

---

[37] U.C.C. §2–719(2); *Office Supply Co., Inc. v. Basic/Four Corp.*, 538 F. Supp. 776, 787, 789–91 (E.D. Wis. 1982) (applying California law); *Chatlos Systems Inc. v. National Cash Register Corp.*, 635 F.2d 1081, 1085 (3d Cir. 1980) (applying New Jersey law).

[38] *Chatlos Systems, Inc. v. National Cash Register Corp.*, 635 F.2d 1081, 1085–1086 (3d Cir. 1980) (applying New Jersey Law).

[39] *See* U.C.C. §2–719(1)(a); *Farris Engineering Corp. v. Service Bureau Corp.*, 276 F.Supp. 643, 645 (D.N.J. 1967).

[40] *See* U.C.C. §2–719 comment 1.

able, the worst that can happen is that the vendor will have to refund the user's money. A typical limitation of liability provision of this type is written as follows:

> Vendor's liability, if any, for loss or damages relating to or arising out of the license of the program products shall not exceed the charges paid by customer for such products.

Burroughs successfully used this limitation in a lawsuit filed by an unhappy customer who had purchased hardware and licensed software which it claimed had never functioned properly.[41] The customer sought significant damages, but at the outset of the lawsuit the court ruled that the contract clause stating "Burroughs liability . . . shall not exceed the charges attributable to [the] program product(s)," was enforceable and limited Burroughs' potential liability to the amounts paid by the customer. But beware of placing total reliance on such a damage limitation clause. Courts in some states will refuse to enforce these clauses in certain situations. In one case, where a vendor was unable to correct the bugs in its software, a court found that its default under the terms of its license agreement was "so total and fundamental" that the exclusive remedy clause failed of its essential purpose and that the customer was entitled to recover all of its damages notwithstanding a contract clause that limited the vendor's liability to the contract price.[42]

10.2.5. Exclusion of Consequential Damages

In addition to limiting the dollar *amount* of its potential liability, the vendor may also limit the *type* of damages for which it can be held liable. Basically there are three types of damages that a user can suffer. They are known as direct damages, incidental damages, and consequential damages.

The lines separating these three types of damages are not clearly drawn. However, in general, direct damages are the damages that are both directly and proximately caused by a software

[41] *Hi-Neighbor Enterprises, Inc. v. Burroughs Corp.*, 492 F. Supp. 823, 826–27 (N.D. Fla. 1980) (applying Florida law); *see also Garden State Food Distributers, Inc. v. Sperry Rand Corp.*, 512 F. Supp. 975, 977–78 (D. N.J. 1981) (applying New Jersey law).
[42] *RRX Industries, Inc. v. Lab-Con, Inc.*, 772 F.2d 543, 546 (9th Cir. 1985).

malfunction. They include, for example, lost computer time, the cost of any necessary software corrections, the cost of rerunning the software, and so forth.

Incidental damages are miscellaneous out-of-pocket expenses which the user incurs as a result of the malfunction. These include the cost of long distance telephone calls to the vendor regarding defects in the software, expenses incurred in shipping the software back to the vendor for analysis, expenses incurred in attempting to locate substitute software, and so forth.

So-called "consequential" damages generally refer to losses that are not directly caused by the failure of a product to perform as warranted but rather as a consequence thereof. For example, if software fails to perform properly, a user's direct damages might be the cost of hiring a programmer to correct the problem, or the cost of obtaining alternate software. But if, as a consequence of the failure, one of the user's customers becomes unhappy with the service it is receiving, and takes its business elsewhere, the user's lost profit is considered as consequential damage. Because they can include such lost profits, consequential damages typically represent a vendor's largest potential exposure.

Under the law a vendor is not liable for consequential damages unless it had reason to know of their potential at the time it entered into the contract,[43] but this protection is more theoretical than real. Given the fact that many users rely on the expertise of a vendor in selecting software, exposure to such damages is often part of a software transaction. Thus it is prudent for the vendor to include a conspicuous clause in its contract which excludes liability for all consequential damages.[44] A clause excluding such liability can be phrased as follows:

IN NO EVENT WILL VENDOR BE LIABLE FOR CONSEQUENTIAL DAMAGES EVEN IF VENDOR HAS BEEN ADVISED OF THE POSSIBILITY OF SUCH DAMAGES.

It should be noted, however, that this exclusion of consequential damages will only apply to economic losses, not to personal injuries.[45]

---

[43] U.C.C. §2–715(2).
[44] U.C.C. §2–719.
[45] U.C.C. §2–719(3).

A good example of the application of this type of damage limitation occurred in a suit for breach of warranty filed by Applied Data Processing, Inc. against Burroughs Corporation.[46] In the late 1960s, ADP had been running assembly language software on its IBM 360 Model 20 computer, but needed a larger system. It agreed to lease a Burroughs B-2500 system based on Burroughs' representations that its system had greater capacity and lower cost than comparable IBM equipment, and thus, that the conversion costs would soon be recovered. The B-2500 computer had serious problems, however, and was ultimately removed by Burroughs about a year after it was installed.

In analyzing the damages suffered by ADP after the computer failed, the court divided them into two categories—direct damages and consequential damages. The direct damages were the cost of transporting the B-2500 back to Burroughs, labor costs in rerunning faulty reports, wages of personnel idled by the malfunctioning of the B-2500, the cost of purchasing outside computer time, and the wages of personnel required to deal with customers because of the B-2500's failure to perform as warranted. The consequential damages were essentially the costs of converting the Burroughs system to a new IBM system, such as the cost of converting from Burroughs COBOL to IBM COBOL. Although ADP was allowed to recover its direct damages, the lease agreement between Burroughs and ADP contained a clause stating that Burroughs was not "liable for indirect or consequential damages." The court held that this clause barred ADP from recovering the consequential damages. Thus, Burroughs' investment in giving careful attention to its contract documents considerably reduced its potential liability.

A limitation of liability clause that excludes consequential damages will not be enforceable if a court finds that it is "unconscionable."[47] The term is hard to define, but the notion of unconscionability is rooted in principles of fairness and public policy. It comes into play where one party, who is in a position of superiority over the other party with respect to skill, knowledge, and resources, takes unfair advantage of the other party by insisting on a

---

[46] *Applied Data Processing, Inc. v. Burroughs Corp.*, 394 F. Supp. 504 (D. Conn. 1975).
[47] U.C.C. §2–719(3).

term which is deemed to be unfair under the circumstances. A finding of unconsionability is rare in the normal commercial context where businesspeople are involved on both sides. It usually arises in consumer situations in which the user is a total neophyte with little or no knowledge of the subject matter of the contract or the world of business itself. Factors that courts frequently consider in determining whether it would be unconscionable to apply a particular limitation of liability provision in a software contract include the following:[48]

1. The relative bargaining power of the two parties;
2. The ability of the user to evaluate the software before entering into the agreement;
3. Whether the limitation of liability was conspicuous;
4. The length of the negotiation process;
5. The length of time the user had to deliberate before signing the contract;
6. The experience or astuteness of the parties;
7. Whether the contract was reviewed by an attorney for the user;
8. Whether the user was a reluctant party to the contract;
9. The nature of the commercial setting and the effect of the allegedly unconscionable clause;
10. The extent of the vendor's default in attempting to fulfill its obligations.

Finally, it should be noted that clauses excluding liability for consequential damages will not be enforced by some courts in situations where the contract contains a limited remedy of repair, and the limited remedy fails of its essential purpose because the vendor is unwilling or unable to fix the software. The theory is that the customer has been deprived of the substantial value of its bargain (i.e., the right to have the software fixed) and thus should be entitled to recover all of its damages.

---

[48] *See A&M Produce Co. v. FMC Corp.*, 135 Cal. App. 3d 473, 489–93, 186 Cal. Rptr. 114, 123-26 (1982); *Office Supply Co. Inc. v. Basic/Four Corp.*, 538 F. Supp. 776, 788–89 (E.D. Wis. 1982) (applying California law); and *Earman Oil Co. v. Burroughs Corp.*, 625 F.2d 1291, 1299 (5th Cir. 1980).

10.2.6.   Reduced Statute of Limitations

Another way in which a vendor's liability may be limited is through the use of a contractual provision which reduces the period of time during which the vendor is exposed to potential liability. This is done by contractually specifying the amount of time that the user has to bring suit against the vendor for breach of the contract. Depending upon which state's law governs the transaction, the user will normally have a right for four years from the date of the breach to sue the vendor for damages. In most states the parties may contractually reduce this period of time to as little as one year.[49] An example of such a clause is the following:

> All suits or causes of action by either party arising out of this agreement will be barred unless commenced within one year from the date of the alleged breach.

A clause like this one was instrumental in overturning an $11.4 million verdict against IBM.[50] An IBM customer, a company that manufactured and distributed jewelry, filed suit against IBM alleging that IBM had breached two contracts, one for the development of production control software and the other for the development of a merchandise control system. After the jury decided in favor of the customer, IBM appealed. The appeals court held that the two contracts were governed by the terms of an IBM Systems Engineering Services agreement, which contained the following limitation of liability clause:

> No action, regardless of form, arising out of the services under this Agreement, may be brought by either party more than one year after the cause of action has accrued.

Because the breach of contract claims had been filed more than one year after the breach allegedly occurred, the court ruled that they were barred. Consequently, IBM could not be held liable for having breached the two contracts.

---

[49] U.C.C. §2–725(1).

[50] *International Business Machines Corp. v. Catamore Enterprises, Inc.*, 548 F.2d 1065, 1074–75, 1076 (1st Cir. 1976) (applying New York law).

Note that although this clause applies to suits by the vendor against the user as well as vice versa, it tends to favor the vendor. The vendor is primarily interested in being paid, and one year is usually more than enough time for the vendor to decide whether the user is going to pay. On the other hand, this clause places the user in a much more difficult position. If the software does not work properly, the first problem the user has is in determining whether the vendor is contractually responsible for the malfunction. And even then the user will often attempt to work with the vendor, sometimes for periods well in excess of a year, in order to attempt to resolve the problems. By doing so, the user may waive its right to sue the vendor for breach. Thus, a prudent user will obtain a written commitment from the vendor to extend the time to sue while the parties try to work out their problems. If the vendor refuses to agree to such an extension, suit can be filed within the original time period.

10.2.7. "No Liability" Clauses

If a vendor can reduce its liability through the use of appropriate contract language, why not contractually eliminate all of its liability by the inclusion of a clause which completely excludes all liability of the vendor for any cause whatsoever?

Normally, the law says that the user must be left with some remedy in the event of a breach by the vendor. When two parties enter into a contract, they must accept the fact that there be at least a fair quantum of remedy for breach of the obligations or duties set forth in the contract. Consequently, any clause purporting to eliminate all liability runs the risk of being unenforceable on the ground of unconscionability.[51] This is exactly what happened in a case involving Burroughs Corp.[52] There, Burroughs sold a computer and corresponding applications software pursuant to a contract stating that "PURCHASER HEREBY EXPRESSLY WAIVES ALL DAMAGES, WHETHER DIRECT, IN-

---

[51] U.C.C. §2–719 Comment 1.

[52] *Chesapeake Petroleum and Supply Co. v. Burroughs Corporation*, 6 Computer L. Serv. Rep. 768, 769 (Montgomery Cty Cir. Ct. Md. 1977), *aff'd* 6 Computer L. Serv. Rep. 782 (Md. App. 1978).

CIDENTAL, OR CONSEQUENTIAL." The court found this to be unconscionable, and refused to enforce it.

As a general proposition, a vendor cannot represent that its product will do certain things and at the same time immunize itself from all liability if it does not. However, in those unusual situations where software has been sold or licensed "as is," "with all faults," or otherwise with no promise that it will perform for the buyer, a court will probably enforce a clause eliminating all of the vendor's liability for software malfunctions. As long as it is clear to the user that the vendor is making no representations whatsoever about the operation of the software, and providing there is no great disparity in bargaining power between the parties, it is proper for the vendor to exclude all of its liability.

Where a transaction is between two businessmen dealing at arms' length, such total exclusions of liability have been upheld in certain cases.[53] But since this type of a clause may be held to be unenforceable in many situations, it should be very sparingly used.

10.3. MISREPRESENTATION

A vendor will often make statements and representations to the user in order to induce the user to enter into a software agreement. Many of these statements will not be included in the contract, and, in fact, the contract will usually state that such statements are not binding on the vendor. (See Sections 9.22 and 10.2.1.) Nonetheless, the user may still rely on them in entering into the agreement. If the statements are false and the user suffers damages as a result, the vendor may be liable for the tort of misrepresentation, or, in other words, for fraud.

Misrepresentation claims against vendors are common. This is in part a natural consequence of transactions involving a great disparity in technical knowledge between the parties. Moreover, a software vendor's sales representative is frequently more interested in closing the deal than in protecting against liability claims. Finally, these claims are sometimes made because of the user's

---

[53] *See W.R. Weber Co. v. Burroughs Corp.*, 580 S.W.2d 76 (Tex. Civ. App. 1979).

need to avoid the effects of a well-written contract, which if enforced in accordance with its terms would leave the user without a remedy. In fact, a successful action for fraud can serve to vitiate contractual limitations on liability.

Misrepresentation claims are governed by each state's "common law," and, consequently, the law will vary somewhat from state to state. Nonetheless, it is generally true that a customer will have a claim for fraud against a vendor if it was induced to enter into the transaction because:

1. The vendor made a misrepresentation of a material fact
2. Which the vendor knew to be false;
3. Which was made with the intent to induce the user to enter into the contract;
4. Which the user justifiably relied upon; and,
5. Which resulted in damage to the user.

If all of these elements are present, the vendor may be liable for any compensatory damages resulting from the misrepresentation. The vendor may also be held liable for punitive damages. Sections 10.3.1–10.3.5 will explain the nature of this liability.

10.3.1. False Statement of a Material Fact

Any statement of fact made by a vendor which is not true can qualify as a misrepresentation. The statement can be oral, as in the case of statements made by the vendor's sales representative, or it can be written, as in the case of representations stated in the vendor's advertising materials, brochures, or correspondence between the vendor and a potential customer. In one case a Hewlett-Packard brochure stated that its APL/3000 computer language would provide "fast response even with multiple users."[54] When a customer experienced unacceptably long response time and sued HP, a court held that HP's statement in its brochure could be the basis of a fraud claim.

---

[54] *APLications, Inc. v. Hewlett-Packard Co.*, 501 F. Supp. 129, 131, 136 (S.D.N.Y. 1980) (applying California and New York law), *aff'd* 672 F.2d 1076 (2d Cir. 1982).

A false "statement" can also be "implied" from other statements made by the vendor. This was what occurred in a case involving the lease of a Honeywell Model 62/40 computer to a company called Systems Information Services.[55] The court found that Honeywell had committed fraud by representing that its 62/40 computer was "best suited for the SIS operation and its projected business expansion." The court acknowledged that there was no testimony at the trial that such a statement had been made verbatim by Honeywell, but concluded that it summarized the fair import of the various statements made by Honeywell's agents.

A fraudulent statement may also be implied from conduct designed to convey a misleading impression. A dummy demonstration of software, for example, could constitute a fraudulent statement if it was designed to give the impression that the system was completely developed and tested, when in fact it was nowhere near completion. Silence can also constitute a misrepresentation in certain cases, such as where the vendor fails to disclose material facts to the user in circumstances where such failure will be misleading. For example, one vendor was found liable for fraud by failing to disclose to a customer that his order was the first one placed for its new model read/write heads, that the heads were still experimental, and that they were still being tested in conjunction with a prototype computer. The court stated that the vendor was under an obligation to disclose the incomplete state of development of its new product in order to avoid the misleading impressions it had created.[56]

In determining whether a statement is false, it is important to distinguish between false statements of fact on the one hand and expressions of opinion, predictions of future performance, or mere "puffing" on the other. The latter, at least in theory, cannot be the basis of a fraud claim. A sales representative's statement that his or her software is the best on the market should be taken as nothing more than a sales pitch. Opinions normally fall in the same category. In one case, a court held that predictions by Burroughs of possible man–hour cost savings by use of the proposed com-

---

[55] *Dunn Appraisal Co. v. Honeywell Information Systems, Inc.*, 687 F.2d 877, 882 (6th Cir. 1982) (applying Ohio law).

[56] *Strand v. Librascope, Inc.*, 197 F. Supp. 743, 753 (E.D. Mich. 1961) (applying Michigan law).

puter were opinions rather than statements of material fact, and the plaintiff's fraud claim was dismissed.[57]

Courts are reluctant, however, to accept a vendor's claim that its representations were merely opinions or puffing, unless the nature of the statements made it clear that they were not intended as statements of fact. Courts take this stand because there is normally a great disparity in knowledge and expertise between the vendor and the user. As a practical matter, where the user is not technically sophisticated, it often relies on statements made by the vendor, without realizing that they are only opinions. In one case, for example, a vendor of read/record heads held itself out as an expert, actually possessed exclusive, superior knowledge, and intimated to its customer either that it knew facts to justify its opinions or knew of no facts to dispute them. Accordingly, the court concluded that the opinions expressed by the vendor could be the basis of a fraud claim since it was reasonable for the customer to have relied upon them under the circumstances of that case.[58] Thus opinions may form the basis of a fraud claim if they are expressed by an expert or by one who holds himself or herself out as specially qualified in the software field.

To impose liability, however, the statement must be a "material" factor in the customer's decision to enter into the transaction. That is, it must be important to the transaction; the mere fact that the statement is false is not enough. If the statement is false, but not material, the vendor will not be liable for misrepresentation. This distinction was illustrated by the facts of a fraud case filed by Iten Leasing Company against Burroughs Corporation.[59] Iten had purchased a computerized accounting system from Burroughs that consisted of an L-8500 accounting machine, internal memory for the system, a data-save device, a reader/feeder/stacker attachment, and various accounting software packages. The court held that Burroughs had made false representations to Iten regarding the reader/feeder/stacker and the data-save device. Nonetheless, it concluded that they were not material to Iten's decision to buy

[57] *Westfield Chemical Corp. v. Burroughs Corp.*, 6 Computer L. Serv. Rep. 438, 442 (Mass. Super. Ct. 1977).

[58] *Strand v. Librascope, Inc.*, 197 F. Supp. 743, 754 (E.D. Mich. 1961).

[59] *Iten Leasing Co. v. Burroughs Corp.*, 684 F.2d 573, 576 (8th Cir. 1982) (applying Minnesota law).

the total accounting system, which had been used by Iten both before and after the problems had developed with those two items. Consequently, the court concluded that Item had failed to establish its claim for misrepresentation.

10.3.2. Knowledge of Falsity—Intent to Deceive

Most states require that the vendor have knowledge of the falsity of its statement before it can be held liable for fraud. It should be noted, however, that some states, for example, Minnesota and Michigan, do not require any knowledge of the falsity by the vendor. That is, if a vendor innocently makes a false statement in those states, it can nonetheless be held liable for fraud.[60] In most states, however, it must be shown that the vendor had a bad intent. Without proof of bad intent, the vendor will not be liable.[61]

Knowledge of the falsity of a statement can take two forms. Either (1) the vendor actually knew that its representation was false at the time that it made the statement, or (2) the vendor lacked an honest belief as to its truth, or made the statement with a reckless disregard as to whether it was true or false. For example, if a sales representative falsely represents that his or her software has been thoroughly tested and debugged, a court will find an intent to deceive if the sales representative either knew that the statement was false or had no idea whether it was true or not.

Knowledge that a statement is false can be shown in a number of ways. In one case in which NCR was found liable for intentional misrepresentation, the court concluded that the following evidence established that NCR had sold its SPIRIT system with knowledge of its defects: (1) an NCR district manager testified that he had notified the SPIRIT support group of problems with the software; (2) the project leader for the SPIRIT development group (who was associated with the support group) testified that

---

[60] *See Clements Auto Co. v. Service Bureau Corp.*, 298 F. Supp. 115, 126 (D. Minn. 1969), *aff'd as modified*, 444 F.2d 169, 176 (8th Cir. 1971) (applying Minnesota law); *Strand v. Librascope, Inc.*, 197 F. Supp. 743, 745, 754 (E.D. Mich. 1961) (applying Michigan law).

[61] *Stahl Management Corp. v. Conceptions Unlimited*, 554 F. Supp. 890, 894 (S.D.N.Y. 1983) (applying New York law).

he was responsible for reporting progress to NCR management; and (3) there was evidence that NCR attempted to hide defects in the system by developing a demonstrator model that gave the impression that it worked better than the actual software.[62] In another case, a court concluded that Honeywell's statement that its Model 62/40 computer was "best suited" for the customer's operation was made with willful disregard for whether it was true or not.[63] This conclusion was based on the fact that a Honeywell employee expressed serious doubts about the suitability of the 62/40 to the salesman who made the statement, but the salesman neither disclosed this to the customer nor modified his own recommendations accordingly.

10.3.3 Justifiable Reliance by the User

In order to prevail on a claim of misrepresentation, the user must actually have relied upon the allegedly false statements in entering into the transaction. If there is no reliance because the statements concern trivial matters, because the user has learned the truth, because it relied on information obtained from other sources, or for any other reason, there can be no recovery for fraud.

A somewhat obvious application of this rule occurred in a case in which a Burroughs employee had stated that the L-5000 computer had sufficient capacity to handle a particular customer's then present business needs and up to double that capacity without adding additional personnel.[64] Instead of accepting this representation, however, the customer conducted its own experiment which proved that the statement was false. It then bought two computers instead of one. Consequently, when the customer later sued Burroughs for fraud, its claim was dismissed by the court on the ground that the customer had not actually relied on this false statement.

---

[62] *Glovatorium, Inc. v. NCR Corp.*, 684 F.2d 658, 660 (9th Cir. 1982).

[63] *Dunn Appraisal Co. v. Honeywell Information Systems, Inc.*, 687 F.2d 877, 883 (6th Cir. 1982) (applying Ohio law).

[64] *Investors Premium Corp. v. Burroughs Corp.*, 389 F. Supp. 39, 44, 46 (D.S.C. 1974); *See also APLications, Inc. v. Hewlitt-Packard Co.*, 501 F. Supp. 129, 136 (S.D.N.Y. 1980), *aff'd* 672 F.2d 1076 (2d Cir. 1982); *Badger Bearing Co. v. Burroughs Corp.*, 444 F. Supp. 919, 924–25 (E.D. Wis. 1977) (applying Wisconsin law).

Even when a customer actually relies on false statements, the reliance must also be justifiable under the circumstances. Given the usual disparity in knowledge and expertise between the vendor and the user, reliance is almost always justifiable. However, in one rather remarkable case it was not. In that case, a certified public accountant purchased a computer in reliance on the salesman's promise that, if he did so, the salesman would procure a nearby oil company as a client for the CPA's accounting service.[65] The CPA never inquired to determine whether the oil company really did intend to employ him, and later admitted that he had been "unreasonable," "naive," and "very stupid" to rely on the salesman's statement without verifying it. Consequently, when he sued the vendor for fraud, his claim was dismissed as "meritless."

Reliance is also not justifiable when the customer knows of facts which indicate that the vendor's representation is not true. This rule was applied in a case in which NCR was accused of fraudulently representing that its NCR 390 computer was suitable, appropriate, and adequate for a particular customer's purposes, when, in fact, the computer's printout rate was too slow.[66] However, the customer had become aware of this fact before purchasing the machine, and the court held that it thus had no right to rely on NCR's representations of adequacy. Statements which are obviously false cannot form the basis of any justifiable reliance.

10.3.4. Damages

The user is entitled to recover all of the losses that it suffered as a result of its reliance on the vendor's fraudulent misrepresentations. In addition, a defrauded customer may seek punitive damages as well.

A wide variety of costs and losses can be awarded as damages in a fraud case. When Service Bureau Corporation was found to have misrepresented the capabilities of a proposed data processing system, it was ordered to repay its customer what it had been charged for data processing services, and to reimburse the customer for its

---

[65] *Shivers v. Sweda Int'l., Inc.*, 146 Ga. App. 758, 247 S.E.2d 576 (1978).

[66] *Fruit Industries Research Foundation v. NCR Corp.*, 406 F.2d 546, 549 (9th Cir. 1969) (applying Washington law).

cost of leasing additional equipment, the cost of maintaining that equipment, the increased cost of clerical personnel, the increased cost of office supplies, a portion of its executive salaries to cover supervision of the data processing system, and interest.[67] In another case, in which Burroughs was alleged to have fraudulently misrepresented the capabilities of its computer, the court held that, if the facts were proven the customer would be entitled to recover its conversion costs, the cost of removing computer equipment from its premises, the cost of purchasing outside computer time, and the cost of physical modifications to the building necessary for installation of the system.[68] In another case the plaintiff was awarded the cost of management time and expenses devoted to installation of the computer and conversion of the computer programs, the cost of labor and machine time to prepare test data, and the cost of hiring an independent consultant to complete the conversion of computer programs.[69]

Substantial punitive damages may also be awarded in an appropriate case. Although the standards vary from one state to another, punitive damages may normally be awarded to punish conduct which the trier of fact, that is, a judge or a jury, determines was "outrageous." Intentional deception of an innocent customer can easily fall into this category, and because punitive damages are normally a function of the defendant's net worth rather than the size of the plaintiff's loss, they can be devastating in amount.

10.3.5. Limiting Liability for Misrepresentation

As a general rule, a disclaimer of warranties or limitation of liability provision contained in a contract will limit liability under a breach of contract claim, but will have no effect on a fraud claim.[70]

---

[67] *Clements Auto Co. v. Service Bureau Corp.*, 444 F.2d 169, 191 (8th Cir. 1971) (applying Minnesota law).

[68] *Applied Data Processing, Inc. v. Burroughs Corp.*, 394 F. Supp. 504, 511 (D.Conn. 1975) (applying Michigan law).

[69] *Dunn Appraisal Co. v. Honeywell Information Systems, Inc.*, 687 F.2d 877, 883–84 (6th Cir. 1982) (applying Ohio law).

[70] *See Clements Auto Co. v. Service Bureau Corp.*, 444 F.2d 169, 178–79, 188–89 (8th Cir. 1971); *APLications, Inc. v. Hewlitt-Packard Co.*, 501 F. Supp. 129, 136 (S.D.N.Y. 1980), *aff'd* 672 F.2d 1076 (2d Cir. 1982); *Badger Bearing Co. v. Burroughs Corp.*, 444 F. Supp. 919, 923 (E.D. Wis. 1977).

Even an "integration" clause, which specifies that all promises or representations pertinent to the transaction are contained, or "integrated," within the written contract, will not necessarily bar a claim that the user was fraudulently induced to sign the contract. In fact, this is the reason that a significant number of computer-related lawsuits contain a claim for fraud. It is the only way a user can get around the fact that the vendor has eliminated or limited its liability for breach of contract.

In the final analysis, limiting liability for fraud is a matter of sound business practices designed to limit the number of claims made. Fraud claims usually arise in the context of representations made to the user to induce it to enter into the transaction. Consequently, limiting claims is a function of responsible product marketing. Products should not be oversold. Sales personnel should be carefully breifed as to what they can and cannot say about the products and the impact of those products on a customer's business. A vendor should not make any promises or representations it is not willing or able to stand behind. And products should not be rushed to market before they are thoroughly tested, at least not without full disclosure to the customer.

10.4. NEGLIGENCE

The law imposes on the software developer an obligation of reasonable care in designing, developing, and testing software, so as to prevent loss or injury to others. If the developer does not fulfill that obligation, it may become liable to someone who suffers a loss as a result of using its software.

Negligence liability is based on obligations imposed by law, in contrast to contract liability (such as breach of warranty), which is based on obligations which the parties have agreed to undertake. A vendor can be liable for breach of contract only to a person with whom it has entered into an agreement, whereas it can be liable to anyone who foreseeably could suffer a loss as a result of its negligent conduct, whether or not they are parties to the same contract.

Negligence is often described as carelessness, that is, the failure to act the way a "reasonably prudent" person would act under substantially the same conditions. A common example is the driver who is not paying attention, fails to see a red light, and, as a result, hits another car in an intersection. The accident was not intentionally caused by the negligent driver, yet he is liable for the damage caused to the car he hit and its occupants, because he failed to live up to his duty to drive carefully.

Negligence can take the form of an act (such as driving too fast on an icy road), or an omission to act (such as failing to warn of a hidden danger). But whether an act or omission is negligent depends on the circumstances. Driving 55 miles per hour on an expressway may be perfectly proper on a warm sunny day in light traffic, but the same conduct may be found to be negligent when the road is covered with ice and snow and the traffic is heavy. Similarly, there are no specific rules as to what will constitute negligence in the development of software. It depends on the circumstances.

The fact that software fails to operate properly does not necessarily imply negligence in its development. If the problem would *not* have been foreseen and prevented by the reasonably prudent software developer, there is no negligence. But what the hypothetical "reasonable person" would have done under a particular set of circumstances must be decided by the judge or jury, after the fact, at the trial of a lawsuit.

The standard of care depends on the status of the person whose conduct has been called into question. Professionals, such as physicians, attorneys, accountants, engineers, and architects, are required to possess and to act in conformity with the level of skill and knowledge expected of other professionals in their respective fields. If they fail to meet this higher standard (regardless of whether they actually possess this higher level of skill), they are guilty of professional negligence or malpractice.

Although the concept of professional negligence or malpractice has not yet been recognized in the software field, it has been raised in some cases,[71] and the courts can be expected to move in that direction. If this heightened standard of care is ever imposed on those who design, develop, and test software, it could result in

---

[71] *Chatlos Systems, Inc. v. National Cash Register Corp.*, 479 F. Supp. 738, 740–41 at n. 1 (D.N.J. 1979); *Triangle Underwriters Inc. v. Honeywell, Inc.*, 457 F. Supp. 765, 770–71 (E.D.N.Y. 1978), *aff'd on this issue*, 604 F.2d 737, 745–46 (2d Cir. 1979) (applying New York law).

the imposition of negligence liability for mere failure to live up to accepted industry practices, regardless of whether the software developer is aware of such practices or possesses the appropriate level of skill.

Nonetheless, regardless of the standard of care that is ultimately applied to persons in the software industry, there are a number of actions or failures to act which might be considered negligent. Perhaps the most obvious is the failure to adequately test and debug the software. What consititutes adequate testing depends on the circumstances, and a "reasonable person" would plainly spend more time testing software designed to control a hospital life-support system than he or she would a new computer game. But there are no rules to establish how much testing is enough. Failure to provide error-handling routines may also constitute negligence, depending upon the nature of the software and the possible harm that might result. Similarly, failure to warn of known and unavoidable problems may also constitute negligence.

To date there have not been many claims against software vendors founded on a theory of negligence. In a number of reported cases in which the user claimed that the vendor has been negligent the courts have held that the negligence claim was really a breach of warranty claim, which is governed by the terms of the contract.[72] Moreover, where only economic losses occur (as opposed to personal injury or property damage), the courts in many states will not permit recovery on a negligence theory in any event.[73] Nevertheless, some courts have indicated that, in the proper circumstances, a claim for damages resulting from defective software can be based on a negligence theory.[74]

In certain cases a negligence standard can greatly expand the scope of a vendor's liability, since under a negligence theory the

---

[72] *Investors Premium Corp. v. Burroughs Corp.*, 389 F. Supp. 39, 42, 46 (D.S.C. 1974); *Westfield Chemical Corp. v. Burroughs Corp.*, 6 Computer L. Serv. Rep. 438, 444 (Mass. Super. Ct. 1977).

[73] *Office Supply Co. Inc. v. Basic/Four Corp.*, 538 F. Supp. 776, 791–92 (E.D. Wis. 1982) (applying California law); *Black, Jackson & Simmons v. International Business Machines Corp.*, 440 N.E.2d 282, 283 (Ill. App. 1982).

[74] *Triangle Underwriters, Inc. v. Honeywell Information Systems, Inc.*, 457 F. Supp. 765, 770–71 (E.D.N.Y. 1978), aff'd, 604 F.2d 737, 744–46 (2d Cir. 1979); *International Business Machines Corp. v. Catamore Enterprises, Inc.*, 548 F.2d 1065, 1072 n. 14, 1076 (1st Cir. 1976) (applying New York law).

vendor can be liable to persons with whom it has never dealt. For example, if a software vendor supplies negligently designed life-support software to a hospital, it does not enter into any agreement with the patients, yet may very well be liable to a patient who is injured if the system fails.

In theory, a vendor may limit or exclude its liability for damages caused by its own negligence by inserting an appropriate provision in the contract.[75] However, such provisions are not favored by the courts and must be carefully drafted to be enforceable. Moreover, such a provision will only cover damage caused to the party who signs the contract, and will not be effective if a court finds that it is unconscionable, that it otherwise violates public policy, or that it is contrary to a state statute.

Where there exists a great disparity in bargaining power and/or technical knowledge between the parties, a court is more likely to hold that a clause limiting or excluding negligence liability is unenforceable. On the other hand, in a negotiated transaction between two businesses such a clause will probably be enforced, on the theory that it represents the parties' agreement as to who should bear the risk of loss arising out of the performance of the contract.

10.5. PRODUCTS LIABILITY

"Products liability" refers to a legal theory under which a manufacturer can be held liable for physical injuries or property damage caused by defects in its products, regardless of whether they resulted from negligence. It is, therefore, a species of "absolute" liability or liability "without fault."

In order to recover under a products liability theory, as applied to software, the injured party must prove that:

1. The software was "defective";
2. The defective condition of the software rendered it "unreasonably dangerous";

---

[75] Restatement (Second) of Contracts §195 and comment a (1979).

3. The defective condition of the software was the "cause" of the plaintiff's injuries (whether to his or her person or property);

4. The developer and/or the vendor placed the software in the stream of commerce; and

5. The software was "defective" at the time it left the control of the developer or vendor.

A product can be "defective" for these purposes in either of two ways. First, if it does not work the way it is supposed to, it will be considered "defective." Thus, for example, process control software designed to control the flow of gas to a furnace will be deemed defective if it fails to determine whether the pilot light is on before permitting the flow of gas. Second, it is possible for a product to be found "defective" even though properly designed if it was "in a condition not contemplated by the ultimate consumer, which will be unreasonably dangerous to him."[76] This situation commonly arises in the case of drugs. Even though a medicine may be 100 percent pure and faultlessly made, consumption in combination with certain other drugs, or by persons with certain physical conditions, or simple overconsumption, may result in dangers unknown to the user. In such a case, the manufacturer is required to give adequate warning of the dangers involved and instructions which, if followed by the user, will permit those dangers to be reduced to "reasonable" levels.[77]

To date, no reported court decision has held the developer or vendor of software liable on a products liability theory, although the claim has been raised in a few cases.[78] Several important restrictions apply to the products liability theory which exempt most, but not all, software transactions. First, products liability applies only to *goods*, not to services. The problem, however, is that many transactions, especially in the software area, are a combination of goods and services. Software can be viewed as a good (the contents of a tape or a floppy disk), or as a service (a product to be developed by a vendor to the user's specifications). Second,

---

[76] Restatement (Second) of Torts §402A comment g (1965).
[77] Restatement (Second) of Torts §402A comment h (1965).
[78] *Chatlos Systems Inc. v. NCR Corp.*, 479 F. Supp. 738, 740–41 at n. 1 (D.N.J. 1979).

products liability applies only to *sales*. It does not apply to licenses—the form of most software transactions. Third, products liability only applies when *personal injury or property damage* results from use of the product. If the user suffers only economic losses, recovery under a products liability theory will not be allowed.[79] Should the products liability theory be applied to software, it would render a vendor liable to a user for any physical injuries or property damage sustained by the user even though the vendor did everything that it possibly could in designing, developing, and testing the software to insure that there were no defects in it.

[79] *Prosser on Torts* §101 (1971); *Office Supply Co. Inc. v. Basic/Four Corp.*, 538 F. Supp. 776, 791–92 (E.D. Wis. 1982) (applying California law).

CHAPTER ELEVEN

TAX TREATMENT OF SOFTWARE

The federal income tax laws and the tax laws enacted by individual states can have a significant impact on the development, sale, purchase, and license of computer software. The tax considerations in software transactions are frequently left to legal and accounting professionals. However, the successful software entrepreneur gains an important edge in any transaction, be it major or routine, by having a sense of its tax consequences before consulting with tax professionals. While this chapter will not attempt to explain every aspect of the federal and state tax consequences of each type of software transaction, it should alert the reader to the major tax issues involved with basic software transactions. However, because the tax laws are very technical and constantly changing,[1] there is no substitute for the counsel of a trusted tax professional in any important transaction.

[1] The federal tax laws have recently undergone a number of major revisions. Three major tax bills have already been enacted in the 1980s: the Economic Recovery Tax Act of 1981, Pub.L. No. 97–34, the Tax Equity and Fiscal Responsibility Act of 1982, Pub.L. No. 97–248, and the Tax Reform Act of 1984, Pub.L. No. 98–369. In May, 1985, President Reagan proposed a sweeping tax reform plan ("Reagan Proposal") that would reduce tax rates and eliminate tax preferences for individuals and corporations alike. At the time this book went to press, Congress was beginning to work on the Reagan Proposal. Although the individual states do not change their tax laws as often as the federal government, the

The federal and state tax laws affect software transactions in different ways. For purposes of the federal income tax, it is important to determine to what extent money or other property received for software products is taxable as "income" and to what extent amounts expended for software products may be deducted from gross income or applied as a credit against taxes owed. At the state level, the primary issue is whether the state's sales, use, or personal property taxes will be imposed on the software transaction.

11.1. INTRODUCTION TO FEDERAL TAX ISSUES

The federal income tax applies to software businesses in the same manner as it applies to any other business. The tax is computed as a percentage of the "taxable income" of the business, with the percentage increasing as the taxable income grows.[2]

Generally, taxable income is the gross income earned by a business minus allowable deductions. However, the apparent simplicity of this formula masks the enormous complexity of the federal tax laws. In fact, the formula is more easily expressed than applied; the gross income of a business is not necessarily the same as the amount of money earned or received, the allowable deductions do not include every expenditure made, the computation of the tax will depend on whether the taxpayer is an individual or corporation, and the applicable percentage of taxable income will not always equal the tax owed because of various tax credits, exemptions, penalties, and additional taxes.

Despite the complexity of the federal tax laws, three basic tax questions are at the core of most software transactions: (1) "How much of the amount received is taxable income?"; (2) "How much of expenses incurred can be deducted?"; and (3) "How much tax

---

changes that are enacted emerge with far less fanfare and commentary than federal changes.

[2] The tax rates are different for individuals and corporations. Under §1 of the Internal Revenue Code (I.R.C.), the tax rates for individuals range from 11 to 50 percent of taxable income, and are adjusted annually for inflation. Under I.R.C. § 11, a corporation is taxed at rates ranging from 15 to 46 percent of its taxable income. There is no adjustment for inflation for these rates. Under the Reagan Proposal, individual tax rates would be set at 15, 25, and 35 percent, and the corporate tax rate would be 33 percent.

will be due?" Following a brief overview of the underlying tax concepts, this chapter will attempt to provide general answers to these questions.

11.1.1. Income

The definition of gross income provided by the Internal Revenue Code (the "Code") encompasses almost all types of proceeds that could be received by an individual or business.[3] The commission a sales representative earns on sales, the wage a laborer receives for a day's work, the dividend an investor is paid on his or her stock, and the rent the landlord receives for his or her office space will all be part of the recipient's income. However, not every dollar received is subject to tax as "income." For example, the principal portion of a loan repayment is not income to the lender. Thus if a lender loans $100 to a borrower on January 1st and the borrower pays back $105 on July 1st, the lender's income from this transaction will not be $105, but only $5, the amount representing the borrower's interest payment for use of the loan principal.

One of the most important distinctions of which businesspeople should be aware is the difference between the "amount realized" from a sale and the taxable income that arises from the sale. The taxable income from any sale is measured by the excess, if any, of the total amount realized from the sale of the item over its cost, or "basis."[4] For example, suppose Nancy Jones pays $100 for a copy of a software package on January 1 and sells it on July 1 for $150. Her income from the transaction, also known as her taxable gain, will be the excess of the "amount realized" ($150) over the "basis" or cost ($100), or $50. On the other hand, if Jones sold the software for $95 there would be no excess of amount realized over basis, hence there would be no taxable gain (and, in fact, there would be a loss). This formula for computing taxable gain, that is, amount realized less basis, is used to determine the income from sales by most manufacturers and merchants, including those in the software industry.

---

[3] *See* I.R.C. §61(a).
[4] I.R.C. §1001; Treasury Regulation ("Treas. Reg.") §1.1001-1(a).

11.1.2. Character of Income

When a taxpayer's income is determined, a closely related step
is to determine its "character" for tax purposes, since the character of income partly determines the amount of taxes owed. The
overwhelming majority of income is considered "ordinary income," every dollar of which is subject to taxation at regular rates.
Most compensation for services, interest, and dividends is considered ordinary income. The taxable gain realized by merchants
from the sale of their inventory is generally "ordinary income,"
and is taxed at normal rates. A far more advantageous category of
income is "long-term capital gain," which is the taxable gain from
the sale of what are known as "capital assets,"[5] provided the item
was owned for an adequate period of time.[6] Long-term capital
gains are advantageous because 60 percent of an individual's net
capital gains is excluded from regular taxation[7] while the net capital gain of a corporation is subject to a maximum tax of 28%.[8]

To illustrate the advantageous tax treatment accorded to capital
gains, we return to our previous example in which Nancy Jones
has $50 of taxable gain from the sale of a software package. If
Jones is in the business of selling these software packages, the
copy she sold on July 1 will not be a capital asset and her taxable
gain is considered ordinary income. Accordingly, the entire $50
must be included in her taxable income. However, if Jones is not
in the business of selling software but merely decided to sell a

---

[5] I.R.C. §1221 defines capital assets to include all property except (1) inventory items
and other property held for sale to customers, (2) depreciable property used in the taxpayer's business, (3) copyrights, artistic, musical or literary compositions, letters, memoranda
and similar property held by a person who created the property, (4) certain accounts and
notes receivable received in the ordinary course of business, and (5) certain governmental
publications.

[6] Under I.R.C. §1222, capital assets acquired after June 22, 1984 and before January 1,
1988 must be held for more than six months to qualify for long-term capital gain tax
treatment. All other assets must be held for more than one year to qualify for long-term
capital gain tax treatment.

[7] I.R.C. §1202. It should be noted that the amount of an individual's net capital gain
which is not subject to regular taxation may be subject to an alternative minimum tax,
which is imposed only if it exceeds the regular income tax. See I.R.C. §55. The Reagan
Proposal would reduce the exclusion for net capital gains of individuals from 60 percent to
50 percent.

[8] I.R.C. §1201. Corporations are not subject to the alternative minimum tax, but a portion of their net capital gains are subject to the minimum tax of I.R.C. §56.

copy of a software package she had bought for her personal use, the software will probably be a capital asset and her gain will be characterized as "capital gain." Thus 60 percent of the $50 gain, or $30, will not be included in her taxable income. This exclusion provides a major incentive for taxpayers to strive for capital gains rather than ordinary income.

11.1.3. Deductibility of Costs

Almost all amounts paid by a taxpayer can be classified as either personal or business expenses. When calculating taxable income, an individual taxpayer may subtract some personal expenses from gross income. These deductible expenses, commonly known as itemized deductions, include medical expenses, state and local taxes, interest expenses, and charitable contributions.[9] For example, in a routine purchase of a quart of milk, the 79¢ paid for the milk will likely be a nondeductible personal expense, but the 4¢ in sales tax is a personal expense that the purchaser is entitled to deduct.

On the other hand, almost all expenses incurred in connection with a business can be deducted in one way or another. Generally, expenses incurred for items such as wages or rent can be "currently expensed," which means that they can be deducted fully in the year they are paid or incurred. The immediate deduction of these expenses is permitted because they are incurred for items having a "useful life" of less than one year, and therefore their deduction should not be deferred until future tax years. For example, suppose Nancy Jones runs a small computer store in the local shopping center. The monthly rent paid to the shopping center and the weekly salary paid to her clerk can be treated as current expenses. However, to be fully deducted from gross income, such expenses must be "ordinary and necessary" expenses for the business.[10] For example, a full deduction is permitted for a

---

[9] *See, e.g.*, I.R.C. §213 (medical expenses), §164 (taxes), §163 (interest), §170 (charitable contributions). For a more extensive listing of available itemized deductions, consult publications such as the *United States Master Tax Guide* (Commerce Clearing House, Inc.) or *Bender's Dictionary of 1040 Deductions* (Matthew Bender).

[10] I.R.C. §162.

"reasonable" allowance for compensation for services actually rendered.[11] Hence if Jones' clerk is her husband who does no work for her business, the $100,000 salary she pays to him may not be considered an ordinary and necessary expense and thus would not be fully deductible.

Capital expenditures, as distinguished from other business expenses, are amounts paid for items which have a useful life of more than one year. Rather than being deducted in full in the year they are paid, capital expenditures must be depreciated, or gradually deducted, over a number of years. Depreciation is permitted for property used in a trade or business that has a useful life of more than one year[12] and the depreciation deduction is intended to reflect the gradual decrease in value of such items. For example, if Jones pays $10,000 for a flashing neon sign for her store, she could not deduct the full amount of the sign's cost in the year she pays for it because the sign would be treated as having a useful life of more than one year. However, she could depreciate the sign and deduct approximately 20 percent of its cost ($2,000) in each of the next five years.[13]

Although Jones has some discretion as to how she will depreciate her capital expenditures, the fundamental decision of whether she currently expenses or gradually depreciates the cost of an item is dictated by the nature (i.e., its "useful life") of the item. As will be discussed in Section 11.2.1, substantially greater discretion is given to software developers, who can decide whether to expense or to depreciate software development costs, regardless of the useful life of the software.

---

[11] I.R.C. §162(a)(l); Treas. Reg. §1.162–7.

[12] I.R.C. §167(a); Treas. Reg. §1.167(a)-1.

[13] For assets acquired for business purposes, depreciation deductions are determined according to the Accelerated Cost Recovery System ("ACRS") prescribed by I.R.C. §168. ACRS classifies all depreciable property as either 3-year property, 5-year property, 10-year property, or 19-year property based on the nature of the asset and its useful life. The overwhelming majority of assets are considered 5-year property. Depending on the category of the property, a certain percentage of the property's cost can be deducted each year. See the tables in I.R.C. §168(b)(l) and Treasury Department News Release R-2890 (10/22/84). ACRS permits the cost of most assets to be deducted more rapidly than their actual useful lives, which, from a business standpoint, has been one of the most favorable aspects of the Economic Recovery Tax Act of 1981. The Reagan Proposal would replace ACRS with a "capital cost recovery system" that increases the amount of time over which an asset's cost is recovered. It should be noted that, as an alternative to depreciation, I.R.C. §179 permits taxpayers to deduct annually up to $5,000 of the cost of depreciable property purchased for use in a business. See explanation in Section 11.3.1 at note 65.

An important consequence of the current expensing or depreciation of business property is the mandatory reduction in the basis of the property.[14] Whenever an item is expensed or depreciated, its basis must be reduced by the allowable deductions. This reduction will affect the taxable gain or loss from the eventual sale of the item. For example, assume Nancy Jones owns her flashing neon sign for three full years, claims depreciation deductions of $2,000 in each year, and then sells the sign for $5,000 in the fourth year. Although she originally paid $10,000 for the sign, she will have a taxable gain of $1,000 from its sale, which is the $5,000 amount realized less the $4,000 "adjusted basis" for the sign (its $10,000 cost minus the three depreciation deductions of $2,000 each).[15]

11.1.4. Tax Credits

The federal income tax owed by a taxpayer is calculated as a percentage of his or her taxable income. However, in addition to the income tax, a taxpayer may have to pay additional taxes such as the minimum taxes[16] or the self-employment tax.[17] On the brighter side, Congress has decided that certain activities should be encouraged through tax credits. Tax credits are distinguished from tax deductions in that tax credits reduce the amount of taxes owed while tax deductions reduce the amount of income subject to tax; hence tax credits may be more valuable than tax deductions. Tax credits available to individuals include child care credits and political contribution credits.[18]

The most sought-after tax credit by business is the investment tax credit, which was created to encourage the purchase of business assets. The investment tax credit is equal to a percentage of the cost of tangible personal property that is used in a business,

---

[14] I.R.C. §1016.

[15] Although the sign would not be a capital asset because it was used in Jones' business (*see* Section 11.1.2 at n. 5), the gain from its sale would be eligible for capital gain treatment pursuant to I.R.C. §1231, which provides that the gain from a sale of depreciable assets used in a trade or business and held for more than six months will be treated as long-term capital gain. However, the depreciation recapture rules of I.R.C. §1245 may still require the gain to be taxed as ordinary income. *See* Section 11.3.2.

[16] I.R.C. §§55, 56.

[17] I.R.C. §1401.

[18] I.R.C. §§21-26.

and can be claimed in addition to allowable depreciation deductions.[19] If the Code requires the property to be depreciated over five years or more, the credit is 10 percent, while the credit is 6 percent if the property must be depreciated over a period of less than five years.[20] If Jones' flashing neon sign is to be depreciated over five years, she can claim an investment tax credit of 10 percent of its cost, or $1,000, in the year of its purchase.

The availability of the investment tax credit is generally not questioned for most depreciable assets, although its availability for computer software is the subject of considerable controversy.[21] Another tax credit relevant to software entrepreneurs is the research credit, which was a half-hearted attempt to encourage research, but which may be headed for extinction.[22]

11.1.5. The Taxpayer

Who will be required to pay the federal income tax owed by a business will depend on the type of entity chosen for the business. A business can be run as a sole proprietorship, a partnership, a corporation, or an "S" corporation, which is a hybrid form of a partnership and corporation. The federal tax laws generally do not require the use of one entity as opposed to another, and in fact, the choice of entity will be influenced by more than just its tax consequences. For example, the limited liability offered to shareholders of a corporation may justify the use of the corporate form rather than the simpler arrangement offered by a proprietorship. Nevertheless, the choice of which entity to use will definitely have tax consequences and it should not be made without some consideration of the tax effects. The following is a very brief comparison of some important tax characteristics of each of the entities.

---

[19] It should be noted that under I.R.C. §48(q) the depreciable basis of property eligible for an investment tax credit must be reduced by one-half of the investment credit. Alternatively, the investment credit can be reduced to either 8 or 4 percent depending on whether a 10 or 6 percent credit would ordinarily be allowed. Furthermore, under I.R.C. §47 part or all of the investment tax credit can be "recaptured" by the Internal Revenue Service ("IRS") in the event the depreciable property is sold before a specified period of time has passed. The Reagan Proposal would repeal the investment tax credit beginning in 1986.

[20] I.R.C. §§46(b)(1), 46(c)(7).

[21] See Section 11.3.1.

[22] See Section 11.2.5.

1. *Sole Proprietorship.* The income of a proprietorship is taxed directly to the proprietor, who reports the income on Schedule C of his or her IRS Form 1040. If allowable deductions of the proprietorship exceed its gross income, the resulting loss can be deducted from the proprietor's other income. The proprietorship must use the same taxable year as the proprietor.

2. *Partnerships.* Although the partnership files an annual tax return, it is not a taxpaying entity. Rather, the partners of the partnership are taxed on their proportionate shares of the partnership's income.[23] If the partnership has a loss, the partners may claim their proportionate shares of the loss as a deduction against their other income, subject to certain limitations.[24] Generally, the partnership's taxable year must be the same as the taxable year adopted by its principal partners.[25]

3. *Corporations.* Unlike the sole proprietorship or partnership, the corporation is treated as a separate taxpayer and its income is taxed at corporate tax rates. Distributions made to shareholders from a corporation's taxable net earnings may be considered dividends, which will also be included in the shareholder's taxable income. This potential double taxation of a corporation's earnings can be a trap for the unwary who select the corporate form, although it can be avoided through careful planning. Losses incurred by a corporation cannot be "passed through" to shareholders, although they can be used to offset prior or future income of the corporation as a "net operating loss."[26] Unlike proprietorships and partnerships, some corporations may be subject to the 50 percent personal holding company tax if they fail to distribute certain passive income to shareholders,[27] or to an accumulated earnings tax if they accumulate earn-

---

[23] I.R.C. §701.

[24] These limitations include the basis of a partner's partnership interest (I.R.C. §704(d)) and the amount of money or other property which the partner has "at risk" (I.R.C. §465).

[25] I.R.C. §706(b).

[26] I.R.C. §172.

[27] I.R.C. §§541-547. This tax may be a major concern for software licensors. *See* Section 11.4.3.

ings beyond those necessary for the reasonable needs of the business.[28] On the plus side, the corporation can adopt the taxable year of its choice without regard to the tax years chosen by its shareholders.[29]

4. *"S Corporation."* Certain corporations with 35 or fewer shareholders can elect to be treated as an "S corporation."[30] This election allows shareholders to be taxed on their proportionate shares of the corporation's income without a double taxation at the corporate level. Furthermore, losses of the corporation are passed down to the shareholders who can use their share of the loss as a deduction against their other income.[31] Prior restrictions on the type of income earned by an S corporation, such as royalties earned by software licensors, were significantly relaxed in 1982, and thus most software companies can elect to be taxed as S corporations.[32] S corporations are not subject to the personal holding company tax or the accumulated earnings tax.[33] An S corporation must use a taxable year which ends on December 31 unless a business purpose can be established for the use of a different year.[34]

11.2. FEDERAL TAX TREATMENT OF SOFTWARE DEVELOPMENT COSTS

The rules for determining the appropriate federal tax treatment of the costs of developing software were first specified by the Internal Revenue Service (IRS) in 1969. Prior to that time the IRS had devoted little attention to the software industry. However, on October 7, 1969, the IRS announced that the tax treatment of soft-

---

[28] I.R.C. §§531–37. *See* Section 11.4.3.

[29] I.R.C. §441.

[30] I.R.C. §1361.

[31] I.R.C. §1366-1368.

[32] Previously, corporations which received an excessive amount of passive income, such as royalties, could not be treated as an S corporation. In 1982, this rule was relaxed for most corporations. *But see* I.R.C. §§1362(d)(3), 1375.

[33] *See* I.R.C. §1363(a), which provides that S corporations will not be subject to taxes, including the personal holding company and accumulated earnings taxes.

[34] I.R.C. §1378; Rev. Proc. 83–25, 1983-1 C.B. 689.

ware development costs should follow the rules of Revenue Procedure 69–21.[35] Software was broadly defined in Revenue Procedure 69–21 as "all programs or routines used to cause a computer to perform a desired task or set of tasks, and the documentation required to describe and maintain those programs,"[36] which includes everything from operating systems to application programs.

11.2.1. Deduction or Amortization

In Revenue Procedure 69–21, the IRS concluded that the costs of developing software so closely resembled "research and experimental expenditures" that the special tax treatment accorded to that category of expenditures[37] should be extended to software development expenditures as well.[38] As a result, a software developer may treat the costs of developing software, for tax purposes, in one of two ways. The developer can treat the costs of developing software as a "current expense," which means that the costs may be deducted from the income of the business in the year in which the costs are incurred. Alternatively, the software developer can capitalize the development costs by ratably amortizing them over a period of five years beginning on the date the software development is completed.[39] Ratable amortization means that the costs are deducted on a "straight-line" basis, which generally provides for a constant amount of deductions over the recovery period, rather than by means of an accelerated method which provides for larger deductions in the initial years of recovery.

---

[35] Rev. Proc. 69–21 is reproduced in Section A.5. It should be noted that the vagueness and overbreadth of this Revenue Procedure can be attributed to the fact that it was published at a time when the software industry was just evolving from a poorly understood cottage industry.

[36] Rev. Proc. 69–21, 1969–2 C.B. 303 (Sec. 2). (Reproduced in Section A.5.)

[37] Under I.R.C. §174, research and experimental expenditures may be fully deducted in the year they were incurred or gradually amortized over five years. This is an exception to the general rule that prohibits the immediate deduction of the start-up costs of a business. I.R.C. §195(a).

[38] Rev. Proc. 69–21, 1969–2 C.B. 303 (Sec. 3). (Reproduced in Section A.5.)

[39] The deductions could be spread over a shorter period of time if the developer can establish that the software has a useful life which is less than five years.

Although the developer may choose either one of these alternatives for treating the costs of developing software, the developer must consistently apply the method chosen to all software development costs. Once an alternative has been selected, the election cannot be changed without the consent of the IRS.[40] Thus the developer does not have the option of deducting the cost of one software project as a current expense, while capitalizing and amortizing the cost of another project.

Most software developers elect to treat their development costs as current expenses. This will reduce their taxable income by the full amount of the expenditures incurred to create their software; in effect, the government subsidizes part of the cost of the development.[41] However, other developers prefer to capitalize their development costs for various reasons. In particular, some companies strive to report higher earnings to their shareholders, since higher earnings favorably reflect the company's recent performance and may trigger price increases for the company's stock. If all development costs are currently deducted, lower earnings would be reported in the year of deduction. For example, IBM's 1983 per-share earnings would have dropped from $9.04 to $8.60 if it did not capitalize its software development costs. The effect on small companies would be even more dramatic. Other developers choose the capitalization option because it permits them to list development costs as "assets" on their balance sheets, an item to which lenders look when deciding whether to make loans. For these reasons, the decision to expense or capitalize software development costs is one of the most important bottom-line issues for the growing software company.

Some developers seek to have the best of both worlds by maintaining two sets of books, one for their shareholders and lenders and one for the IRS. This practice has led accounting and securi-

---

[40] Rev. Proc. 69–21, 1969–2 C.B. 303 (Sec. 6.01) (Reproduced in Section A.5.); Rev. Rul. 71-248, 1971-1 C.B. 55 (IRS consent necessary when taxpayer wants to change to a different treatment of software development costs). *See also* the general rules for changing an accounting method in I.R.C. §§446(e) and 481 and Treas. Reg. §1.446-l(e)(2).

[41] Since the highest tax rate for corporations is 46 percent and for individuals is 50 percent, every deductible dollar can result in a tax saving of as much as 46¢ to 50¢.

ties officials to push for a standardized treatment of all software development costs for financial reporting purposes.[42]

11.2.2. Software Development Costs Defined

The IRS has not defined which costs are eligible to be treated as "costs of developing software." However, since the IRS has analogized software development costs to research and experimental expenditures in Revenue Procedure 69–21, it is appropriate to refer to the definition of the latter for guidance on what constitutes software development costs.[43] Based on this analogy, software development costs would include the costs of labor, nondepreciable materials, computer time, and other similar costs incurred by a business in the actual development of software, but would not include costs incurred for items that can be expected to last for more than one year, such as the cost of a computer (although depreciation deductions for such items would be included), or for routine inspections or nondevelopmental testing of the software product.

If a business utilizes the services of an outside firm for the

[42] In April 1983, the Securities and Exchange Commission (SEC) imposed a moratorium that prevented companies from capitalizing the costs of developing computer software if they had not previously done so. The SEC promised to lift the moratorium after the accounting industry provided guidance on the subject. On August 9, 1985, the Financial Accounting Standards Board (FASB) issued its Statement of Financial Accounting Standards No. 86, "Accounting for the Costs of Computer Software to be Sold, Leased, or Otherwise Marketed," effective for fiscal years beginning on or after December 15, 1985. The Standard requires costs incurred to purchase or develop software to be currently deducted until "technological feasibility" is established. Thereafter, all coding, testing, and other production costs must be capitalized. Technological feasibility is established when a detailed program design is completed, or in its absence, upon completion of a working model.

[43] See Treas. Reg. 1.174–2(a) which defines "research and experimental expenditures" to include "all costs incident to the development of an experimental or pilot model, a plant process, a product, a formula, an invention, or similar property, and the improvement of already existing property of the type mentioned" as well as the costs of obtaining certain patents. The definition excludes the costs of routine testing or inspection of materials and the cost of depreciable items which would be owned by the taxpayer. (See Treas. Reg. §1.174–2(b)(l).) However, the IRS proposed regulations in 1983 which stated that "generally, the costs of developing computer software are not research or experimental expenditures within the meaning of section 174." Proposed Treas. Reg. §1.174–2(a)(3). For a discussion of the controversy created by the proposal and the IRS response, see Section 11.2.3.

development of new software, the amounts paid to the outside firm may qualify as "software development costs." However, this tax treatment will be available only if the business for which the software is being developed (the "sponsor") bears the economic risk of development.[44] This means that the development contract must not contain any guarantees or warranties that the software will operate in a certain manner or produce specified results. It will not be enough for the sponsor to bear the risk that the software will be a commercial success. If the software fails to perform as desired, the sponsor, not the developer, must be the economic loser. However, this general rule should not prevent the contract from requiring the finished product to meet specifications unrelated to its economic success. Thus in one case the IRS concluded that the sponsor bore the "risk of the utility" of the software developed by a third party because it was responsible for all costs of correcting malfunctions in the program unless they were due to errors or omissions of the developer's employees.[45] If the sponsor of the software development project does not bear the appropriate risks, the sponsor will be treated as having purchased the software (assuming that the sponsor becomes the owner of the software after it is developed), and the software development costs must be treated in the same way as the cost of purchased software. This was the result reached in another case, which involved the conversion of existing computer programs to run on different hardware, pursuant to a fixed price contract. There the IRS concluded that the sponsor did not bear sufficient risks because neither the operational feasibility nor the cost of the software were in doubt at the time the contract was entered into, and because the developer was responsible for the expense of correcting all errors in the software, and would be required to pay a specified sum for every day the software was not delivered to the sponsor.[46]

To illustrate, assume Nancy Jones hires Computer Consultants, Inc. (CCI) to develop software which translates English into Japa-

---

[44] Under Treas. Reg. §1.174–2(b)(3) research and experimentation expenditures are deductible when paid to a third party contractor only if "made upon the taxpayer's order and at his risk." See generally Battaglia and Herskovitz, "Organizing a Computer Software Research and Development Program for Top Tax Advantage," 58 J. Tax'n. 92 (1983).

[45] IRS Private Letter Ruling No. 8136024 (5/27/81).

[46] IRS Private Letter Ruling No. 7804007 (10/12/77); see also Section 11.2.4.

nese. If the agreement between Jones and CCI provides that Jones does not have to pay unless the software developed by CCI has a 90 percent translation accuracy rate, Jones is probably not bearing the economic risk of development and her payment should be treated as the cost of purchased software. On the other hand, if the only conditions to Jones' obligation to pay are that the software be written in assembler and that CCI correct at its expense any malfunction due to errors of its employees, Jones would presumably bear the risk of development of the software and she should be able to treat her payment as a software development cost.

Although there is some question whether the sponsor bears sufficient risk in a contract for the development of software for which there is no doubt as to its eventual operability, it is likely that a contract for such software, in which the contractor is paid a flat fee to use its best efforts within a specified time frame, but without any guarantee of success, will suffice. Under such an arrangement the sponsor would bear the risk that the software can be developed within the time frame and for the costs specified in the contract.

11.2.3. IRS Challenges to Software Development

Recently, a more troublesome controversy has emerged regarding the level of novelty that must be present in order for costs to qualify as software development costs. In Revenue Procedure 69–21 the IRS permitted full deduction for development of software regardless of the uniqueness of the program. Within a short time after 1969, however, the IRS attempted to narrow the scope of this allowance by asserting that because most software development costs do not really resemble research and experimentation expenditures, they should be capitalized rather than currently deducted.[47] In 1983, the IRS proposed regulations which would

---

[47] The IRS contended that most software development costs were not experimental or investigative in a laboratory sense, and thus did not satisfy the requirements of research and experimental expenditures. Additionally, the IRS argued that the costs should be capitalized because of the expectation of benefits beyond the year in which the costs are incurred. *See* General Counsel Memorandum ("G.C.M.") 38618 (1/23/81); G.C.M. 36053 (10/9/74); G.C.M. 34681 (11/12/71).

have established a general rule that denies a current deduction for the costs of developing most computer software.[48] Under these proposed regulations, software development costs could be currently deducted only if the software is "new or significantly improved" and its operational feasibility is "seriously in doubt."[49]

The proposed regulations were met with intense criticism from software industry groups, lawyers, accountants, and numerous legislators. Many expressed bewilderment over the confusing description of when the operational feasibility of software would be considered seriously in doubt and feared that the proposal would foreclose almost all software development costs from the favorable tax treatment that had been available since 1969.

The IRS eventually responded to the outcry by announcing that the proposed regulations would not change the treatment of software development costs allowed under Revenue Procedure 69–21.[50] Thus software developers continue to be able to choose between the alternatives of currently deducting or capitalizing and amortizing their development costs. Nevertheless, it is clear that the IRS has set its sights on narrowing the generous advan-

---

[48] *See* Proposed Treas. Reg. §1.174–2(a)(3), which provides as follows:
Generally, the costs of developing computer software are not research or experimental expenditures within the meaning of section 174. However, the term "research or experimental expenditures," as used in section 174, includes the programming costs paid or incurred for new or significantly improved computer software. The term does not include costs paid or incurred for the development of software the operational feasibility of which is not seriously in doubt. The costs of modifying previously developed computer software programs, such as the costs of adapting an existing program to specific customer needs, or the costs of translating an existing program for use with other equipment, do not constitute research or experimental expenditures. Whether software is "new or significantly improved" will be determined with regard to the computer program itself rather than the end use of the program. For example, the costs of developing a program to perform economic analysis which involves only standard or well known programming techniques are not research or experimental expenditures even if the economic principles embodied in the program are novel. However, if the programming itself involves a significant risk that it cannot be written, the costs of developing the program are research or experimental expenditures regardless of whether the economic principles or formulas embodied in the program are novel.

[49] *See* Proposed Treas. Reg. §1.174–2(a)(3).

[50] *See* IRS Information Release 83–71 (4/19/83), which stated that "the method of accounting for computer software development costs established in 1969 will not be superseded by amendments to proposed regulations under Internal Revenue Code section 174, concerning research and experimental expenditures." *See also* General Counsel Memorandum 38996 (6/2/83), in which the IRS overruled prior rulings (cited in footnote 47) which required the capitalization of software development costs.

tages now available for software development costs. The first target of an IRS attack will likely be the costs of routine software development, such as in-house inventory control programs, which in the future will probably not be eligible for deduction as a current expense because of their lack of resemblance to research and experimental expenditures.

11.2.4. Research and Development Partnerships

Entrepreneurs seeking to enter the software development business are finding that they need more and more capital for research and development. Traditional lines of credit are usually unavailable to the fledgling developer. Thus many entrepreneurs have formed research and development partnerships ("R&D partnerships") to finance the development of software. R&D partnerships have provided needed capital for software developers and attractive tax incentives to investors. However, recent developments could considerably reduce the benefits of investing in R&D partnerships.

Although there is a wide range of possible financing arrangements involving R&D partnerships, most follow a similar pattern. The developer in need of capital contributes all of its rights to the software concept to a limited partnership, of which the developer or the developer's controlled corporation will serve as the general or managing partner. Investors contribute money to this partnership in exchange for limited partnership interests, which entitle the investors to a share of the partnership's profits and tax losses, but not of its management. The R&D partnership then enters into an agreement with a research company, which is often controlled by or related to the developer, to produce the software on behalf of and at the risk of the R&D partnership in exchange for the immediate payment of a fixed fee to the research company. The R&D partnership uses the investors' contributions to make this payment and claims a deduction for research and experimental expenditures which can be passed through to the investors. Other nonexclusive license agreements may have to be entered into to permit the R&D partnership to use previously developed technology or to allow the research company to produce and sell products based on the software technology.

The research company will typically be granted an option to purchase the rights to the finished software product from the partnership. The proceeds of such a sale could be eligible for treatment as long-term capital gains even if cast in the form of royalties.[51] If the software product is patentable, individual partners can claim long-term capital gain treatment regardless of the length of time the software was held prior to sale.[52] If the software is not patentable, long-term capital gains may still be available if the software qualifies as depreciable property held for use in the partnership's business.[53] Because investors believed they could deduct most of their contributions to the R&D partnership and could also receive advantageous tax treatment for any returns on their investment, the R&D partnership was viewed as not only a source of financing for developers, but also as an attractive tax-sheltered investment.

R&D partnerships have recently lost some of their lustre as a tax-favored investment. In March 1984, the IRS announced that any gain realized from the sale of patent rights and technical know-how developed as a result of deductible research work would not be eligible for capital gain tax treatment to the extent of prior research deductions.[54] Furthermore, the Tax Reform Act of 1984, enacted in July 1984, made a number of changes that will influence the structure of future R&D partnerships. The most significant is a new requirement that prepayments for services, such as that made by the R&D partnership to the research company, can no longer be deducted until the year in which the services are performed.[55] Under this new rule the R&D partnership could not claim a deduction for the full amount of payment made to the research company unless the work paid for had been completed within 90 days after the end of the year in which the payment was

---

[51] Rev. Rul. 60–226, 1960–1 C.B. 26.

[52] I.R.C. §1235; Treas. Reg. §§1.1235–1, 1.1235–2.

[53] I.R.C. §1231.

[54] *See* IRS Private Letter Ruling No. 8409009 (11/23/83); Note, however, that the IRS recently reversed this position. *See* Rev. Rul. 85–186.

[55] I.R.C. §461(i). An exception is provided for services which are performed within ninety days after the close of the taxable year in which the payment is made. I.R.C. §461(i)(2)(A).

made.[56] Finally, a recent Tax Court decision requiring R&D partnerships to be engaged in a trade or business may prevent their
use as a financing device.[57] Despite the repeated acknowledg-
ment by Congress of the need to encourage research efforts by our
nation's entrepreneurs, these changes threaten to reduce the tax-
attractiveness of R&D partnerships and to force entrepreneurs to
seek other sources of capital.

11.2.5. Research and Development Tax Credit

Beginning in 1981, businesses already engaged in software development were able to claim a 25 percent research and experimentation tax credit for research expenditures.[58] This credit was of
limited usefulness to start-up companies because Congress decided to restrict the availability of the credit to enterprises that
were actually engaged in a trade or business.[59] Although Congress
intended that some software development costs would qualify as
research expenditures eligible for the credit,[60] the IRS proposed
regulations which would have eliminated the credit for all software research expenditures other than those incurred to develop
new and improved software, the operational feasibility of which is
seriously in doubt.[61] The credit was scheduled to expire at the end
of 1985, and Congress passed up the chance to make the credit
permanent as part of the Tax Reform Act of 1984. Nonetheless,
there is a chance it will be continued.[62]

[56] Thus it may be necessary to restructure the arrangement between the R&D partnership and the company so that payments are made only for that portion of the work anticipated to be completed within 90 days after the close of the taxable year of the partnership.

[57] In *Green v. Commissioner*, 83 T.C. 667, 687 (1984), the Tax Court held that a research
and development partnership was not engaged in a trade or business but rather was only "a
vehicle for injecting risk capital into the development and commercialization of the inventions." Accordingly, the court held the R&D partnership was not entitled to deductions
under I.R.C. §174.

[58] I.R.C. §30 (formerly I.R.C. §44F).

[59] I.R.C. §30(b)(1).

[60] *See* H. Rep. No. 97-201, 97th Cong., 1st Sess. 114 (1981).

[61] Proposed Treas. Reg. §§1.44F-4(a), 1.174-2(a)(3).

[62] Two bills which would make this credit permanent (S.58 and H.R. 1188) were introduced in Congress in early 1985. Both would specifically extend the credit to software
research activities. Furthermore, the Reagan Proposal would retain the credit until the end
of 1988, but with an increased emphasis on expenditures that would result in "technological innovation."

11.3. FEDERAL TAX TREATMENT OF SOFTWARE PURCHASES AND SALES

The tax treatment of purchased software will be important in more situations than just the outright purchase of software for use in a business. As discussed in Section 11.2.2, the development costs of custom software for which the sponsor does not bear sufficient risk will be treated as a purchase. Also, as discussed in Section 11.4.2 a license or lease of software could be treated as a purchase. If a transfer of software is treated as a sale for tax purposes, the chief issues for the seller will be how much of the sales proceeds will be taxable and whether the taxable portion can be treated as a capital gain. For the buyer, the major issues are the amortization of the purchase price and the availability of the investment tax credit. This section examines the tax consequences of purchases and sales of software.

11.3.1. Purchase of Software—Bundled or Unbundled?

When software is purchased for use in a business, the IRS has contended that the tax consequences will depend upon whether or not the software was purchased as part of a "bundled" transaction. If the software is purchased in a "bundled" package that includes both software and hardware for a single price, and in which the price of the software is not separately stated, the IRS will treat the software as an integral part of the hardware.[63] This is favorable tax treatment for the software purchaser for three reasons. First, the purchase price of the software can be depreciated in the same manner as the hardware.[64] Subject to some special

---

[63] Rev. Proc. 69–21, 1969–2 C.B. 303 (Sec. 4.01(1)). (Reproduced in Section A.5.)

[64] Provided the bundled hardware and software are first used in the taxpayer's business after 1980, they would be depreciated according to the Accelerated Cost Recovery System ("ACRS") under I.R.C. §168. *See* Section 11.1.3. Usually, the bundled package will be treated as "5-year property" under ACRS; accordingly, under I.R.C. §168(b)(1) the following percentages of the purchase price of the package could be deducted by the purchaser:

Year	Recovery Percentage
1	15%
2	22
3	21
4	21
5	21

However, if the computer package is used in the development or improvement of a product

rules, depreciation will allow the purchaser to deduct the entire cost of the bundled package over five years. Second, because it will be considered part of the cost of the hardware, the cost of the software could be included as an amount eligible for the first-year expensing election.[65] Third, if the investment tax credit is available for the cost of the hardware, it will extend to the cost of the software as well.[66]

The following example illustrates the tax advantages of a "bundled" purchase. Assume ABC Computers pays $5,000 in 1986 for a microcomputer and compatible software for use exclusively in its business. If the software's price is not separately stated by the seller, ABC may claim for its first year of ownership of the computer an investment tax credit of $500 (10 percent of $5,000) and a depreciation deduction of $712.50.[67] Alternatively, ABC can take advantage of the first-year expensing election, which allows it to deduct up to $5,000 of the cost of business property purchased in any year.[68] In that case, if the computer and software are ABC's only business property purchased during 1986, ABC could elect

---

or invention, it could be considered "used in connection with research and experimentation;" accordingly, the package will be treated as "3-year property" under ACRS (I.R.C. §168(c)(2)(A)) which is depreciated according to the following percentages prescribed by I.R.C. §168(b)(1):

Year	Recovery Percentage
1	25%
2	38
3	37

The Reagan Proposal would replace ACRS with a less favorable "capital cost recovery system."

[65] Under I.R.C. §179 a taxpayer can annually elect to expense rather than to depreciate the cost of tangible depreciable property purchased for use in a business, up to a certain dollar amount. Through 1987, this option, known as the expensing election, is limited to $5,000, but will increase to $7,500 in 1988 and to $10,000 in 1990. I.R.C. §179(b)(1). The Reagan Proposal would set the expensing election permanently at $5,000. No investment credit is available for amounts for which the expensing election is made. I.R.C. §179(d)(9).

[66] See Rev. Rul. 71-177, 1971–1 C.B. 5. The investment credit will be ten percent of the cost of the package, unless it qualifies as three-year property, for which the credit is six percent. (See Section 11.1.4.)

[67] Assuming the microcomputer is five-year property under ACRS, the first-year's depreciation deduction would be 15 percent of the cost of the microcomputer. (See I.R.C. §168(b)(1).) However, I.R.C. §48(q) requires the depreciable basis of recovery property to be reduced by one-half of the investment credit. Accordingly, ABC's depreciation deduction for the first year of ownership of the computer is 15 percent of $4,750 ($5,000 original cost less $250, one-half of investment tax credit), or $712.50.

[68] I.R.C. §179. See footnote 65.

to deduct the entire $5,000 cost in 1986 rather than waiting five years to recover such cost.

The Tax Reform Act of 1984 attempts to curb the tax benefits for computers that are only partly used for business purposes. If the computer is used 50 percent or less for business purposes the investment credit and the first-year expensing deduction are not available and the depreciation deductions are curtailed.[69]

In today's software market, the bundled transaction has become very rare. Instead, most software is purchased in a transaction which is not connected with the hardware acquisition. Since 1969, if the software is purchased in a separate transaction or even if its price is stated separately from the price of any concurrently purchased hardware, the IRS requires the software to be treated as an intangible asset.[70] The IRS has never explained why the intangibility of software should depend on whether its price is stated separately from that of the hardware and the connection between the fortuitous manner in which software costs are stated and the difficult concept of tangibility is not at all logical. Because the unbundled software is treated as an intangible asset, it is not eligible for accelerated depreciation; instead, its cost is recovered by ratable amortization deductions over five years unless the purchaser can establish that the software has a shorter useful life.[71]

A much more critical consequence of the treatment of separately purchased software as an intangible asset is the loss of both the investment credit and the annual expensing election, which are only available for tangible assets.[72] The IRS contends that software is an intangible asset that does not qualify for the investment tax credit.[73] In a recent private ruling, the IRS held that a

[69] I.R.C. §280F(b).

[70] Rev. Proc. 69–21, 1969–2 C.B. 303 (Sec. 4.01(2)). (Reproduced in Section A.5.)

[71] *Id.* The ratable amortization required to recover the separately stated software purchase costs means that a straight-line method, rather than an accelerated method (such as ACRS), must be used to recover the cost of the software. Because as much as 20 percent of the cost of the software would be recovered annually under the ratable amortization rule, there is little if any disadvantage to this method of cost recovery when compared to the ACRS rates for five-year property (*see* I.R.C. §168(b)(1)). However, five-year ratable amortization will be much less desirable than the ACRS rates for assets used in connection with research, which can be depreciated as three-year property.

[72] The investment credit and the expensing election are only available for "section 38 property," which is defined in I.R.C. §48(a)(l) to include only tangible property.

[73] General Counsel Memorandum 38618 (1/23/81). It should be noted that the IRS may

computer video game master tape was an intangible asset ineligible for the investment credit because any profit derived from sales of the video game, and hence any real value, depended on the "audience or public appeal of the intangible video game" as opposed to the tangible tape on which the game is recorded.[74]

Although the IRS maintains that unbundled software is an intangible asset for federal tax purposes, federal courts have not decided the issue and, in fact, have leaned toward tangibility in analogous cases. For example, one court held that computer-generated tape recordings of seismic information were tangible property eligible for the investment tax credit.[75] This court concluded that the value of the intangible information recorded on the tapes could not be separated from the value of the tangible tapes because "[a]n investment in the data simply does not exist without recording of the data on tangible property."[76] Another court held that film negatives were eligible for the investment tax credit by analogizing the negative to a machine used in production, and noted that "[w]ithout this negative, no positive print would be available to plaintiff to carry out its everyday business."[77] Although these decisions support an argument that unbundled software should be treated as a tangible asset eligible for the investment tax credit and the expensing election, the issue is far from clear and will have to be resolved by Congress or by a definitive court decision. In the meantime, purchasers of unbundled software and their tax advisers must decide whether claiming the investment credit and the expensing election is worth possible IRS challenges.

11.3.2. Sale of Software

The tax rules applicable to a sale of software depend on the nature of the item being transferred. Generally, there are three ways in

---

be reconsidering this position. *See* Notice of Proposed Rulemaking, 49 Fed. Reg. 5940–41 (1984).

[74] IRS Private Letter Ruling No. 8408049 (11/23/83).

[75] *Texas Instruments, Inc. v. United States*, 551 F.2d 599 (5th Cir. 1977).

[76] *Id.* at 611.

[77] *Walt Disney Productions v. United States*, 327 F. Supp 189, 192 (C.D. Cal. 1971), *modified* 480 F.2d 66 (9th Cir. 1973), *cert. denied*, 415 U.S. 934 (1973).

which software can be sold:

1. The developer (or subsequent owner of all rights to the software) can sell individual copies, retaining the right to make and sell as many more copies as possible
2. The developer (or subsequent owner of all rights to the software) can sell all of its rights to the software (including its copyright and trade secret rights) in a one-time transaction, thereby forfeiting the right to make any more sales
3. A customer who has purchased a single copy of software from the developer can sell its copy to someone else

The tax consequences to the seller (i.e., whether the income from the sale will be ordinary income or capital gains) is different in each of these transactions.

In the first case, advantageous capital gains treatment is not available for the seller because the transactions do not qualify as sales for tax purposes. To qualify as a sale for tax purposes, all substantial rights in the software must be transferred.[78] A transaction will not qualify as a sale if the transferor retains its copyright and trade secret rights, places geographical, time or use restrictions on the transferee, or retains any other significant right in the software.[79] If the software is considered "trade secret" property, the transferee must also be given the right to prevent unauthorized disclosure for a "sale" to be present.[80] Thus the typical software marketing situation, in which the vendor sells or licenses only a copy and retains ownership of all copyright and trade secret rights, will not constitute a "sale" for tax purposes. Moreover, if the vendor is in the business of selling copies of software, that fact itself will also preclude the availability of capital gains treatment.[81]

The second case is more complex. There, a business which owns all rights to a software package and licenses or sells copies of it to its customers would probably be able to claim long-term

---

[78] This rule is based on I.R.C. §1235, which has been extended to transfers of nonpatented technology. *See Pickren v. United States*, 378 F.2d 595, 599 (5th Cir. 1967).

[79] Treas. Reg. §1.1235–2(b).

[80] *Graham v. United States*, 79–1 U.S. Tax Cases ¶9274, at 86,584 (N.D. Tex. 1979).

[81] I.R.C. §§1221(1), 1231(b)(1)(A) and 1231(b)(1)(B) preclude capital gain treatment for the sale of property held for resale to customers.

capital gains treatment for the sale of all rights to the package. However, such capital gains treatment is not available for copyrightable software when all rights are sold by the taxpayer whose personal efforts created the software.[82] This category includes individual creators and small companies whose shareholders created the software. It does not apply to larger corporations whose fully compensated employees created the software,[83] or to sales by someone other than the creator.[84] Alternatively, if the software is patentable, any seller, including an individual author, may be able to obtain capital gains upon a transfer of all substantial rights to the software.[85]

The third case is easy. The general tax principles governing all sales[86] may apply to the mere transfer of a copy of software from one customer to another, and capital gains treatment may apply.

Remember, however, that software must be held for at least six months to qualify for long-term capital gain treatment.[87] The six-month holding period begins when the software is ready for commercial use, which is that point at which the software can do what it was designed to do, has been debugged and tested, and is operable.[88] Unless the software is completely altered, updates should not affect the holding period.[89]

Even when capital gains tax treatment is available, not all of the taxable gain will be eligible for the capital gains exclusion. To the extent the gain is attributable to previous depreciation, amortization, or expense deductions, it will be "recaptured" as ordinary income.[90] Moreover, if an investment credit was claimed for the

[82] I.R.C. §§1221(3), 1231(b)(1)(C).

[83] Rev. Rul. 55–706, 1955–2 C.B. 300, superseded on other grounds by Rev. Rul. 62–141, 1962–2 C.B. 182.

[84] For example, if an individual software author sold all of his or her rights in the software to a publisher who later resold all of the rights to a third party, the sale by the publisher would qualify for capital gain treatment but the sale by the author would not.

[85] I.R.C. §1235.

[86] See Sections 11.1.1 and 11.1.2.

[87] I.R.C. §§1222(3), 1231(b)(1). But see I.R.C. §1235, which provides long-term capital gains for holders of patents regardless of the holding period.

[88] Myers v. Commissioner, 6 T.C. 258 (1946); Treas. Reg. §1.1235–2(e).

[89] Computer Sciences Corp. v. Commissioner, 63 T.C. 327, 353 (1974).

[90] I.R.C. §1245. It is also conceivable that the IRS position requiring §174 deductions to be recaptured as ordinary income upon the sale of the developed product could be extended to software development. See Private Letter Ruling No. 8409009, discussed in Section 11.2.4.

software and the software is sold before a certain period of time has elapsed, some of the investment credit may be recaptured as well.[91]

To illustrate these problems, assume that ABC Computer purchased software for $2,000 on January 1, 1983 and sold it for $1,500 on January 1, 1985. Assume ABC took an aggressive tax position and treated the software as tangible five-year property and claimed a $200 investment credit and $700 in depreciation deductions. ABC will have a taxable gain of $300, which is the difference between its sale price ($1,500) and the adjusted tax basis of the software ($1,200).[92] Although this gain would ordinarily be eligible for capital gains treatment, all of it is attributable to prior depreciation deductions and must be "recaptured" as ordinary income. Moreover, 60 percent of the $200 investment credit, or $120, will also be recaptured as additional tax because, for investment tax credit purposes, the software was prematurely sold.[93]

11.4. FEDERAL TAX TREATMENT OF SOFTWARE LICENSE FEES

Most software is licensed rather than sold. The IRS treats these two types of transactions differently in many cases, both for the vendor and the customer.

11.4.1. Tax Consequences of License Payments

The tax treatment of the cost of licensing software is similar to the tax treatment of the cost of renting equipment. Accordingly, the licensee may deduct its license payments as a current expense in the year in which they are paid.[94] For example, in an arrangement where a software distributor licenses the right to market someone

---

[91] I.R.C. §47.

[92] The adjustments to ABC's original basis of $2,000 are attributable to the $700 in depreciation deductions and one-half of the $200 investment credit.

[93] I.R.C. §47(a)(5)(B).

[94] Rev. Proc. 69–21, 1969–2 C.B. 303 (Sec. 5); Treas. Reg. §1.62-11.

else's software in exchange for royalty payments, the royalty payments should be deductible in the year in which they are made.[95] On the other hand, it is not clear whether a full deduction in the year of payment will be allowed for a one-time fee paid for a perpetual software license. By analogy to the equipment leasing context, a one-time up-front advance payment would have to be capitalized and gradually deducted over the useful life of the software. However, in one case deciding the issue with respect to software, a court permitted a bank to currently deduct a one-time license fee which it paid for the perpetual use of certain credit card software.[96]

11.4.2. License or Sale?

Normally, if a software transaction is structured as a license, the licensor (vendor) of the software will continue to be considered its owner, and hence will be entitled to take depreciation or amortization deductions and will not be subject to investment tax credit recapture. In addition, the licensee will be entitled to deduct its license fee payments as current expenses. However, if the license provides for a transfer to the purported licensee of all substantial rights in the software (i.e., not just rights to a single copy), and such license is for a perpetual term, the license could be treated as a sale for tax purposes by the IRS.[97] If this occurs, the user (licensee) will be deemed the owner of the software for tax purposes and its license payments may not be fully deductible as a current expense but will be treated as installments of the "purchase price," which can be recovered gradually through depreciation or amortization deductions.[98] Further, the vendor (licensor) will not only be unable to claim further depreciation deductions for the licensed software, but it will also be forced to recognize taxable gain or loss from the transaction. These tax consequences will usually not be a concern in most licenses, however, since the vendor rarely tansfers all of its rights to the software involved in the transaction.

[95] *Leisure Dynamics, Inc. v. Commissioner*, 494 F.2d 1340, 1346–47 (8th Cir. 1974).
[96] *First Sec. Bank of Idaho v. Commissioner*, 592 F.2d 1050 (9th Cir. 1979).
[97] *See* Section 11.3.2.
[98] Rev. Rul. 72–408, 1972–2 C.B. 86.

11.4.3. Personal Holding Company Tax Trap

Software companies in which more than 50 percent of the stock is held by five or fewer individuals and which derive most of their income from software license fees may be subject to the personal holding company tax.[99] The personal holding company tax was originally enacted at a time when corporations were taxed at a much lower rate than individuals, in order to prevent small groups of investors from using corporations to receive their passive investment income. This tax, which is assessed in addition to the regular income tax, is 50 percent of the company's undistributed "personal holding company income," which generally includes various types of "passive income," such as rents and royalties.[100]

In a recent private letter ruling, the IRS applied the personal holding company tax to a small company engaged in developing, marketing, maintaining, and distributing software products.[101] The company derived most of its income from a one-time license fee paid by new customers for the nonexclusive, perpetual right to use its software products and from annual maintenance fees paid by existing customers for updates to the software. The IRS ruled that this income was subject to the personal holding company tax because it fell within the definition of royalties; that is, amounts received for the privilege of using secret processes and formulas and other like property.[102] The IRS rejected the company's argument that its income should not be considered passive income subject to the personal holding company tax because it was derived from an active, ongoing business. Unfortunately, the ruling does not even consider characterizing the company's income as something other than royalties. For example, the license fees could arguably have been treated as sales income since customers obtained the perpetual use of the software for a fixed fee while the maintenance fees could have been considered service income.

Careful tax planning will be necessary to avoid or at least to minimize a software company's exposure to this tax trap. For ex-

---

[99] I.R.C. §542(a).
[100] I.R.C. §§541, 543(a).
[101] Private Letter Ruling No. 8450025.
[102] Treas. Reg. §1.543–1(b)(3).

ample, the personal holding company tax will not apply to an S corporation,[103] which may be an important reason for making the election to be taxed as an S corporation. The distribution of sufficient dividends to shareholders will limit or eliminate the tax for corporations which do not make the S election. Corporations creating software products through the efforts of employees who are not shareholders may also be able to take advantage of the limited exception for copyright royalties.[104] If license fees for the right to use copyrighted software constitute more than half of a company's income, such income will not be considered personal holding company income if (a) other personal holding company income is 10 percent or less of gross income, and (b) the ordinary business expenses are at least 25 percent of net royalties. Although this exception appears to apply to many software companies, it would not cover software royalties for products even partly created by holders of 10 percent or more of the corporation's stock. Strategies such as these may not be necessary, however, if legislation presently pending in Congress succeeds in carving out an exception for active businesses receiving software royalties.

11.5. INTRODUCTION TO STATE TAXES ON SOFTWARE TRANSACTIONS

Software businesses can be subject to a variety of taxes imposed by the individual states. The most common concern for software vendors is the applicability of a state's sales and use taxes to their transactions. If applicable, these taxes are imposed on each software transaction rather than on the annual income of the business. The different states have applied their sales and use taxes to software transactions in a wide variety of ways, which has led to considerable confusion for vendors.

Some states also levy personal property tax on software located within the state. Usually this tax will be imposed on software only if the state law treats it as tangible property.

---

[103] I.R.C. §1363(a).
[104] I.R.C. §543(a)(4).

11.6.   STATE SALES AND USE TAXES

A sales tax is imposed directly on a retail sale of tangible property. It is usually a percentage of the "gross receipts" derived from the sale. Under most sales tax statutes the tax is imposed upon the seller for the privilege of selling tangible personal property within the state, although the retailer is usually permitted or required to pass the tax on to the buyer. Nevertheless, the retailer is usually responsible for collecting the tax and paying it to the state. Retailers should be aware that not only the state, but also the local municipality or county may levy a sales tax on transactions that occur within their boundaries.

In most states that have sales taxes the tax applies not only to sales of tangible personal property, but also to the rental or leasing of such property. These states extend their taxes to leases and licenses by defining the "retail sale" to include leases and rentals,[105] or by imposing the sales tax on rental receipts,[106] or by instituting a separate leasing tax.[107] It should be noted that the sales tax is intended to tax each article only once; hence, sales for resale are usually exempt.

Use taxes are imposed on the use, storage, or consumption of tangible personal property within a state. These taxes are generally equal to the sales taxes and are designed to apply to sales transactions which fall outside the scope of the sales tax. Use taxes are imposed only on tangible personal property which has not been subject to a sales tax because, for example, it was purchased in State A by someone in State B for use in State B. Usually in computing the use tax due a credit is allowed for sales taxes paid to the state in which the purchase or lease occurred. Furthermore, the sale or lease for resale or re-lease will usually be exempt from the use tax, just as it is from the sales tax. In analyzing the applicability of sales taxes and uses taxes to software, they may be generally treated as identical. That is, if the sales tax would apply to the sale or licensing of software within the state, then the use tax would also apply to the software obtained from a vendor outside of the state.

---

[105] *See, e.g.,* Ark. Stat. Ann. §84-1902(c).
[106] *See, e.g.,* Idaho Code §63–3612(a), (d), (h).
[107] *See, e.g.,* Ala. Code §40–12–222.

11.6.1. Software as Tangible or Intangible

State laws determining the applicability of sales and use taxes to computer software generally fall into one of three categories: (1) a minority of states impose no tax whatsoever on any transaction involving software;[108] (2) a somewhat larger minority of states impose sales and use taxes on all forms of computer software;[109] and (3) the vast majority of states distinguish between pre-written, or "canned," software and "custom" software. In these states, canned software is subject to sales and use taxes as tangible property, whereas custom software is generally considered an incidental part of the programming services which are not taxable.

In many states, the question of whether the sale or license of software is a transaction subject to sales or use tax turns on whether the courts of the state consider the software to be "tangible" or "intangible". Generally, if the courts consider software to be tangible property it will be subject to the tax, whereas if it is considered to be intangible it will not be subject to the tax. Thus, contrary to federal tax law in which most tax benefits are available for tangible property, the state tax laws provide the most favorable treatment for intangible property. Unfortunately, the states have not adopted consistent standards for the imposition of sales and use taxes on software, or even for the determination of whether software is tangible property. For that reason, the software vendor is well advised to seek professional assistance in determining the applicability of a particular state's sales and use taxes to its products.

In determining whether computer software is tangible or intangible, and hence subject to sales and use taxes, state courts have relied on a variety of theories to support their conclusions. The most favorable theory for the taxpayer is the "essence of the transaction" concept, in which the courts look to the object of the taxpayer's purchase and determine whether it was a tangible or

---

[108] This category includes those states which do not impose a sales tax at all (Alaska, New Hampshire, Oregon, Montana), and those states which exempt all software from sales and use taxation, such as Illinois (86 Ill. Adm. Code §130.1935), and Louisiana (La. Sales Tax Law & Regulations, Art. 47:301(16)).

[109] States in this category include Arkansas (House Bill 51 (Nov. 3, 1983)), Kansas (Kan. Stat. Ann. §79–3603(s)), and Tennessee (Tenn. Code Ann. §67–6–102(14)(B)).

intangible item. Frequently, courts using this theory conclude that the object of a software purchase is not the tangible transporting media but the intangible knowledge contained therein.[110] However, other state courts have rejected the "essence" test and applied a "container" theory which maintains that the intangible computer programs are inseparable from their transporting media, or container, and hence the software should be treated as a tangible item subject to tax.[111] In states which rely on this theory, it may be possible to use electronic transfers of software by means of phone lines to avoid sales tax although the necessity for transferring tangible documentation to the customer may hinder this attempt.

11.6.2. Software as Custom or Canned

In many states the question of whether a software transaction will be taxed is defined by statute or regulation, and turns on whether the software involved is canned or custom software. The distinction between canned and custom software, however, is not easily made. Although the general definitions vary widely from state to state, custom software is most often defined as software prepared specially to meet the needs of one user,[112] or as software prepared to the special order of the customer.[113] By contrast, "standard," "prewritten" or "canned" software is generally defined by the states as software "not written specifically for one user,"[114] or as software "prepared, held, or existing for general or repeated use."[115] In most of these states custom software is not subject to sales or use taxes because the custom software is interpreted to be essentially services rather than property.[116] On the other hand,

---

[110] *See, e.g., State of Alabama v. Central Computer Services, Inc.*, 349 So.2d 1160 (Ala. 1977); *Janesville Data Center, Inc. v. Wisconsin Dept. of Revenue*, 267 N.W.2d 656 (Wis. 1978); *First National Bank of Fort Worth v. Bullock*, 584 S.W.2d 548 (Tex. Civ. App. 1979); *First National Bank of Springfield v. Illinois Department of Revenue*, 421 N.E.2d 175 (Ill. 1981); *James v. Tres Computer Systems, Inc.* 642 S.W.2d 347 (Mo. 1982).

[111] *See, e.g., Comptroller of the Treasury v. Equitable Trust Co.*, 464 A.2d 248 (Md. 1983); *Chittenden Trust Co. v. Commissioner*, 465 A.2d 1100 (Vt. 1983).

[112] *See, e.g.*, Mass. Sales & Use Tax Regulations 64H.06(6)(c).

[113] *See, e.g.*, Cal. Rev. & Tax Code §6010.9(d).

[114] *See, e.g.*, New York Tech. Serv. Bulletin 1978–1(S).

[115] *See, e.g.*, Cal. Sales & Use Tax Regulations 1502(f)(l).

[116] *See, e.g., Maccabees Mutual Life Insurance Co. v. Dept. of Treasury*, 332 N.W.2d 561 (Mich. App. 1983).

canned software is analogized to prerecorded records or tapes and is therefore taxable.[117] Software which was originally developed for in-house use (and thus would presumably be custom software) will be considered canned or prewritten software subject to tax if it is subsequently held or offered for sale or lease.[118]

A significant area of controversy relates to the sale or lease of canned software which must be modified in order to meet the requirements of a particular customer. Most states have specific rules dealing with this situation, but the rules are not at all uniform. In some states, for example, canned software is always subject to the tax, regardless of whether any modifications must be made to meet customer requirements.[119] In other states, any modification to a canned software package will render it nontaxable.[120] Many states, however, impose certain requirements before a modification to a canned software package will render software nontaxable. In New Jersey and New York, for example, modifications render software nontaxable if the software requires adaptations by the vendor in order to be used in a specific environment, that is, a particular make and model of computer utilizing a specified output device.[121] In Nebraska modifications render the software nontaxable if they are required to complete software otherwise unusable by the customer, or if they materially change the operation of the software.[122] In Maryland any modification of ten percent or more of the software will render the transaction nontaxable, whereas in Missouri, only when the charges for a modified program exceed those for an unmodified program by 100 percent will the modified program be exempt.[123]

Some other states have found the medium by which the software is transferred to be significant for purposes of the sales and use taxes. In most of these states canned software is considered tangible property subject to tax regardless of the medium used. However, custom software transferred to the customer by means

---

[117] *See Comptroller of the Treasury v. Equitable Trust Co.,* 464 A.2d 248 (Md. 1983).
[118] *See, e.g.,* Cal. Rev. & Tax Code §6010.9(d).
[119] *See, e.g.,* Iowa Admin. Code, Rule 730-18.34(2)(c); Indiana Sales Tax Division Information Bulletin #8 (5/23/83).
[120] *See, e.g.,* Fla. Admin. Code §12A–1.32(4).
[121] *See* N.Y. Tech. Services Bureau Bulletin 1978–1(S); N.J. Adm. Code 18:24–25.2(b).
[122] Neb. Rev. Stat. §77–2702(23).
[123] 12 Mo. CSR 10–3.588(6).

of machine-readable media such as disk, tape, or punched cards will also be treated by these states as tangible property subject to tax. But if the custom software is transferred in the form of written procedures, such as program instructions transferred on coding sheets, the software will be exempt from tax.[124] In these states as well as any other state which relies on the tangible/intangible distinction, an argument against imposition of the tax will be strengthened by an invoice to the software customers which separates charges for services such as programming and consultation from charges for tangible items such as cards or tapes.

The analysis above is only intended to provide an idea of the variety of ways the states have applied their sales and use taxes to computer software. For software vendors involved in the sale or license of software in a variety of states, it would be wise to consult various compilations of state tax laws and regulations affecting software.[125] However, because of the rapid changes in these laws, vendors should consult with local tax counsel to determine the current status of the local sales and use taxes.

11.7. STATE PROPERTY TAXES

Some states impose an annual personal property tax on the owner of tangible personal property located in the jurisdiction on a specified tax or lien day. The tax is a percentage of the current value of the property and can be as much as seven percent of such value.

The applicability of property taxes to computer software once again depends on whether the state interprets software to be tangible property. Many of the courts which have considered the question have held that software should be treated as intangible property which is not subject to the property tax.[126] At least one

---

[124] Wisconsin Technical Information Memorandum S–38.4(III)(D) (8/7/78); Rhode Island Sales & Use Tax Reg. Regarding Computers and Related Systems; Iowa Admin. Code, Rule 730–18.34(3)(a).

[125] *See, e.g., ADAPSO Sales and Use Tax Survey,* published by Association of Data Processing Service Organizations, Inc., 1300 N. Seventeenth Street, Arlington, Va; and *State Computer Tax Report,* published by Bigelow & Saltzberg, 100 Tower Office Park, Suite L, Woburn, Ma.

[126] *See, e.g., District of Columbia* v. *Universal Computer Associates, Inc.,* 465 F.2d 615 (D.C. Cir. 1972).

court, however, ruled that the property tax could be applied to the tangible media in which the software is contained (i.e., the tape or disk), even though such items would probably have a far smaller value than the intangible software services.[127] Where software is bundled with hardware and the unit is sold for a single price, the property tax will generally not be assessed against the value of the intangible software services.[128]

Since 1972 California has adopted a different approach to the property taxation of software. All software other than "basic operational programs" are exempt from the California property tax.[129] The California statute presumes that any program which is bundled with the hardware is a basic operational program subject to the property tax unless the software can be purchased or leased separately. Basic operational programs are defined to include operating systems, assemblers, compilers, and utility programs, that is, those items which are fundamental and necessary to the functioning of the computer.[130]

[127] *Greyhound Computer Corp. v. State Dept. of Assessment & Taxation*, 320 A.2d 52 (Md. 1974).

[128] *Honeywell Information Systems v. Maricopa County*, 575 P.2d 801 (Ariz. Ct. App. 1977).

[129] Cal. Rev. & Tax. Code §§995–995.2.

[130] Cal. Prop. Tax Rules & Regs. No. 152 (1972).

CHAPTER TWELVE

SOFTWARE AND THE CRIMINAL LAW

As society becomes increasingly dependent upon the computer, the opportunities for computer crime will expand accordingly. So-called computer crime can include almost any sort of activity directed against, or involving the use of, a computer system. This chapter will examine the current state of the criminal law as it relates to illegal activities involving software. Software-related computer crime can be divided into three general areas: theft of software; unauthorized use, modification, or destruction of software; and the use of software for illegal or fraudulent purposes.

These software-related criminal activities can generally be prosecuted in one of three ways at the state level:

1. As a violation of the state's theft statute;

2. As a violation of the state's trade secret statute (if one exists); or

3. As a violation of the state's computer crime statute (if one exists).

Some software-related criminal activity may also be prosecuted under federal criminal statutes governing copyright infringement, wire fraud, mail fraud, interstate transportation of stolen property, and receipt of stolen property moving in interstate commerce. A federal computer crime statute also exists, but its coverage is limited to computers owned by the federal government and to specified classes of information.

The most important vehicles for prosecuting computer crime, however, are the computer crime statutes. Such statutes are relatively new at both the state and federal level, although they have been enacted in some form in over 30 states as well as by the federal government.[1] These statutes are designed to fill the gap left by theft and trade secret statutes, which in many cases simply do not cover all of the various types of computer crime. They deal specifically with criminal acts involving computers, computer networks, computer systems, computer software, and data stored within computer systems. This chapter will examine only the portions of those statutes that identify criminal activity relating to computer software, although in most cases, the same activities are prohibited with respect to all of the other items listed as well. Because of the rapidly changing nature of the law in this area, it is virtually impossible to present a comprehensive summary of all of

---

[1] 18 U.S.C. §§1029, 1030; Ariz. Rev. Stat. Ann. §§13–2301E, 13–2316; Cal. Penal Code §502; Colo. Rev. Stat. §§18–5.5-101 and 102; Conn. Pub. Act No. 84–206, 1984; Del. Code Ann. tit. 11, §858; Fla. Stat. Ann. §§815.01–815.07; Ga. Code Ann. §16–9-90 through 16–9-94; Haw. Rev. Stat. §708; Idaho Code §§18–2201, 18–2202; Ill. Rev. Stat. ch. 38, §§15–1, 16–9; Iowa Code §§716A.1, .2, .3 and .9; Ky. Rev. Stat. §§434.840—834.860; Md. Ann. Code art. 27, §146; Mich. Stat. Ann. §§28.529, M.C.L.A §§752.791–797; Minn. Stat. §§609.87 through .89; Mo. Rev. Stat. §§569.093 through .097; Mont. Rev. Code Ann. §§45-2-101, 45-6-310, 45–6-311; Nev. Rev. Stat. §§205.473 through .477; N.M. Stat. Ann. §§30–16A; N.C. Gen. Stat. §§14.453 through .457; N.D. Cent. Code §12.1–06.1-08; Okla. Stat. Ann. tit. 21, §§1951 through 1956; Pa. Cons. Stat. Ann. §3933; R.I. Gen. Laws §§11–52-2, 3 and 4; S.C. Code Ann. §§ 16–16-10 and 16–16-20; S.D. Codified Laws Ann. §43–43B; Tenn. Code Ann. §39–3-1401 through 1406; Utah Code Ann. §§76–6-701 through 704; Va. Code §§18.2–152.1 through .14; Wash. Rev. Code §9A.52; Wis. Stat. Ann. §943.70; Wyo. Stat. §§6–3-501 through 505.

these computer crime statutes. Moreover, the laws in each state are different, and it is thus dangerous to make assumptions about the legality or illegality of particular conduct without consulting the statute of the state involved. Consequently, the discussion that follows represents an attempt to generalize about the computer crime laws which have been passed to date.

State computer crime statutes generally follow a similar pattern, although each one contains somewhat different language and definitions. The computer crime statute of Idaho is typical and reads as follows:[2]

> (1) Any person who knowingly accesses, attempts to access or uses, or attempts to use any computer, computer system, computer network, or any part thereof for the purpose of: devising or executing any scheme or artifice to defraud; obtaining money, property, or services by means of false or fraudulent pretenses, representations, or promises; or committing theft, commits computer crime.

> (2) Any person who knowingly and without authorization alters, damages, or destroys any computer, computer system, or computer network described in section 18-2201, Idaho Code, or any computer software, program, documentation, or data contained in such computer, computer system, or computer network commits computer crime.

> (3) Any person who knowingly and without authorization uses, accesses, or attempts to access any computer, computer system, or computer network described in section 18-2201, Idaho Code, or any computer software, program, documentation, or data contained in such computer, computer system, or computer network, commits computer crime.

This chapter will examine the application of these statutes to the three areas of software crime described above.

12.1. THEFT OF SOFTWARE

Probably the most common form of software-related computer crime is the theft of software. It can occur in one of two ways.

---

[2] Idaho Code §18–2202.

First, someone can physically steal the media on which the software resides, such as paper listings, disks, diskettes, or tapes containing software. Second, software can be stolen electronically (i.e., copied). For example, software can be electronically copied from one disk to another either on the same computer or to a remote computer over cable or phone lines. With the first form of theft, the original copy of the software is taken from the owner, who is permanently deprived of its possession and use. In the second case, the original copy of the software remains with the owner and, in fact, the owner may not even be aware that a theft has occurred. Although both cases represent theft of software, they may be treated very differently under the laws of the various states.

Surprisingly, the computer crime statutes in only a few states specifically make theft of software a crime.[3] Included in this group are the states of Florida, Iowa, Minnesota, Missouri, Nevada, Oklahoma, Rhode Island, Wisconsin, and Wyoming.[4] Some of these statutes appear to prohibit both the theft of the media containing software as well as unauthorized copying. For example, a section of the Florida computer crime statute[5] provides that:

> Whoever willfully, knowingly, and without authorization discloses or takes data, programs or supporting documentation which is a trade secret as defined in Section 812.081 or is confidential as provided by law residing or existing internal or external to a computer, computer system, or computer network commits an offense against intellectual property.

Because this statute refers to software that resides either within or outside of a computer, it appears to cover both theft of the media containing the software as well as unauthorized copying. Such theft is a felony in Florida. The computer theft statutes in Mis-

---

[3] As discussed in Section 12.2, most of the computer crime statutes cover unauthorized access, modification, or destruction of software. Theft of software may also be covered under the general provisions of other state statutes.

[4] Fla. Stat. Ann. §815.04; Iowa Code §716A.9; Minn. Stat. §609.89; Mo. Rev. Stat. §569.095; Nev. Rev. Stat. §205.4765; Okla. Stat. Ann. tit. 21, §1953; R.I. Gen. Laws, §11-52-4; Wis. Stat. Ann. §943.70(2); and Wyo. Stat. §6-3-502.

[5] Fla. Stat. Ann. §815.04(3).

souri, Nevada, and Wyoming also appear to cover both types of software theft.

In Iowa and Rhode Island, by contrast, the computer theft statutes appear to be limited to theft of the physical media containing software and do not cover copying, although it is not entirely clear. The Rhode Island statute,[6] for example, states that:

> Whoever, intentionally and without claim of right, and with intent to permanently deprive the owner of possession, takes, transfers, conceals or retains possession of any computer, computer system, computer network, computer software, computer program or data contained in such computer, computer system, computer program or computer network with a value in excess of $500.00 shall be guilty of a felony and shall be subject to the penalties set forth in Section 11-52–5.

Note that one commits a crime under this statute only if the software is taken "with intent to permanently deprive the owner of possession." It can certainly be argued that, under this statute, making a copy of the software (which would not deprive the owner of the possession of his or her original copy) is not a crime. (The Iowa statute is similar.) This is an issue which will have to be resolved in the courts.

The Minnesota computer statute appears to take yet another approach, and prohibits electronic copying, but not taking the physical media.[7] It provides that anyone who

> Intentionally and without claim of right, and with intent to permanently deprive the owner of possession, takes, transfers, conceals or retains possession of any computer, computer system or any computer software or data contained in a computer, computer system or computer network, . . . is guilty of computer theft.

In Minnesota violation of this provision is a crime punishable by up to ten years in prison and a $50,000 fine. Note that because the word "or" comes before the words "any computer software" this statute appears to cover theft of software and data *only* if it is

---

[6] R.I. Gen. Laws §11–52–4.
[7] Minn. Stat. §609.89.

"contained in a computer." Thus, it would seem to cover electronic copying of software resident in a computer, but not the physical taking of a disk or tape. Moreover, a person accused under this statute could also argue that, because he or she merely made a copy of software contained in a computer, he or she could not have intended permanently to deprive the owner of possession. However, this statute would probably cover a situation in which software was taken and the original copy erased from the system. These are issues that will have to be sorted out by the courts and merely illustrate some of the problems that legislators have in trying to deal with computer technology.

Finally, it is worth pointing out that the issue does not arise under the statutes in Oklahoma and Wisconsin. In Wisconsin, for example, the statute[8] simply makes it a crime if someone:

> . . . [w]illfully, knowingly and without authorization . . . takes possession of data, computer programs or supporting documentation.

The statute contains nothing to suggest that it is limited to either theft of media or electronic copying, and thus presumably covers both situations.

The computer crime statutes in most of the states[9] do not utilize the words "copy" or "take" to describe a crime involving computer software. Thus they do not cover theft of software, either by a physical taking or electronic copying. In these states, as well as in the states that have no computer crime statutes at all, it is necessary to look to the more traditional criminal statutes, such as those dealing with theft or larceny, to determine whether such a taking of software constitutes a crime.

When theft occurs by removal of the physical media on which the software is located, the theft can be prosecuted under the standard larceny statutes in most states. That is, it can be treated the same as the theft of any other physical item. In one case, for example, a Texas Instruments employee photocopied 59 of TI's

---

[8] Wis. Stat. §943.70(2).

[9] Arizona, California, Delaware, Georgia, Hawaii, Kentucky, Maryland, Michigan, New Mexico, North Carolina, North Dakota, Pennsylvania, South Carolina, Tennessee, Utah and Virginia.

computer programs and attempted to sell them to Texaco, one of TI's clients, for $5 million. He was indicted and convicted under the Texas felony theft law, and sentenced to five years in prison.[10]

A problem arises in some states, however, in determining whether the theft is a misdemeanor or a felony. Generally, state larceny statutes will make this determination on the basis of the value of the item taken. This raises a question. If the software is stolen by the removal of a floppy disk, is the item taken considered to be the floppy disk, which has a relatively low cost, or is it considered to be the software residing on that disk, which may have a much more significant value? If the value of the item taken is considered to be the cost of the diskette, then the theft may be considered nothing more than a misdemeanor. However, if that disk contains software worth a significant amount of money, and the theft is analyzed on the basis of the value of the software, then a felony may have occurred. The states do not treat this problem uniformly.

The TI employee who stole 59 programs, for example, argued that at most he stole $35 worth of paper. The court rejected this argument, however, and held that the value of the items taken was the value of the software, rather than the relatively minor value of the paper on which the source code was printed.[11] However, in another case a court reached a different conclusion, holding that computer printouts obtained by the defendant had no more value than scrap paper. Under the circumstances the defendant could not be convicted of grand larceny for his unauthorized use of the computer, since it required proof that he took something valued at $100 or more.[12]

When the theft of software is not accomplished by removal of the physical media on which the software is located, but rather through electronic copying, state theft statutes may not cover the crime at all. In one California case, for example, an employee of a

---

[10] *Hancock v. State*, 402 S.W.2d 906, 1 Computer L. Serv. Rep. 562 (Crim. App. Tex. 1966); *aff'd*, *Hancock v. Decker*, 379 F.2d 552, 1 Computer L. Serv. Rep. 858 (5th Cir. 1967).

[11] *Id.*

[12] *Lund v. Commonwealth of Virginia*, 7 Computer L. Serv. Rep. 1581, 1585–86, 232 S.E.2d 745 (Va. 1977).

computer service company called UCC was charged with theft of a computer program from a competitor, ISD. He was accused of dialing up the ISD computer over telephone lines and transferring a copy of the source code to the computer at his own office. The theft statute under which he was prosecuted, however, required that something *tangible* be taken, and the court ruled that the electronic impulses by which the source code was transmitted over the telephone lines from the ISD computer to the UCC computer were not tangible. The court avoided this problem, however, by finding probable cause to believe that the defendant had made a copy of the source code through the use of the UCC computer, and that this act of copying had violated the statute.[13]

Thus on the basis of this opinion, one can conclude that at the time this case was decided, it was not a crime in California to copy software from one computer to another electronically and to use the unauthorized copy in the second computer, unless a printout was made of the unauthorized copy.[14] This strange situation results from trying to fit old law to new technology.

A few states have attempted to deal with computer related crimes by adding new definitions to existing criminal statutes. Massachusetts has amended the definition of "property" in its larceny statute to include items that are "electronically processed or stored" and has redefined "trade secrets" to include anything "electronically kept or stored." Both of these changes were almost certainly made with computer data and computer software in mind.[15] Similarly, Ohio has extended the scope of its general theft statute by amending its definition of property to include computer programs.[16] And in the State of Washington, the "malicious mischief" provision of the statute relating to the physical damage of property, has been amended to redefine the term "physical damage" to include "the alteration, damage or erasure of records, information, data or computer programs which are electronically recorded for use in computers . . . ."[17]

---

[13] *Ward v. Superior Court*, 3 Computer L. Serv. Rep. 206, 208–09 (Superior Ct., Alameda Cty. Calif., March 22, 1972).

[14] California has since enacted a computer crime statute which eliminates this problem.

[15] Mass. Ann. Laws. ch. 266, §30.

[16] Ohio Rev. Code Ann. §§2901.01(J)(1), (2) and §§2913.01, 02.

[17] Wash. Rev. Code Ann. §§9A.48.100.

As an alternative to prosecuting the theft of software on the basis of a state's larceny statute, it is possible in some states to use statutes which specifically prohibit the theft of trade secrets, if it can be established that the software was or contained a trade secret. This may be a more viable alternative for the prosecution of this type of crime, especially in a state in which the offense of larceny depends on the value of the media on which the software resides.

California, for example, has a comprehensive statute imposing criminal liability for the theft or wrongful appropriation of trade secrets.[18] It covers trade secrets taken by theft or fraud, and trade secrets appropriated by employees. The California statute reads in part as follows:

> Every person is guilty of theft who, with intent to deprive or with-hold from the owner thereof the control of a trade secret, or with an intent to appropriate a trade secret to his own use or to the use of another, does any of the following:
>
> 1. Steals, takes, or carries away any article representing a trade secret.
>
> 2. Fraudulently appropriates any article representing a trade secret entrusted to him.
>
> 3. Having unlawfully obtained access to the article, without authority makes or causes to be made a copy of any article representing a trade secret.
>
> 4. Having obtained access to the article through a relationship of trust and confidence, without authority and in breach of the obligations created by such relationship makes or causes to be made, directly from and in the presence of the article, a copy of any article representing a trade secret.

This statute has been used in California to prosecute individuals accused of stealing software.

In the case of *People v. Serrata*,[19] for example, an IBM employee was convicted of stealing trade secrets from his employer. In *Ward v. Superior Court*,[20] a computer programmer accessed a

---

[18] Cal. Penal Code §499c.

[19] *People v. Serrata*, 62 Cal. App. 3rd 9, 133 Cal. Rptr. 144 (1976).

[20] *Ward v. Superior Court*, 3 Computer L. Serv. Rep. 206, (Super. Ct. Alameda Cty. Calif., March 22, 1972).

competitor's computer over phone lines and printed out the source code for the competitor's software on his employer's computer. The court considered the competitor's program to be a trade secret and therefore ruled that there was probable cause to believe that the defendant committed the offenses specified in the California Trade Secrets Statute.

Some federal statutes also cover the theft of software. The copyright law is one example. If the theft is accomplished by unauthorized copying, either electronically or mechanically (as opposed to stealing a listing, disk or tape), a copyright infringement is involved. If the copy was made "willfully and for purposes of commercial advantage or private financial gain," it will constitute criminal copyright infringement,[21] a federal crime punishable by up to one year in prison and a fine of up to $25,000.

Federal criminal statutes governing interstate transportation[22] and receipt of stolen property[23] can also be applied to software theft, provided that the theft occurs by means of a physical taking of media on which the software is stored (e.g., disk, tape, etc.), and the software has a value of at least $5,000. If the software is stolen electronically, however, the statutes will probably not apply.

The federal wire fraud statute[24] has been used to prosecute interstate electronic theft of software via telephone lines. In the case of *United States v. Seidlitz*,[25] a former employee of a company called Optimum Systems, Inc. used a telephone to dial up the OSI computer and copy the source code to a software system known as WYLBUR. His unauthorized access was detected by OSI and the calls were traced electronically to the defendant's office. After a number of such calls had occurred and were traced, the FBI obtained a warrant to search the defendant's office, and seized 40 rolls of computer paper upon which the source code had been printed. The defendant was then indicted and convicted of transmitting telephone calls in interstate commerce as part of a scheme to defraud OSI of property—that is, the WYLBUR source code.

---

[21] 17 U.S.C. § 506.
[22] 18 U.S.C. §2314.
[23] 18 U.S.C. §2315.
[24] 18 U.S.C. §1343.
[25] *United States v. Seidlitz*, 589 F.2d 152 (4th Cir. 1978).

12.2. UNAUTHORIZED ACCESS, MODIFICATION, OR DESTRUCTION OF SOFTWARE

Software is accessed, modified, or destroyed without authorization for a variety of reasons. These can range from motives as simple as sabotage and vandalism to more sophisticated schemes whereby software is modified in order to embezzle funds, deliver goods to particular persons, or for other similarly fraudulent purposes. Virtually all of the states that have passed computer crime legislation prohibit the unauthorized access, modification, or destruction of software, regardless of whether it is done by an insider who is otherwise authorized to have access to the computer (such as an employee), or an outsider who gains access to the computer in an unauthorized manner (such as a "hacker"). Such an offense can be either a misdemeanor or a felony depending upon the state in which it occurs. An example of such a statute is that passed in Colorado[26] which provides that:

> Any person who knowingly and without authorization uses, alters, damages or destroys any computer, computer system, or computer network described in section 18–5.5-101 or a computer software program, documentation, or data contained in such computer, computer system, or computer network commits computer crime.

A slightly different version was enacted in Georgia,[27] and provides as follows:

> Any person who intentionally and without authorization, directly or indirectly accesses, alters, damages, destroys, or attempts to damage or destroy any computer, computer system, or computer network, or any computer software, program, or data, upon conviction thereof, shall be fined not more than $50,000.00 or imprisoned not more than 15 years, or both.

Note that these statutes apply to "any person." It makes no difference whether the person committing the crime is an employee or an outsider. Note also that two conditions must be satis-

---

[26] Colo. Rev. Stat. §18–5.5-102(2).
[27] Ga. Code Ann. §16–9-93.

fied before the act will be criminal. It must be done "intentionally" and it must be done "without authorization." Thus if an employee accidentally deletes a key program, or carelessly modifies one while attempting to fix a problem, no crime is committed because the required "intent" is missing. But if the employee modifies the payroll program so that it automatically adds 10 percent to his or her own paycheck, the employee is acting intentionally and without authorization and is guilty of a crime. Similarly, when an employee engaged in software development modifies a program as part of his or her job, or deletes one no longer needed, the employee is acting with authorization, and no crime is committed.

12.3. USE OF SOFTWARE AS PART OF A FRAUDULENT SCHEME

The computer crime statutes passed in most states also make criminal the fraudulent use of a computer or computer software. A good example is the California statute[28] which provides that:

> Any person who intentionally accesses or causes to be accessed any computer system or computer network for the purpose of (1) devising or executing any scheme or artifice to defraud or extort or (2) obtaining money, property, or services with false or fraudulent intent, representations, or promises shall be guilty of a public offense.

Thus even when someone has the authority to access, use, and modify software, such an act will constitute a criminal offense if it is done for any fraudulent purpose.

12.4. CONCLUSION

Government has only recently begun to give serious consideration to the criminal misuse of computers, and the subject is

---

[28] Cal. Penal Code §502(b).

fraught with much uncertainty. As more attention is given to this area of the law, which is inevitable given the expanding importance of computer crime, much of this uncertainty will be resolved. In the meantime, the victims of intentional wrongdoing related to computers should complain to law enforcement authorities and press for vigorous prosecution of those responsible.

APPENDICES

A.1. COPYRIGHT REGISTRATION FORM AND INSTRUCTIONS FOR COMPLETING IT

FORM TX
UNITED STATES COPYRIGHT OFFICE

REGISTRATION NUMBER

TX   TXU

EFFECTIVE DATE OF REGISTRATION

Month   Day   Year

DO NOT WRITE ABOVE THIS LINE. IF YOU NEED MORE SPACE, USE A SEPARATE CONTINUATION SHEET.

1

TITLE OF THIS WORK ▼

PREVIOUS OR ALTERNATIVE TITLES ▼

PUBLICATION AS A CONTRIBUTION If this work was published as a contribution to a periodical, serial, or collection, give information about the collective work in which the contribution appeared. **Title of Collective Work ▼**

If published in a periodical or serial give: **Volume ▼**   **Number ▼**   **Issue Date ▼**   **On Pages ▼**

2 a

NAME OF AUTHOR ▼

DATES OF BIRTH AND DEATH
Year Born ▼   Year Died ▼

Was this contribution to the work a "work made for hire"? ☐ Yes ☐ No

AUTHOR'S NATIONALITY OR DOMICILE
Name of Country
OR { Citizen of ▶_____
Domiciled in ▶_____

WAS THIS AUTHOR'S CONTRIBUTION TO THE WORK
Anonymous? ☐ Yes ☐ No
Pseudonymous? ☐ Yes ☐ No
If the answer to either of these questions is "Yes," see detailed instructions.

NATURE OF AUTHORSHIP Briefly describe nature of the material created by this author in which copyright is claimed. ▼

NOTE
Under the law, the "author" of a "work made for hire" is generally the employer, not the employee (see instructions). For any part of this work that was "made for hire" check "Yes" in the space provided, give the employer (or other person for whom the work was prepared) as "Author" of that part, and leave the space for dates of birth and death blank.

b

NAME OF AUTHOR ▼

DATES OF BIRTH AND DEATH
Year Born ▼   Year Died ▼

Was this contribution to the work a "work made for hire"? ☐ Yes ☐ No

AUTHOR'S NATIONALITY OR DOMICILE
Name of country
OR { Citizen of ▶_____
Domiciled in ▶_____

WAS THIS AUTHOR'S CONTRIBUTION TO THE WORK
Anonymous? ☐ Yes ☐ No
Pseudonymous? ☐ Yes ☐ No
If the answer to either of these questions is "Yes," see detailed instructions.

NATURE OF AUTHORSHIP Briefly describe nature of the material created by this author in which copyright is claimed. ▼

c

NAME OF AUTHOR ▼

DATES OF BIRTH AND DEATH
Year Born ▼   Year Died ▼

Was this contribution to the work a "work made for hire"? ☐ Yes ☐ No

AUTHOR'S NATIONALITY OR DOMICILE
Name of Country
OR { Citizen of ▶_____
Domiciled in ▶_____

WAS THIS AUTHOR'S CONTRIBUTION TO THE WORK
Anonymous? ☐ Yes ☐ No
Pseudonymous? ☐ Yes ☐ No
If the answer to either of these questions is "Yes," see detailed instructions.

NATURE OF AUTHORSHIP Briefly describe nature of the material created by this author in which copyright is claimed. ▼

3

YEAR IN WHICH CREATION OF THIS WORK WAS COMPLETED This information must be given in all cases. ◀ Year

DATE AND NATION OF FIRST PUBLICATION OF THIS PARTICULAR WORK
Complete this information ONLY if this work has been published.
Month ▶_____ Day ▶_____ Year ▶_____ ◀ Nation

4

COPYRIGHT CLAIMANT(S) Name and address must be given even if the claimant is the same as the author given in space 2.▼

APPLICATION RECEIVED
ONE DEPOSIT RECEIVED
TWO DEPOSITS RECEIVED
REMITTANCE NUMBER AND DATE

DO NOT WRITE HERE — OFFICE USE ONLY

See instructions before completing this space.

TRANSFER If the claimant(s) named here in space 4 are different from the author(s) named in space 2, give a brief statement of how the claimant(s) obtained ownership of the copyright.▼

MORE ON BACK ▶ • Complete all applicable spaces (numbers 5-11) on the reverse side of this page. • See detailed instructions. • Sign the form at line 10.

DO NOT WRITE HERE
Page 1 of_____pages

EXAMINED BY	**FORM TX**
CHECKED BY	
☐ CORRESPONDENCE Yes	FOR COPYRIGHT OFFICE USE ONLY
☐ DEPOSIT ACCOUNT FUNDS USED	

DO NOT WRITE ABOVE THIS LINE. IF YOU NEED MORE SPACE, USE A SEPARATE CONTINUATION SHEET.

PREVIOUS REGISTRATION Has registration for this work, or for an earlier version of this work, already been made in the Copyright Office?
☐ Yes ☐ No If your answer is "Yes," why is another registration being sought? (Check appropriate box) ▼
☐ This is the first published edition of a work previously registered in unpublished form.
☐ This is the first application submitted by this author as copyright claimant.
☐ This is a changed version of the work, as shown by space 6 on this application.
If your answer is "Yes," give: **Previous Registration Number ▼**   **Year of Registration ▼**

5

DERIVATIVE WORK OR COMPILATION Complete both space 6a & 6b for a derivative work; complete only 6b for a compilation.
a. Preexisting Material Identify any preexisting work or works that this work is based on or incorporates. ▼

b. Material Added to This Work Give a brief, general statement of the material that has been added to this work and in which copyright is claimed. ▼

See instructions before completing this space

6

MANUFACTURERS AND LOCATIONS If this is a published work consisting preponderantly of nondramatic literary material in English, the law may require that the copies be manufactured in the United States or Canada for full protection. If so, the names of the manufacturers who performed certain processes, and the places where these processes were performed **must** be given. See instructions for details.
Names of Manufacturers ▼   **Places of Manufacture ▼**

7

REPRODUCTION FOR USE OF BLIND OR PHYSICALLY HANDICAPPED INDIVIDUALS   A signature on this form at space 10, and a check in one of the boxes here in space 8, constitutes a non-exclusive grant of permission to the Library of Congress to reproduce and distribute solely for the blind and physically handicapped and under the conditions and limitations prescribed by the regulations of the Copyright Office: (1) copies of the work identified in space 1 of this application in Braille (or similar tactile symbols); or (2) phonorecords embodying a fixation of a reading of that work; or (3) both.
a ☐ Copies and Phonorecords   b ☐ Copies Only   c ☐ Phonorecords Only

See instructions

8

DEPOSIT ACCOUNT If the registration fee is to be charged to a Deposit Account established in the Copyright Office, give name and number of Account.
Name ▼   **Account Number ▼**

9

CORRESPONDENCE Give name and address to which correspondence about this application should be sent. Name/Address/Apt/City/State/Zip ▼

Area Code & Telephone Number ▶

Be sure to give your daytime phone ◀ number

CERTIFICATION* I, the undersigned, hereby certify that I am the
Check one ▶
☐ author
☐ other copyright claimant
☐ owner of exclusive right(s)
☐ authorized agent of
of the work identified in this application and that the statements made by me in this application are correct to the best of my knowledge.
Name of author or other copyright claimant, or owner of exclusive right(s) ▲

Typed or printed name and date ▼ If this is a published work, this date must be the same as or later than the date of publication given in space 3.

_____ date ▶ _____

☞ **Handwritten signature (X) ▼**

10

MAIL CERTIFI-CATE TO	Name ▼	**Have you:** • Completed all necessary spaces? • Signed your application in space 10?
Certificate will be mailed in window envelope	Number/Street/Apartment Number ▼	• Enclosed check or money order for $10 payable to *Register of Copyrights*? • Enclosed your deposit material with the application and fee?
	City/State/ZIP ▼	**MAIL TO:** Register of Copyrights Library of Congress. Washington D C 20559

11

* 17 U.S.C. § 506(e): Any person who knowingly makes a false representation of a material fact in the application for copyright registration provided for by section 409, or in any written statement filed in connection with the application, shall be fined not more than $2.500.

☆ U.S. GOVERNMENT PRINTING OFFICE: 1983: 381-278/507

Sept. 1983—600,000

1. *Filling Out Section 1*

   a. *Title of this Work.*   Enter the name of the program or software package being registered on this line. All software submitted for copyright registration must be given a title so that it can be identified and indexed by the Copyright Office. If the software has been or will be marketed with different versions, it is a good idea to include the version number in the title, for example, "Multicalc Version 5.2." Remember that the copyright law does not provide any protection for this title (See Section 2.2.5), although it may be protectible as a trademark. (See Sections 6.1 and 6.2.)

   b. *Previous or Alternate Titles.*   This line should be filled in only if the software has previously been registered with the Copyright Office under a different title. If the software was not previously registered, the fact that it was previously called by a different name does not require that the old name be inserted in this line.

   c. *Publication as a Contribution.*   If the software has been published as a contribution to a periodical, serial, or collection, such as in a magazine or as part of a larger system owned by someone else, the information requested in this space should be provided about the larger work in which the software appeared. Otherwise this section should be left blank.

2. *Filling out Section 2*

   a. *Name of Author.*   The name of the author of the software should be entered here. Note that parts a, b, and c of Section 2 provide space for three authors. If there are more than three authors an additional form is available to list the additional authors (Form TX/CON). Remember that the author is not necessarily the person who wrote the software. If the software was written by an employee in the scope of his or her employment, then the employer is considered the author under the "work for hire" doctrine, and the name of the employer should be inserted as the name of the author. (This is discussed in Sections 3.1.3 and 3.1.4.) In such a case, the box indicating that the software was a "work made for hire" should be checked. Otherwise, the individual who actually wrote the software should be named as the author.

b. *Dates of Birth and Death.* The year of birth and death (if relevant) should be entered for each individual author. If the software was a "work made for hire," this space should be left blank.

c. *Author's Nationality or Domicile.* Specify either the country in which the author is a citizen or the country in which the author lives (i.e., is domiciled). This must be done for both individual authors and employers who own the copyright under the "work for hire" doctrine, including corporations.

d. *This Author's Contribution to the Work.* An author's contribution to a work is considered "anonymous" if that author is not identified on the copies of the software. An author's contribution to the software is pseudonymous if that author is identified on the copies under a fictitious name. Check the appropriate box. If the software is a "work made for hire," this box should be left blank.

e. *Nature of Authorship.* This section is very important. It is intended to provide the Copyright Office with a brief general statement of the nature of the author's contribution to the software, and is used to help determine whether the software qualifies for registration. No special language is required, but the description of the author's contribution must refer to copyrightable subject matter. Where they are applicable, the following descriptions of the nature of the authorship will be accepted by the Copyright Office:[1]

computer program
entire computer code
entire program
entire program code

---

[1] Compendium II §325.02(a).

entire text

entire work

module, new modules, revised modules

program

program instructions

program listing

program text, programming text

revised program

routine, new routines, revised routines

software, computer software

subroutine, new subroutines, revised subroutines

text

text of computer game

text of . . . . (except "text of object code" or "text of algorithm")

text of program translation from (one programming language) to (another programming language)

wrote program.

The Copyright Office will generally question an application describing the claim of the authorship in terms which may or may not represent copyrightable authorship. Examples of questionable descriptions of the nature of authorship include the following:[2]

adaptation or translation (where program appears to have been adapted merely to run on different hardware)

compilation

debugging

enhancements

error correction

features

patching

translation (listed alone).

The Copyright Office will refuse registration when terms such as the following, which clearly indicate non-copyrightable subject matter, are used to describe the nature of authorship:[3]

[2] Compendium II §325.02(b).

[3] Compendium II §325.02(c).

algorithm (or text of algorithm)
analysis
cassette
chip
disk
encripting
EPROM
firmware
formatting
functions
language (alone)
logic
nemonics
printout
PROM
ROM
software methodology
system
system design(er).

If the software to be registered is a modified version of previously registered or public domain software, the "Nature of Authorship" section should refer only to the changes that have been made to the previous version, as this is all the registration will cover. The new version can be registered only if the changes or additions are enough to be separately copyrightable. (See Section 2.6.5).

3. *Filling out Section 3*

a. *Year in Which Creation of this Work was Completed.* Specify the year in which the version of the software being registered was completed. Note that this may be earlier than the year in which the software was first published. If a software package containing multiple programs is being registered as a single work, use the latest year in which any portion of the package was completed.

b. *Date and Nation of First Publication of this Particular Work.* This section should be filled out only if the software has been published. (See Section 2.4 for a definition of when software has been published.) Note that the year of publication (if the software has been published) must be the same as the year that appears in the copyright notice on the software.

4. *Filling out Section 4*

    a. *Copyright Claimants.* Enter the name and address of the person or company claiming to be the owner of the copyright. The owner is the author identified in Section 2 of the form unless the author has transferred the copyright to someone else.

    b. *Transfer.* If the copyright has been transfered to someone else, this section should include a brief statement as to how the copyright claimant obtained ownership of the copyright. For example, if the software was transferred to a publisher by a written agreement, then it is appropriate to say that the publisher obtained the copyright "by contract."

5. *Filling Out Section 5—Previous Registration*

    The purpose of Section 5 is to enable the Copyright Office to determine whether a previous version of this software has been registered, or whether it incorporates software that has been previously registered. If not, simply check the box titled "No." Otherwise, check "Yes" and fill out the rest of Section 5. This requires that the applicant supply the previous registration number and the year of the previous registration. The applicant must also indicate (by checking the appropriate box) why another registration is being sought—that is, whether this is the first published edition of software prevously registered in unpublished form; whether this is the first application submitted by this author as a copyright claimant; or whether this is a changed version of the work as shown by Section 6 on the application. A second registration is not allowed for any other reason.

6. *Filling Out Section 6—Derivative Work or Compilation*

    Section 6 must be filled out only if the third box in Section 5 (asking whether this is a changed version of the work) was checked. If so, the "preexisting material" portion of Section 6 requires an identification of the previous work on which the new software is based, or which is incorporated within the new software.

The application for registration of software that incorporates previously registered software (i.e., a derivative work), must limit the copyright claim to the copyrightable new material, excluding any preexisting material that was previously registered or published or that is in the public domain. To limit the copyright claim appropriately in such cases, the "material added to this work" statement on the application should be completed.[4] The "material added" statement is not required when the preexisting material has never been registered or published or when the amount of preexisting material is not substantial.

For example, a software package incorporating material from two earlier developmental versions that remained unregistered and unpublished would not be considered a derivative computer program for registration purposes and no "material added" statement would be required. Similarly, the application for a derivative program containing a total of 5,000 lines of program text, 50 of which were previously published, would not be required to give a "material added" statement.[5] The Copyright Office will require a "material added" statement on an application for a derivative computer program only when the previously published or registered or public domain materials contained in the new version of the program are substantial or, in relation to the work as a whole, represent a significant portion of the work.[6]

7. *Filling Out Section 7—Manufacturers and Locations*

Section 7 can be skipped if only software is being registered. If documentation, advertising brochures, or other printed material is being registered, then Section 7 must be completed. It requires the name of the company that manu-

---

[4] Compendium II §325.01.
[5] Compendium II §325.01(a).
[6] Compendium II §325.01(b).

factured the copies, as well as where the manufacturing took place.

8. *Filling Out Section 8—Reproduction for Use of Blind or Physically Handicapped Persons*

Section 8 allows the Copyright Office to reproduce and distribute copies of the copyrighted work for the blind and physically handicapped. It is an optional license, and may be terminated by the copyright owner on 90 days notice. It applies to printed text, not computer programs.

9. *Filling Out Section 9*

    a. *Deposit Account.* For organizations which file a large number of copyright applications, it is possible to maintain a deposit account with the Copyright Office and to have the fee for each copyright registration deducted automatically. If the applicant has such an account, the name of the account and the account number should be specified. In most cases, such an account will not exist and this can be skipped.

    b. *Correspondence.* Enter the name, address, and daytime telephone number of the person with whom the Copyright Office should correspond in the event that there are any questions regarding the copyright application.

10. *Filling Out Section 10—Certification*

The Copyright Office requires that all applications for copyright registration be signed by the author, the copyright claimant, the owner of the exclusive rights, or an authorized agent of the copyright owner (usually an attorney). The name of this person must be printed or typewritten in Section 10 and his or her handwritten signature must also be included.

11. *Filling Out Section 11—Mail Certificate To*

Section 11 merely provides for the name and address of the person to whom the copyright registration certificate should be mailed once it is issued by the Copyright Office.

A.2. SECTIONS OF THE COPYRIGHT ACT SPECIFICALLY DEALING WITH SOFTWARE[1]

1. *Section 101—Definition of a Computer Program.* A "computer program" is a set of statements or instructions to be used directly or indirectly in a computer in order to bring about a certain result.

2. *Section 117—Right to Copy or Adapt Computer Programs in Limited Circumstances*

    Notwithstanding the provisions of section 106,[2] it is not an infringement for the owner of a copy of a computer program to make or authorize the making of another copy or adaptation of that computer program provided:

    (1) that such a new copy or adaptation is created as an essential step in the utilization of the computer program in conjunction with a machine that is used in no other manner; or

    (2) that such new copy or adaptation is for archival purposes only and that all archival copies are destroyed in the event that continued possession of the computer program should cease to be rightful.

    Any exact copies prepared in accordance with the provisions of this section may be leased, sold, or otherwise transferred, along with the copy from which such copies were prepared, only as part of the lease, sale, or other transfer of all rights in the program. Adaptations so prepared may be transferred only with the authorization of the copyright owner.

---

[1] These sections of the Copyright Act were added in 1980 as a result of the recommendations of CONTU and formed what is known as the Computer Software Copyright Act of 1980.

[2] Section 106 of the Copyright Act gives copyright owners the exclusive right to make copies of the work, prepare derivative works, distribute copies to the public by sale, lease or lending to perform the work publicly, and to display the work publicly. See Section 2.1.2.

A.3. EXAMPLE OF A SOFTWARE PATENT

United States Patent [19]

Torkelsen et al.

[11] **Patent Number:** **4,460,975**

[45] **Date of Patent:** **Jul. 17, 1984**

[54] **EASILY ACCESSIBLE FORMATING OF COMPUTER PRINTOUTS**

[75] Inventors: **John B. Torkelsen**, Princeton; **Kevin M. Hooliban**, Plainsboro, both of N.J.

[73] Assignee: **Saga Data, Inc.**, Princeton, N.J.

[21] Appl. No.: **420,182**

[22] Filed: **Sep. 17, 1982**

[51] Int. Cl.³ G06F 3/12
[52] U.S. Cl. 364/900
[58] Field of Search .... 364/900 MS File

[56]   **References Cited**

U.S. PATENT DOCUMENTS

4,097,924 6/1978 Figini 364/900
4,425,629 1/1984 Cason et al. 364/900

Primary Examiner—Raulfe B. Zache
Attorney, Agent, or Firm—Russell J. Barron; Lester J. Savit

[57]   **ABSTRACT**

A process for allowing non-programmers to generate customized formats for computer printouts according to user specifications. The process allows a user to create a report or other formatted representation of data by responding to a sequence of prompting stimuli. Each stimulus is presented to the user by a computer processor in combination with a menu of command choices or in combination with instructions for responding by alphanumeric command or designation. The sequence of prompting stimuli is dependent on previous command choices to present only relevant stimuli to the user. A list of generic default format commands specifies parameters not specified by the user. Consequently, the user needs to respond only to a few stimuli in order to generate a completely formatted representation of data. The generic default format commands may be changed and stored in the long-term memory as custom default format commands for easy and quick retrieval and regeneration of desired formats with updated data or with other variations. The process is accomplished by a transfer of default format commands from the long-term memory to the processor memory followed by modification of the default format commands by the user's commands given in response to the prompting stimuli. The series of commands are converted to electrical impulses suitable to direct a printer to print out the designated data according to the specifications of the user.

52 Claims, 4 Drawing Figures

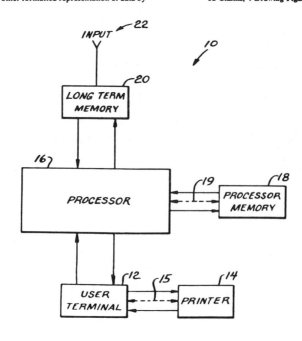

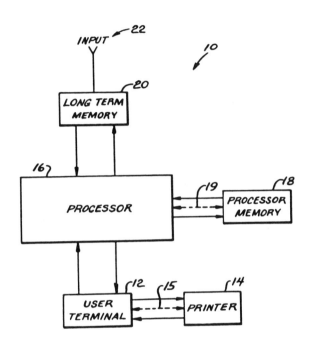

FIG. 1

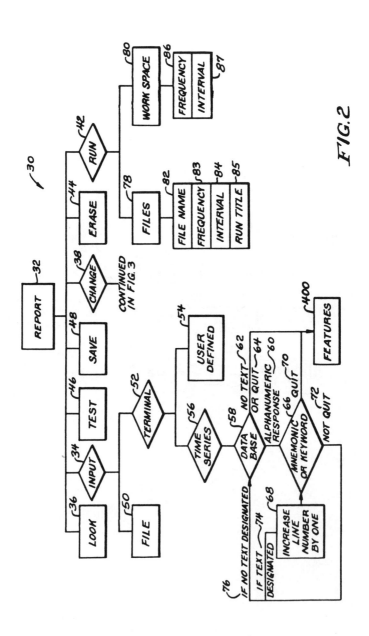

FIG. 2

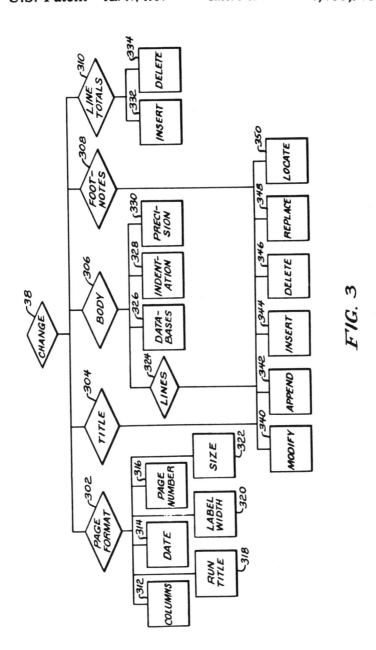

FIG. 3

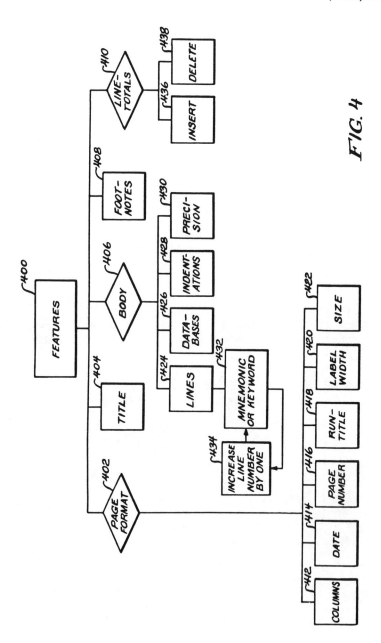

FIG. 4

4,460,975

1

EASILY ACCESSIBLE FORMATING OF COMPUTER PRINTOUTS

BACKGROUND OF THE INVENTION

The invention pertains to computer generated printed representations of data. In particular, the invention relates to processes for interfacing a non-programmer user with a digital computer to produce a desired format of a computer printout.

The invention is ideally suited for quick and easy generation and regeneration of business and economic reports containing lists of data and transformations of data. It is also well suited for incorporation as part of a broader computer program including aspects of co-pending patent application Ser. No. 409,783.

In the past, computers have been used to format business reports or other types of representations or tables of data. Such formatting is very desirable because it produces printouts of raw or transformed data that are easily understood and further facilitates comparison of categories of data or transformations of categories of data. However, past programs for formatting computer printouts have required that the user know the specific language used by the program. Only a computer programmer skilled in the use of these languages or a non-programmer extensively trained in a specific formatting language could generate desired formats of computer printouts. For example, universal computer languages such as FORTRAN and COBOL have been used to format printouts in the past. Also, commercial software formatting packages such as Impact, created by United Information Services, and Focus, created by Information Builders, Inc. are available. However, both universal computer languages and previous commercial software formatting packages require many pages of user instruction with which the user must familiarize himself before becoming proficient enough to generate even the simplest desired formats. Consequently, prior to the present invention, only programmers or other users willing to spend the considerable time and energy necessary to learn how to use a complex computer language and syntax were able to specify formats for computer generated reports or tables.

It is an object of the present invention to provide a process for making formatting of computer printouts accessible to non-programmer users.

It is another object of the present invention to provide a process for non-programmer users to be able to generate, store and retrieve user specified formats of computer printouts of data.

It is another object of the present invention to provide a process for quickly and easily regenerating customized formats of computer printouts with new or updated data.

It is a further object of the present invention to provide a process utilizing a logical sequence of prompting stimuli to create a list of user commands to be combined with stored default format commands to specify the entirety of a format of a computer printout of data in a short period of time.

It is yet another object of the present invention to provide a system and a process for generation of computer printout formats according to non-programmer user specifications giving the user control to modify a great number of parameters of the format.

It is yet another object of the present invention to provide a process for teaching non-programmer users

2

how to specify the desired format at the same time the user first attempts to produce a format for a computer printout.

The foregoing and other objects, features, and advantages of this invention will be apparent from the following descriptions and illustrations of the preferred embodiment of this invention.

SUMMARY OF THE INVENTION

The present invention provides a process and a system for generating an infinite variety of formats of computer displays of selected data from a variable number of prompted user commands. The user may define a format, specifying only a few parameters such as designation of data, frequency of data to be printed and interval of time to be represented. The user may, alternatively, define a format specifying a great number of parameters such as titles, subtitles, footnotes and other details. The user may print out data according to a previously defined format by specifying only frequency of data points and the interval of time to be represented.

The process utilizes a general purpose digital computer having a processor with a memory. The processor communicates with a long-term memory and a user operated terminal. The terminal communicates with a printer for printing the data in a specific format.

The revolutionary results of the present invention are produced by a method for easily compiling user commands with computer supplied default format commands to specify all the parameters necessary to generate a completely formatted printout. The user need only respond to a sequence of prompting stimuli to generate the commands needed to produce the desired format. The sequence of prompting stimuli is a logical progression dependent upon previous user command choices. In this manner, the user is presented with only relevant stimuli and command choices. Consequently, the sequence of prompting stimuli is as long or as short as necessary for the user to specify desired changes or additions to the default format commands without the user needing to consciously decide what needs to be changed in advance of being presented with the appropriate stimulus. Once a desired format has been generated, the command list can be stored in long-term memory for latter retrieval and regeneration with new or updated data.

The generic default format commands are stored in the long-term memory. At the beginning of program, the default format commands are reproduced in the processor memory. The default format commands are then modified and supplemented according to user commands selected from menus of command choices presented in combination with prompting stimuli.

A prompting stimulus may require the user to respond in one of several ways to the prompting stimulus. If the prompting stimulus is presented in combination with a menu of command choices, the user may respond by designating one of the commands listed on the menu. Normally this is done by depressing the terminal keys corresponding to the first or first two letters of the command words. If the prompting stimulus seeks to elicit a designation of data or other text in the body of the format, the user may respond by depressing the terminal keys corresponding to a desired data base and mnemonic designating the data within the data base to be printed on a line. Alternatively, a specific transformation of the data may be printed. Also, the user may

4,460,975

3

designate by alphanumeric command that a line contain a subhead or some other labeling. If the user does not know what options of response are available, a question mark response will result in the computer instructing the user as to what alphanumeric commands may be 5 designated. Similarly, proper syntax, where necessary, is taught when the question mark is designated by the user. If the prompting stimulus indicates that the user may designate a word or label to be printed on the printout, such as a title, footnote, subhead or other label, 10 the user may simply key the appropriate letters spelling the label on the terminal keyboard.

The user may enter the data to be represented directly into the processor memory or may designate data stored in the long-term memory. Designated data stored 15 in the long-term memory is reproduced in the processor memory upon the appropriate user command. The user need only specify the parameters which the user desires to be different from the default parameters and the data to be included in the body of the printout. 20

Upon command, the processor converts the list of commands into electrical impulses to direct a printer to print out the data according to the specified parameters. Prior to converting the data, the processor presents the 25 user with two prompting stimuli. First, the user is presented with a choice of frequency of data in combination with a menu of command choices, e.g., monthly, quarterly or annually. Second, the user is presented with a choice of interval of time to be included in the format in 30 combination with a space to designate the appropriate time span, e.g., if monthly frequency is selected then beginning month and year and ending month and year are to be designated.

After the frequency and interval have been desig- 35 nated, the processor automatically compiles the designated data from the long-term memory into the processor memory. The list of commands, e.g., the default format commands modified and supplemented by user commands, is then electronically converted into electri- 40 cal impulses to direct a printer to print out according to the specified parameters.

The list of commands automatically generating a desired format may be saved for later reference in the long-term memory. Such a list of user commands incor- 45 porated into generic default format commands are custom default format commands. If a user so chooses, the custom default format commands can be instantly retrieved from the long-term memory and further modified or supplemented as desired. In this manner, either a 50 previously defined format or a modification of a previously defined format may be generated in a very short period of time.

The default format commands are stored separately from the data but not separately from data designation. 55 Consequently, the desired format can be regenerated by a secretary or other agent of the original user at a later time with updated or new data. After the original user defined the desired format, periodic printouts are a simple, quick ministerial task. Many different sets of 60 custom default commands may be stored in the long-term memory for later retrieval. Accordingly, a whole set of reports can be custom designed by an original user and periodically updated by agents of the user.

BRIEF DESCRIPTION OF THE DRAWINGS

A better understanding of the invention may be had from a consideration of the following detailed descrip-

4

tion taken in conjunction with the following drawings, in which:

FIG. 1 is a schematic diagram showing the preferred arrangement of component parts used in practice of the present invention;

FIG. 2 shows a flow diagram of the sequence of prompting stimuli;

FIG. 3 shows a continuation of the flow diagram of the sequence of prompting stimuli depicted as "change" in FIG. 2; and

FIG. 4 shows a detailed flow diagram of prompting stimuli depicted as "features" in FIG. 1.

DETAILED DESCRIPTION OF THE INVENTION

The process and system of the present invention may be understood by reference to the diagrams described above. Referring to FIG. 1, the general arrangement of component parts is depicted by the numeral 10. The processor 16 can be any general purpose computer but, preferably, is a main frame digital computer such as the IBM 370. The processor 16 has a processor memory 18 which is used for storage of information such as the object code, data, and commands. The processor memory 18 is the work space of the processor, that is, the transformations run on information are done in the processor memory 18. While FIG. 1 shows the processor memory as separate from the processor, in fact processor memory 18 will normally be part of the processor as indicated by the double headed arrow 19 between processor 16 and processor memory 18.

The processor 16 further communicates with the long-term memory 20. Long-term memory 20 is used to store software, command lists, data, and other information which can be retrieved by the processor 16, and reproduced on the processor memory 18 for desired transformations. Normally, information in the long-term memory 20 can be retrieved any number of times without erasing the information in the long-term memory 20. Information can be entered into the long-term memory by direct input 22 into the memory or by entry through the processor 16. Direct input 22 may be accomplished by entry on discs carrying the information or by recordation on any memory storage device. Information may also be entered into the long-term memory 20 through the processor 16 from the processor memory 18 or from the user terminal 12. In this manner, the user can enter information into the long-term memory 20 by direct transcription. Or, alternatively, information can be compiled on the processor memory 18 by the user and then transferred in bulk into the long-term memory 20.

The user terminal 12 communicates both with the processor 16 and a printer 14. The printer 14 may be incorporated between the processor 16 and user terminal 12 or as a separate component, as shown in FIG. 1. Alternatively, the printer may be incorporated in the user terminal as indicated by the double-headed arrow 15 between user terminal 12 and printer 14.

The printer 14 may be any device for printing letters or words. Such devices include user terminals with any type of output device, daisy wheel printers, ink jet printers, computer controlled typewriters as well as any other electromechanical printers. Alternatively, the 65 printout could appear on a CRT or other "soft" display. Later, this soft display could be transformed to "hard" copy by photograhic or other methods. The present invention is not limited to use of only the above listed

4,460,975

5

type printers but further contemplates that any method of printing can be incorporated into the system. In fact, the system could direct any type of commercial computer controlled printer which can be driven by electrical impulses. New printers developed in the future could be easily incorporated into the system because of industry standardization of the printer code.

A user communicates with the processor through the user terminal 12, which usually contains a keyboard having alphanumeric keys. The user is preferably a human being, but, alternatively, could be another computer or electronic or electromechanical device.

The process allows non-programmer users to compile a list of specifications and both generate printouts from those specifications for later modification or regeneration of the printout. This increase is accessibility of the format of a printout is accomplished by a process involving several steps.

In particular, after the user has begun communicating with the processor 16 and designates the report generator program, the process of user specification of the desired format starts.

The user is confronted with a sequence of prompting stimuli generated by the processor 16. Preferably, the prompting stimulus is a descriptive word presented on a video screen but, alternatively, it could be a picture, an audio stimulus, a depiction of a report or any other indication of the decision to be made. The stimulus can be presented by either a video device, an audio producing device, or any other device or method of indicating to the user that a certain decision is to be made and that the processor 16 awaits the user's decision.

Each prompting stimulus is presented in combination with a menu of command choices or instructions for an alphanumeric response. Preferably, the menu of command choices is a list of descriptive words presented in combination with the prompting stimulus on a video monitor but, alternatively, it could be presented in any manner in which the stimulus can be presented, as discussed above. The descriptive words describe the command they represent. Commands are selected from each menu by choosing the first or first two letters of the descriptive words. Preferably, this is accomplished by depression of the keys representing the appropriate letters on the terminal 12 keyboard. However, the entire descriptive word is recognized by the processor so that entry of an inappropriate command word coincidentally having first letter or letters corresponding to a command found on the menu will not be confused as the menu command choice. If the user does not wish to change the default command because it is the desired command or because the user does not wish to take the time to specify parameters of the format, the user may choose to not respond and depress the send signal. The sequence progresses as if the default format command was selected by the user.

The user may also designate an alphanumeric response when appropriate by "typing" or keying the response word on the keyboard of the user terminal. If the user is learning to use the program or is otherwise confused, an entry of a question mark will result in the processor presenting brief instructions of user options to the stimulus and/or appropriate syntax required to properly respond to the stimulus. It will also, where appropriate, give instructions on what keywords may be used and what syntax is required for a coherent response. The sequence of prompting stimuli does not progress until a recognizable user response is made.

6

The sequence of prompting stimuli is a logical progression related to the particular commands previously chosen by the user. Referring now to FIG. 2, the sequence of prompting stimuli is generally indicated by number 30. After the user logs on to the report format program 32, the user is presented with the stimulus indicating that a choice of operations is to be made, such as the word "report" or "format." The stimulus is prescribed in combination with a menu of command choices indicating different operations. The menu list of the descriptive words includes: "input" 34, indicating that the user wishes to input commands; "change" 38, indicating that the user wishes to change a set of commands; and "run" 42, indicating that the user wishes to print out a list of commands present in the processor memory 18 or the long-term memory 20. In addition, other operations listed on the menu could be: "look" 36, directing the processor 16 to present the list of commands for review; "save" 48, directing the processor 16 to save the list of commands found in the processor memory 16 in the long-term memory 20; "erase" 44, directing the processor 16 to erase a specified list of commands; and "test" 46, directing the processor to print out the format without the data.

The user selects the input operation by depressing the "i" key on the keyboard and then sends the signal to the processor. The user is subsequently presented with a prompting stimulus indicating that a choice of a source of the input is to be made. This, preferably would be the word "input." The prompting stimulus "input" 34 is presented in combination with a menu of command choices "file" 50, indicating that the source is a file containing previously stored commands, and "terminal" 52, indicating that the commands will be produced on the terminal.

If the user selects the terminal source, by depressing "t" on the keyboard, the user is presented with a prompting stimulus indicating that a choice of type of format definition mode is to be made. A menu of command choices is also presented. The menu includes "user defined" 54, directing that the user is an experienced user familiar with the computer language and that the user desires less prompting of responses, and "time-series" 56, directing that the user is inexperienced and desires maximum interaction between user and processor 16.

If the user selects the user defined 54 command, the user is free to specify parameters without the necessity of going in order of the sequence of prompting stimuli. This allows the user who is familiar with the language of the program to avoid passing through parts of the sequence to get to the part that is desired. In this manner, a user who has used the process many times before will not be slowed down by the remedial nature of the sequence. Consequently, anyone, skilled or non-skilled, can use the process but all users will be able to move through the sequence at a rate corresponding to his familiarity with the system.

If the user selects the "time-series" 56 command, the user is presented with a prompting stimulus indicating that a choice of text to make up the body of the printout is to be made. The user is presented with a stimulus indicating that a choice of data base 58 is to be made. If the user designates an data base by keying in an alphanumeric response 60, the user is next presented with a prompting stimulus indicating that a designation of text 66 is to be made. If the user responds by selecting nothing 62 and hitting the send signal or "q" for quit 64 and

4,460,975

7

the send signal, the sequence of prompting stimuli continues through the features **400** selection of the sequence.

The prompting stimulus indicating that a designation of text **66** is to be made is preferably the words mnemonic or keyword presented to the user. A mnemonic is an alphanumeric designation of data stored within the data base specified as a response to the data base **58** prompting stimulus. The mnemonic designation will direct the computer to print the data on the designated line. A keyword, on the other hand, is an alphanumeric designation of a transformation of data or a non-data entry on to a specified line. If the user is not familiar with the possible keywords options, the question mark response results in a complete description of each possible keyword. For example, the preferred embodiment includes keywords "&BLANK," inserting a blank line into the report; "&CENTER," inserting a centered labeled line without data; "&NEWPAGE," starting next line on a new page; "&SUBHEAD," inserting a labeled line without data; "&%," inserting percent change from the previous period; "&%P," inserting percent change from the same period of the previous year; "&%A," inserting compound annual growth rate; "&REPEAT," beginning repeating line definition for each keyword and mnemonic designated by the user; "&END," ending repeating line definition; "&LIST," identifying a list of mnemonics-file name immediately follows; "&MNCLAB," indicating whether to print mnemonics on a line above label; and "&LABMNC," indicating whether to print labels on a line above mnemonics. Of course, the present invention is not limited to these keywords or operations but contemplates use of different keywords and further operations than those listed.

If the user designates text, e.g., a keyword or a mnemonic, the processor increases the line number by one **68** and again presents the prompting stimulus, this indicating that line two of the text is to be designated by a keyword or mnemonic. This process is repeated as long as a keyword or mnemonic is designated for each line. The text of each line of the body is designated in order. If the user completes this process the "q" or quit **70** key is depressed and the sequence of prompting stimuli continues to the features **400** section.

If the user desires to change a data base, the user depresses the send signal only, designating neither keyword, mnemonic nor "quit." The user is then again presented with the prompting stimulus indicating that a data base is to be designated.

FIG. 2 shows this process of designating the text of the body of the report line-by-line as a series of logical "loops". As previously discussed, the user may continue designating keywords and mnemonics as long as a keyword or mnemonic is entered as a response. If the user desires to exit the "loop", the user can designate "q" **64** and **70** to enter the features **400** sequence. This is also accomplished by designating no response **62** when a data base **58** designation is requested by the processor **16**. If "q" is not designated **72** when a mnemonic or keyword **66** is requested, the user will remain in the loop. If the text was designated **74** by the user, the line number is increased by one and the user is again presented with the prompting stimulus indicating that a mnemonic or keyword **66** is to be designated. If text was not designated **76**, the user is presented with the prompting stimulus indicating that a designation of a data base **58** is to be made.

8

Referring to FIG. **4**, when the user has finished designating lines of text in the body of the report, the features **400** sequence is represented. A prompting stimulus indicating that the user may now specify further format features of the report is presented in combination with a menu of command choices including "page format" **402**, directing that the page format is to be specified; "title" **404**, directing that the title is to be specified; "body" **406**, directing that the body of the report is to be specified; "footnotes" **408**, directing that the footnotes or text below the body of the report is to be specified; and "line-totals" **410**, directing that columns of totals of a quarter of a year or a year be displayed in the body.

If the user selects the page format **402** command, the user is presented with a prompting stimulus indicating that a choice of type of change to the page format is to be made. The stimulus is presented in combination with a menu of command choices including "columns" **412**, directing that the width or spacing of the columns be changed; "date" **414**, directing that the position of the date be changed or the date eliminated; "page number" **416**, directing that the position of the page number be changed or the page number eliminated; "run-title" **418**, directing that a run title be included in the title of report, the title to be specified at the time of command or at the time of printing out; "label width" **420**, directing the maximum space allotted for labels of the data entered in the lines of text; "size" **422**, directing that the length and width of the printout is to be specified.

If the user selects the body **406** command, the user is presented with a prompting stimulus indicating that a choice of type of change to the body format is to be made. The prompting stimulus is presented in combination with a menu of command choices including "lines" **424**, directing that more lines of text are to be added; "data bases" **426**, directing that a new data base is to be designated; "indentations" **428**, directing that a line or lines are to be indented from the left margin; and "precision" **430**, directing that the number of digits to the right of the decimal in the data of a line or lines are to be specified by the user. If the user selects the lines **424** command the user is presented with a prompting stimulus indicating that a mnemonic or keyword **432** is to be designated. As long as a mnemonic or keyword is designated the prompting stimulus again is presented indicating a line number, each time the line number is increased by one **434**.

If the user selects the line-totals **410** command, the user is presented with a prompting stimulus indicating that a choice of whether to insert or delete a line total is to be made. The prompting stimulus is presented in combination with a menu of command choices including "insert" **436**, directing that a line total be inserted in the body of a report, and "delete" **438** directing that a line total be deleted from the body of a report.

Referring now to FIGS. 1 and 2 in conjunction with FIG. 3, the user may select change **38** if the user desires to change a set of commands present in the processor memory **18**. If the user selects the change **38** command, the user is presented with a prompting stimulus indicating that a choice of part of the format to be changed is to be made. The prompting stimulus is presented in combination with a menu of command choices including "page format" **302**, directing that the format of the page is to be changed; "title" **304**, directing that the text of the title is to be changed; "body" **306**, directing that the body of the report is to be changed; "footnotes" **308**,

4,460,975

9

directing that the footnotes or text below the body is to be changed; and "line-totals" 310, directing that columns of totals of a year or part of a year be included or taken out of the body.

If the user selects the page format 302 command, the user is presented with a prompting stimulus indicating that a choice of type of change to the page format is to be made. The stimulus is presented in combination with a menu of command choices including "columns" 312, directing that the width or spacing of the columns be changed; "date" 314, directing that the position of the date be changed or the date eliminated; "page number" 316, directing that the position of the page number be changed or the page number eliminated; "run-title" 318, directing that a run title be included in the title of report, the title to be specified at the time of command or at the time of printing out; "label width" 320, directing the maximum space allotted for labels of the data entered in the lines of text; "size" 322, directing that the length and width of the printout is to be specified.

If the user selects the body 306 command, the user is presented with a prompting stimulus indicating that a choice of type of change of the body format is to be made. The prompting stimulus is presented in combination with a menu of command choices including "lines" 324, directing that lines of text are to be changed; "data bases" 326, directing that the data base designation is to be changed; "indentations" 328, directing that indentations of a line or lines from the left margin are to be changed and "precision" 330, directing that the number of digits to the right of the decimal in the data of a line or lines are to be changed.

If the user selects the line-totals 310 command the user is presented with a prompting stimulus indicating that a choice of whether to insert a line total or to delete a line total is to be made. The prompting stimulus is presented in combination with a menu of command choices including "insert" 332, directing that a line total be inserted in the body of the report and "delete" 334, directing that a line total be taken out of the body of the report.

If the user selects the title 304 command, the footnote 308 command or the lines 324 command, the user is presented with a prompting stimulus indicating that a choice of type of change to the title, footnote or lines, respectively, is to be made. The prompting stimulus is presented in combination with a menu of command choices. These command choices are the editing functions. A question mark or "function" designation in this part of the sequence results in presentation to the user of instructions of which editing functions are available, what their function is, and the required syntax to make a coherent entry. The editing functions listed on the menu may include "modify" 340, directing that a line be changed as specified; "append" 342, directing that a line be appended to the end of a line as specified; "insert" 344, directing that a specified insertion be made in a line; "delete" 346, directing that a specified line be taken out; "replace" 348, directing that a specified entry be replaced by another in a line; and "locate" 350, directing that a line with a specified entry be located.

Of course, the present invention is not limited to the specific words or operations of the editor listed here. It contemplates that any number of standard editing functions could be included into this list as useful commands. For example, other functions such as "up", directing the editor to move up a specified number of lines; "go," directing the editor to go to the specified

10

line; "bottom," directing that the editor go to the last line of the body of the format; and "top", directing the editor to go to the first line of the body. Similarly, the descriptive names used here could be different. For example, "modify" could be "change", "append" could be "add" and "locate" could be "find".

If the user selects the run 42 command, the user is presented with a prompting stimulus indicating that a choice of source of commands to be printed out is to be made. The prompting stimulus is presented in combination with a menu of command choices including "files" 78, directing that the printout be made from commands found in the long-term memory, and "work space" 80, directing that the printout be made from commands found in the processor memory 18.

If the user selects the files 78 command, the user is presented with a sequence of four prompting stimuli indicating that the user is to designate the file name 82 of the list of commands stored in the long-term memory and desired to be retrieved, frequency 83 of data points to be printed in the body, interval 84 of time to be represented in the report, and run title 85 of the printout.

If the user selects work space as the source of the list of commands, the user is presented with two prompting stimulus indicating that the frequency 86 of data points is to be designated and that the interval 87 of data to be represented in the report is to be specified.

The distinction between command descriptive words and the correlated command should be clarified. Each menu of command choices in the preferred embodiment contains a list of descriptive words which describe the command directed or indicated. This descriptive word, indicated by quotation marks, should not be confused with the command it represents. The invention is not limited to the particular descriptive words in the menus, but contemplates use of any word, signal, or other form of communication to the processor 16 which indicates the command choice desired by the user. However, the particular words used in the preferred embodiment were chosen to represent the specific commands they direct. For purposes of this application, use of a descriptive word designates the command represented by the descriptive word and not the descriptive word, unless the descriptive word is enclosed in quotation marks.

The present invention is not limited to specific menus of command choices described above but contemplates use of command choices in addition to those listed in the menus. In particular, additional graph-types, plots and charts can be added to increase user options of type of graphic representation to display data.

In the preferred embodiment of the present invention, a set of generic default format commands are initially stored in the long-term memory 20. Upon appropriate user command at the beginning of the format program the generic default format commands are reproduced in the processor memory 18 electronically by the processor 16. The commands selected from the menus presented in combination with the prompting stimuli modify the default format commands in the processor memory 18. Alphanumeric keywords, mnemonics and labels are also incorporated into the command list. The user can move through the sequence of prompting stimuli as the logical sequence progresses, only needing to specify parameters which the user desires to be different from the generic default format commands. The user may also move upward one step in the logical sequence by designating "q" or back to the original choice of operations by designating "qq." Of course, the invention

4,460,975

11

contemplates any designation of letters, numbers, combinations of letters and numbers, or any other method of communication with the processor 16 to indicate a reverse step in the prompting sequence. The user may utilize this capability to move between input 34, change 38, run 42, test 46 and other operations. Consequently, the user has full control to decide to modify none of the generic default format commands or to specify as many parameters as the user desires to be different from the default format commands. To define a format of a printout, the process minimally requires only designation of data, frequency and interval.

After the user has completed the desired modification of the generic default format commands, creating custom default format commands, the report is ready to be printed. The user has by this point either designated data designating a data base and a mnemonic to designate data in the data base or has entered data through the terminal 12 into the processor memory 18. A maximum of 100 lines of data may be entered as desired. If the user prints out the data according to the commands, the user is presented with a prompting stimulus indicating that the user is to choose a frequency. After the user chooses a frequency of data points to be represented, e.g., monthly, quarterly, annually, the user is presented with a prompting stimulus indicating that the user is to choose an interval of time to be represented. If the user designated a monthly frequency, then a beginning month and year and ending month and year should be specified by the user. If the user designated a quarterly frequency, then a beginning quarter and year and ending quarter and year should be specified. If annual frequency is selected only a beginning year and ending year are required to be designated.

Subsequent to user specification of frequency and interval, the processor 16 electronically reproduces designated data from the long-term memory 20 in the processor memory 18. Alternatively, the data is already present in the processor memory 18 because it was entered there directly by the user of the terminal 12. The processor 16 then electronically converts the custom default format commands and data recorded on the processor memory 18 into electrical impulses to direct a printer 14 to print out the data according to the parameters specified by the commands.

The conversion of the commands into electrical impulses is accomplished by line-by-line translation of the command list into the universal code for running a printer. Because this code is standardized, any commercial printer will be directed by the resulting electrical impulses or code.

As an alternative to immediate incorporation of user commands with default commands, the user commands can be stored in the processor memory 18 and, at an appropriate time incorporated with the generic default format commands to specify any parameters which the user chooses not to specify.

The custom default format commands may be stored in the long-term memory 20 for later retrieval. They are retrieved from the long-term memory 20 and repro-

12

duced on the processor memory 18 upon appropriate user command. The custom default commands are then ready to be run or may be modified exactly as if they were the generic default format commands. Many different sets of custom default commands can be stored in the long-term memory 20 so that desired graphic representations may be periodically reproduced without the user needing to again specify any of the desired parameters.

The sets of custom default format commands include designations of data but do not include the data itself. This is advantageous because the user does not need to redesignate data or erase old data. The custom default format commands, when run, will designate data from the long-term memory 20 to be printed out. This means that new or updated data stored in the long-term memory 20 is automatically printed. Also, the frequency and interval of updated runs can be modified without modifying a list of custom default format commands.

The present invention is not limited to operation of the present process in a general purpose computer. It is contemplated that any electronic, electromagnetic, electromechanical or mechanical components may be used. It is understood that any electronic communications between processor 16 and the user terminal could be accomplished by mechanical, electromechanical or electromagnetic means as well as electronic means.

Communication between the processor 16 and the long-term memory 20 will, preferably, be by electronic means. However, the invention contemplates that other means of communication, such as electromechanic, electromagnetic and mechanical mean may be used.

The term "reproduction" in reference to data or commands refers to transfer of data without erasing the originally stored data. For example, reproduction of data from the long-term memory 20 into the processor memory 18 means that the data remains intact in the long-term memory 20 but now also appears in the processor memory 18. The term "record" means to place data or commands into the location referred to without indication of what occurs to the source. For example, recording data in the processor memory 18 implies only that it is put into the processor memory 18. The term "to store" implies that the information, i.e., data, commands, object code etc., is available for retrieval.

The present invention is further explicated by the following examples of the preferred embodiment.

EXAMPLE I

The user logs on to the computer and enters the format or report generator program. The following prompting stimuli are presented on the user terminal by the computer. The following responses are responses given by the user by keying in the letters and depressing the send key. Explanations of commands are given inside parenthesis. The period at the beginning of the user command is presented by the computer to indicate that the processor is ready to receive a command and does not need to be designated by the user.

```
Prompting Stimulus - REPORTS: INPUT, LOOK, TEST, CHANGE, RUN, SAVE OR ERASE
Command - .i (chooses the INPUT operation)
Prompting Stimulus - FROM FILE OR TERMINAL
Command - .t (Input from terminal)
Prompting Stimulus - TYPE: TIME SERIES OR USER DEFINED
Command - .t (Maximum interaction, unexperienced user)
Prompting Stimulus - BODY ENTER DATABASE NAME.
Command - .us (US database designated)
```

4,460,975

-continued

Prompting Stimulus - LINES: ENTER MNEMONIC/KEYWORD SPECIFICATIONS OR
LINE 1
Command - .- (a dashed line appears in line 1, separating the
body from the title)
Prompting Stimulus - LINE 2
Command - .& subhead output (creates subheading "output")
Prompting Stimulus - LINE 3
Command - .& subhead - (underscores the subheading)
Prompting Stimulus - LINE 4
Command - gnp$ gnp-current dollars   (Mnemonic designating data for
                                        GNP in current dollars, the
                                        data will appear on line 4
                                        preceded by label "GNP -
                                        Current Dollars")
Prompting Stimulus - LINE 5
Command - .& % (line 5 will contain percent change in GNP$ from
previous quarter - subhead of "% Change" will appear)
Prompting Stimulus - LINE 6
Command - .& % p (line 6 will contain percent change in GNP$ from the
same quarter of the previous year - subhead "% Change
Year-to-Year" will appear)
Prompting Stimulus - LINE 7
Command - .& blank (line 7 will contain a blank space)
Prompting Stimulus - LINE 8
Command - . (no text designated may indicate user's desire to
change data base designation)
Prompting Stimulus - BODY: ENTER DATABASE NAME
Command - .usefile (Mnemonic for user created database, different from
US database for data above)
Prompting Stimulus - LINES: ENTER MNEMONIC/KEYWORD SPECIFICATION OR?
LINE 8
Command - .pdgnp implicit price deflator (data and label in line 8)
Prompting Stimulus - LINE 9
Command - .& % (line 9 will contain present change in PDGNP from
previous quarter)
Prompting Stimulus - LINE 10
Command - .& % p (line 10 will contain percent change in PDGNP
from the same quarter of the previous year)
Prompting Stimulus - LINE 11
Command - .& blank (line 11 left blank)
Prompting Stimulus - LINE 12
Command - .- (line 12 contains a continuous dashed line separating
the body of the report from the footnotes)
Prompting Stimulus - LINE 13
Command - .q ("quit" line-by-line text designation is complete)
Prompting Stimulus - FEATURES: BODY, TITLE, FOOTNOTES, PAGE FORMAT,
OR LINE-TOTALS
Command - .b (body of printout to be specified)
Prompting Stimulus - BODY: LINES, DATABASE, INDENTATIONS, OR PRECISION?
Command - .p (precision of data to be set)
Prompting Stimulus - ENTER LINE NUMBER OR MNEMONIC AND NUMBER OF DIGITS
TO THE RIGHT OF THE DECIMAL POINT.
Command - .4 0 (set no digits to the right of decimal in
        .8 0 line 4 - GNP$ and line 8 - PDGNP)
        .q
Prompting Stimulus - BODY: LINES DATABASE, INDENTATIONS, OR PRECISION?
Command - .q (quit)
Prompting Stimulus - FEATURES: BODY, TITLE, FOOTNOTES, PAGE FORMAT,
OR LINE-TOTALS?
Command - .t (Title to be specified)
Prompting Stimulus - ENTER TITLE, MAXIMUM 5 LINES.
Command - indicators (title to be "INDICATORS")
.q
Prompting Stimulus - FEATURES: BODY, TITLE, FOOTNOTES, PAGE FORMAT,
OR LINE-TOTALS?
Command - .f (footnotes to be specified)
Prompting Stimulus - ENTER FOOTNOTES, MAXIMUM 5 LINES.
Command - .data source: bureau of economic analysis
        .all data are seasonably adjusted
        .q (test of footnotes specified line-by-line)
Prompting Stimulus - FEATURES: BODY, TITLE, FOOTNOTES, PAGE FORMAT,
OR LINE-TOTALS?
Command - .q (Input is complete)

EXAMPLE II [65]

The above format commands are printed out by the
following interaction.

```
Prompting Stimulus -REPORTS: INPUT, LOOK, TEST, CHANGE, RUN, SAVE,
OR ERASE?
Command - r (Run designated, command to print out a formatted printout)
Prompting Stimulus - FROM FILE OR WORK SPACE?
Command - .w (commands from work space)
Prompting Stimulus - FREQUENCY: MONTHLY, QUARTERLY, ANNUALLY
Command - .q (quarterly data points to be listed in body of report)
Prompting Stimulus - BEGINNING, ENDING QUARTER AND YEAR
Command - .1 80 4 80 (4 quarters of 1980 to be displayed
in report)
Prompting Stimulus - SET PAPER AND PRESS CARRIAGE RETURN
Command - (carriage return pressed when ready to print out)
```

The resulting report looks like this:

01/26/82				Page 1
	INDICATORS			
	1Q/80	2Q/80	3Q/80	4Q/80
OUTPUT				
GNP-CURRENT DOLLARS	2572	2565	2637	2731
% CHANGE	3.0	−0.3	2.8	3.5
% CHANGE - YR TO YR	9.9	8.0	7.9	9.4
IMPLICIT PRICE DE- FLATOR	171	175	179	183
% CHANGE	2.2	2.4	2.2	2.6
% CHANGE - YR TO YR	8.3	8.8	9.1	9.8

DATA SOURCE: BUREAU OF ECONOMIC ANALYSIS
ALL DATA ARE SEASONALLY ADJUSTED

Example III

The following interaction illustrates the change operation.

```
Prompting Stimulus - REPORTS: INPUT, LOOK, TEST,
CHANGE, RUN, SAVE OR ERASE
Command - .c (enter change section)
Prompting Stimulus - CHANGE: BODY, TITLE, FOOT-
NOTES, PAGE FORMAT, OR LINE-TOTALS?
Command - .b (body to be changed)
Prompting Stimulus - BODY: LINES, DATABASES,
INDENTATIONS, OR PRECISION?
Command - .l (lines in body to be changed)
Prompting Stimulus - LINES: MODIFY, APPEND, INSERT,
DELETE, REPLACE, OR LOCATE?
Command - .l (locate specified alphanumeric string)
Prompting Stimulus - ENTER STRING TO BE LOCATED
Command - .output (locate "output" string)
Prompting Stimulus - 2. SUBHEAD OUTPUT
       LINES: MODIFY, APPEND, INSERT, DETELE,
       REPLACE, OR LOCATE?
Command - .a (append "output" line)
Prompting Stimulus - ENTER LINE NUMBER FOLLOWED BY
CHARACTER STRING TO BE APPENDED ON TO LINE.
Command - .2 gnp (line 2 will now printout as "OUTPUT GNP")
```

It is thus clearly seen that the present invention provides a significant increase in accessibility to computer generated, versatile, highly variable formatted printouts of data. Periodic regeneration of desired formats with new or updated data is now simple and easy for untrained users.

From the above description it will be apparent that there is thus provided a process and system of the advantage before mentioned as desirable, but which obviously is susceptible to modification in its form, method, operation, detailed construction and arrangement without departing from the principles involved or sacrificing any of its advantages.

It is to be understood that the invention is not limited to the specific features shown, but that the means, method and construction herein disclosed comprise the preferred form of several modes of putting the invention into effect, and the invention is, therefore, claimed in any of its forms or modifications within the legitimate and valid scope of the appended claims.

We claim:

1. A process for electronically generating a format for a computer printout according to commands of a user communicating with a processor, the processor having a memory and further communicating with a long-term memory, the long-term memory storing a set of generic default format commands, the process comprising the steps of:
   (a) reproducing the default format commands in the processor memory;
   (b) modifying the default format commands reproduced in the processor memory according to prompted user format commands to create a set of custom default format commands;
   (c) recording data in the processor memory;
   (d) converting the custom default format commands and data recorded in the processor memory into electrical impulses to direct a printer to represent the data according to the format specified by the commands.

2. The process of claim 1 wherein the sequence of steps in first (a), second (b), third (c) and fourth (d).

3. The process of claim 1 wherein each prompted user format command is selected from a menu of format command choices presented in combination with each of a sequence of prompting stimuli.

4. The process of claim 1 or 2 wherein substantially simultaneous to the conversion of the custom default format commands and data into electrical impulses to direct a printer, the custom default format commands are reproduced in the long-term memory.

5. The process of claim 1 wherein the default format commands reproduced in the processor memory from the long-term memory are custom default format commands previously stored in the long-term memory.

6. The process of claim 1 wherein the modifications of the generic default format commands are accomplished by a logical sequence of prompting stimuli.

7. The process of claim 6 wherein succeeding prompting stimuli are determined by the prior format command choices, thereby shortening the sequence of prompting stimuli presented to the user to only those prompting stimuli relevant to the particular format and data specified by previous commands.

8. The process of claim 1 wherein the data is recorded in the processor memory directly by the user.

9. The process of claim 1 wherein the data is stored in the long-term memory and wherein the data is recorded in the processor memory by user designation of data stored in the long-term memory followed by reproduction of the designated data in the processor memory.

4,460,975

17

10. The process of claim 3 wherein the sequence of prompting stimuli includes a request for an alphanumerical response as a command.

11. The process of claim 10 wherein the alphanumeric response is a data base designation.

12. The process of claim 10 wherein the alphanumeric response is a file name designation.

13. The process of claim 10 wherein the alphanumeric response is a mnemonic designation.

14. The process of claim 10 wherein the alphanumeric response is a word to be included in the printout of data.

15. The process of claim 1 wherein the generic default format commands specify all the parameters of the format except for the data, an interval of time to be represented and a frequency of data to be represented.

16. A process for electronically generating a format for a computer printout from a series of commands comprising the steps of:

(a) prompting a series of commands by a user, the commands defining the format;

(b) recording the series of user commands;

(c) incorporating a series of generic default format commands with the user commands;

(d) recording data designated by the user; and

(e) converting the recorded commands and data into electrical impulses to direct a printer to represent the data according to the format specified by the commands.

17. The process of claim 16 wherein the electronic prompting includes a sequence of presentation of prompting stimuli, and wherein each prompting stimulus is presented in combination with a menu of possible command choices relating to the particular prompting stimulus.

18. The process of claim 17 wherein the sequence of prompting stimuli also includes a request for an alphanumeric response as a command.

19. The process of claim 18 wherein the sequence of presentation of prompting stimuli is determined by preceding commands.

20. The process of claim 16 wherein the series of user commands are recorded in the processor memory of the computer.

21. The process of claim 16 wherein the default format commands are stored in a long-term memory and are reproduced in the processor memory and wherein the user commands modify the default format commands in the processor memory and wherein the modified default format commands are stored in the long-term memory as custom default format commands, thereby allowing the user to later retrieve the custom default commands.

22. The process of claim 16 wherein the user communicates with a processor which further communicates with a processor memory and wherein the commands and data are recorded in the processor memory.

23. The process of claim 22 wherein the recording of data is accomplished by user designation of data stored in a long-term memory communicating with the processor, followed by reproduction of the data in the processor memory.

24. A process for electronically generating a format for a computer printout according to commands of a user, the user communicating with a processor having a memory, the process comprising the steps of:

(a) presenting a sequence of prompting stimuli to the user;

18

(b) presenting a menu of command choices in combination with the prompting stimuli; and

(c) the user selecting commands from the menus;

wherein the sequence of prompting stimuli comprises:

first, presenting the user with prompting stimuli indicating that a choice of operations is to be made, the stimuli is presented in combination with a menu of command choices including to input new commands, to change commands already stored in the processor memory and to print out according to commands already stored; and

second, a further prompting stimulus dependent upon the command choice selected by the user.

25. The process of claim 24 wherin the user selects the command to input new commands and wherein the second prompting stimulus indicates that a choice of a source of the input is to be made, the stimulus is presented in combination with a menu of command choices including from previously stored commands and from the terminal.

26. The process of claim 25 wherein the user selects the command to input from the terminal and further comprising a third prompting stimulus indicating that a choice of type of format definition mode is to be made, the stimulus is presented in combination with a menu of command choices including to require maximum interaction and to require language responses.

27. The process of claim 26 wherein the user selects the command to require maximum interaction and further comprising a fourth prompting stimulus indicating that a choice of text to make up the body of the printout is to be designated and indicating a line number of the body wherein each designation of text by the user is followed by the iteration of the fourth prompting stimulus with the line number increased by one.

28. The process of claim 26 wherein the user selects the command to require maximum interaction and further comprising a fourth prompting stimulus indicating that a designation of a data base is to be made, wherein user selection of a data base results in presentation of a fifth prompting stimulus indicating that the user is to designate text by an alphanumeric response selected from the group consisting of a mnemonic and a keyword, the fifth prompting stimulus is presented with an indication of a line number of the body to contain the designated text.

29. The process of claim 28 wherein each alphanumeric response is followed by an indication that another alphanumeric response is to be designated for the text of the next line of the body.

30. The process of claim 29 wherein the user may respond to presentation of the fifth stimulus by directing to change the data base designation and wherein the fourth stimulus again is presented.

31. The process of claim 30 wherein the user responds to presentation of fifth stimulus by directing that no further text of lines in the body is designated and further comprising a sixth prompting stimulus indicating that a choice of format feature is to be made, the sixth prompting stimulus is presented in combination with a menu of command choices including page format feature, body feature and line-totals feature.

32. The process of claim 30 wherein the user responds to the presentation of the fourth stimulus by directing that no further lines of text in the body are designated and further comprising a sixth prompting stimulus indicating that a choice of format feature is to be made, the sixth prompting stimulus is presented in combination

4,460,975

19

with a menu of command choices, including page format feature, body feature, and line-totals feature.

33. The process of claim 31 or 32 wherein the user selects the page format feature and further comprising a seventh prompting stimuli indicating that a choice of type of change to the page format is to be made, the seventh prompting stimulus is presented in combination with a menu of command choices including columns, date, page number, run-title, label width and size.

34. The process of claim 31 or 32 wherein the user selects the body format feature and further comprising a seventh prompting stimuli indicating that a choice of type of change to the body is to be made, the seventh prompting stimulus is presented in combination with a menu of command choices including lines, data-base, indentation and precision.

35. The process of claim 34 wherein the user selects to change lines, and further comprising an eighth stimulus indicating the line number immediately subsequent to the last line of text designated and further indicating that a choice of text to make up that line is to be selected.

36. The process of claim 35 wherein each time the user chooses a designation of text the eighth stimulus is presented with line number increased by one.

37. The process of claim 31 or 32 wheren the user selects the line totals feature and further comprising a seventh prompting stimuli indicating that a choice of whether to insert or delete line totals is to be made, the seventh prompting stimulus is presented in combination with a menu of command choices including insert and delete.

38. The process of claim 24 wherein the user selects to change commands in the processor memory and wherein the second prompting stimulus indicates that a choice of the part of the format to be changed is to be made, the second prompting stimulus is presented in combination with a menu of command choices including page format, title, body, footnotes and line-totals.

39. The process of claim 38 wherein the user selects to change the page format and further comprising a third prompting stimulus indicating that a choice of type of change to the page format is to be made, the third prompting stimulus is presented in combination with a menu of command choices including columns, run title, date, label width, page number and size.

40. The process of claim 38 wherein the user selects to change the title and further comprising a third prompting stimulus indicating that a type of change to the title is to be made, the third prompting stimulus is presented in combination with a menu of command choices including modify, append, insert, delete, replace and locate.

41. The process of claim 38 wherein the user selects to change the body and further comprising a third prompting stimulus indicating that a choice of part of the body to be changed is to be made, the third prompting stimulus is presented in combination with a menu of command choices including lines, data bases, indentation and precision.

42. The process of claim 41 wherein the user selects to change the lines of the body and further comprising a fourth prompting stimulus indicating that the type of change to the lines is to be made, the fourth prompting stimulus is presented in combination with a menu of command choices including modify, append, insert, delete, replace and locate.

20

43. The process of claim 38 wherein the user selects to change the footnotes part of the format and further comprising a third prompting stimulus indicating that a choice of type of change to the footnotes is to be made, the third prompting stimulus is presented in combination with a menu of command choices including modify, append, insert, delete, replace and locate.

44. The process of claim 38 wherein the user selects to change the line-totals and further comprising a third prompting stimulus indicating that a choice of whether to insert or delete line totals is to be made, the third prompting stimulus is presented in combination with a menu of command choices including to insert and to delete.

45. The process of claim 24 wherein the user selects to print out according to commands already stored and wherein the second prompting stimulus indicating that a choice of source of the commands to be printed out is to be made, the second prompting stimulus is presented in combination with a menu of command choices including from workspace and from file.

46. The process of claim 25 wherein the user selects to print out commands stored in the workspace and further comprising a third stimulus and a fourth stimulus indicating that a choice is to be made of frequency of data to be printed out and of interval of data to be printed out.

47. The process of claim 45 wherein the user selects to print out commands stored in the files and further comprising third, fourth, fifth and sixth stimuli indicating that a choice is to be made of file name designating the commands to print out that a choice is to be made of frequency of data to be printed out, that a choice is to be made of interval of data to be printed out, and that a choice is to be made of run title.

48. A system for electronically generating a format for a computer print out according to commands of a user communicating with a processor, the processor having a memory and further communicating with a long-term memory, the long term memory storing a set of generic default format commands, the system comprising:

    (a) means for reproducing the generic default format commands in the processor memory;

    (b) means for modifying the generic default format commands reproduced in the processor memory according to prompted user commands to create a set of custom default commands wherein each command is selected from a menu of command choices presented in combination with each of a sequence of prompting stimuli;

    (c) means for recording data with the default format commands on the processor memory; and

    (d) means for converting the custom default format commands and data recorded on the processor memory into electrical impulses to direct a printer to print out the data according to the commands.

49. A method for designating lines of text, to be printed by a computer controlled printer, the user communicating with a computer and computer further communicating with a printer, the method comprising the steps of:

    (a) the computer requesting that the user designate text for the first line to be printed;

    (b) the user communicating a designation of text to the computer;

4,460,975

(c) the computer responding to every user designation of text by requesting that the user designate text for the next line to be printed.

50. The method of claim 49 wherein the user may designate data to be printed on a line by specifying a mnemonic association with particular data stored in the computer.

51. The method of claim 50 wherein the user may

designate text selected from the class consisting of a blank line, a row of hyphens, a centered label, a subheading, and a percentage of data.

52. The method of claim 51 further comprising a long-term memory communicating with the computer wherein data is stored in the long-term memory.

* * * * *

10

15

20

25

30

35

40

45

50

55

60

65

A.4.   TRADEMARK REGISTRATION FORM

TRADEMARK APPLICATION, PRINCIPAL REGISTER, WITH DECLARATION (Corporation)	MARK (identify the mark)
	CLASS NO. (if known)

TO THE COMMISSIONER OF PATENTS AND TRADEMARKS:

NAME OF CORPORATION [1]

STATE OR COUNTRY OF INCORPORATION

BUSINESS ADDRESS OF CORPORATION

The above identified applicant has adopted and is using the trademark shown in the accompanying drawing[2] for the following goods: _____

and requests that said mark be registered in the United States Patent and Trademark Office on the Principal Register established by the Act of July 5, 1946.

The trademark was first used on the goods[3] on _____ ; was first used on the goods[3] in

_____ commerce[4] on _____ ; and is now in use in
        (type of commerce)   *(date)*
such commerce.

5

The mark is used by applying it to[6] _____

and five specimens showing the mark as actually used are presented herewith.

7

_____ ,
                              (name of officer of corporation)
being hereby warned that willful false statements and the like so made are punishable by fine or imprisonment, or both. under Section 1001 of Title 18 of the United States Code and that such willful false statements may jeopardize the validity of the application or any registration resulting therefrom, declares that he/she is

_____
                                    (official title)
of applicant corporation and is authorized to execute this instrument on behalf of said corporation; he/she believes said corporation to be the owner of the trademark sought to be registered; to the best of his/her knowledge and belief no other person, firm, corporation, or association has the right to use said mark in commerce, either in the identical form or in such near resemblance thereto as may be likely, when applied to the goods of such other person, to cause confusion, or to cause mistake, or to deceive; the facts set forth in this application are true; and all statements made of his/her own knowledge are true and all statements made on information and belief are believed to be true.

_____
                  (name of corporation)
By _____
       (signature of officer of corporation, and official title of officer)

_____
                  (date)

Form PTO 1478 (Rev. 10-82) *(Instructions on reverse side)*   Patent and Trademark Office - U.S. DEPT. of COMMERCE
                                                                                              (over)

REPRESENTATION

If the applicant is not domiciled in the United States, a domestic representative must be designated. See Form 4.4.

If applicant wishes to furnish a power of attorney, see Form 4.2. An attorney at law is not required to furnish a power.

FOOTNOTES

1   If applicant is an association or other similar type of juristic entity, change "corporation" throughout to an appropriate designation.

2   If registration is sought for a word or numeral mark not depicted in any special form, the drawing may be the mark typed in capital letters on letter-size bond paper; otherwise, the drawing should be made with india ink on a good grade of bond paper or on bristol board.

3   If more than one item of goods in a class is set forth and the dates given for that class apply to only one of the items listed, insert the name of the item to which the dates apply.

4   Type of commerce should be specified as "interstate," "territorial," "foreign," or other type of commerce which may lawfully be regulated by Congress. Foreign applicants relying upon use must specify commerce which Congress may regulate, using wording such as commerce with the United States or commerce between the United States and a foreign country.

5   If the mark is other than a coined, arbitrary or fanciful mark, and the mark is believed to have acquired a secondary meaning, insert whichever of the following paragraphs is applicable:

a) The mark has become distinctive of applicant's goods as a result of substantially exclusive and continuous

use in _____ commerce for the five years next preceding the date of filing
                    (type of commerce)
of this application.

b) The mark has become distinctive of applicant's goods as evidenced by the showing submitted separately.

6   Insert the manner or method of using the mark with the goods, i.e., "the goods," "the containers for the goods," "displays associated with the goods," "tags or labels affixed to the goods," or other method which may be in use.

7   The required fee of $175.00 for each class must be submitted. (An application to register the same mark for goods and/or services in more than one class may be filed; however, goods and/or services, and dates of use, by class, must be set out separately, and specimens and a fee for each class are required.)

A.5. IRS REVENUE PROCEDURE 69–21

Section 1. Purpose.

The purpose of this Revenue Procedure is to provide guidelines to be used in connection with the examination of Federal income tax returns involving the costs of computer software.

Section 2. Background.

For the purpose of this Revenue Procedure, "computer software" includes all programs or routines used to cause a computer to perform a desired task or set of tasks, and the documentation required to describe and maintain those programs. Computer programs of all classes, for example, operating systems, executive systems, monitors, compilers and translators, assembly routines, and utility programs as well as application programs are included. "Computer software" does not include procedures which are external to computer operations, such as instructions to transcription operators and external control procedures.

Section 3. Costs of Developing Software.

.01 The costs of developing software (whether or not the particular software is patented or copyrighted) in many respects so closely resemble the kind of research and experimental expenditures that fall within the purview of section 174 of the Internal Revenue Code of 1954 as to warrant accounting treatment similar to that accorded such costs under that section. Accordingly, the Internal Revenue Service will not disturb a taxpayer's treatment of costs incurred in developing software, either for his own use or to be held by him for sale or lease to others, where:

1. All of the costs properly attributable to the development of software by the taxpayer are consistently treated as current expenses and deducted in full in accordance with rules similar to those applicable under section 174(a) of the Code; or

2. All of the costs properly attributable to the development of software by the taxpayer are consistently treated as capital expenditures that are recoverable through deductions for ratable amortization, in accordance with rules similar to those provided by section 174(b) of the Code and the regulations thereunder, over a period of five years from the date of completion of such development or over a shorter period where such costs are attributable to

the development of software that the taxpayer clearly establishes has a useful life of less than five years.

Section 4.   Costs of Purchased Software.

.01 With respect to costs of purchased software, the Service will not disturb the taxpayer's treatment of such costs if the following practices are consistently followed:

1. Where such costs are included, without being separately stated, in the cost of the hardware (computer) and such costs are treated as a part of the cost of the hardware that is capitalized and depreciated; or

2. Where such costs are separately stated, and the software is treated by the taxpayer as an intangible asset the cost of which is to be recovered by amortization deductions ratably over a period of five years or such shorter period as can be established by the taxpayer as appropriate in any particular case if the useful life of the software in his hands will be less than five years.

Section 5.   Leased Software.

Where a taxpayer leases software for use in his trade or business, the Service will not disturb a deduction allowable under the provisions of section 1.162-11 of the Income Tax Regulations, for rental.

Section 6.   Application.

.01 The costs of development of software in accordance with the above procedures will be treated as a method of accounting. Any change in the treatment of such costs is a change in method of accounting subject to the provisions of sections 446 and 481 of the Code and the regulations thereunder.

.02 For taxable years ending after October 27, 1969, the date of publication of this Revenue Procedure, the Service will not disturb the taxpayer's treatment of software costs that are handled in accordance with the practices described in this Revenue Procedure.

.03 For taxable years ending prior to the date of publication of this Revenue Procedure, the Service will not disturb the taxpayer's treatment of software costs except to the extent that such treatment is markedly inconsistent with the practices described in this Revenue Procedure. For the purpose of applying the preceding sentence, the absence of any formal election similar to that

required by section 174 of the Code, or the amortization of capitalized software costs over a period other than the five-year period
specified in section 174(b) of the Code, will not characterize the
taxpayer's treatment of such costs as markedly inconsistent with
the principles of this Revenue Procedure.

A.6. CHECKLIST FOR A SOFTWARE LICENSE AGREEMENT

[Between the owner or distributor of software ("Vendor") and
the end–user customer ("User")]

1. *Introduction*
    a. What is the date of the agreement?
    b. Who are the parties to the contract?
    c. What is the background of the agreement?

2. *Definitions*
    a. What terms must be defined for purposes of the contract?
    b. Consider the following—
        (1) Software
        (2) Licensed Software
        (3) Documentation
        (4) Designated Equipment
        (5) Minimum System Configuration
        (6) Updates
        (7) Enhancements
        (8) Use

3. *Grant of License to Use the Software*
    a. Is it exclusive or nonexclusive?
    b. Is it transferable or not?
    c. Is the use restricted to specific hardware?
    d. Is the use restricted to a specific operating system?
    e. Is the use restricted to a specific location?
    f. Is sublicensing allowed?
    g. Is the user allowed to modify the software?

h.   Can the user allow third parties to access the software on a time sharing basis?

i.   Are there any other restrictions imposed on the user?

4. *Term*

a.   When does the right to use the software begin?

b.   When does it end (or how long does it last)?

c.   Does the user have the right to renew the license when it expires?

d.   Does either party have the right to terminate the agreement for any reason before it would otherwise end?

5. *License Fee*

a.   What type of fee is charged?

  (1)   Fixed lump sum

  (2)   Fixed periodic fee

  (3)   Variable fee based on usage

b.   What is the amount of the fee?

c.   What is covered by the license fee? Consider the following possibilities—

  (1)   Software

  (2)   Custom modifications to the software

  (3)   Subsequent updates and enhancements

  (4)   Documentation

  (5)   Delivery

  (6)   Installation

  (7)   Training

  (8)   Support

  (9)   Maintenance

  (10)   Technical assistance

  (11)   Warranty

  (12)   Taxes

  (13)   Travel and other vendor expenses

  (14)   Vendor programming assistance

d.   When is payment due? Consider the following possibilities—

  (1)   Upon execution of contract

  (2)   Upon delivery

        (3)   Upon installation

        (4)   Upon completion of training

        (5)   Upon acceptance

        (6)   On the date the software becomes operational

        (7)   When the software is "ready for use"

        (8)   Specified number of days after any of these events

6. *Taxes*

   Who pays for any state or local taxes imposed on the license transaction?

7. *Ownership of Software*

   a. Does the vendor represent that it owns the software or that it has the right to license it?

   b. Does the user acknowledge that the vendor owns the software and that it is only acquiring a right to use it?

8. *Confidentiality*

   a. Is the user obligated to keep the software and documentation confidential?

   b. What specific steps must the user take to insure that the software remains confidential?

   c. Does this confidentiality obligation continue after the license agreement ends?

9. *Right to Copy*

   a. Does the user have the right to make copies of the software?

   b. If so, is use of the copies limited to back-up?

   c. If so, is there a limit on the number of copies that can be made?

   d. Does the user have the right to make extra copies of the documentation?

   e. Do all authorized copies remain property of the vendor?

10. *Indemnification*

    a. Will the vendor pay any damages or expense suffered by the user if the vendor's ownership rights to the software are challenged by anyone?

    b. What types of damages and expenses are covered?

    c. What are the conditions for such coverage?

11. *Delivery*
    a. When will the software be delivered to the user?
    b. What is the user's remedy for late delivery?
        (1) Right to cancel and get refund
        (2) Liquidated damages
        (3) Vendor not liable for delays outside its control

12. *Installation*
    a. Who installs the software?
    b. If the vendor will install the software, when will it be installed?
    c. Is there any charge for vendor installation?

13. *Training*
    a. Will the vendor provide training?
    b. How much training will be provided?
    c. What is the cost of training?
    d. When and where will training take place?
    e. Is future training for new personnel available at a later date? If so, under what terms?
    f. Who gets trained?
        (1) Operators
        (2) Programmers
        (3) Management
    g. How many people will be trained?

14. *Warranties*
    a. Is the software licensed "AS IS" or does the vendor make any express warranties?
    b. What express warranties (if any) are included?
        (1) Warranty that the vendor owns the software
        (2) Warranty of power and authority to grant licenses (if the vendor is not the owner of the software)
        (3) Warranty of software functions
        (4) Warranty of performance
        (5) Warranty of adequacy of documentation
        (6) Warranty of noninfringement of patents, copyrights, and trade secrets

  (7) Warranty as to the minimum equipment required to support the software

  (8) Warranty as to the operating system and any other software required to support the software

  (9) Warranty that the vendor will modify the software to adapt to any future hardware and/or operating system changes

  (10) Warranty of file compatability

c. How long does the warranty last?

d. Has the vendor disclaimed all express warranties not specifically included in the contract?

e. Has the vendor disclaimed the warranties implied by law?

  (1) Merchantability

  (2) Fitness for particular purpose

f. If the software fails to work as warranted, is the user's remedy limited to repair or some other specified remedy (e.g., refund)?

g. What conditions will void the warranty?

  (1) Installation on unauthorized CPU

  (2) Designated equipment does not meet minimum system requirements

  (3) Software modified by user

15. *Limitations of Liability*

a. Is there a limit on the dollar amount of damages to which the vendor is exposed in the event the software fails to work properly?

b. Is there a limit on the type of damages to which the vendor is exposed; i.e., has the vendor excluded liability for—

  (1) Consequential damages (such as lost profits)

  (2) Claims by third parties

  (3) Damages caused by improper use

c. Is there a contractual limit on the time in which either party can file a lawsuit against the other?

16. *Software Maintenance*

a. Is the vendor obligated to provide maintenance?

   b. What maintenance (if any) is provided by the vendor during the warranty period?

   c. What maintenance (if any) is provided by the vendor after the warranty expires?

   d. Is maintenance optional or required?

   e. What is excluded from maintenance coverage?

      (1) User modifications to the software

      (2) Failure to comply with the terms of the license

      (3) Failure to install updates

   f. Does the vendor have the right to terminate maintenance?

   g. Does the user have an obligation to identify errors?

   h. Does the vendor have an obligation to notify the user of errors found?

   i. What is the maintenance fee and when is it due?

17. *Updates and Enhancements*

   a. Does the user have the right to obtain updates and enhancements?

   b. Is the vendor obligated to provide updates and/or enhancements?

   c. On what terms (and price) will they be made available?

18. *Modifications by User*

   a. Does the user have the right to modify the software?

   b. Who owns any user modifications?

   c. Are there any limitations on use of such modifications?

   d. What is the effect of user modifications on the vendor's warranty and maintenance obligations?

19. *Default*

   a. Are there any special circumstances which the parties will consider to be a breach of the contract?

   b. Is the nonbreaching party required to give notice of the breach to the other party before exercising its legal rights?

   c. Does the breaching party have an opportunity to cure its breach?

    d. Is there a right to terminate the license a specified number of days after notice of a breach?

    e. Is there a right to immediate termination upon breach of trade secret confidentiality?

20. *Arbitration of Disputes*

    a. If a dispute arises between the parties, will they be required to submit to arbitration or to some other method of alternate dispute resolution instead of going to court?

    b. If so, where will the arbitration be held?

    c. If so, how will the arbitrator(s) be chosen and what rules will govern the arbitration proceeding?

21. *Termination*

    a. When can either party terminate the license?
- (1) Upon expiration of the term
- (2) At either party's discretion
- (3) On default
- (4) On bankruptcy or insolvency
- (5) On cessation of business
- (6) If the software is not accepted

    b. When is termination effective?
- (1) After notice
- (2) After right to cure expires

    c. What happens on termination?
- (1) User must discontinue use of software
- (2) User must destroy or return all copies of software
- (3) User must return all documentation
- (4) User must certify destruction and/or return of all materials

    d. Do any obligations survive termination?
- (1) Confidentiality
- (2) Indemnification
- (3) Payments due and owing (fees, taxes, royalties, etc.)

22. *Events upon Cessation of Business*

    a. What happens if the vendor ceases doing business?

    b. What happens if the user ceases doing business?

23. *Source Code Access*
    a. Are any arrangements made to provide the user with access to source code in the event the vendor cannot support the software?
    b. If so, what type of access mechanism is used?
        (1) User holds source code
        (2) Vendor releases the source code on the occurrence of a specified event (such as the vendor ceasing to do business)
        (3) Source code escrow
    c. If an escrow is used, what material is included in the escrow?
        (1) Source code
        (2) Documentation
        (3) System design, flowcharts, other data, etc.
    d. Is any procedure established to verify the completeness of the escrow materials?
    e. Are any arrangements made for subsequent deposit into escrow of enhancements, modifications, and corrections?
    f. Who pays the escrow and verification fees?
    g. What are the triggering events for release of the source code?
        (1) Bankruptcy
        (2) Assignment for benefit of creditors
        (3) Dissolution, liquidation, or death of vendor
        (4) Appointment of receiver or trustee
        (5) Levy or execution on any lien, mortgage, or security interest of vendor
        (6) Failure to maintain software
    h. What is the release mechanism?
        (1) Notice from user with consent from vendor
        (2) Notice from user without consent from vendor
        (3) Resolution of disputes regarding release
            (a) Injunctive relief
            (b) Arbitration
            (c) Liquidated damages
    i. What are the user's rights to the software upon release?
        (1) Internal use only
        (2) Subject to terms of license

24. *Assignment Rights*

    a. Does the vendor have the right to assign the license?

    b. Does the user have the right to assign the license?

25. *Miscellaneous*

    a. Is this contract the entire agreement of the parties?

    b. Is there a requirement that all amendments to the contract be in writing?

    c. What state's law will govern any disputes?

26. *Exhibits*

    a. Are any exhibits to be attached?

    b. Possibilities include—

        (1) Licensed software description

        (2) Licensed software specifications

        (3) Hardware facility requirements

        (4) Software facility requirements

        (5) Performance (run time) requirements

        (6) Licensed software documentation

A.7. SAMPLE SOFTWARE LICENSE AGREEMENT*

This Agreement is entered into on ___ _, 19_ by and between Software Marketing Co., an Illinois corporation ("Vendor"), and Software Enduser, Inc., a Delaware corporation ("Licensee").

    1. *Definition of Terms.*

    (a) *Licensed Software.* The term "Licensed Software" means the object code version of the computer software identified on Exhibit A of this Agreement and any subsequent Updates and Enhancements thereto furnished to Licensee by Vendor.

    (b) *Documentation.* The term "Documentation" means the standard user manual supplied by Vendor with the Licensed

---

* This contract is an example of the way a software license agreement might be structured, and the types of provisions that might be included in such an agreement. It is not intended to be used as a form, however, since the structure and content of each contract must be tailored to meet the needs of the situation in which it is to be used.

Software which tells Licensee how to install and use the Licensed Software.

(c) *Updates.* The term "Updates" means all changes, modifications, and improvements to the Licensed Software which affect its operating performance or efficiency, but which do not alter the basic functions that it performs.

(d) *Enhancements.* The term "Enhancements" means all changes and additions to the Licensed Software which render it capable of performing additional basic functions that were not provided by the Licensed Software originally supplied under this Agreement.

(e) *Designated Equipment.* The term "Designated Equipment" means the single computer central processing unit (CPU) and its associated peripheral equipment as identified by serial number on Exhibit B of this Agreement.

(f) *Date of Installation.* The term "Date of Installation" means the date that Vendor installs the Licensed Software on the Designated Equipment at Licensee's place of business, or the date that Vendor is able to demonstrate that the Licensed Software properly executes its standard test data, whichever is later.

2. *License Grant.* Vendor grants to Licensee a nonexclusive license to use the Licensed Software and Documentation, under the terms and conditions set forth below, on the Designated Equipment only. This license does not include any rights to alter, sublicense others, or transfer in any way the Licensed Software or Documentation provided by Vendor. Only Licensee and its employees shall be allowed to use the Licensed Software.

3. *Term.* This license shall commence on the Date of Installation, and shall continue for a Term of 10 years. At the end of this term, Licensee shall have the option of renewing this license for an additional 10-year term, subject to the conditions in this Agreement, by paying Vendor an additional 10 percent of the License Fee paid pursuant to this Agreement.

4. *License Fee.* Licensee agrees to pay Vendor a single License Fee which is specified on Exhibit C. Payment of one-half of this fee shall be due within 30 days of the signing of this Agreement, and the remaining balance shall be paid on the Date of Installation.

5. *Taxes.* Licensee shall pay all taxes (local, state and federal), including all sales and use taxes, which may now or hereafter be imposed upon this license, or the possession or use of the Licensed Software, excluding, however, all taxes on or measured by Vendor's income.

6. *Ownership of Software.* Licensee acknowledges that the Licensed Software and the Documentation are the exclusive property of Vendor and that Licensee has no rights in the Licensed Software except those expressly granted by this Agreement, and that the Licensed Software shall not be used in any way not allowed by this Agreement.

7. *Confidentiality.* Licensee acknowledges that the Licensed Software and Documentation constitute valuable trade secrets of Vendor and are unpublished works on which Vendor holds the sole and exclusive copyright. Licensee agrees to maintain and protect the confidentiality of these trade secrets and agrees not to disclose them or use them for any purpose not contemplated by this Agreement. Licensee agrees to formulate and adopt appropriate safeguards, in light of its own operating activities, to insure protection of the confidentiality of these trade secrets. Licensee shall immediately notify Vendor of any information which comes to its attention which indicates that there has been any loss of confidentiality of Vendor's trade secret information.

8. *Right to Copy Software and Documentation.* Licensee may make no more than three (3) copies of the Licensed Software. Such copies shall be used only by Licensee and solely for backup purposes. All copies shall be the exclusive property of Vendor.

Licensee shall include Vendor's copyright, trade secret, and confidentiality notices on all of its copies of the Licensed Software, and on all tangible media, such as tapes, disks, or diskettes, upon which such copies are stored, in the same mannner as provided on the materials received from Vendor. The Documentation licensed by Vendor to the Licensee may not be reproduced by the Licensee. Additional copies of the Documentation may be licensed from Vendor at the fees then in effect, subject to the terms of this Agreement.

9. *Patent, Copyright, and Trade Secret Indemnity.* In the event that any suit is brought against Licensee based on a claim

that the Licensed Software infringes any existing patent, copyright, or trade secret, Vendor agrees that it will either defend the suit at its expense and pay all damages and costs awarded against Licensee, or procure for Licensee the right to continue using the Licensed Software, or replace or modify the Licensed Software so that infringement will not exist. Vendor shall not be liable for any claim of infringement based upon the use of the Licensed Software in combination with software not supplied by Vendor, or resulting from modifications to any of the Licensed Software made by Licensee.

10. *Delivery.* The Licensed Software and Documentation shall be delivered to Licensee within 90 days of the date of this Agreement.

11. *Installation.* Vendor will install the Licensed Software on the Designated Equipment at Licensee's place of business and demonstrate to Licensee that the Licensed Software has properly executed Vendor's standard test data.

12. *Training.* Vendor will provide up to three (3) days of training in the use of the Licensed Software at Licensee's offices for two (2) employees designated by Licensee. Additional training is available at Vendor's standard published rates.

13. *Warranty and Limitations.*

(a) *Software Functions.* Vendor warrants that the Licensed Software will perform all functions specified in the Documentation. However, Licensee acknowledges that the Licensed Software is of such complexity that it may have inherent defects, and therefore agrees that its remedy shall be limited to that specified in part (b) of this paragraph.

(b) *Licensee's Remedy.* In the event that the Licensed Software fails to perform as warranted, as Licensee's sole and exclusive remedy Vendor shall, within a reasonable time, provide all reasonable programming services to correct documented errors.

(c) *Warranty Period.* This warranty shall be effective for the term of one (1) year after the Date of Installation of the Licensed Software ("Warranty Period"). All claims must be made by Licensee within this Warranty Period.

(d) *Conditions Voiding Warranty.* This warranty shall be null and void in the event that the Licensed Software is installed on any computer equipment other than the Designated Equipment, is modified by the Licensee, or is merged with other software by the Licensee. This warranty shall also be null and void in the event that the Licensed Software is used by any person other than Licensee and Licensee's employees.

(e) *LIMITATIONS OF WARRANTY.* THE FOREGOING WARRANTY IS THE ONLY WARRANTY MADE BY VENDOR. ALL OTHER WARRANTIES, EXPRESS OR IMPLIED, INCLUDING, BUT NOT LIMITED TO, THE IMPLIED WARRANTIES OF MERCHANTABILITY AND FITNESS FOR A PARTICULAR PURPOSE, ARE EXPRESSLY DISCLAIMED.

14. *LIMITATIONS OF LIABILITY.* IT IS UNDERSTOOD AND AGREED THAT VENDOR'S LIABILITY FOR ANY LOSSES SUFFERED BY LICENSEE SHALL NOT EXCEED THE RETURN OF THE AMOUNT OF THE LICENSE FEE PAID BY LICENSEE. IN ADDITION, VENDOR SHALL HAVE NO LIABILITY WHATSOEVER FOR SPECIAL OR CONSEQUENTIAL DAMAGES (INCLUDING LOST PROFITS) OF LICENSEE OR ANY THIRD PARTY, EVEN IF VENDOR HAS BEEN ADVISED OF THE POSSIBILITY OF SUCH DAMAGES. NO ACTION, REGARDLESS OF FORM, ARISING OUT OF THE TRANSACTIONS UNDER THIS AGREEMENT MAY BE BROUGHT BY LICENSEE MORE THAN ONE YEAR AFTER THE CAUSE OF ACTION HAS ACCRUED.

15. *Software Maintenance Support.*

(a) *During Warranty Period.* During the Warranty Period Vendor will provide programming services at no charge to correct any material defects in the operation of the Licensed Software and to maintain it in good working order.

(b) *After Warranty.* At the expiration of the Warranty Period, Licensee may, at its option, elect to continue maintenance on a year-to-year basis by paying the yearly maintenance fee then in effect.

(c) *Exclusions.* If any problem is due to Licensee alterations of the Licensed Software or the Designated Equipment, or failure to comply with the terms of this Agreement, Licensee shall pay for the time and expenses associated with such maintenance effort at Vendor's then-current applicable rates. Furthermore, Vendor may periodically send Updates to Licensee, as described elsewhere in the Agreement. In order to remain eligible for maintenance support, Licensee must apply Updates so that the Licensed Software is up-to-date.

16. *Future Updates and Enhancements.*

(a) *Software Updates.* If Vendor releases any Updates to the Licensed Software, they will be furnished to Licensee at no cost during the Warranty Period. Thereafter, Vendor will continue to furnish any Updates released only if Licensee has paid for continued maintenance.

(b) *Software Enhancements.* If Vendor releases any Enhancements to the Licensed Software after the Date of Installation, Licensee shall have the right to obtain such Enhancements at the license fees then in effect.

17. *Licensee Modifications to Software.* Licensee shall not have any right to alter or modify the Licensed Software.

18. *Default.* In the event Licensee breaches any of the terms of this Agreement, Vendor may, at any time thereafter, give written notice of the breach to Licensee, and demand that the same be cured. In the event that such breach is not cured within thirty (30) days after notice, this Agreement shall terminate. Notwithstanding the foregoing, in the event Licensee breaches any of its obligations of confidentiality under this Agreement, Vendor shall have the right to terminate the Agreement immediately upon notice to Licensee.

19. *Events Upon Termination.* Upon the termination of this Agreement, Licensee hereby agrees to immediately terminate its use of the Licensed Software, and to return to Vendor all copies of the Licensed Software and Documentation. Licensee shall thereafter make no further use of the Licensed Software. Termination of this Agreement shall not relieve either party of the obligations arising hereunder before termination, including the responsibility for paying previously accrued license fees, the responsibility for not disclosing the Licensed Software and the Documentation, and the responsibility for returning these items to Vendor.

20. *Assignment.* This Agreement may not be assigned by Licensee to any other person, firm, or corporation without the express written approval of Vendor, which approval will not be unreasonably withheld.

21. *Entire Agreement.* The parties have read this Agreement and agree to be bound by its terms, and further agree that it constitutes the entire and exclusive agreement of the parties and super-

sedes all previous communications, representations, or agreements, either oral or written, between them. No representations or statements of any kind made by any representative of Vendor which are not stated herein shall be binding on Vendor.

22. *All Amendments in Writing.* Any modification or addition to any provision of this Agreement must be agreed to in writing by a duly authorized representative of each party.

23. *Governing Law.* This contract will be governed by and construed in accordance with the laws of the State of Illinois.

IN WITNESS WHEREOF, the parties have caused this Agreement to be executed by their duly authorized representatives.

SOFTWARE MARKETING CO.

By: _____

Title _____

SOFTWARE ENDUSER, INC.

By: _____

Title _____

A.8. CHECKLIST FOR A SOFTWARE DISTRIBUTORSHIP AGREEMENT

[Between the owner of the software ("Owner") and the distributor of the software ("Distributor")]

1. *Introduction*
   a. What is the date of the agreement?
   b. Who are the parties to the contract?
   c. What is the background of the agreement?

2. *Definitions*
   a. What terms must be defined for purposes of the contract?
   b. Consider the following—
      (1) Software
      (2) Licensed Software
      (3) Documentation
      (4) Updates

    (5) Enhancements
    (6) Use
    (7) Customer
    (8) Territory
    (9) Market

3. *Grant of License to Market the Software*
   a. Is it exclusive or nonexclusive?
   b. Is it transferable or not?
   c. Is the right to market restricted to specific hardware?
   d. Is the right to market restricted to a specific operating system?
   e. Is the right to market restricted to a specific territory?
   f. Is the right to market restricted to a particular market (e.g., the medical services market)?
   g. Is the distributor allowed to modify the software?
   h. Does the distributor have the right to use a copy of the software for its own internal purposes?
   i. Does the distributor have the right to use the owner's trademarks?
   j. Are there any other restrictions imposed on the distributor?

4. *Method of Marketing the Software*
   a. Will the distributor sell copies of the software, sublicense copies of the software, or act as a sales representative facilitating license agreements directly between the software owner and the customer?
   b. Does the distributorship agreement specify any of the terms that must appear in the contract between the distributor and the customer?
   c. Does the distributorship agreement require the distributor to use a form contract drawn up by the software owner when sublicensing software to its customers?

5. *Term*
   a. When does the right to market the software begin?
   b. When does it end (or how long does it last)?
   c. Does the distributor have the right to renew the agreement when it expires?

    d. Is the right to renew conditioned upon the distributor's performance or some other criteria?

    e. Does either party have the right to terminate the agreement before it would otherwise end?

6. *License Fees and Royalties*

    a. Payments by distributor to software owner
   - (1) Will the owner be paid in a lump sum, or on a per copy basis?
   - (2) How much will the distributor pay the software owner for each copy of the software that it sells or licenses to a customer?
   - (3) When is each payment due?
   - (4) Are any discounts allowed for volume?
   - (5) Does the owner have the right to change the royalty during the term of the agreement?

    b. Distributor bookkeeping requirements
   - (1) What record-keeping requirements are imposed on the distributor in order to keep track of all sales or licenses of the software to insure that the software owner is paid all sums owed?
   - (2) What information must the distributor record with respect to each sale or license?
   - (3) How often must the distributor send reports to the software owner?
   - (4) What rights does the software owner have to audit the distributor's books?

    c. Are there any restrictions on the price that the distributor can charge a customer for the software?[1]

    d. What does the owner provide to the distributor in exchange for the license fee? Consider the following—
   - (1) Software
   - (2) Custom modifications to the software
   - (3) Subsequent updates and enhancements
   - (4) Documentation
   - (5) Delivery
   - (6) Installation

---

[1] If the software owner places any restrictions on the distributor's right to set the price for its end–user customer, it may be a violation of the antitrust laws. This should be checked with an attorney.

      (7) Training

      (8) Support

      (9) Maintenance

      (10) Technical assistance

      (11) Warranty

      (12) Taxes

      (13) Travel and other owner expenses

      (14) Owner programming assistance

e. When is payment due from the distributor to the owner? Consider the following—

      (1) Upon execution of the contract between the owner and the distributor (i.e., an advance payment or a single lump sum payment)

      (2) Upon execution of a contract between the distributor and customer

      (3) Upon delivery of software to the customer

      (4) Upon installation at customer's site

      (5) Upon training of customer

      (6) Upon acceptance by customer

      (7) On the date the software becomes operational at a customer's site

      (8) When the software is "ready for use" by a customer

      (9) Specified number of days after any of these events

      (10) Monthly, quarterly, semiannually, or on some other periodic basis.

7. *Taxes*

  a. Who pays for any state or local taxes imposed on the transactions between the owner and the distributor (if any)?

  b. Who pays for any state or local taxes imposed on the sale or license of the software to the end-user customer?

8. *Ownership of Software*

  a. Who owns the software?

  b. Does the owner represent that it owns the software or that it has the right to license it?

  c. Does the distributor acknowledge that the owner owns the software and that it is only acquiring a right to use and market it?

9. *Confidentiality*
    a. Is the distributor obligated to keep the software and documentation confidential?
    b. What specific steps must the distributor take to insure that the software remains confidential?
    c. Does this confidentiality obligation continue after the distributorship agreement ends?
    d. Is either party restricted from making use of the list of customers to whom the distributor has sold or licensed the software?
    e. Is the distributor obligated to inform its customers as to who owns the software?
    f. Is the distributor obligated to require its customers to sign a confidentiality agreement?
    g. Is the distributor required to place the owner's copyright and trade secret notices on all copies of the software?

10. *Right to Copy*
    a. Who will make copies of the software for the customers?
    b. Does the distributor have the right to make copies of the software either for customers or for its own use?
    c. If so, is use of the copies restricted in any way?
    d. If so, is there a limit on the number of copies that can be made?
    e. Does the distributor and/or customer have the right to make extra copies of the documentation?
    f. Do all authorized copies remain property of the software owner?

11. *Indemnification*
    a. Will the owner agree to pay any damages or expenses suffered by the distributor and/or its customers if the owner's ownership rights to the software are challenged by anyone?
    b. What types of damages and expenses are covered?
    c. What must the distributor do to be entitled to such reimbursement?
    d. Will the distributor pay all damages suffered by the owner if the distributor makes any misrepresentations to its customers?

    e. Will the owner pay all damages suffered by the distributor as the result of complaints by customers relating to software problems that are the owner's fault?

12. *Delivery*

    a. Will the owner deliver the software to the distributor or directly to its customer?

    b. When will the software be delivered?

    c. What is the distributor's remedy for late delivery? Consider the following—

        (1) Right to cancel and get refund

        (2) Liquidated damages

        (3) Owner not liable for delays outside its control

13. *Installation*

    a. Who installs the software for the distributor's customer?

    b. When will the software be installed?

    c. Is there any charge for installation?

14. *Training*

    a. Will the owner train the distributor in any of the following areas:

        (1) Use of the software

        (2) Installation of the software

        (3) Maintenance of the software

    b. Will customer training be provided?

    c. If so, who is obligated to provide customer training?

    d. What is the cost of training?

    e. When and where will training take place?

    f. Is future training available?

    g. Who gets trained? Consider the following—

        (1) Operators

        (2) Programmers

        (3) Management

        (4) Customers of distributor

    h. How many people will be trained?

15. *Distributor Performance Obligations*

    a. Is the distributor required to use its "best efforts" to market the software?

    b. Is the distributor required to fulfill any quotas?

    c. Is the distributor required to make any specified marketing efforts (e.g., devote a specified dollar amount to advertising, employ a specified number of salespersons devoted full time to marketing the software, etc.)?

    d. Is the distributor restricted from marketing competing software?[2]

    e. Is the distributor required to make any commitments with respect to providing installation, training, warranty service, or maintenance for its customers?

16. *Warranties (From Owner to Distributor)*

    a. Is the software provided "AS IS" or does the owner make any express warranties to the distributor?

    b. What express warranties (if any) does the owner make to the distributor?

       (1) Warranty that the owner owns the software

       (2) Warranty of power and authority to grant distributorship

       (3) Warranty of software functions

       (4) Warranty of performance

       (5) Warranty of adequacy of documentation

       (6) Warranty of noninfringement of patents, copyrights, and trade secrets

       (7) Warranty as to minimum equipment required to support the software

       (8) Warranty as to the operating system and any other software required to support the software

       (9) Warranty that the owner will modify the software to adapt to any future hardware and/or operating system changes

     (10) Warranty of file compatability

    c. How long does the warranty last?

    d. Is the distributor authorized by the owner to make any warranties to the end–user customer?

---

[2] Such a restriction may violate the antitrust laws and should not be included without prior consultation with an attorney.

   e. Has the owner disclaimed all express warranties not specifically included in the contract?

   f. Has the owner disclaimed the warranties implied by law?

     (1) Merchantability

     (2) Fitness for particular purpose

   g. If the software fails to work as warranted, is the distributor's remedy limited to repair or some other specified remedy (e.g., refund)?

   h. What conditions will void the warranty?

     (1) Installation on unauthorized hardware

     (2) Designated equipment does not meet minimum system requirements

     (3) Software modified by distributor or customer

17. *Limitations of Liability*

   a. Is there a limit on the dollar amount of damages to which the owner is exposed in the event the software fails to work properly?

   b. Is there a limit on the type of damages to which the owner is exposed, i.e., has the owner excluded liability for—

     (1) Consequential damages (such as lost profits)

     (2) Claims by customers and other third parties

     (3) Damages caused by improper use

   c. Is there a contractual limit on the time in which either party can file a lawsuit against the other?

18. *Software Maintenance*

   a. Who provides maintenance for the distributor's customers (owner or distributor)?

   b. What maintenance (if any) is provided by the owner during the warranty period?

   c. What maintenance (if any) is provided by the owner after the warranty period expires?

   d. Is maintenance optional or required?

   e. What is excluded from maintenance coverage?

     (1) Distributor and/or customer modifications to the software

(2) Failure to comply with the terms of the license

(3) Failure to apply updates

f. Does the owner have the right to terminate mainte-nance?

g. Does the distributor have an obligation to identify er-rors?

h. Does the owner have an obligation to notify the distribu-tor of errors found?

i. What is the maintenance fee and when is it due?

19. *Updates and Enhancements*

a. Does the distributor have the right to obtain updates and enhancements?

b. Is the owner obligated to provide the distributor with updates and/or enhancements?

c. On what terms (and price) will they be made available?

20. *Modifications by Distributor*

a. Does the distributor have the right to modify the soft-ware?

b. Who owns any distributor modifications?

c. Are there any limitations on use of such modifications?

d. What is the effect of distributor modifications on the owner's warranty and maintenance obligations?

21. *Default*

a. Are their any special circumstances that the parties will consider to be a breach of the contract?

b. Is the nonbreaching party required to give notice of the breach to the other party before exercising its legal rights?

c. Does the breaching party have an opportunity to cure its breach?

d. Is there a right to terminate the distributorship agree-ment a specified number of days after notice of a breach?

e. Is there a right to immediate termination upon breach of trade secret confidentiality?

22. *Arbitration of Disputes*

a. If a dispute arises between the parties, will they be re-

quired to submit to arbitration or some other method of alternate dispute resolution instead of going to court?
b. If so, where will the arbitration be held?
c. If so, how will the arbitrator be chosen and what rules will govern the arbitration proceeding?

23. *Termination*
   a. When can either party terminte the distributorship agreement?
      (1) Upon expiration of the term
      (2) At either party's discretion
      (3) On default
      (4) On bankruptcy or insolvency
      (5) On cessation of business
      (6) If the distributor fails to fulfill its quotas
   b. When is termination effective?
      (1) After notice
      (2) After right to cure expires
   c. What happens on termination?
      (1) Distributor must discontinue use and marketing of software
      (2) Distributor must destroy or return all copies of software
      (3) Distributor must return all documentation
      (4) Distributor must return all other materials supplied by owner
      (5) Distributor must certify destruction and/or return of all materials
   d. What happens to licenses with customers when the distributorship ends?
   e. If the distributor was maintaining the software for its customers, who will provide such maintenance after the distributorship ends?
   f. Do any obligations survive termination?
      (1) Confidentiality
      (2) Indemnification
      (3) Payments due and owing (fees, taxes, royalties, etc.)

24. *Events upon Cessation of Business*
    a. What happens if the owner ceases doing business?
    b. What happens if the distributor ceases doing business?

25. *Source Code Access*
    a. Are any arrangements made to provide the distributor with access to source code in the event the owner cannot support the software?
    b. What type of access mechanism is used?
       (1) Distributor holds source code
       (2) Owner releases the source code on the occurrence of a specified event (such as owner ceasing to do business)
       (3) Source code escrow
    c. If an escrow is used, what material is included in the escrow?
       (1) Source code
       (2) Documentation
       (3) System design, flowcharts, other data, etc.
    d. Is any procedure established to verify the completeness of the escrow materials?
    e. Are any arrangements made for subsequent deposit into escrow of enhancements, modifications, and corrections?
    f. Who pays the escrow and verification fees?
    g. What are the triggering events for release of the source code?
       (1) Bankruptcy
       (2) Assignment for benefit of creditors
       (3) Dissolution, liquidation, or death of owner
       (4) Appointment of receiver or trustee
       (5) Levy or execution on any lien, mortgage, or security interest of owner
       (6) Failure to maintain software
    h. What is the release mechanism?
       (1) Notice from distributor with consent from owner
       (2) Notice from distributor without consent from owner
       (3) Resolution of disputes regarding release
          (a) Injunctive relief
          (b) Arbitration

      (c)   Liquidated damages

  i. What are the distributor's rights to the software upon release?

     (1)   Internal use only

     (2)   Subject to terms of distributorship agreement

26. *Assignment Rights*

  a.   Does the owner have the right to assign the distributorship agreement?

  b.   Does the distributor have the right to assign the distribution agreement?

27. *Miscellaneous*

  a.   Is this contract the entire agreement of the parties?

  b.   Is there a requirement that all amendments to the contract be in writing?

  c.   What state's law will govern any disputes?

28. *Exhibits*

  a.   Are any exhibits to be attached?

  b.   Possibilities include—

     (1)   Licensed software description

     (2)   Licensed software specifications

     (3)   Hardware facility requirements

     (4)   Software facility requirements

     (5)   Performance (run time) statistics

     (6)   Licensed software documentation

     (7)   License agreement to be used with customers

     (8)   Prices and discounts for software

A.9.   SAMPLE SOFTWARE DISTRIBUTORSHIP AGREEMENT*

THIS AGREEMENT is entered into on _____ , 19 __ , by and between BUSINESS SOFTWARE DEVELOPERS, INC.

---

* This contract is an example of the way a software distributorship agreement might be structured, and the types of provisions that might be included in such an agreement. It is not intended to be used as a form, however, since the structure and content of each contract must be tailored to meet the needs of the situation in which it is to be used.

("Owner") and XYZ SOFTWARE DISTRIBUTORS, INC. ("Distributor").

1. *Background.* This Agreement is made with reference to the following facts:

(a) Owner is the developer and owner of all rights to the computer Software Product identified on Exhibit A;

(b) Owner desires to license Distributor to use, market, and sublicense the Software Product upon the terms and conditions of this Agreement;

(c) Distributor desires to obtain a license to use, market, and sublicense the Software Product in accordance with the terms and conditions of this Agreement.

2. *Definition of Terms.*

(a) *Software Product.* The term "Software Product" means the object code version of the proprietary computer software identified on Exhibit A of this Agreement, and any subsequent revisions or modifications thereto furnished to Distributor by Owner.

(b) *Documentation.* The term "Documentation" means Owner's standard instruction manual normally provided to customers who license the Software Product.

(c) *Customer.* The term "Customer" means any person to whom Distributor sublicenses a copy of any of the Software Product.

(d) *Territory.* The term "Territory" means the geographical area described in Exhibit B.

(e) *Sublicense Agreement.* The term "Sublicense Agreement" means the standard form license agreement attached to this Agreement as Exhibit C.

3. *License Grant.*

(a) *Right to Sublicense.* Owner grants to Distributor a nonexclusive, nontransferrable, license to use, market, and sublicense the current version of the Software Product to Customers located in the Territory.

(b) *Form of Sublicense Agreement.* When sublicensing the Software Product to Customers, Distributor will use only the Sublicense Agreement attached as Exhibit C as its sublicense agreement with its Customers. Any modification of this form must be approved by Owner in writing.

(c) *Demonstration Copy.* Owner shall provide Distributor with an initial demonstration copy of the Software Product and Documentation at no charge.

4. *Term.* This Agreement shall commence immediately and shall continue for a period of three (3) years. It shall automatically be renewed on a year-to-year basis thereafter unless terminated by either party by written notice delivered to the other party at least 90 days before the end of the term.

5. *Payment.*

(a) *Software.* For each copy of the Software Product sublicensed to a Customer, Distributor agrees to pay Owner the license fee set forth in Exhibit D, subject to the applicable discounts also set forth therein. Owner reserves the right to change the license fee on 90 days written notice.

(b) *Payments.* Payment of the license fee shall be made within 30 days of the date that the Software Product is shipped to Distributor pursuant to paragraph 11.

(c) *Books and Records.* Distributor shall maintain its books and records so as to establish the payments due to Owner under this Agreement. Such books and records shall be made available at their place of keeping for inspection on a confidential basis during normal business hours by Owner solely for the purpose of verifying the payments due to Owner.

(d) *Reports.* Distributor shall furnish to Owner quarterly reports setting forth the name and address of all Customers to whom the Software Product has been delivered.

6. *Taxes.* Distributor will pay all taxes of any type that are imposed on this Agreement or on the use or sublicensing of the Software Product by Distributor.

7. *Ownership of Software.* Distributor acknowledges that the Software Product is the sole property of Owner and that Distributor has no rights in the Software Product except those expressly granted by this Agreement.

8. *Confidentiality.* Distributor acknowledges that the Software Product and Documentation contain valuable trade secrets which are the sole property of Owner, and agrees to use reasonable care to prevent other parties from learning of these trade secrets. Distributor will take all reasonable steps to prevent unauthorized access to or duplication of the Software Product and Doc-

umentation. Distributor is authorized, however, to make a limited disclosure of the nature and function of the Software Product to prospective Customers in the course of its marketing efforts.

The obligations of this paragraph shall not extend to any information which is or becomes publicly available (through no fault of Distributor), or is rightfully obtained from third parties.

9. *Rights to Copy Software and Documentation.* The Software Product, Documentaton, and other printed materials provided by Owner to Distributor may be reproduced by Distributor, provided that such reproduction is made solely for uses consistent with the terms of this Agreement, and provided that all of Owner's copyright and confidentiality notices are reproduced on each copy.

10. *Patent, Copyright, and Trade Secret Indemnity.*

(a) In the event that any suit is brought against Distributor based on a claim that the Software Product infringes any existing patent, copyright, or trade secret, Owner agrees that it will:

(1) Defend the suit at its expense, as long as Owner is notified promptly in writing and is given complete authority and information required to defend the suit; and

(2) Pay all damages and costs awarded against Distributor, but Owner will not be responsible for any cost, expense, or compromise made by Distributor without Owner's written consent.

(b) In the event the Software Product is, or in Owner's opinion is likely to become, the subject of a claim for patent, copyright, or trade secret infringement, Owner may at its option and expense procure for Distributor the right to continue using, marketing, and sublicensing same, or replace or modify the Software Product so that infringement will not exist.

(c) Owner shall not be liable for any claim of infringement based upon the use of the Software Product in combination with software not supplied by Owner, or resulting from modifications to the Software Product made by Distributor or any third party.

11. *Delivery.* Owner will ship a copy of the Software Product and Documentation to Distributor as soon as is reasonably practical after Owner's receipt of Distributor's order enclosing a copy of the Sublicense Agreement executed by the Customer.

Distributor is responsible for delivering the Software Product and Documentation to its Customer.

12. *Installation.* Distributor shall be responsible for installation of the Software Product at the Customer's site.

13. *Training.*

(a) *For Distributor.* Owner shall conduct a five (5) day training session at a mutually agreeable time and location to assist and train up to five (5) of Distributor's employees in the installation, use, and maintenance of the Software Product. Owner shall provide all necessary personnel and materials needed for such training sessions.

(b) *For Customers.* It is understood and agreed that any training necessary for Distributor's Customers shall be provided by Distributor.

(c) *Availability for Consultation.* Owner will be available for telephone consultation with Distributor and its personnel at such times and for such periods as Distributor may reasonably request.

14. *Obligations of Distributor.*

(a) *Marketing.* Distributor shall use its best efforts to market the Software Product within the Territory.

(b) *Training and Support.* Distributor shall establish a training and support service for Customers and employ qualified personnel to enable it to perform these obligations.

(c) *Reporting of Problems.* Distributor shall promptly inform Owner of any problems with the Software Product that come to its attention.

15. *Warranties.*

(a) *Authorization.* Owner warrants that it has full power and right to license the Software Product and Documentation and to perform all other terms of this Agreement.

(b) *Operation.* Each copy of the Software Product sublicensed by Distributor to its Customers is warranted for a period of three (3) months from the date of delivery to the Customer (the "Warranty Period") from any failure to perform all functions and operations set forth in the Documentation. During such period, Owner will furnish all maintenance and service necessary to maintain the copy of the Software Product in operation and in working order at no cost to Distributor or to the Customer.

(c) *Indemnification for Breach of Warranty.* Owner will indemnify and hold Distributor harmless from and against any loss, cost, liability, and expenses (including reasonable attorneys' fees) arising out of any breach of any of the warranties or representations of Owner in this Agreement.

(d) *WARRANTY DISCLAIMER.* THE FOREGOING WARRANTY IS IN LIEU OF ALL OTHER WARRANTIES EXPRESS OR IMPLIED, INCLUDING, BUT NOT LIMITED TO, THE IMPLIED WARRANTIES OF MERCHANTABILITY AND FITNESS FOR A PARTICULAR PURPOSE.

16. *LIMITATION OF LIABILITY.* IT IS UNDERSTOOD AND AGREED THAT OWNER'S LIABILITY TO DISTRIBUTOR, WHETHER IN CONTRACT, IN TORT, UNDER ANY WARRANTY, IN NEGLIGENCE, OR OTHERWISE, SHALL NOT EXCEED THE RETURN OF THE LICENSE FEE PAID BY DISTRIBUTOR FOR THE TRANSACTION INVOLVED. UNDER NO CIRCUMSTANCES SHALL OWNER BE LIABLE FOR SPECIAL OR CONSEQUENTIAL DAMAGES (INCLUDING LOST PROFITS) OF DISTRIBUTOR, ANY CUSTOMER, OR ANY OTHER THIRD PARTY, EVEN IF OWNER HAS BEEN PREVIOUSLY ADVISED OF THE POSSIBILITY OF SUCH DAMAGES. NO ACTION, REGARDLESS OF FORM, ARISING OUT OF THE TRANSACTIONS UNDER THIS AGREEMENT MAY BE BROUGHT BY EITHER PARTY MORE THAN ONE (1) YEAR AFTER THE EVENT(S) WHICH GAVE RISE TO THE CAUSE OF ACTION HAS (HAVE) OCCURRED.

17. *Indemnification by Distributor.* Distributor shall indemnify Owner from all claims, losses, and damages which may arise from its marketing, installation, or support of the Software Product, including claims based on misrepresentations made by Distributor, inadequate installation, support or assistance by Distributor, or any other act or failure to act on the part of Distributor.

18. *Maintenance.* All maintenance necessary to correct any errors in the Software Product found by Distributor or any Customer after the Warranty Period for the applicable Customer shall be provided by Owner pursuant to the terms of its standard maintenance agreement.

19. *Updates and Enhancements.* Owner will provide Dis-

tributor with copies of any updates to the Software Product released by Owner for the purpose of correcting defects, and Distributor agrees to make them available, at no charge to its Customers who have paid for maintenance. Owner shall notify Distributor of the release of any enhancements, and they shall be made available at Owner's then current license fee.

20. *Modifications by Distributor.* Distributor shall not alter or modify the Software Product in any way.

21. *Termination.*

(a) *By Owner.* Owner may terminate this Agreement prior to its expiration on the occurrence of any of the following events:

(1) A default by Distributor which has not been cured within 30 days of notice given to Distributor by Owner;

(2) Distributor's violation of the confidentiality provisions of this Agreement;

(3) If Distributor ceases to do business or becomes insolvent;

(4) If Distributor attempts to assign this Agreement without permission from Owner.

(b) *By Distributor.* Distributor may terminate this Agreement at any time by giving 90 days written notice to Owner.

(c) *Duties on Termination.* Upon expiration or termination of this Agreement, Distributor agrees to cease using, marketing, and sublicensing the Software Product, and to return to Owner all copies of the Software Product and Documentation in its possession. Distributor also agrees to pay all accrued license fees to Owner and to provide a full accounting as required by paragraph 5. The obligation of confidentiality set forth in paragraph 8 shall remain in effect.

(d) *Customer Rights On Termination.* Termination of this Agreement shall not affect the rights of any Customer to use the Software Product, and all sublicense agreements with Customers shall be automatically assigned to Owner upon termination of this Agreement.

22. *Arbitration of Disputes.* Any dispute arising under this Agreement shall be submitted to binding arbitration in the City of Chicago, Illinois, under the rules then prevailing of the American Arbitration Association, and judgment upon the award rendered

may be entered and enforced in any court of competent jurisdiction.

23. *Assignment.* This Agreement may not be assigned by Distributor to any other person, firm, or corporation without the express written approval of Owner.

24. *Entire Agreement.* The parties have read this Agreement and agree to be bound by its terms, and further agree that it constitutes the complete and exclusive statement of the agreement between them which supersedes all proposals, oral or written, and all other communications between them relating to the license and use of the Software Product.

25. *All Amendments in Writing.* This Agreement may not be changed or modified except by a written agreement signed by both parties.

26. *Governing Law.* This Agreement will be governed by and construed in accordance with the laws of the State of Illinois.

27. *Relationship of the Parties.* Each party is acting as an independent contractor and not as an agent, partner, or joint venturer with the other party for any purpose. Except as provided in this Agreement, neither party shall have any right, power, or authority to act or to create any obligation, express or implied, on behalf of the other.

28. *Nonsolicitation.*

(a) *Employees.* During the term of this Agreement, and for a period of one year after its termination, each party agrees that it will not employ or solicit the employment of any employee of, or any independent contractor utilized by, the other party in the performance of this Agreement, without the prior written consent of the other party.

(b) *Customers.* Owner agrees that it will not knowingly solicit any Customer or potential Customer with whom Distributor has made prior contact.

IN WITNESS WHEREOF, the parties have caused this Agreement to be executed by their duly authorized representatives.

BUSINESS SOFTWARE DEVELOPERS, INC.

By: _____

Title _____

Date: _____

XYZ SOFTWARE DISTRIBUTORS, INC.

By: _____

Title _____

Date: _____

A.10. CHECKLIST FOR A SOFTWARE DEVELOPMENT AGREEMENT

[Between the developer of the software ("Developer") and the client for whom the software is developed ("Client")]

1. *Introduction*
   a. What is the date of the agreement?
   b. Who are the parties to the contract?
   c. What is the background of the agreement?

2. *Definitions*
   a. What terms must be defined for purposes of the contract?
   b. Consider the following—
      (1) Functional specifications
      (2) Detailed system specifications
      (3) Software
      (4) User
      (5) Documentation

3. *Work to be Performed by Developer*
   a. What has the developer agreed to do? Consider—
      (1) Analyze the client's requirements
      (2) Develop functional specifications
      (3) Develop detailed system specifications
      (4) Design the software
      (5) Code the software
      (6) Test the software
      (7) Install the software
      (8) Train the client
   b. Will the work be done in separate phases?
   c. If so, how will each phase be defined?
   d. What specifications govern the developer's work?

    e. How will the parties handle client-requested changes in the work being done by the developer?

    f. What is the extent of the resources to be committed to the project?

4. *Term*

    a. When does the developer begin work?

    b. When is the project scheduled to be completed?

    c. Does either party have the right to terminate the project before it is finished?

5. *Payment*

    a. What type of fee is charged?

        (1) Fixed lump sum

        (2) Hourly rate plus out-of-pocket expenses

    b. What is the amount of the fixed fee or the hourly rate?

    c. What does the fee cover? Consider the following—

        (1) Client requirements analysis

        (2) Development of specifications

        (3) Software development

        (4) Documentation

        (5) Installation

        (6) Training

        (7) Warranty

        (8) Taxes

        (9) Travel and other developer expenses

    d. When is payment due? Consider the following possibilities—

        (1) Upon execution of contract

        (2) In installments, such as weekly, monthly, etc.

        (3) At the completion of the work to be performed in each phase

        (4) Upon delivery of the software

        (5) Upon installation

        (6) Upon completion of client training

        (7) Upon acceptance of the software

        (8) On the date the software becomes operational

        (9) When the software is "ready for use"

     (10) Specified number of days after any of these events

    e. Does the developer have the right to stop work if any invoices remain unpaid for a specified number of days after they are due?

    f. What happens to the price if the client requests any changes to the specifications during the life of the project?

6. *Taxes*

Who pays for any state or local taxes imposed on the software development transaction?

7. *Ownership of Software*
    a. Who owns the software developed?
       (1) The developer
       (2) The client
       (3) Both parties
    b. Does the developer represent that it will not use any software that is owned by others, or that it will not do so without obtaining their permission?
    c. Does the party that will not own the software have the right to market the software, or to share in any income received by the other party from marketing the software?

8. *Confidentiality*
    a. Is the party who does not own the software obligated to keep it confidential?
    b. What specific steps must that party take to insure that the software remains confidential?
    c. Does each party agree that it will not use or disclose any confidential information that it learns about the business or products of the other?

9. *Right to Copy*
    a. Does the party who does not own the software have the right to make copies of the software?
    b. If so, is use of copies limited in any way?
    c. If so, is there a limit on the number of copies?
    d. Does this also include the right to make extra copies of the documentation?

e. Do all authorized copies remain property of the software owner?

10. *Indemnification*

a. Will the developer pay any damages or expenses suffered by the client if someone challenges the developer's ownership rights to the software that is delivered to the client?
b. What types of damages or expenses are covered?
c. What are the conditions for such coverage?

11. *Delivery*

a. When will the software be delivered to the client?
b. What is the client's remedy for late delivery?
   (1) Right to cancel and get full or partial refund
   (2) Liquidated damages
   (3) Developer not liable for delays outside its control
c. What happens to the delivery schedule if the client requests any changes in the specifications during the life of the project?

12. *Installation*

a. Who installs the software?
b. If the developer will install the software, when will it be installed?
c. Is there any extra charge for developer installation?

13. *Training*

a. Will the developer provide any training?
b. If so, how much training will be provided?
c. What is the cost of training?
d. When and where will the training take place?
e. Is future training for new personnel available at a later date? If so, under what terms?
f. Who gets trained
   (1) Operators
   (2) Programmers
   (3) Management
   (4) Users
g. How many people will be trained?

14. *Acceptance*

    a. When is the client deemed to have "accepted" the software? Consider the following—

        (1) Upon delivery of the product due in each phase

        (2) Upon delivery of the final product

        (3) Upon installation

        (4) When the software is "ready for use"

        (5) Upon completion of training

        (6) Upon completion of the developer's standard tests

        (7) Upon developer certification that installed software meets contract specifications

        (8) Upon completion of a contractually predefined acceptance test

        (9) Upon use by client

       (10) When client is "satisfied"

    b. What happens on acceptance? Consider the following—

        (1) Final payment is due

        (2) The warranty period begins

        (3) Risk of loss passes

        (4) Right of possession (or title) is transferred

        (5) Maintenance fees are due

        (6) The term of the license begins to run

    c. If there is an acceptance test—

        (1) What requirements must the software meet

        (2) Who performs the test

        (3) When does the test start

        (4) What type of test will be conducted

        (5) What is the length of the test

        (6) What data will be used for the test

        (7) What are the client's obligations during the test

        (8) What are the developer's obligations during the test

        (9) What happens if the test fails

       (10) Who decides when the test is passed

       (11) When does acceptance occur

15. *Warranties*

    a. Does the developer make any express warranties about the performance of the software?

    b. What express warranties (if any) are included?
- (1) Warranty that the developer owns the software
- (2) Warranty of power and authority to grant licenses (if developer is not the owner of all the software to be provided)
- (3) Warranty that software conforms to specifications
- (4) Warranty of performance
- (5) Warranty of adequacy of documentation
- (6) Warranty of noninfringement of patents, copyrights, and trade secrets
- (7) Warranty as to the minimum equipment required to support the software
- (8) Warranty as to the operating system and any other software required to support the newly developed software
- (9) Warranty of file compatability
- (10) Warranty of compatibility with other software

    c. How long does the warranty last?

    d. Has the developer disclaimed all express warranties not specifically included in the contract?

    e. Has the developer disclaimed the warranties implied by law?
- (1) Merchantability
- (2) Fitness for particular purpose

    f. If the software fails to work as warranted, is the client's remedy limited to repair or some other specified remedy (e.g., refund)?

    g. What conditions will void the warranty?
- (1) Software modified by client
- (2) Failure to make final payment

16. *Limitations of Liability*

    a. Is there a limit on the dollar amount of damages to which the developer is exposed in the event the software fails to work properly?

    b. Is there a limit on the type of damages to which the developer is exposed, i.e., has the developer excluded liability for—
- (1) Consequential damages (such as lost profits)
- (2) Claims by third parties

        (3) Damages caused by improper use
   c. Is there a contractual limit on the time in which either party can file a lawsuit against the other?

17. *Software Maintenance*
   a. Is the developer obligated to provide any maintenance?
   b. What maintenance (if any) is provided by the developer during the warranty period?
   c. What maintenance (if any) is provided by the developer after the warranty period expires?
   d. Is maintenance optional or required?
   e. What is excluded from maintenance coverage?
        (1) Client modifications to software
        (2) Failure to comply with terms of license
        (3) Failure to apply updates
   f. Does the developer have the right to terminate maintenance?
   g. Does the developer have an obligation to notify the client of errors found?
   h. What is the maintenance fee and when is it due?

18. *Updates and Enhancements*
   a. Does the client have the right to obtain updates and enhancements?
   b. Is the developer obligated to provide updates and enhancements?
   c. On what terms (and price) will they be made available?

19. *Modifications by Client*
   a. If the client does not own the software, does the client have the right to modify the software?
   b. Who owns any client modifications?
   c. Are there any limitations on the client's use of such modifications?
   d. What is the effect of modifications made by the client on the developer's warranty and maintenance obligations?

20. *Default*
   a. Are there any special circumstances that the parties will consider to be a breach of the contract?
   b. Is the nonbreaching party required to give notice of the

breach to the other party before exercising its legal rights?

c. Does the breaching party have an opportunity to cure its breach?

d. Is there a right to terminate the contract a specified number of days after notice of a breach?

e. Is there a right to immediate termination upon breach of trade secret confidentiality?

21. *Arbitration of Disputes*

a. If a dispute arises between the parties, will they be required to submit to arbitration or to some other method of alternate dispute resolution instead of going to court?

b. If so, where will the arbitration be held?

c. If so, how will the arbitrator(s) be chosen and what rules will govern the arbitration proceeding?

22. *Termination*

a. Can either party terminate the development agreement before it is completed?

b. If so, when?

    (1) On default of other party

    (2) On a specified number of days notice

    (3) At the terminating party's discretion

    (4) On bankruptcy or insolvency of the other party

c. When is termination effective?

    (1) After notice

    (2) After right to cure expires

d. What happens on termination?

    (1) Discontinue development

    (2) All work to date turned over to client or retained by developer

    (3) All past due payments must be made

e. Do any obligations survive termination?

    (1) Confidentiality

    (2) Indemnification

    (3) Payments due and owing (fees, taxes, royalties, etc.)

f. Is there any penalty for early termination?

23. *Events upon Cessation of Business*
    a. What happens if the developer ceases doing business?
    b. What happens if the client ceases doing business?

24. *Source Code Access*
    a. If the client does not get source code, are any arrangements made to provide the client with access to source code in the event the developer cannot support the software?
    b. What type of access mechanism is used?
        (1) Client holds source
        (2) Developer releases the source code on the occurrence of a specified event (such as the developer ceasing to do business)
        (3) Source code escrow
    c. If an escrow is used, what material is included in the escrow?
        (1) Source code
        (2) Documentation
        (3) System design, flowcharts, other data, etc.
    d. Is any procedure established to verify the completeness of the escrow materials?
    e. Are any arrangements made for subsequent deposit into escrow of enhancements, modifications, and corrections?
    f. Who pays the escrow and verification fees?
    g. What are the triggering events for release of the source code?
        (1) Bankruptcy
        (2) Assignment for benefit of creditors
        (3) Dissolution, liquidation, or death of developer
        (4) Appointment of receiver or trustee
        (5) Levy or execution on any lien, mortgage, or security interest of developer
        (6) Failure to maintain software
    h. What is the release mechanism?
        (1) Notice from client with consent of developer
        (2) Notice from client without consent of developer
        (3) Resolution of disputes regarding release
            (a) Injunctive relief

         (b)   Arbitration

         (c)   Liquidated damages

   i. What are the client's rights to the software upon release

         (1)   Internal use only

         (2)   Subject to terms of license

25. *Assignment Rights*

    a. Does the developer have the right to assign the contract?

    b. Does the client have the right to assign the contract?

26. *Miscellaneous*

    a. Is this contract the entire agreement of the parties?

    b. Is there a requirement that all amendments to the contract be in writing?

    c. What state's law will govern any disputes?

27. *Exhibits*

    a. Are any exhibits to be attached?

    b. Possibilities include—

         (1)   Functional specifications

         (2)   Detailed design specifications

         (3)   Hardware facility requirements

         (4)   Software facility requirements

         (5)   Performance (run time) requirements

         (6)   Documentation requirements

A.11. SAMPLE SOFTWARE DEVELOPMENT AGREEMENT*

This Agreement is entered into on _____ , 19 __ by SOFTWARE DEVELOPMENT CORP. ("Developer") and SOFTWARE CUSTOMER, INC. ("Client").

---

* This contract is an example of the way a software development agreement might be structured, and the types of provisions that might be included in such an agreement. It is not intended to be used as a form, however, since the structure and content of each contract must be tailored to meet the needs of the situation in which it is to be used.

1. *Definitions*

(a) *Products.* The term "Products" means the Functional Specifications, the Detailed Technical Design Specifications, the Software, and the Documentation to be produced by Developer under the terms of this Agreement.

(b) *Software.* The term "Software" means all computer programs, subroutines, translations, compilers, diagnostic routines, control software or special software produced, provided or modified by Developer under the terms of this Agreement.

(c) *Functional Specifications.* The term "Functional Specifications" means the list of the tasks and functions that must be performed by the Software in order to fulfill the specific needs of Client's business.

(d) *Detailed Technical Design Specifications.* The term "Detailed Technical Design Specifications" means the software design specifications which define the way the Software must be organized and programmed in order to accomplish the tasks and functions identified in the Functional Specifications. They must contain sufficient specificity so as to enable an average computer programmer to write and/or modify the necessary computer programs to perform the tasks identified in the Functional Specifications.

(e) *Documentation.* The term "Documentation" means the user documentation necessary to instruct users in the operation of the Software and all of its features.

(f) *Services.* The term "Services" means all work to be provided by Developer under this Agreement, including analysis, design, programming, testing, conversion, implementation, maintenance, consulting, and support services.

(g) *Software Maintenance.* The term "Software Maintenance" means any and all Services necessary to rectify errors or problems in the Software. Software Maintenance shall not include on-site support or on-site maintenance.

2. *Scope of Services.* Developer agrees to perform the following Services for Client:

(a) *Phase 1.* With the advice and assistance of client, Developer shall analyze Client's business requirements and develop Functional Specifications for a software package designed to perform the general function specified on Exhibit A.

(b) *Phase 2.* Upon completion of Phase 1, and receipt of Client's written acceptance of the Functional Specifications developed in Phase 1, Developer will prepare Detailed Technical Design Specifications for the development of Software capable of performing the Functional Specifications on the hardware and software environment specified in Exhibit A.

(c) *Phase 3.* Upon completion of Phase 2, and receipt of Client's written acceptance of the Detailed Technical Design Specifications, Developer will code, test, and debug Software pursuant to the Detailed Technical Design Specifications, prepare the Documentation, and install the Software on the equipment specified in Exhibit A.

3. *Modifications to Specifications.* Developer shall develop the Detailed Design Specifications in Phase 2 on the basis of the Functional Specifications as accepted by Client, and shall develop the Software and Documentation in Phase 3 on the basis of the Functional Specifications and Detailed Technical Design Specifications as accepted by Client, which specifications shall be deemed to be part of this Agreement. No changes in or deviations from the specifications will be permitted unless the following procedure is followed:

(a) Client must submit a written request detailing the changes that it desires.

(b) Within 10 business days of the receipt of the request, Developer will inform Client, in writing, of any change in price or schedule that will be caused by the proposed change in specifications.

(c) Unless Client accepts the change, in writing, within 10 business days thereafter, the change will not be made. If the change is accepted, the written request for change and Developer's response thereto will be deemed to constitute an amendment to this Agreement.

4. *Charges and Payment.*

(a) *Phase 1.* The Products to be developed under Phase 1 shall be provided on a fixed fee basis, for the amount specified in Exhibit B. One-half of the amount specified shall be due prior to the commencement of work, and the balance shall be due upon acceptance of the Phase 1 Products.

(b) *Phase 2.* The Products to be developed under Phase 2 shall be provided on a fixed-fee basis, for the amount specified in Exhibit B. One-half of the amount specified shall be due prior to the commencement of work, and the balance shall be due upon acceptance of the Phase 2 Products.

(c) *Phase 3.* The Products to be delivered under Phase 3 shall be developed on a time-and-expense basis. Client shall pay Developer at the hourly rate set forth on Exhibit B for all time expended, plus reimbursement of all reasonable out-of-pocket expenses incurred by Developer. Developer will submit invoices monthly. Client will pay 90% of the amount invoiced within 10 days of receipt, with the balance to be paid within 20 days of the Acceptance Date of the Phase 3 Products.

5. *Taxes.* Developer's price for its Services under this Agreement does not include any taxes that may be levied upon the Services or Products provided under this Agreement. If, during the term of this Agreement, or thereafter, taxes on the data processing Services or Products should be imposed, Client agrees that it will pay all such taxes and that it will hold Developer harmless for the payment of any and all such taxes.

6. *Acceptance—Phases 1 and 2.* Upon delivery of the Products to be developed in Phases 1 and 2 of this Agreement, Client shall have 10 business days to examine the Products in order to determine whether or not they conform to the specifications of this Agreement. If the Products conform to such specifications, Client shall notify Developer in writing of its acceptance and Developer will begin work on the next Phase. If any of the Products delivered under Phases 1 or 2 fail to conform to such specifications, Client shall notify Developer, specifying the deficiency, and Developer shall correct, modify, or improve the Products to meet all requirements of this Agreement.

7. *Acceptance of Software—Phase 3.* Following delivery of the Software and Documentation to Client, Client shall, with Developer's assistance, operate the Software on its own hardware for a period not to exceed 15 business days to determine whether:

(a) The Software conforms to the Functional Specifications and the Detailed Technical Design Specifications developed under this Agreement;

(b)   The Software is capable of running on a repetitive basis on a variety of Client's actual data, without failure; and

(c)   The Documentation for the Software meets the requirements of this Agreement.

(d)   If the Software and Documentation successfully meet this Acceptance Test, based upon reasonable judgment of pass or fail, Client shall so notify Developer in writing within five (5) business days and the Products shall be deemed to be accepted. In such case, the Acceptance Date shall be the date that the Products satisfactorily complete all of the tests specified above.

(e)   If the Software and Documentation fail to meet the above-specified Acceptance Test, Client shall notify Developer of such failure in writing and Developer shall correct, modify, or improve the Software so that it conforms to the specifications. Thereafter, Client shall have 10 additional business days in which to re-conduct the Acceptance Test specified above. This process shall be repeated as may be necessary until the Products are deemed to be accepted hereunder; provided, however, that if the Products have not successfully completed the Acceptance Test within 180 days after Developer's initial delivery, Client shall have the option, following ten (10) days' advance written notice to Developer (during which period Developer shall have the right to cure by full performance of its obligations hereunder), to declare Developer to be in default of this Agreement.

8.   *Warranties.*

(a)   *Warranty of Software Functions.*   Developer represents and warrants that the Software delivered hereunder will meet the Functional Specifications, the Detailed Design Specifications, and the other requirements described or incorporated in this Agreement. Developer will, for a period of six (6) months following the Acceptance Date, without additional charge to Client, correct any problems or defects discovered in the Software and reported to Developer by Client, excluding defects or problems arising from misuse or modification by Client, computer hardware defects, or power or other environmental related problems, and will use its best efforts to make such additions, modifications, or adjustments to the Software as may be necessary for it to operate in accordance with such specifications.

(b) *Warranty Limitations.* This warranty shall be null and void in the event that all or any part of the Software is modified by Client or is merged with other software by Client.

(c) *Exclusive Remedy For Warranty Breach.* In the event that the Software fails to perform as warranted, and as Client's sole and exclusive remedy, Developer shall, within a reasonable time, provide all reasonable programming services to correct documented errors.

(d) *WARRANTY DISCLAIMERS.* THE FOREGOING WARRANTY IS IN LIEU OF ALL OTHER WARRANTIES EXPRESS OR IMPLIED, INCLUDING, BUT NOT LIMITED TO, THE IMPLIED WARRANTIES OF MERCHANTABILITY AND FITNESS FOR A PARTICULAR PURPOSE.

9. *LIMITATIONS OF LIABILITY.* DEVELOPER'S LIABILITY TO CLIENT ON ANY CLAIM FOR DAMAGES ARISING OUT OF THIS AGREEMENT SHALL BE LIMITED TO DIRECT DAMAGES AND SHALL NOT EXCEED THE AMOUNT OF THE FEES PAID BY CLIENT UNDER THIS AGREEMENT. DEVELOPER SHALL HAVE NO LIABILITY WHATSOEVER FOR SPECIAL OR CONSEQUENTIAL DAMAGES (INCLUDING LOST PROFITS) OF CLIENT OR ANY THIRD PARTY, EVEN IF DEVELOPER HAS BEEN ADVISED OF THE POSSIBILITY OF SUCH DAMAGES. NO ACTION, REGARDLESS OF FORM, ARISING OUT OF THE TRANSACTIONS UNDER THIS AGREEMENT, MAY BE BROUGHT BY CLIENT MORE THAN ONE YEAR AFTER THE CAUSE OF ACTION HAS ACCRUED.

10. *Software Maintenance.* Following expiration of the warranty, Developer agrees to provide all Software Maintenance necessary to correct and resolve any errors or defects which appear in the Software as a result of its use by Client. Developer's obligation to provide such Software Maintenance is contingent upon advance payment of the yearly maintenance fee specified in Exhibit B, and the accurate and timely reporting of any errors or problems in the Software by Client. Software Maintenance shall not apply to any problems resulting from modifications to the Software by Client or any third party.

11. *Confidentiality.* Each party acknowledges that, during

the course of this Agreement, it will be entrusted with confidential information relating to the business and products of the other party. Each party agrees that it will not use such confidential information for any purpose except the performance of this Agreement, and that it will not disclose any such confidential information to any person unless such disclosure is authorized by the other party in writing.

12. *Ownership of Software Developed.* All Software and other Products developed pursuant to this Agreement, and all corresponding copyrights, trade secrets, and patents, shall be jointly owned by both Developer and Client, and may be freely used by either party without any accounting between them. Each party agrees to execute all documents reasonably necessary to effect this intent.

13. *Patent, Copyright, and Trade Secret Indemnification.* Developer agrees to indemnify Client against any liability to third parties resulting from claims that the Software developed pursuant to this Agreement infringes on or violates any patents, copyrights, or trade secrets of such third parties. This indemnification is contingent upon Client providing prompt written notice of such a claim to Developer, and granting Developer the sole right to defend such claim.

14. *Termination.* Client may, for any reason, terminate this Agreement at any time effective upon Developer's receipt of written notice thereof. In the event of termination, Client will pay all sums due to Developer, including pro-rated fees and expenses for items partially complete at time of termination, as well as any expenses associated with termination, plus a termination penalty calculated in accordance with the formula specified in Exhibit B. After receipt of the payment of such sums, Developer will deliver to Client copies of its work product completed to that date.

15. *Default.* In the event either party shall be in material default of its obligations under this Agreement, the party not in default shall have the right to terminate this Agreement if the defaulting party fails to cure such default within 30 days of receiving written notice of the default.

16. *Arbitration.* Any dispute arising under this Agreement shall be submitted to binding arbitration in the city of Detroit, Michigan, under the rules then prevailing of the American Arbi-

tration Association, and judgment upon the award rendered may be entered and enforced in any court of competent jurisdiction.

The party submitting such dispute shall request the American Arbitration Association to:

(a)   Appoint an arbitrator who is knowledgeable in the data processing area and familiar with the data processing industry and who will follow substantive rules of law;

(b)   Require the testimony to be transcribed; and

(c)   Require the award to be accompanied by findings of fact and a statement of reasons for the decision.

Except where clearly prevented by the area in dispute, both parties agree to continue performing their respective obligations under this Agreement while the dispute is being resolved.

17.   *Entire Agreement.*   The parties have read this Agreement and agree to be bound by its terms, and further agree that it constitutes the complete and exclusive statement of the agreement between them which supersedes all proposals, oral or written, and all other communications between them relating to the subject matter of this Agreement.

18.   *Governing Law.*   This contract will be governed by and construed in accordance with the laws of the State of Michigan.

19.   *Force Majeure.*   Neither party shall be liable for delays or failure to deliver or perform due to causes beyond its reasonable control, acts of God, acts of the other party, acts of civil or military authorities, fires, strikes, floods, epidemics, wars, riots, delays in transportation, or the unavailability of information or material to be furnished by the other party.

20.   *Relationship of the Parties.*   Each party is an independent contractor and shall be free to exercise its discretion and independent judgement as to the method and means of performance its obligations hereunder. The employees of each party shall in no sense be considered employees of the other and shall not, by virtue of this Agreement, be entitled or eligible to participate in any benefits or privileges given by the other to its employees.

21.   *All Amendments in Writing.*   This Agreement may not be changed or modified except by a written agreement, executed on behalf of Developer and Client.

IN WITNESS WHEREOF, the parties hereto, by their respective duly authorized officers or representatives, have each executed this Agreement, effective as of the date first above written.

SOFTWARE   SOFTWARE
DEVELOPMENT CORP.   CUSTOMER, INC.
By: _____   By: _____
Title: _____   Title: _____

A.12.   CHECKLIST FOR AN EMPLOYEE CONFIDENTIALITY AGREEMENT

[Between the employer ("Company") and the employee ("Employee")]

1. *Introduction*
    a. What is the date of the agreement?
    b. Who are the parties to the agreement?

2. *Consideration*
    a. Does the agreement specify what the employee is receiving as consideration for signing the contract?
    b. Consider the following possibilities—
        (1) Employment
        (2) Continuing employment
        (3) Promotion
        (4) Raise
        (5) Bonus

3. *Confidentiality Obligation*
    a. Does the agreement impose an obligation of confidentiality on the employee?
    b. What is the employee obligated to keep confidential?
    c. Does the obligation remain in effect after the employment is terminated? If so, for how long?

4. *Assignment of Rights to Inventions*

   a. Is the employee obligated to disclose all new inventions, developments, discoveries, etc., to the company?

   b. Is the employee obligated to assign all rights he or she may have in any such new inventions, developments, ideas, etc., to the company?

   c. What new inventions, developments, and ideas are covered by this provision? Consider—

      (1) Inventions made on company time

      (2) Inventions made using company resources

      (3) Inventions made using company trade secrets

      (4) Inventions made which relate to the company's business

5. *Noncompetition*[1]

   a. Is the employee prohibited from competing with the company or from working for a competitor of the company after the employee terminates his or her employment?

   b. How long does the restriction last?

   c. In what geographical area does the restriction apply?

   d. To what type of work does the restriction apply?

6. *Conflicting Obligations*

   Does the employee represent that he or she is not precluded from taking this job or disclosing any information because of a prior agreement to which he or she is a party?

7. *Duty on Termination*

   Does the employee agree to return all company documents when his or her employment ends?

8. *Solicitation of Employees*

   Is the employee prohibited from soliciting other employees of the company to work elsewhere?

---

[1] Note that noncompetition agreements are not allowed in certain states.

A.13. SAMPLE EMPLOYEE CONFIDENTIALITY AND NONCOMPETITION AGREEMENT*

THIS AGREEMENT is made on ――――――― , 19 __ , be-tween ABC Software Corporation, an Illinois corporation ("Com-pany"), and John Smith ("Employee").

BACKGROUND

A. The Company is engaged in the research, design, develop-ment, testing, marketing, distribution, and licensing of a variety of computer software products, and now has, and expects to develop, trade secrets and other Confidential Information relating thereto; and

B. The Company desires to hire Employee, and Employee desires to be employed by the Company in the position of systems analyst, and as a result of such employment Employee may have access to the Company's Confidential Information and may be involved in the further development thereof; and

C. To induce the Company to hire him, Employee desires to insure the Company that he will not disclose any of the Compa-ny's Confidential Information and that he will assign all new de-velopments for which he is responsible in whole or in part to the Company;

THEREFORE, Company and Employee hereby agree as fol-lows:

1. *Definitions.*

(a) *Confidential Information.* The term "Confidential Information" shall mean all information not generally known in the relevant trade or industry which was obtained from Company, or which was learned, discovered, developed, conceived, origi-nated, or prepared by Employee in the scope of his employment, and which falls within the following general categories:

---

* This contract is an example of the way a formal employee confidentiality, invention assignment, and noncompetition agreement might be structured, and the types of provi-sions that might be included in such an agreement. It is not intended to be used as a form, however, since the structure and content of each contract must be tailored to meet the needs of the situation in which it is to be used. Note also that the noncompetition clause contained in this Agreement is unenforceable in many states. (*See* Section 7.3.)

(i)   Software products and services of the Company either currently existing or under development, including all New Developments;

(ii)   Business plans, product development plans, sales or marketing methods, and internal business procedures of the Company;

(iii)   Customer lists, and specific requirements of the Company's customers;

(iv)   Any other information which the Company informs Employee is to be kept confidential.

(b)   *New Developments.*   The term "New Developments" means all ideas, inventions, and discoveries, including but not limited to software, algorithms, designs, innovations, and improvements to existing Confidential Information, which were conceived or developed by Employee in the course of his employment or by using any Confidential Information.

2.   *Nondisclosure and Nonuse of Confidential Information.* During Employee's term of employment with Company, and at all times thereafter, Employee agrees that he will not disclose to others, use for his own benefit, or otherwise appropriate or copy any Confidential Information, whether or not developed by Employee, except as required in the performance of Employee's duties to Company. This paragraph shall apply only so long as the information in question is secret or confidential in the trade or industry.

3.   *Warranty of Original Development.*   Employee represents and warrants that all work performed for Company and all work product he produces will be of original development, and will be specifically developed for the fulfillment of this Agreement and will not knowingly infringe upon or violate any patent, copyright, trade secret, or other proprietary right of any former employer or any other third party.

4.   *Rights to New Developments.*

(a)   Employee agrees to promptly disclose all New Developments to the Company.

(b)   Employee acknowledges that all copyrightable New Developments are "works made for hire" and consequently that the Company owns all copyrights thereto.

(c)   Employee hereby assigns to Company all other rights to any New Developments, including but not limited to United States and foreign letters patent, trade secrets, trade names, and trademarks granted upon such New Developments. However, this provision does *not* apply to a New Development for which no equipment, supplies, facility, or trade secret information of the Company was used *and* which was developed entirely on the Employee's own time, unless the New Development:

(i)   relates to the business of the Company, *or*

(ii)   relates to the actual or demonstrable anticipated research or development of the Company, *or*

(iii)   results from any work performed by the Employee for the Company.

(d)   Employee agrees to execute all documents reasonably requested by Company to assist the Company in perfecting or protecting any or all of its rights in the New Developments.

5.   *Covenant Not To Employ.*   During Employee's term of employment, and for a period of one (1) year from the date of its termination, Employee agrees that he will not employ or solicit the employment of any Company employee.

6.   *Noncompetition Agreement.*   During the period of his employment with Company, and for a period of one (1) year after its termination, Employee agrees that he will not render, directly or indirectly, any services of an advisory or consulting nature or as an employee or otherwise to any business located in Illinois which is a competitor of Company.

7.   *Duty Upon Termination of Employment.*

(a)   Upon termination of employment with Company for any reason, Employee agrees to deliver to Company all writings, designs, documents, records, data, memoranda, computer source code listings, file layouts, record layouts, system design information, models, manuals, documentation, notes, and other material of any nature which are in his possession or control and which are or contain Confidential Information.

(b)   Employee further agrees to retain in the strictest confidence any Confidential Information he learned during his term of employment unless and until such information has been made generally available to the trade other than by breach of this Agreement.

8. *Other Agreements.* Employee represents and warrants that, to the best of his knowledge, signing this Agreement and performing services for the Company will not be in violation of any other contract, agreement, or understanding to which he is a party.

9. *Severability.* In case a court determines that any provision in this Agreement is illegal or unenforceable, such determination shall solely affect such provision and shall not impair the remaining provisions of this Agreement.

IN WITNESS WHEREOF, the parties have hereto executed this Agreement as of the day and year first above written.

COMPANY

By: _____   _____
                                     Employee's Signature

　　Its _____   _____
　　　　　　　　Title   Employee's Address

　　　　　　　　　　　　　　　　　　　　　　_____
                                     City   State   Zip

A.14. SAMPLE EMPLOYEE CONFIDENTIALITY AGREEMENT*

I understand that ABC Software Corporation, an Illinois corporation (the "Company"), is engaged in the research, design, development, testing, marketing, distribution, licensing, and sale of a variety of computer software products (hereinafter referred to as the "Software"). I understand further that the Software is to be used in, and is of substantial value to, the Company's business,

---

* This contract is an example of the way an informal employee confidentiality and invention assignment agreement (without a noncompetition clause) might be structured, and the types of provisions that might be included in such an agreement. It is not intended to be used as a form, however, since the structure and content of each contract must be tailored to meet the needs of the situation in which it is to be used.

and that it embodies confidential information and trade secrets which, if appropriated, may do serious damage to the Company.

Accordingly, in consideration of my employment by the Company, and in further consideration of the position of trust and responsibility which I assume, I, _____ , hereby agree as follows:

1. *Nondisclosure.* During the term of my employment and at all times thereafter I will not disclose to others, use for my own benefit, or otherwise appropriate any trade secrets, confidential information, or any other knowledge or information of or relating to the Software, except as authorized by the Company in writing.

2. *Discoveries and Improvements.* I will disclose promptly to the Company any improvements in or modifications to the Software which I may discover or develop. I hereby assign to the Company, free from any obligations to me, all right, title, and interest which I may have in and to any and all discoveries, improvements, extensions, or advancements made, conceived, devised, developed, or perfected by me during the term of my employment, whether on duty or off, which relate to the Software. However, this provision does *not* apply to any software for which no equipment, supplies, facility, or trade secret information of the Company was used *and* which was developed entirely on my own time, unless the software:

(a)　relates to the business of the Company, *or*

(b)　relates to the actual or demonstrable anticipated research or development of the Company, *or*

(c)　results from any work performed by me for the Company.

3. *Duty Upon Termination of Employment.*

(a)　Upon termination of my employment with the Company for any reason, I will deliver to the Company all listings, printouts, records, data, memoranda, manuals, notes, and other material of any nature which are in my possession or control and which relate to the Software.

(b)　I agree to retain in the strictest confidence trade secrets and confidential information embodied in the Software after the termination of my employment with the Company for whatever reason unless and until such information has been made generally available to the trade other than by breach of this Agreement.

Dated: _____

_____
                                                    Employee

A.15. SAMPLE CLIENT CONFIDENTIALITY AGREEMENT*

This Agreement is entered into between Computer System Services, Inc., an Illinois corporation ("CSSI"), and the Client identified below, and is made to induce CSSI to disclose certain information to Client regarding the CSSI System software (the "Software") for purposes of evaluation by Client.

1.   Client agrees that any information regarding any Software which is disclosed to it by CSSI is confidential and proprietary information, and constitutes trade secrets owned solely by CSSI.

2.   Client agrees to maintain such information in confidence, and agrees that it will not, at any time, without the prior written consent of CSSI, disclose to others, use for its own benefit, or otherwise appropriate or copy any such information disclosed to it by CSSI.

3.   Client acknowledges that this obligation of confidentiality shall not apply to information that:

    a.   was already known to Client at the time of its disclosure by CSSI;

    b.   after being disclosed to Client by CSSI is subsequently disclosed to Client by a third party having no obligations to CSSI;

---

* This contract is an example of the way a client confidentiality agreement might be structured, and the types of provisions that might be included in such an agreement. It is not intended to be used as a form, however, since the structure and content of each contract must be tailored to meet the needs of the situation in which it is to be used.

c. currently is or later becomes public knowledge through no fault of Client.

4. In consideration of this Agreement of confidentiality, CSSI agrees to disclose, at its discretion, certain information relating to its Software for purposes of evaluation by Client.

5. Client acknowledges receipt of a copy of this Agreement.

DATE: _____

_____   COMPUTER SYSTEM
              CLIENT   SERVICES, INC.

By: _____   By: _____

   Title: _____   Title: _____

GLOSSARY

Acceptance   Acceptance is the act by which a buyer or licensee indicates that the software as delivered conforms to the requirements of the contract. Acceptance can occur formally, such as by the signing of a document indicating that the software has been accepted, or informally, such as through delivery followed by use without objection.

Amortization   Amortization is the gradual deduction of the cost of certain business items over a specified number of years. It is often used to recover the cost of intangible property such as patents and copyrights. It is similar to depreciation.

Assign, Assignment   An assignment is the transfer or sale of property or of rights granted by a contract. For example, if a user licenses software from a vendor and then transfers his or her right to use the software (granted in the license agreement) to another person, he or she will have "assigned" the license agreement.

C.B.   See "Cumulative Bulletin."

C.F.R.   See "Code of Federal Regulations."

Cir.   This is an abbreviation for "Circuit" used in the citation of a federal court case and refers to the United States Circuit Courts of Appeal. At present there are 12 federal appeals courts. Eleven of them cover certain geographical areas and the twelfth, the Federal Circuit, hears appeals in patent, trademark, and certain other subject matter areas.

Code of Federal Regulations   This is a compiliation of all of the regulations issued by the administrative agencies of the federal government.

Commission on New Technological Uses of Copyrighted Works This is a commission that was established by Congress on December 31, 1974, to analyze the impact of the computer on copyrighted works. This commission, which is generally referred to as "CONTU," collected data and held hearings over a period of three years. On July 31, 1978, it issued its final report titled, "Final Report of the National Commission on New Technological Uses of Copyrighted Works, 1978." In this report CONTU recommended amendments to the Copyright Act designed to deal with the issues raised by software. CONTU's recommendations were enacted, with minor modification, in the Computer Software Copyright Act of 1980, which is reproduced in Section A.2.

Common Law Common law is the law established through the decisions of our courts. It is to be distinguished from statutory laws enacted by the Congress or state legislatures.

Compendium II See "Compendium of Copyright Office Practices."

Compendium of Copyright Office Practices The Compendium of Copyright Office Practices is a manual intended primarily for use by the staff of the Copyright Office as a general guide to its examining practices and operations. It is amended from time to time by the Copyright Office to reflect changes in practice. The Compendium currently in effect was released in early 1985 and is known as Compendium II.

Computer L. Serv. Rep. This is an abbreviation for Computer Law Service Reporter, a seven-volume compiliation of computer law cases covering the period from 1951 through 1980, published by Callaghan & Company. It is no longer in print, but is available in many law libraries.

Computer Program (as used in the Copyright Act) Under the Copyright Act a computer program is defined as "a set of statements or instructions to be used directly or indirectly in a computer in order to bring about a certain result." 17 U.S.C. §101.

Computer Software Copyright Act of 1980 The amendments to §101 (definition of computer program) and §117 (right to copy and modify software in limited circumstances) of the Copyright Act are referred to as the Computer Software Copyright Act of 1980. These amendments resulted from recommendations made by CONTU. They are reproduced in Section A.2.

Confidentiality Agreement   This is an agreement that secret information disclosed by its owner to an individual or organization will be kept confidential and not disclosed to anyone else. This agreement is a binding contract which places the person to whom the information has been disclosed under a legal obligation not to use the information in a manner not authorized by its owner, and not to disclose the information to anyone else.

Consequential Damages   Consequential damages are losses which do not flow directly and immediately from the breach of contract or tortious act of another party, but only from the consequences of the act. They are also referred to as indirect damages. The loss of an expectancy of income, such as a loss of potential future profits, is usually considered to be consequential damages.

Consideration   Consideration is what one party gives or promises to give to another as an inducement to enter into a contract. In a software license agreement, for example, the consideration given by the vendor to the user is the right to use the software, in exchange for the user's promise to pay money for the right to use of that software.

CONTU   See "Commission on New Technological Uses of Copyrighted Works."

Copy (as used in the Copyright Act)   A "copy," as that term is used in the Copyright Act, is any material object, other than phonorecords, in which a work is fixed by any method now known or later developed, and from which the work can be perceived, reproduced, or otherwise communicated, either directly or with the aid of a machine or device. 17 U.S.C. §101.

Copyright   Copyright is the exclusive right granted "to authors" under the U.S. Copyright Act to copy, sell, license, modify, perform, and display their works of authorship, such as software. Copyright is further defined in Section 2.1.

Cumulative Bulletin   The Cumulative Bulletin is a collection of IRS revenue rulings, revenue procedures, and treasury decisions published semi-annually by the Treasury Department.

D. This is an abbreviation for "District" in the citation of a federal court case. It is used to identify the federal trial court in a particular state in which the decision was rendered. If there is more than one federal district court in the state, each district is identified separately, such as Northern District (N.D.), Southern District (S.D.), Central District (C.D.), and so forth. For example, the federal trial court in Chicago is known as the United States District Court for the Northern District of Illinois, abbreviated "N.D. Ill."

Damages Damages are any loss suffered by a person as the result of a breach of contract or tortious act committed by another person. Such losses can include out-of-pocket expenses, lost profits, lost time, injury to goodwill, and a host of other types of injuries which individuals and business entities may suffer.

Defendant The defendant is the individual or business entity being sued in a lawsuit.

Depreciation This is the method by which taxpayers gradually recover the cost of business or investment property that has a useful life of more than one year, by claiming tax deductions equal to a percentage of the cost of such property in each of several years.

Derivative Work As defined in the Copyright Act, "a derivative work is a work based upon one or more preexisting works, such as a translation, musical arrangement, dramatization, fictionalization, motion picture version, sound recording, art reproduction, abridgment, condensation, or any other form in which a work may be recast, transformed, or adapted. A work consisting of editorial revisions, annotations, elaborations, or other modifications which, as a whole, represent an original work of authorship is a derivative work." 17 U.S.C. §101. For example, enhancements to an original software package will constitute a derivative work, as will the translation of a software package from one programming language to another.

Direct Damages Direct damages are the damages that arise naturally or ordinarily (i.e., as a direct result) of a breach of contract or tortious act of another person. Direct damages should be distinguished from consequential (or indirect) damages, which refer to losses which do not flow directly from the act of another, but only from the consequences of such an act, such as the more speculative loss of business, and should be distinguished from punitive damages which are not a measure of any damages, but more in the nature of a penalty intended to punish the wrongdoer.

Entire Agreement Clause   The entire agreement clause in a contract is also known as an "integration clause" or a "merger clause." This type of contract clause typically states that the written contract is the entire agreement of the parties and that there are no other oral or written understandings between the parties relating to the subject matter of the contract which are not included in the contract, that is, not integrated within the agreement. For a detailed discussion of this clause, see Section 9.22.

Exemplary Damages   See "Punitive Damages."

Expensing Election   A taxpayer has the option to deduct, in the year of payment, up to $5,000 of the cost of tangible personal property which would otherwise be recovered over a number of years through depreciation. This is known as the "expensing election."

F.   This is an abbreviation for "Federal Reporter," a series of books containing copies of the decisions of the Federal Courts of Appeals from the years 1800 to 1924. The Federal Reporter series consists of 300 volumes and is published by West Publishing Company.

F.2d   This is an abbreviation for "Federal Reporter 2d Series," which is a continuation of the Federal Reporter. It contains decisions from all of the Federal Courts of Appeals from 1924 through the present. The F.2d series of Federal Reporters consists of over 750 volumes and is published by West Publishing Company.

F. Supp.   This is an abbreviation for "Federal Supplement," a series of books containing the decisions of the Federal District Courts (i.e., the trial courts) from 1932 through the present. At present, the F. Supp. series of Reporters consists of over 600 volumes.

Force Majeure   This term refers to events which are beyond the control of either party, such as hurricanes, tornados, floods, earthquakes, wars, riots, fire, etc. which prevent or delay performance of the contract. The purpose of a force majeure clause in a contract is to specify how the contract will be treated in such a case. It typically provides that the party who is prevented from performing the contract as a result of force majeure will not be in breach of the contract as a result. For a discussion of the force majeure clause see Section 9.24.

Franchise Tax This is a state tax imposed on the privilege of carrying on a business.

Fraud Fraud is a false statement of a material fact made by one party to another which induces the other party to act in a way which causes him or her damage. For a detailed discussion of the nature of fraud see Section 10.3.

Federal Register The Federal Register is a daily government publication which includes information regarding new and proposed regulations of the various federal agencies. It is used to solicit comments on any proposed regulations and to announce newly adopted regulations. Newly adopted regulations are subsequently printed in the Code of Federal Regulations.

General Counsel's Memorandum This is a document prepared by the legal staff of the Internal Revenue Service outlining the legal reasoning for certain Private Letter Rulings or Revenue Rulings.

Indemnity An indemnity agreement is an undertaking by one party to reimburse a second party for payments the second party is required to make to a third party. An insurance policy is a classic example of an indemnity agreement. The indemnity clause typically found in a software license agreement obligates the vendor to indemnify the user for any loss or expense incurred by the user as a result of a dispute over ownership of the software.

Indirect Damages See "Consequential Damages."

Infringement The concept of infringement arises in patent, copyright, or trademark law. When someone copies software without permission of the copyright or patent owner, or uses a trademark to identify software without the permission of the trademark owner, he or she has committed an act of infringement, that is, he or she has infringed the rights of the copyright, patent, and/or trademark owner.

Injunction An injunction is a court order directing a party to a lawsuit to do or refrain from doing something.

Intangible Asset An intangible asset is a property right having no physical substance such as patent rights, copyrights, trademark rights, trade secret rights, and, according to many courts, software itself.

Integration Clause   See "Entire Agreement Clause."

Internal Revenue Code   This is the compilation of the federal tax laws, including the federal income tax laws.

Investment Tax Credit   The investment tax credit (or "ITC") is a credit applied against tax liability, equal to a percentage of the amount paid for tangible personal property used in a trade or business.

I.R.C.   See "Internal Revenue Code."

IRS Private Letter Ruling   See "Private Letter Ruling."

Jurisdiction   Personal jurisdiction refers to the power which a particular court has over the parties to a lawsuit. Subject matter jurisdiction refers to the court's power to decide the particular kind of case before it. A court cannot render a binding decision unless it has jurisdiction over both the parties to the litigation and the subject matter involved. For example, a court in California will not normally have personal jurisdiction over a person who lives in Florida and does not do business in California. Similarly, a California state court does not have subject matter jurisdiction to hear a case involving the federal copyright laws.

Licensee   The licensee is the party who receives the right to use the software, subject to the terms and conditions imposed by the licensor in the license agreement. A licensee obtains no ownership rights in the copy of the software that he or she receives.

Licensor   The licensor is the party who grants to another the right to possess and use a copy of the software.

Limitations, Statute of   See "Statute of Limitations."

Liquidated Damages   When the parties agree, at the time that they enter into a contract, that a future breach of the contract by one party will be compensated by the other in damages of a specified sum of money, that sum of money is referred to as liquidated damages.

Magnuson-Moss Warranty Act   This is a federal consumer protection statute designed to govern the terms of warranties in certain types of consumer transactions. See Section 10.1.3 for a brief discussion of this statute.

Merger Clause   See "Entire Agreement Clause."

Misappropriation   Misappropriation refers to the theft or other improper use or disclosure of the trade secrets of one party by another.

Misrepresentation   The term "misrepresentation" is often used interchangeably with the term "fraud." It refers to a false statement of material fact made by one party to induce another to enter into a transaction with the first party. It may be intentional or innocent. In some states innocent as well as intentional misrepresentations are considered wrongful acts for which the wrongdoer must pay damages. For a further discussion of the law of misrepresentation see Section 10.3.

National Commission on New Technological Uses of Copyrighted Works   See "Commission on New Technological Uses of Copyrighted Works."

Negligence   Technically, negligence is the failure to do something which a "reasonably prudent person" would do under the same circumstances, or the doing of something that the "reasonably prudent person" would not do. In practice it is the same as carelessness. Driving too fast on an icy road is an example of negligent conduct, since it is done without exercising due care for the safety of others. See Section 10.4.

Noncompetition Agreement   This is an agreement in which one party agrees not to engage in competition with the other for a specified period of time within a specified geographical area. See Section 7.3.

Nondisclosure Agreement   See "Confidentiality Agreement."

Patent   A patent is a grant of exclusive rights issued by the U.S. Patent Office which gives an inventor a 17-year monopoly on the right to "practice" or make, use, and sell his or her invention.

Permanent Injunction   An injunction issued by the court at the conclusion of a lawsuit. See "Injunction" and "Preliminary Injunction."

Personal Property Tax   This is a state or local tax measured by the value of the personal property owned by the individual being taxed.

Plaintiff   The plaintiff is the person who brings suit against someone, the defendant, whom the plaintiff believes is responsible for doing him or her harm.

P.L.R. See "Private Letter Ruling."

Preliminary Injunction A preliminary injunction is a temporary injunction entered at the beginning or during the course of a lawsuit which lasts only until a trial is held and a decision reached. Its purpose is to preserve the status quo pending the conclusion of the lawsuit. The preliminary injunction will either be terminated or converted into a permanent injunction after the trial is over. See Section 4.11.1.

Prima Facia Case Evidence introduced during the trial of a lawsuit which, if unrebutted, would entitle the person having the burden of proof to the relief he or she is seeking. Stated another way, it is enough evidence to require the opponent to introduce evidence in his or her defense or risk losing the case.

Private Letter Ruling This is a ruling by the Internal Revenue Service directed to a particular taxpayer or group of taxpayers on a specific factual situation. Although it may not be relied on as authority for actions by other taxpayers, it is useful as a guide to the position the IRS may take in similar situations.

Products Liability Products liability normally refers to a legal theory which holds the manufacturer of a product liable for any injuries caused by a "defect" in the product that makes it unreasonably dangerous, whether or not the defect resulted from the manufacturer's negligence. See Section 10.5.

Proprietary Rights The term proprietary rights, as used in this book, refers to the rights that the owner of software has in the software, such as the copyright, trade secret, and patent rights (if applicable). These are rights (such as the right to copy or the right to license) which no one else possesses unless they are granted by the owner of the original proprietary rights.

Punitive Damages Punitive damages are damages awarded to the plaintiff separate from those awarded as compensation for the loss that he or she actually suffered; they are awarded for the purpose of punishing or making an example of the defendant. Punitive damages are not available in breach of contract cases, and are generally only available in cases involving intentional torts, such as fraud or misrepresentation.

Published (Publication) Publication, under the Copyright Act, is the distribution of copies of software to the public by sale or other transfer of ownership, or by rental, lease, or lending. The offering to distribute copies to a group of persons for purposes of further distribution, public performance, or public display also constitutes publication. A public performance or display of software does not of itself constitute publication. 17 U.S.C. §101.

Research & Development Tax Credit   This is a credit against tax liability based on 25 percent of a taxpayer's qualified research expenditures.

Rev. Proc.   See "Revenue Procedure."

Revenue Procedure   A Revenue Procedure is a statement of procedure by the Internal Revenue Service that affects the rights and duties of taxpayers under the Internal Revenue Code. It usually reflects the contents of internal management documents of the Internal Revenue Service.

Rev. Rul.   See "Revenue Ruling."

Revenue Ruling   This is an official interpretation of the tax laws, issued by the National Office of the Internal Revenue Service, for the information and guidance of taxpayers and IRS officials. Revenue rulings can be relied on by taxpayers to the extent they are not affected by subsequently issued Treasury Regulations, revisions of the Internal Revenue Code, or court decisions.

Sales Tax   This is a tax imposed by a state or municipality upon sales and lease transactions that occur within its borders. It is usually measured as a percentage of the sales price.

Secondary Meaning   This is a trademark term which refers to a mark that is initially merely descriptive but which over time acquires a meaning over and above the meaning ordinarily ascribed to it. It is further explained in Section 6.2.2.

Software   See "Computer Program."

Special Damages   See "Consequential Damages."

Statute of Limitations   The statute of limitations is the law which determines the amount of time that an injured party has to file a lawsuit against the party allegedly responsible for the injury following the date of the wrongful act. Once a statute of limitations has expired, the action may no longer be filed.

Statutory Damages   In situations where the plaintiff is unable to prove the actual damages that he or she sustained as a result of the wrongful acts of the defendant, some statutes provide for limited damages in any event. One such statute is the Copyright Act, which provides that the plaintiff may recover between $250 and $10,000 dollars for each copyright infringement regardless of whether he or she is able to prove in court that he or she has actually been damaged.

Temporary Restraining Order A temporary restraining order is an injunction issued by the court for a very short period of time (usually no more than 10 days) in order to prevent some immediate harm from occurring before the court can have a hearing on a motion for a preliminary injunction. For example, if a defendant in a lawsuit is about to destroy the only copy of the source code for software over which the ownership was in dispute, a court might issue a temporary order prohibiting such destruction for 10 days until it had time to hold a hearing into the dispute.

Tort A tort is a wrong for which the injured person has a right to recover damages under the common law. Examples include negligence, fraud, theft, and defamation.

Trademark Any word, name, symbol, or device, or any combination thereof adopted and used by a manufacturer or merchant to identify his or her goods and distinguish them from those manufactured or sold by others. 15 U.S.C. §1127. See Section 6.1.

Trade Secret Any secret formula, pattern, device, or compilation of information which is used in one's business and which gives an advantage over competitors who do not know or use it is considered to be a trade secret. See discussion of trade secret definition at Section 4.1.

Treas. Reg. See "Treasury Regulations."

Treasury Regulations Treasury Regulations are official interpretations of the Internal Revenue Code by the Internal Revenue Service, which will have the force and effect of law when the Internal Revenue Code requires their publication. They are also referred to as "Income Tax Regulations."

TRO. See "Temporary Restraining Order."

U.C.C. See "Uniform Commercial Code."

U.S.C. This is an abbreviation for United States Code. This is a codification of all laws passed by the federal government. References to these laws are usually expressed in the format of x U.S.C. y, where "x" refers to the "title" or chapter of the statute and "y" refers to the section of the statute. The Copyright Act, for example, begins at 17 U.S.C. §101.

U.S.P.Q.   This is an abbreviation for United States Patent Quarterly, a series of volumes of a reporter that contains copies of all patent cases decided by the U.S. courts.

Uniform Commercial Code   The Uniform Commercial Code is a body of law governing the sale of goods, banking transactions, and security interests, among other things, which has been adopted (with minor variations) in all states except Louisiana. All sales of goods, such as the sale of hardware, are governed by the Uniform Commercial Code. It is unclear whether a software license agreement is also covered by the U.C.C., since it is not clear that such a license involves a sale of goods.

Unpublished   This is a copyright term which indicates that a work (such as software) has not yet been "published" as that term is defined in the copyright law.

Use Tax   A use tax is a tax imposed by a state or local municipality upon property that was purchased outside of the state which imposed the tax. The use tax is usually equal to the sales tax and is levied to prevent avoidance of the sales tax by purchasing goods outside of the state and later bringing them into the state for use there.

INDEX